Raw judicial power?

The Supreme Court and American society

Robert J. McKeever

Second edition

MANCHESTER UNIVERSITY PRESS
Manchester and New York

distributed exclusively in the USA and Canada by St. Martin's Press

Copyright © Robert J. McKeever 1995

Published by Manchester University Press
Oxford Road, Manchester M13 9NR, UK
and Room 400, 175 Fifth Avenue, New York, NY 10010, USA

Distributed exclusively in the USA and Canada
by St. Martin's Press, Inc., 175 Fifth Avenue, New York,
NY 10010, USA

British Library Cataloguing-in-Publication Data

A catalogue record for this book is available from the British Library

Library of Congress Cataloging-in-Publication Data
McKeever, Robert J., 1951–
    Raw judicial power? : the Supreme Court and American society /
Robert J. McKeever. — 2nd ed.
        p.   cm.
    Includes bibliographical references and index.
    ISBN 0–7190–4873–7 (alk. paper)
    1. United States. Supreme Court.   2. United States–
–Constitutional law—Interpretation and construction.   3. Judicial
review—United States.   4. Political questions and judicial power–
–United States.   5. United States—Social conditions.   I. Title.
KF8742.M35   1996
347.73'26—dc20
[347.30735]

ISBN 0 7190 4873 7 *paperback*

First edition published 1993

99 98 97 96 95   10 9 8 7 6 5 4 3 2 1

Photoset in Linotron Ehrhardt
by Northern Phototypesetting Co. Ltd., Bolton
Printed in Great Britain
by Biddles Ltd., Guildford and King's Lynn

19.99

Raw judicial power?

Published here with a new chapter covering judgements from 1993 to 1995, *Raw judicial power?* is established as the definitive analysis of the powerful forces shaping the United States Supreme Court today.

Robert J. McKeever analyses the approach of the Court to the most pressing contemporary social issues, such as capital punishment, abortion, race and affirmative action, gender equality and religion, sex and politics. He shows how social policy initiatives in the US have often come from the judicial rather than the legislative branch of government, leading to charges that the Supreme Court has been exercising 'raw judicial power'. He examines the policy decisions the Court has made, and argues that the Court has increasingly jettisoned traditional notions of constitutional interpretation in order to tackle the conflicts in contemporary American society.

Students of American politics, constitutional law and social policy will all find this book invaluable.

Robert J. McKeever is Lecturer in Politics at the University of Reading.

This book is dedicated to Joan, my mother

As an act of raw judicial power, the Court perhaps has authority to do what it does today; but in my view its judgement is an improvident and extravagant exercise of the power of judicial review that the Constitution extends to this Court.

Supreme Court Justice Byron White, *Roe v. Wade*

Contents

Preface and acknowledgements

The urge to write this book stemmed mainly from a long-standing fascination with the United States Supreme Court as a political institution. The Court's blend of legal and political characteristics, combined with its power to make important policy decisions on behalf of the federal government, makes it a rich and unique field of study. Above all, perhaps, the attraction of the Supreme Court is that, unlike the other major institutions of American government, it seeks to make (or, at least, justify) its policy decisions by calm, reasoned application of basic principles. The Justices of the Supreme Court are, then, about as near to philosopher kings as modern democracy allows.

The attraction of studying the Court is clearly of a different kind from that of studying the President or the Congress. The politics of the elected branches of government in the United States is brash, populist, sometimes glamorous, sometimes sleazy. The Court, by contrast, is staid, intellectual, lacking in glitz and impressively virtuous. While these distinctions may make Congress and the presidency more exciting on the surface, they seem to me also to make the substance of the Court's work all the more worthy of detailed examination.

I do, however, have some reservations about the way academics cover the Court. For one thing, the accepted wisdom that the Court is both a legal and a political institution, is too often more honoured in the breach than in the observance. As a result, either judicial opinions are dissected and analysed as if they have no connection with the political and historical frameworks within which the Court acts; or treated simply as products of the Justices' personal policy predilections, as if those who sit on the Court are no more than politicians in judges' robes. This book, therefore, is a modest attempt to analyse the modern Supreme Court, taking full account of both its legal and political aspects. I offer no grand theories. I do hope to show, however, that the Supreme Court is a political institution whose legal characteristics make it different from other political institutions. And that it is just as important to take Supreme Court opinions seriously (though not uncritically), as it is to recognise that the Court does not operate in a political vacuum.

A second reservation I have about the current literature on the Court is that it is far too normative. There is a seemingly inexhaustible supply of books and articles arguing what the role of the Supreme Court should be in American government, but a comparative dearth of those describing and analysing in detail what it actually does. This book, then, has an unashamedly empirical bias. If nothing else, I hope that readers will feel that they have at least acquired the necessary knowledge of the Court's decisions to enable them to evaluate, or even devise, normative arguments.

The structure of the book is, therefore, as follows. Chapter one examines the political and social forces which brought to prominence the kind of social issues which have formed the staple constitutional diet of the Court in recent decades. Chapter two traces the legal and judicial developments that have occurred roughly in parallel to, and sometimes in direct connection with, the rise of the Social Issue in American politics. Chapters three to seven analyse the Court's decisions in the major policy areas affected by these political and judicial dynamics. Respectively, they are capital punishment, abortion, affirmative action for racial minorities and women; and finally a mixed bag of other cases arising out of the contemporary conflict over traditional morality, including gay rights, pornography and governmental support for religious values. In each of these chapters, I try to show how the Court interacts with the outside political world in its exercise of judicial review, without, I hope, offering simplistic and mechanistic explanations of the decisions involved. In chapter eight, I draw some conclusions from all this as to the Supreme Court's suitability to continue carrying the heavy political burden that it has acquired.

Perhaps I should make one further comment at this point. Just as it is often a mistake to assume that a Justice's vote to uphold or condemn a statute implies approval or disapproval of that statute on policy grounds, so too it would be wrong to read any criticisms I make of the Justices' opinions as an expression of my own policy preferences. However, to avoid any misunderstandings, let me say that, in the terms used in chapter one, my views on the Social Issue coincide almost unreservedly with those of the New Class. Whether, however, constitutional interpretation is the best method of persuading more Americans that these values are superior to traditional ones, is by no means as clear to me.

I would like to thank those who have been particularly helpful in enabling me to write this book. I was grateful for financial assistance received from the British Academy, the United States Embassy in London, the Department of Politics and the Research Board at Reading University. Not for the first time, I benefited greatly from access to the excellent resources of the Supreme Court Library and Library of Congress in Washington, DC, and The Institute of Advanced Legal Studies in London. While carrying out research for this book in the United States, some very busy people working at the heart of the issues it examines, took time to enlighten me on how their organisations approach their work: John Katz, lawyer and member of the Board of the National Organisation for Women; Lois Murphy, of the National Abortion Rights Action League; and Ed Hirschfeld, Associate General Counsel of the American Medical Association. My colleague and friend Christine Macleod proof-read the draft meticulously and did what she could to improve my writing skills.

Preface to the second edition

In the three years since I wrote the first edition of this book, there have been some significant developments both on the Court and in its political environment. For the first time since 1976, a Democrat was elected to the presidency in 1992 and, within two years, President Clinton had appointed Justices Ginsburg and Breyer to the Court as replacements for Justices White and Blackmun. This strengthened the liberal-moderate wing of the Court. The Republican capture of Congress in 1994, however, may augur a swing of the pendulum back towards the conservative wing, especially if the White House changes hands in 1996.

In tackling cases involving the Social Issue, therefore, the Court has continued much as before to juggle law and politics in its thankless task of trying to arrive at authoritative resolutions of some of the nation's most controversial policy questions. There have, of course, been developments in the Court's jurisprudence since 1992, though no cases perhaps of the stature of a *Roe*, *Bakke* or *Furman*. These I have dealt with in a new *Epilogue*, which I hope will serve to keep the reader abreast of such developments up until the Spring of 1995. Since the *Epilogue* was written, some of the cases mentioned as being on the Court's docket have actually been decided. Thus *Adarand* has further restricted the scope for affirmative action by the federal government and *Miller* has followed *Shaw* in threatening the very existence of 'majority-minority' legislative districts.

I trust readers will find, however, that these cases are readily comprehensible within the structure laid out in the first edition. Certainly there have been no developments which have caused me to question the political and judicial premises on which I originally based the book. Most importantly, however, I hope readers will continue to find the Court's unique blend of law and politics to be a source of intellectual fascination and pleasure.

Robert J. McKeever
July, 1995

One—The rise of the 'Social Issue'

> The American judicial tradition has important elements of continuity, but its predominant feature is that of a reflection of cultural change.[1]

Never has this been more true of the United States Supreme Court than during the last three decades. Since the 1960s its decisions have reflected the fact that there has arisen a new dimension to the nation's political agenda in the form of 'the Social Issue', 'lifestyle issues' or simply 'social issues', as they have variously been called.[2] In addition to traditional debates over economic and foreign policy, the political system has had to deal with acrimonious divisions over such issues as abortion, affirmative action for women and ethnic minority groups, crime and punishment, drug use, sexual mores and attitudes to God and country. In the words of one partisan, politics in the United States is now beset by 'culture wars'.[3] While many of these concerns have long been a feature of American society, a variety of factors has combined to give them unprecedented political prominence in recent years. In order to understand both the role of the Court and the substance of its decisions in these culture wars, it is first essential to understand the changing political context in which the Court has been operating.

The politics of post-industrial society

Since the end of the Second World War, the United States has been transformed into a post-industrial society. Many things may be said to distinguish such a society from an industrial one, but perhaps most important is its dependence upon advanced technology in economic production and communications.[4] This in turn has stimulated a vast expansion of education, particularly higher education, in order to meet the new society's need for a work-force which can cope with the increased complexities of economic and social intercourse. One of the leading exponents of post-industrial theory, Everett Ladd, encapsulates these developments by contrasting the fortunes of coal miners and college professors as a result of post-industrialism: the coal miners, he says, can be viewed as the prototypical employees of industrial America and in 1936 they outnumbered professors nine-to-one. By 1978, professors outnumbered miners four-to-one and they may justifiably be viewed as the prototypical employee of post-industrial society. The demand for professors was, of course, created by the new demand for college credentials and in the same period, college enrolments increased 700 per cent.[5]

This explosion of higher education had important social and political consequences. Some went so far as to suggest that it created a broad 'New Class', made up of 'knowledge workers', whose values and aspirations differed significantly from those who had previously occupied a similar position in the American class structure.[6] In particular, the New Class of salaried professionals and technically-trained managers was said to be a rival for power and status with the 'old' business class, which had until now occupied the middle and upper-middle strata of American society.

Although the conceptualisation of 'knowledge workers' as a *class* has failed to withstand empirical scrutiny,[7] significant elements of New Class theory remain central to an understanding of contemporary politics in the United States. Most important is the fact that it is the educated middle class which is the most liberal section of American society on a wide range of social issues: 'The rise of left-of-centre political views in broad sections of the educated middle class has been one of the distinctive – and one of the more surprising – features of post-war American politics. By the early 1970s, college graduate professionals were the leading liberal stratum on many social and foreign policy issues . . .'[8] Ladd concurred and stressed the contrast between the liberalism of the professional middle class and the conservatism of lower classes: 'Nowhere are present-day differences between the upper and lower socioeconomic-status groups more striking than on attitudes toward the social, cultural, and lifestyle issues that have thrust into prominence since the mid-1960s.'[9] This, of course, represents a reversal of the usual relationship that is posited between socioeconomic status and political ideology: the greater one's stake in the present social order, the more likely one is to hold conservative attitudes and to oppose change. Even in the New Deal and post war eras, the college educated and the middle class were more conservative on social issues than those of lesser education and lower class. This was true of both Republicans and Democrats. For example, in 1952 88 per cent of college educated Republicans opposed Medicare, compared with 74 per cent of all Republicans. For Democrats, the figures were 52 per cent and 39 per cent, respectively.[10]

The picture forty years later is very different and education is a major factor explaining contemporary middle-class liberalism on social issues. Even those least enthusiastic about New Class theory have found that education has a liberalising effect on issues such as rights of minorities, abortion, marijuana use and pornography.[11] An analysis of six major opinion surveys in the 1970s demonstrated the point with great clarity. For example, among those with four years of college education, 52 per cent agreed with the view that homosexuality is not always wrong; among those educated to high school level, only 26 per cent agreed. A similar question on adultery revealed a split of of 43 per cent to 26 per cent. On race and sex equality, abortion, pornography and premarital sex, similar differentials appeared. Moreover, the gap between attitudes grew almost invariably in relation to the gap in years of education. Thus, on the homosexuality issue, the difference between those with postgraduate education and those with less than high school education was 57 per cent to 14 per cent.[12]

It is by no means clear why education should have a liberalising effect on social issues but not economic issues.[13] Education does tend to produce greater cognitive sophistication and this leads, perhaps, to greater levels of political tolerance towards others, even when the group involved is neither liked nor otherwise respected.[14] This tolerance factor may come into play when material redistribution is not a primary element in policy and where a gain for the group concerned is not viewed as a threat to the existing status structure.

Others, however, particularly those on the political right, offer a cultural explanation of contemporary middle-class liberalism on social issues. Norman Podhoretz, for example, believes that the vast expansion of higher education has simply exposed millions more Americans to the 'adversary culture' which has always existed in the country's intellectual and cultural institutions, especially universities.[15] The adversary culture is anti-business and anti-materialist, despising the bourgeois values associated with the 'old' middle class. There was a lull in the advocacy of the adversary culture around mid-century, as Nazism and Stalinism made American values look good in comparison. Then came the 1960s: poverty, racism and Vietnam all helped convince the new vast cohort of young college students that the United States was in need of radical change. They rejected the '. . . "Puritan ethic" and indeed all middle-class values: work, ambition, discipline, monogamy, and the family.'[16] Despite electoral failure, Podhoretz continues, the adversary culture's values were spread throughout the education system and other cultural institutions: 'The ascendant ethic

preached in the public schools, in the mass media, and even in comic
books and pornographic magazines now seemed to be that nothing –
not wives, not husbands, not children, and certainly not the state – must
stand in the way of the individual's right to self-fulfilment and self-
expression in the realm of morals, sex and personal relations . . .'[17]
Ladd strikes a similar note when he argues that the American upper-
middle class has been transformed into an intelligentsia at odds with
'business values':

> . . . the upper-middle class in the United States has shed much of its
> identification with the business world. Increasingly, large segments of the
> broad, new upper-middle classes, primarily those who are at once the most
> affluent, the most secure and most closely associated with advanced tech-
> nology, think of themselves as professionals – business administrators,
> engineers, accountants, lawyers and so on – all responding to intellectual
> values and orientations rather than those traditionally associated with
> business. Along with their counterparts in the public sector, these new
> upper-middle-class professionals have become the core of the current
> 'intelligentsia'.[18]

The opposition to business values extended to an attack upon
economic individualism and called for government policy promoting
'. . . equality, social justice, and state regulation of the private economy
. . .'[19] This produced affirmative action programmes, held by many to
be antithetical to traditional values '. . . by making rewards contingent
upon membership in a group favoured for one reason or another by
government rather than upon individual effort and achievement. It
could be understood, then, as an extension into concrete social policy
of the adversary culture's assault on the "Protestant ethic".'[20] Jeanne
Kirkpatrick also emphasised the use of government by the new intelligentsia: 'I believe it is demonstrable that new class power has increased
in the last decade or so, and that the most important consequences of
this increase have been the decline of consensus, the progressive
involvement of broader cultural forces in politics . . . and in the ever-
increasing use of government power and organisations to achieve
"rationalist" goals.'[21]

   The transformation of the middle and upper-middle classes into an
intelligentsia is, however, only half of the story. At the same time that
the number of those espousing bourgeois values was being depleted by
this development, they were replaced by the newly-affluent members
of what until now had been termed the working class. In the twenty-five
years from 1947, the median income for all American families virtually
doubled in real terms.[22] Many of the blue-collar workers who were

'have-nots' before the war have moved decisively into the category of 'haves'. As they seek to protect their newly-acquired stake in the status quo, and with less experience of the liberalising effect of higher education, the working class has become a 'New Bourgeoisie', or lower-middle class, which opposes the values of the new intelligentsia.[23]

As noted above, the precise bases of upper-middle class liberalism and lower-middle-class conservatism on social issues is open to debate. It is, however, clear that this phenomenon has been a major feature of electoral politics since 1968. Indeed, according to Walter Dean Burnham, it played a significant role in the disintegration of the political order that had existed since the 1930's – 'post-New Deal interest-group liberalism'.[24] That regime crumbled partly due to economic problems and partly due to foreign affairs; but there was a third aspect: 'The 1970s were marked no less by the emergence of crisis in the culture: traditional standards of morality and, what was worse, the nuclear family itself, seemed to many to be in danger.'[25] Out of the wreckage of the old order came, on the left, the New Politics and, in opposition to it, the Reconstituted Right.[26]

The New Politics movement '. . . was spearheaded by young members of the upper-middle class for whom the civil rights and antiwar movements were formative experiences . . .'[27] Their opposition to the war in Vietnam developed into a critique of what they saw as American militarism and imperialism in the Cold War era. By thus impugning their country's role and self-image, they appeared as unpatriotic to traditionalists, many of whom were to be found among blue-collar workers. A famous illustration of this class conflict came when a group of 'hard-hat' construction workers physically attacked participants in an anti-war demonstration in New York on 8 May 1970. A sympathetic historian of the anti-war movement recognised the problem, as did others at the time: 'The prowar mobilisation of labourers illustrated the class lines that antiwar activists had encountered before. Contemporary observers interpreted them as the great failure of the white, middle-class antiwar movement – what Jimmy Breslin termed "its arrogance toward people who work with their hands for a living and its willingness not only to ignore them, but to go even further and alienate them completely." Policy-shaping elites in Wall Street and on Ivy League campuses might be shifting in their attitudes toward the war, Breslin noted, but nobody bothered to inform the steamfitters in the country that the signals had been changed.'[28] George Wallace, one of several candidates who tried to appeal to traditionalist sentiment in the

1968 presidential election, also took a robust stand on antiwar demonstrators: 'If any demonstrator lies down in front of my car when I'm President, that'll be the last car he lies down in front of.'[29]

The Vietnam war and patriotism was just one of a cluster of issues which animated the election of 1968. Race, crime and the 'counterculture' of the young, particularly its advocacy of recreational drug use, sexual liberation and unconventional dress, all played their part in smashing the social and cultural consensus of earlier decades. American society did indeed seem to be 'coming apart'.[30] Several presidential candidacies were constructed upon these tensions. On the left, Robert Kennedy, Eugene McCarthy and George McGovern tried to tap the dissatisfactions of the young, their disillusionment with 'the system' and its values. None of them were radicals but their opposition to the war made them suitable mainstream vehicles for antiwar activists.[31] On the right, George Wallace and Ronald Reagan were the most strident purveyors of traditional values and their campaigns presaged the emergence of the 'New Right' in the late 1970s. One biographer described Reagan as '... an evangelist warning of the destruction of the American dream.'[32] He certainly painted an apocalyptic vision of the direction in which he saw the country heading: 'This country is totally out of control ... It cannot afford politicians who demand that Social Security be tripled; that the national duty in Vietnam be discarded to provide huge make-work programmes in the city slums with money provided from Vietnam; that no youth need honour the draft; that Negroes need not obey the law ...'[33]

Some of the Wallace rhetoric revealed a particularly interesting aspect of the conservative critique of American society, as in inimitable populist fashion, he identified the intelligentsia and their allies in the federal government as the source of many of the country's problems: 'Our lives are being taken over by bureaucrats, and most of them have beards!' was a campaign speech line that invariably drew great applause.[34] He also made repeated attacks on the 'pointy-heads', that is, intellectuals, who were challenging accepted values and practices from their positions of power in the media and the universities, as well as in the federal government. As David Broder noted, this is the theme which enabled Wallace to transcend his status as a mere Southern racist: he played on '... all the fears and resentments of lower-income whites, not only their dislike of Negroes but also their frustration with rising taxes, with bureaucracy and with the machinations of all those "pointy-heads" Wallace told them were running the country into the ground.'[35]

Wallace also made frequent, explicit attacks upon the United States Supreme Court and the federal judiciary in general. The platform of his American Independent Party attacked the courts for encouraging lawlessness, permissiveness and moral decay, ignoring the American people's love of God and country and, of course, for unwarranted interference in the school system. It concluded that federal district court judges should be popularly elected and Supreme Court justices should be subjected to periodic reconfirmation.[36] On the campaign trail, he decried 'Federal judges playing God' and said that Chief Justice Earl Warren '. . . doesn't have enough legal brains in his head to try a chicken thief in my home county . . .'[37]

However, the winner that year, Richard Nixon, and his vice-presidential running mate, Spiro Agnew, also sought to profit from the conservative backlash against the upheavals of the 1960s. Like Wallace and Reagan, Nixon attacked the judiciary, although in more measured tones. In his speech accepting his party's nomination at the Republican Convention in Miami Beach, he said: 'Let us always respect, as I do, our courts and those who serve on them, but let us also recognise that some of our courts have gone too far in weakening the peace forces as against the criminal forces in this country.'[38] Earlier at the Convention, when meeting with Southern delegates, Nixon stated his opposition to court-ordered busing of school children to achieve desegregation. He said courts, including the Supreme Court, should not try to act as a school board and policy should not be aimed at satisfying 'some professional civil-rights group'.[39]

The 1968 presidential election thus made clear that social issues were now a significant factor in American politics and that the Supreme Court was likely to be caught up in this development. From that time on until the present day, the situation has only intensified. The 1972 presidential election saw the Democratic candidacy of Senator George McGovern, who friend and foe alike viewed as the representative of young, upper-middle class liberalism. Between 1968 and 1972, the so-called New Politics movement had greatly strengthened its position within the Democratic Party. Most important, the McGovern-Fraser commission had rewritten the rules of the Democratic nominating process in ways which increased the representation of women, young and black activists. The New Politics movement aimed at a coalition of the disaffected, but the leadership was supplied by '. . . upper-middle-class professionals'.[40] Kevin Phillips found empirical data to support this connection between class, ideology and McGovern's candidacy: 'Some 40 percent of the

McGovern delegates to the 1972 Democratic convention had master's degrees or better, and much of McGovern's doctrine was quintessential New Class ideology'.[41] In policy terms, this meant support for affirmative action, women's rights, pollution controls and the redistribution of wealth to the advantage of the poor. It also meant cutting defence expenditure in line with a new vision of a less militaristic foreign policy. That McGovern was crushed in the presidential election was due not least to the fact that these policies were viewed by many blue-collar workers as inimical to their interests and values. The environmental and welfare measures appeared to threaten their jobs and economic position, while the proposals on racial justice, women and foreign policy threatened their conservative social values. Furthermore, 'This conflict of interest was exacerbated by the disdain – verging on class hatred – often exhibited by the upper-middle-class proponents of the New Politics toward members of the working class.'[42] McGovern's Republican opponents tried, successfully, to capitalise on his identification with New Class values by depicting him as the candidate of the three A's – 'amnesty, acid and abortion'.[43] As a result, George McGovern's defeat was perceived not simply as a routine failure to unseat an incumbent President with some recent foreign policy triumphs to his credit, but as a decisive rejection by the electorate of upper-middle-class liberalism on social issues.

It was around this very time, however, that such liberalism scored some notable victories in the Supreme Court. In 1971 the Court, for the first time, struck down a legal distinction based on gender because it violated women's constitutional equality.[44] The same year, it authorised the use of busing to overcome segregated schooling.[45] In 1972, the Court ruled that all existing death penalty statutes involved 'cruel and unusual punishments', as defined by the Eighth Amendment to the Constitution.[46] In 1973, and most controversial of all, the Court announced the new constitutional right of a woman to choose to terminate a pregnancy by abortion.[47] This decision was to have enormous political consequences. It immediately supplied the anti-abortion movement with a dynamism that it had hitherto lacked.[48] As the self-styled pro-life forces gathered political strength, the abortion issue was used as a rallying point for the broader New Right movement: 'The antiabortion movement . . . has been a central vehicle through which the New Right has crystallised and developed its mass base and mass ideology. This particular crusade . . . has provided the perfect issue to "freeze" the political process into an absolute struggle between good and evil . . .'[49] Since the mid-1970s on, the New Right has been the most prominent, and most extreme, movement combating the social and cultural values associated with the New Class. It is ideologically anti-elitist and seeks to mobilise lower-middle-class Americans. One of its earliest chroniclers described the movement thus:

> Collecting millions of dollars in small contributions from blue-collar workers and housewives, the New Right feeds on discontent, anger, insecurity, and resentment, and flourishes on backlash politics. Through its interlocking network, it seeks to veto whatever it perceives to threaten its way of life – busing, women's liberation, gay rights, pornography, loss of the Panama Canal – and promotes a beefed-up defence budget, lower taxes, and reduced federal regulation of small businesses. Moreover, the New Right exploits social protest and encourages class hostility by trying to fuel the hostilities of lower-middle-class Americans against those above and below them on the economic ladder.[50]

In other words, the New Right became the political vanguard of Ladd's New Bourgeoisie, Nixon's Silent Majority, or Scammon and Wattenburg's Real Majority. Politicians who identified with the New Right achieved significant victories very quickly. Most obviously, Ronald Reagan almost wrested the Republican presidential nomination from the incumbent, Gerald Ford, in 1976, and then went on to two overwhelming electoral triumphs in 1980 and 1984. In 1978, the New Right was credited with the defeat of three Senate liberals and their replacement by New Right sympathisers – Roger Jepsen (Iowa), Gordon Humphrey (New Hampshire) and William Armstrong (Colorado).[51] That year's elections also saw the astonishing defeat of the liberal Governor of Massachusetts, Michael Dukakis, in the Democratic primary. His opponent, Edward J. King, adopted the strategy of appealing to blue-collar Democrats on the basis of the Social Issue, reminding them of Dukakis' New Class liberalism on abortion, the death penalty and minimum prison sentences, for example. It paid off handsomely with King taking 51 per cent of the vote to Dukakis' 42 per cent.[52]

It is debatable whether the New Right itself should take most of the credit for these conservative successes and others which followed in 1980. Social issues were, however, clearly an important factor, either because they mobilised conservative activists or because significant numbers of Americans find them decisive in determining their vote. For Jerome Himmelstein, the impact of social issues has been limited but significant, particularly in relation to the Religious Right: '. . . they played a big role in the mobilisation of cadres of conservative activists and contributors, and they provided the terrain for the politicisation of evangelical Christians and the rise of the New Religious Right.'[53]

Others, however, argue persuasively that the presidential election of 1988 provides evidence to suggest that the importance of the Social Issue is more extensive. Marjorie Hershey recalls how, in May 1988, George Bush trailed Michael Dukakis by ten points in the opinion polls. The response of the Bush campaign was to assemble two small groups of Democrats who had voted for Ronald Reagan but who now intended to vote for Dukakis. These returning Democrats were presented by the Bush team with materials indicating Dukakis' position on a wide variety of issues, in order to identify which produced the most powerful negative reaction. The two issues found to be most productive in changing the voting intentions of the focus groups' members were prominent components of the Social Issue. First was Governor Dukakis' veto of a Massachusetts law requiring teachers to lead pupils in a daily recital of the Pledge of Allegiance. The second was the now infamous issue of the release on Governor Dukakis' parole of the convicted black murderer, Willie Horton. Out on a weekend pass, Horton raped a white woman and brutalised her boyfriend. The Bush team decided that their best bet was to try to pin the label of 'Liberal' on Dukakis. Defence and economic issues would feature in this strategy, but: 'Even more, the Bush staff intended to define Dukakis as a *social* liberal: overly concerned with the rights of criminals, unconcerned with other people's fears of crime, happy to defend any group or belief, no matter how objectionable to the majority.'[54] Both national and state Republicans ran vicious advertisements on the Willie Horton issue. The Illinois Republican party produced a leaflet saying 'all the murderers and rapists and drug pushers and child molesters in Massachusetts vote for Michael Dukakis.'[55] In October, George Bush personally took up the issue, saying: 'Clint Eastwood's answer to crime is, "Go ahead, make my day". My opponent's answer is slightly different. His answer is, "Go ahead, have a nice weekend".'[56] The Republican strategy was vile, but highly successful, and Dukakis never recovered from it.

Gerald Pomper saw the victory of George Bush as an election which confirmed the recent trend favouring presidential majoritarianism for the Republicans: 'It is the accumulated result of population changes, weakening party loyalties, innovative campaign methods, *and changes in the issue agenda of American politics from economic issues to basic values.*[57]

Pomper also believes that the Social Issue, particularly in its moral dimension, is coming increasingly to define the two major political parties. For the Republicans, their contemporary concern with such issues as pornography, school prayer and the death penalty continues their party's historic moralism.[58] The Democrats, too, are now a more morally coherent party: 'Democrats now espouse moral liberalism, which makes a sharp distinction between private and public life. In this philosophy, individuals, not society, decide whether and where to pray, whether and when to abort a fetus, whether and how to salute the flag. Emphasising individualism, Democrats are more tolerant of different life styles, even of eccentricity, sometimes of deviance.'[59]

Looking to the future, Pomper concludes that the importance of social values is likely to remain in presidential elections, and may even be decisive. If the Republicans are to be defeated, he argues, then 'Most of all, presidential Democrats must understand the value of values . . . Democrats must first assure the electorate that they truly endorse its basic and emotional commitments to national defence, public safety, *and moral stability*.'[60]

It is the moral base of so many social issues that makes them so difficult to resolve by traditional American political methods. The essence of policy making in the United States is compromise and incrementalism, methods dictated by the fragmented nature of government established by the Constitution. The system has worked reasonably well in relation to the distribution of material goods, but is less well suited to moral issues which, by their very nature, are less susceptible to compromise.[61] William Lunch argues that this dilemma is a major element in a distinctive new political system in the United States: '. . . the new, nationalised system is driven in large measure by political ideas rather than political interests. This means that the crass, but reliable, materialism that was the foundation of the old system is being rendered increasingly obsolete by a politics frequently dominated by abstract ideas that have mobilised a new class of political activists on both the left and the right.'[62] Material goods can be divided on an acceptable basis, but morality often involves stark issues of right and wrong and in the eyes of many of the interested parties, compromise means sell-out and defeat. As Lunch observed: '. . . demands for purity, whatever their source, are impossible to meet.'[63]

This brief survey of the rise to prominence of the Social Issue in American politics is the first step in explaining the contemporary role and jurisprudence of the Supreme Court. For, to some extent, the caseload of the Supreme Court always mirrors the agenda of the wider world of politics. Yet this alone cannot account for the Court's decisions on abortion, the death penalty, affirmative action and so on. If

the Court has always been confronted with claims arising from controversies in politics, it has also been adept at avoiding them when
judicial deference to the elected branches of government has seemed
in the interests of self-preservation. In this respect, the right of the
Supreme Court to select its own docket is invaluable. Every year,
thousands of petitions for judicial review arrive at the Court: the vast
majority are denied and less than two hundred are chosen for full
consideration by the Justices. Thus although some cases carry such
obvious and important constitutional implications that the Court finds
them difficult to avoid, the fact remains that every decision taken by the
Court is, to some extent, a voluntary action of the Justices.[64] It is
necessary to explain, therefore, both why the Court decided to take on
many aspects of the Social Issue and why it decided them in such
controversial fashion. One important step towards answering the first
of those questions is to examine the systemic changes which have taken
place in the political process in recent American history. For these have
affected the role of the Supreme Court, just as they have the role of the
other branches of government. Furthermore, some observers argue
that the particular effect on the federal judiciary has been to 'assign' the
resolution of social controversies to the courts, whether the judges like
it or not.

The 'New' judicial activism

The surest way to change the role of the Supreme Court is to change its
personnel. Or at least that is how it seemed until recently. Perhaps
because the role of the Supreme Court was never defined in the
Constitution or in any other authoritative source, the Justices themselves have had a great say in how the institution operates at any given
moment. Everyone familiar with the history of the Court knows that
Chief Justice John Marshall virtually invented a new role for the Court
in 1803[65] when he developed his concept of the power of judicial
review. Equally familiar is the story of President Franklin D.
Roosevelt's struggle with the 'Nine Old Men' of the Supreme Court in
the 1930s over the constitutionality of the New Deal. When legal
reasoning failed to persuade the Court to permit unprecedented
government intervention in the economy, Roosevelt tried brute political force in the form of the 'court-packing plan', which, had it succeeded, would have enabled Roosevelt to appoint six additional
Justices. Although the pressure on the Justices is usually regarded as
the reason for their climb-down in 1937, it was only when Roosevelt

was eventually able to appoint new Justices in the normal way that the New Deal was finally secured against further judicial resistance. Roosevelt replaced 'judicial activists' with those who professed 'judicial restraint' and the Court duly entered a period of passivity. Presidents simply have to accept that it is usually easier to change a Justice than it is to change a Justice's mind.

When Richard Nixon won the presidential election of 1968, then, he looked to his power of judicial appointment to bring an end to the liberal judicial activism of the Warren Court. He would nominate Justices who would practise judicial restraint through 'strict construction' of the Constitution. However, despite making four new appointments, with a fifth being added by his Republican successor, the expected 'counter-revolution' on the Court failed to materialise.[66] Indeed, although the Burger Court did cut back some of the rights of the accused advanced by the Warren Court, it also took some strikingly activist decisions on gender equality, the death penalty and abortion, as already noted. The Burger Court presented a puzzle: why was a Supreme Court with a nominal conservative-restraintist majority handing down decisions which were both liberal and activist? In response, Court analysts began to look beyond the subjective philosophies of the Justices and asked whether the judicial process itself had not undergone a fundamental change. In 1983, Vincent Blasi expressed the idea thus:

> In the future, the 1970s and early 1980s may well be looked upon as the period during which the activist approach to judicial review solidified its position in American judicial practice. If so, this development has not been a matter of professed ideology; the opinions of the last thirteen years abound with essays on the virtues of judicial self-restraint. Nevertheless, by almost any measure the Burger Court has been an activist court. And if a court with the make-up and mandate of this one has chosen not to resist the temptations of activism, that fact says something important about the imperatives of the judicial process, if not the legitimacy of the activist philosophy.[67]

In an earlier article, Nathan Glazer argued that '. . . we must at least consider the possibility that there has been a permanent change in the character of the courts and their role in the commonwealth, rather than simply a somewhat extended activist cycle.'[68] He cited three main reasons for this change, all of which were also highlighted by other judicial scholars of various political standpoints.

First, Glazer argued, the Warren Court had taken decisions that were not only difficult to reverse, but which had also developed a momentum that was difficult to slow. Some of these were doctrinal, others technical. Both had the effect of encouraging greater resort to the courts as a forum for settling political conflicts. On the technical side, for example, the Warren Court relaxed the requirements of 'standing' and 'justiciability'. The former requires that in order to bring a case before the Court, a litigant must demonstrate a real personal stake in the outcome, not merely an interest or putative stake. 'Justiciability' concerns the question of whether the judiciary can fashion a remedy for the alleged ill. In a series of decisions in the 1960s, the Court granted standing to taxpayers over federal expenditures affecting First Amendment rights; effectively abandoned the 'abstention doctrine', which kept the Court out of cases where the constitutional issue rested on an unsettled point of state law; and, of course, took on the reapportionment cases, thus for the first time entering, and cutting a swathe through, what it had previously described as 'a political thicket'.[69]

The Warren Court also allowed greater use of 'class actions', in which individuals may not only sue on behalf of themselves, but for all similarly situated individuals. This device allows the involvement, knowing or otherwise, of an unlimited number of people who share a constitutional grievance. It is, therefore, admirably suited to the needs of those who pursue social reform through litigation, as it can result in a victory for the 'class' or group, without all the expense and effort of mounting a campaign in the legislature. Its importance is immediately demonstrated by the fact that it was used in *Brown v. Board of Education*[70] on behalf of blacks and in *Roe v. Wade*[71] on behalf of pregnant women seeking abortions. In 1966, the Court amended Rule 23 of the Federal Rules of Civil Procedure to make class actions easier: 'Within a few years . . . the class-action suit became a powerful tool in the hands of upper-middle-class professionals and intellectuals who during the 1960s and 1970s organised a variety of groups and movements that attempted to bring about significant changes in American government and society. Hence, in addition to civil rights claims on behalf of minority groups, the class action became a powerful weapon in the arsenals of the consumer, environmental, feminist, and anti-nuclear movements.'[72] Such was the proliferation of class action suits – they doubled between 1970 and 1975 – that the Burger Court did eventually take action to restrict them in certain respects.[73] Nevertheless, it has by no means reversed the more relaxed policy of the Warren Court.[74]

The same is true of the Warren Court's doctrinal innovations. The classic example here is that of the constitutional 'right to privacy', first announced in *Griswold v. Connecticut*[75] in 1965. In that case, the new right was held to protect married couples wishing to use contraceptives. In 1972, however, the Burger Court extended its logic to cover unmarried couples.[76] In 1973, the privacy right was extended to women seeking abortions.[77] As Glazer put it, 'The Court must work out the logic of positions once taken, and it cannot easily withdraw from the implications of these positions.'[78] As long as it wishes to be perceived as a court of law, the Supreme Court must demonstrate some commitment to stability, continuity and logic in its rulings. Justice Potter Stewart illustrated this factor in his opinions in *Griswold* and *Roe*. In the former, he dissented from the judicial creation of a right to privacy because he considered it an usurpation of legislative power, reminiscent of the substantive due process decisions of the anti-New Deal Court in the 1930s.[79] Eight years later, in *Roe*, however, he joined the majority in extending that very same privacy right. He gave his explanation in his concurring opinion: '. . . the *Griswold* decision can be rationally understood only as a holding that the Connecticut statute substantively invaded the "liberty" that is protected by the Due Process Clause of the Fourteenth Amendment. As so understood, *Griswold* stands as one in a long line of . . . cases decided under the doctrine of substantive due process, and I now accept it as such.'[80] Thus, while such considerations do not preclude cutting back or wholesale reversal in some areas of the law, they do not facilitate frequent or widespread constitutional counter-revolutions.[81]

Glazer identified the second factor behind the new judicial activism as, '. . . the enormous increase in the reach of government itself. When government expands, it would seem reasonable that the Court must extend its reach also. It must consider issues of equity and due process and equal protection in all the varied areas of education, health care, housing, and access to government services of all types.'[82] This explanation sees the Court being dragged into further activism as part of the constitutional system of checks and balances. As governmental intrusion into ever more spheres of life has proliferated since the New Deal, the Court must execute its historic function of policing the boundaries of government action. Stephen Halpern explained this in greater detail:

> The widened range of judicial policymaking is primarily attributable to the enormous growth in the scope and power of American government in the last twenty-five years. The central development in American domestic politics in the last quarter century has been the vast and virtually incompre-

hensible growth in the range and complexity of activities regulated by government, especially the federal government ... We need reminding that extensive federal regulation of such matters as racial and sexual discrimination, education, health care, water and air pollution, urban and consumer affairs, and national economic development, to name only a few, either did not exist or were in early developmental stages two short decades ago.[83]

There is also, however, a more radical alternative to this liberal explanation of increased judicial activism. It holds that far from being a counterbalance to expanding government, the Supreme Court has played an independent and creative role in that expansion. Certain theorists of the modern state in advanced capitalist society have suggested that the state is an autonomous or semi-autonomous entity which rules on behalf of, but not necessarily at the behest of, the ruling class.[84] In seeking to create social stability and consensus, the state 'negotiates' with subordinate groups in society in order to win their acquiescence to the leadership of the ruling class. Such negotiation entails reforms which make concessions to subordinate and dissident groups and, it is argued, much of modern American liberalism, from the New Deal to the Great Society, has involved precisely this type of state-sponsored reform.

It is not surprising that this analysis has been applied to the modern Supreme Court. If some degree of autonomy is required to carry out these reforms, then the life tenure of the Justices provides it. Furthermore, by claiming to speak through the Constitution, the Court is able to confer a high degree of symbolic reward to groups with political grievances, thus helping to bind them to the system with assurances that they have power and status within it. Many writers, for example, have argued that the *Brown* decision gave an enormous boost to the civil rights movement in the 1950s, by encouraging it to believe that the state was on its side. At the same time, however, it has also been noted that the Court's decision alone achieved little by way of desegregating the schools of the Deep South.[85] Joan Roelofs argues that *Brown*, and other Warren Court reforms, constituted the judicial version of progressive social engineering on behalf of the capitalist state:

In the short run, the *Brown* decision was in accordance with the interests of corporate capitalism. It was viewed as a threat only by lower-status whites and black school personnel. It announced to the world that a capitalist society could be just and concerned with human rights. Insofar as *Brown* did lead to genuine progress for blacks ... it brought them into the American *consumer* class, while dispelling any ideas of revolution that might be circulating. The New Deal had done little for blacks; the *Brown* decision supplied this part of the 'conservative revolution'.[86]

Arthur S. Miller developed a more detailed statist explanation of the Court in his work *Toward Increased Judicial Activism* in 1982. He argued that the myth of the Court as a neutral umpire in the political system has promoted social consensus and helped to quell discontent: 'If people . . . could think that they were getting a fair shake of the social dice, they would be more willing to accept social inequities. The Myth served as a unifying, and even at times a civilising element, in society, helping to bind people together, an intangible cement that aided in making a "united state" out of the United States.'[87] In fact, he says, the Court's decisions subtly amend the Constitution '. . . in the interests of a never-defined entity called "society"', which in reality turns out to be only a small segment of society.[88] In analysing who benefits from Court decisions, Miller says, 'The interests of the State, and of those who in fact (although not in theory) control the State, have always been and still are preeminent.'[89] Reforms initiated by the Court, therefore, are prompted by a desire to deal with potentially destabilising social and political developments in a way which allows certain changes within the system without altering the basic configuration of power within the system: 'As a political institution, the Supreme Court's function is to produce decisions that are both systems maintaining and system developing . . . It tries to create a constantly shifting equilibrium as new problems emerge.'[90]

Whether the liberal or neo-Marxist explanation of the Court's role in governmental expansion is correct, both at least agree that developments in the nature of government generally have required greater judicial activism of the Justices in recent years, even where they professed a desire for restraint.

The third factor identified by Glazer as promoting increased judicial activism is that, 'The courts will not be allowed to withdraw from the broadened positions they have seized, or have been forced to move into, because of the creation of new and powerful interests, chief among them the public advocacy law centres.'[91] Glazer observed that prior to the 1960s, there was only one prominent such group, the National Association for the Advancement of Coloured People Legal Defence Fund. Since then, however, legal interest groups have emerged in virtually every field of social policy and representing virtually every group of potential clients.[92] The list of the causes advanced by these groups in the courts is almost limitless, but prominent among them have been those concerned with the Social Issue: for example, feminist and New Right groups, ethnic minority groups, civil liberties groups and religious groups. Aryeh Neier, who spent fifteen years as a lawyer for the American Civil Liberties Union, agreed with Glazer that what the Warren Court era began, the Burger Court era saw flourish: '. . . the cause litigation bar is larger, better financed, more sophisticated, and more resourceful in the era of the Burger Court than it was earlier. By bringing into existence the robust public law bar that exists today, the Warren Court's decisions helped to maintain their own momentum.'[93]

These groups intervene in the judicial process in two main ways. Some, most notably the NAACP Legal Defence Fund, try to take full control over Supreme Court cases by finding and sponsoring clients to act as parties in the litigation. This may be part of a long-term strategy to achieve a major reform in the law, as with the campaigns to end racially restrictive housing covenants[94] and the death penalty.[95] Most groups, however, lack the resources to engage in such full campaigns. For that reason, their preferred means of judicial lobbying is the *amicus curiae* brief. Literally meaning 'friend of the court', and having its origins in Roman law, the *amicus curiae* in the United States has long since ceased to be a disinterested third party with expertise to give the court on a particular issue. As Samuel Krislov put it: 'The *amicus* is no longer a neutral, amorphous embodiment of justice, but an active participant in the interest group struggle.'[96] And empirical research by Karen O'Connor and Lee Epstein has demonstrated just how far and how fast the use of the *amicus* brief has progressed in recent times. Before the Second World War, interest group *amicus* participation in non-commercial cases was almost non-existent, occurring in only 1.6 per cent of such cases in the period 1928–40.[97] A steady increase took place over the next twenty-five years and then there was a rapid acceleration from the mid-1960s onwards. In the period from 1970–80, interest group *amicus* briefs were filed in 53.4 per cent of non-commercial cases decided by the Court, a virtual doubling of the number for the period 1953–66.[98] Moreover, prominent among the types of cases attracting interest group briefs were those involving social issues, for example, sex discrimination, race discrimination, church-state relations, obscenity and conscientious objectors.[99] Lee and Epstein also reported that cases which attract multiple briefs are now common: of those non-commercial cases where a brief was filed, 26.7 per cent involved four or more briefs.[100] Their conclusion was that '. . . *amicus curiae* participation by private groups is now the norm rather than the exception.'[101]

There are several possible reasons for this explosion of judicial lobbying. Glazer suggests that its origins can be traced to the popularity of public law for students in the late 1950s. This in turn reflected the simultaneous rise in the prevalence of the adversary culture among the young and their growing disillusionment with the ineffectiveness and unfairness of the elected branches of government in dealing with perceived social grievances. They flocked to the new public law interest groups as a means of pursuing social reform.[102]

Others highlight the ways in which the federal judiciary itself has encouraged the participation of interest groups. As discussed earlier, the Warren Court relaxed the rules on standing and class actions. It also positively welcomed *amicus* briefs by interest groups, even when the actual parties to cases did not. In 1949, the Court had tightened the rules governing the participation of *amici*, in the belief that many of the briefs being submitted were little more than propaganda without legal merit. The 1949 measures included one which required interest groups who wished to participate in a case to present a motion for leave to file with the Court whenever permission had been denied by any party to the case. There was an immediate drop in the number of *amicus* briefs filed.[103] In the face of the criticism in the scholarly community and, indeed, by some of the Justices, that the Court was excluding groups with legitimate interests, that was quickly reversed and it once again became relatively easy to file an *amicus* brief. Empirical analysis of the Court's response, from the 1969 Term to the 1981 Term, to interest group motions for leave to file a brief shows that only 11 per cent of such motions were refused. The obvious suggestion is that the Court welcomes the intervention of interest groups as *amici*, since it could otherwise reject many of the briefs.[104]

It has often been observed that the Court's decisions on desegregation also gave substantial encouragement to many interest groups to bring their causes to the federal judiciary. *Brown* and its progeny were read as a signal that those groups who were disadvantaged in the political arena might fare better with appointed judges than with elected politicians.[105] As the Court proved receptive to the claims of groups such as blacks, Jehovah's Witnesses, the poor and those accused of crime, other groups who had failed in the electoral arena tried litigation. As Donald Horowitz put it, 'The (desegregation) decisions created a magnetic field around the courts, attracting litigation in areas where judicial intervention had earlier seemed implausible.'[106] By the time of the Burger Court, women, a statistical majority of the population, took this path to advance gender equality, with considerable success.[107] Combined with doctrinal developments that convinced many federal judges that they could and should provide solutions to a wide range of social problems,[108] the liberal, humanitarian impulses of many of the Warren and Burger Court Justices made litigation a major instrument of social reform. As early as 1963, Samuel Krislov recognised that these factors were important in '. . . the encouragement of group representation *by a self-conscious bench.* The judges have sought to gain information from political groups as well as to give them a feeling of participation in the process of decision. Access to the legal process on the part of such organisations is a logical extension of realistic awareness of law as a process of social choice and policy making.'[109]

Interest groups who were initially 'invited' to take their causes to the judiciary naturally became defenders of judicial activism and the Supreme Court. In effect, they became clients of the Court, with a vested interest in protecting it from attacks by other groups and political institutions. As with the other factors discussed here, there is a self-perpetuating dynamic inherent in interest group use of the courts for social reform which is difficult, though not impossible, to reverse.

One other major factor needs to be considered here: changes in the relationship of the Supreme Court to the other two branches of the Federal Government. It has generally been accepted that the Court has never long been able to resist the combined might of the Presidency and Congress in any major policy struggle.[110] At the least, the Court needs an 'alliance' with one of the other major institutions, if its more controversial decisions are not to be reversed. Historically, the Court has been closer to the presidency than the Congress and this alliance was particularly powerful from the inception of the post-New Deal Court in 1937 until the end of the Warren Court. During this period, the Court first acquiesced in the nationalisation of political power in the socio-economic sphere and then rediscovered judicial activism to promote the nationalisation of the Bill of Rights. The Court and the presidency were generally fellow travellers down the road to a nationalised political system, with the presidency at its centre: 'Thus for all the controversy engendered by many of its decisions, the Warren Court of the 1960s enjoyed strong executive support because its activism served the interests of the occupants of the White House.'[111]

Since 1968, however, this relationship has altered dramatically. Conservative Republicans, bent on curbing the Court's power and reversing its decisions, have had a virtual monopoly of presidential power. At the same time, the Democrats have retained control of both houses of the Congress, with the exception of the first six years of the Reagan presidency. Although the weight of the Reagan and Bush Court appointees is gradually being felt, the liberal elements of the Burger and Rehnquist Courts have been able to count on strong support from Congressional Democrats, as well as the client groups whose interests the Court has served. The power of this alliance's support for the Court's modern jurisprudence was graphically demonstrated when it defeated President Reagan's attempt to put Judge Robert Bork on the Supreme Court. As the most articulate and outspoken critic of modern judicial review, the successful nomination of Bork would have been more than the addition of yet another Justice dedicated to judicial restraint. It would have been a symbolic rejection of all that the modern Supreme Court has come to stand for.[112]

Moreover, as Cornell Clayton and Christopher McMahon have recently demonstrated, the new 'dealignment' or 'bifurcated' politics, in which Congress and presidency are controlled by different parties, has made legislative action more difficult. The result has been that both Congress and presidency have sought to draw the federal judiciary into their own political struggle: 'An activist judiciary and a dealigned electoral system heighten the value of litigation and law enforcement as policy instruments'.[113] This has taken a variety of forms. One is that the legal bureaucracy of both Congress and the presidency has become highly politicised, especially in the Department of Justice and its two leading offices, the Attorney-General and the Solicitor-General. This, in turn, led the Senate to cease its historic reliance upon the Attorney-General's office to defend Congressional legislation in the courts. In 1978 it created the Office of the Senate Legal Counsel as a non-partisan defender of Congress in the courts.[114] Clayton and McMahon argue that beyond fragmenting and politicising government legal bureaucracy, 'The SLC's office has ramifications for the federal judiciary as well. The operation of specialised legal offices tends to redirect political disputes in the courts, increasing the scope of judicial policymaking. Moreover, litigation by the SLC may provide an additional institutional source for judicial independence. Whatever else may result, regularised confrontations between Congress and the President allow the judiciary to pick and choose which "electoral mandate" it wishes to follow.'[115]

A second manifestation of the greater use of the courts by the other branches of government is the way in which legislation is deliberately left vague, either to overcome divisions within the Congress or to avoid the antagonism of the President and the exercise of his veto power: 'Members of Congress . . . may find it useful to rely on the Court to resolve difficult problems, although congressional reliance on the Court varies from one policy question to the next. When an issue is particularly complex, Congress may stop when it has made a general policy statement – usually a result of legislative compromise – and thus leave it up to the justices to make policy as the Court applies the laws.'[116]

Third, Congress may simply wish to avoid pronouncing on certain issues at all. As noted above,[117] the social issues analysed here are bitterly divisive. While for some politicians, like George Wallace or George McGovern, they present a golden opportunity to mobilise a particular segment of the electorate, for others who rely on consensus they offer only the danger of alienating a group of erstwhile or potential supporters. Abortion is one such issue. President George Bush is a notable example of a politician whose position on abortion has 'evolved' to meet the imperatives of the electoral process. Having entered the 1980 Republican presidential primaries with a pro-choice position, he switched to an anti-abortion position on becoming Vice-President. He continued that way until the 1989 Supreme Court decision in *Webster v. Reproductive Health Services*[118] threw the abortion conflict back into the state legislative arena with a vengeance. When the 1989 state elections turned up some important victories for pro-choice candidates, the President felt the need to soften his pro-life stand. He publicly reassured pro-choice voters that, 'We have room in our party for people that feel one way, pro-life or pro-choice.'*(sic)*[119] Politicians may well, therefore, positively welcome the fact that the Supreme Court is willing to take the lead on some controversial issues simply because it deflects the heat from them. John Hart Ely believed this was true of the Court's decision in *Roe*: 'The sighs of relief as this particular albatross was cut from the legislative and executive necks seemed to me audible.'[120]

For all the reasons outlined above, it can be argued that the role of the Supreme Court in the policy-making process has undergone a significant change in the last few decades. Because of changes in the political system and political environment in which it operates, the Court has acquired a greater autonomy than it has ever had before; and it has responded to those changes by instituting modifications in judicial procedures that help reinforce its increased independence in policy making. Many Court observers believe that these developments have become institutionalised and, therefore, are unlikely to be reversed in the foreseeable future. William Lasser recently expressed the thought forcefully, writing that the Court's '. . . unprecedented activism, far from endangering its place in American politics, seems to have given the Court even more power. Its critics have been unable to reverse outright even one of the Court's controversial decisions, and the Court shows no sign of retreating from its activist approach to constitutional decision making.'[121] While this may underestimate the impact of new and recent Supreme Court appointments, the essence of the statement is correct. As Donald Horowitz succinctly put it: 'The tendency to commit the resolution of social policy issues to the courts is not likely to be arrested in the near future. The nature of the forces undergirding the tendency makes them not readily reversible'.[122]

One factor which does place considerable limitations on the expansion of judicial power, in theory at least, is the fact that the Justices have always been held obliged to make their decisions according to law, not politics. To do otherwise would simply make them politicians disguised in judicial robes. More than anything else, this has meant basing their decisions on an interpretation of some clause or another in the Constitution. Although constitutional interpretation leaves the Justices with considerable latitude for innovation, the need to justify their decisions in public, with a well-reasoned argument proceeding from a premise contained in the Constitution, helped to set the broad parameters of judicial policy making. However, at the very same time that political developments were stimulating increased judicial activism, this fundamental constraint was also under attack by many of those who make up the legal and intellectual community. This attack, too, is an important factor in explaining the contemporary role of the Supreme Court in American politics and so is analysed in the next chapter.

Notes

1 G. E. White, *The American Judicial Tradition* (expanded ed.), Oxford, 1988, p. 459.
2 I shall use these terms interchangeably for the sake of variety, although I prefer 'the Social Issue' simply because it is most closely associated with a specific political moment in American history. It was first employed, as far as I know, in 1970, by Richard Scammon and Ben Wattenberg in their influential book; *The Real Majority*, to identify what they saw as 'A New Tide' in American politics, New York, pp. 35–44.
3 R. Bork, *The Tempting of America: The Political Seduction Of The Law*, New York, 1990. 'War' is Bork's preferred term to describe the political and legal conflict over social issues, judging by the frequency with which he uses it in this work. For example, 'My nomination was, as I have said, merely one battleground in a long-running war for control of our legal culture, which, in turn, was part of a larger war for control of our

general culture.', p. 271.

4 D. Bell, *The Coming of Post-Industrial Society*, New York, 1973.

5 E. Ladd, Jr, 'The New lines are drawn: class and ideology in America', *Public Opinion*, July/August 1978, pp. 48–53, 49–51.

6 B. Bruce-Briggs (ed.), *The New Class?*, New York, 1981; S. Brint, ' "New Class" and cumulative trend explanations of the liberal political attitudes of professionals', *American Journal of Sociology*, XC, 1984, pp. 30–71.

7 J. L. Himmelstein and J. A. McRae, Jr, 'Social issues and socioeconomic status', *Public Opinion Quarterly*, LII, 1988, pp. 492–512; Brint, *op. cit.*

8 Brint, *op. cit.*, p. 30.

9 E. C. Ladd, Jr, 'Pursuing the New Class: social theory and survey data', in Bruce-Briggs, *op. cit.*, p. 107.

10 Ladd, 1978, *op. cit.*, p. 49. See also Ladd, *Transformations Of The American Party System*, New York, 1978.

11 Himmelstein and McRae, *op. cit.*, p. 505. See also Brint, *op. cit.*

12 Ladd 1978, *op. cit.*, Table 2, p. 51.

13 The distinction between these types of issue is not always neat: for example, the public funding of abortions may invoke both social and economic concerns. Himmelstein and McRae, *op. cit*, p. 507. Nevertheless both these researchers and Brint, *op. cit.*, found a clear difference between the effects of education on social, as opposed to economic opinion. For example, on policy to reduce income differentials, Brint found that 'Both business and new-class groups were overwhelmingly conservative . . . They were much more conservative, in fact, than either blue-collar wage workers or the population at large.', p. 37.

14 L. Bobo and F. C. Licari, 'Education and political tolerance: testing the effects of cognitive sophistication and target group effect', *Public Opinion Quarterly*, XIII, 1987, pp. 285–308, 303.

15 'The adversary culture and the new class', in Bruce-Briggs, *op. cit.*

16 *Ibid.* p. 29.

17 *Ibid.* p. 30

18 Ladd 1978, *op. cit.*, p. 49.

19 Brint, *op. cit.*, p. 32.

20 Podhoretz, *op. cit.*, p. 31.

21 'Politics and the New Class', Bruce-Briggs, *op. cit.*, p. 34.

22 Ladd, 1978, *op. cit.*, p. 50.

23 *Ibid.*, pp. 49–51.

24 'The Reagan heritage', in G. Pomper *et al.*, *The Election of 1988*, Chatham, 1989.

25 *Ibid.*, p. 5.

26 B. Ginsberg and M. Shefter, 'A critical realignment? The New Politics, the Reconstituted Right, and the 1984 election', in M. Nelson (ed.), *The Elections of 1984*, Washington, DC, 1985.

27 *Ibid.*, p. 6.

28 C. DeBenedetti, *An American Ordeal: The Antiwar Movement of the Vietnam Era*, Syracuse, 1990, p. 283.

29 L. Chester, G. Hodgson and B. Page, *An American Melodrama: The Presidential Campaign of 1968*, London, p. 305.

30 W. O'Neill, *Coming Apart: An Informal History of America in the 1960's*, New York, 1971.

31 Chester *et al.*, *op. cit.*, recounts the search of Al Lowenstein, a radical with links to both the establishment and the student movement, for an anti-war candidate within the Democratic party to oppose President Lyndon Johnson's renomination. Kennedy, McCarthy and McGovern were among a sizeable number approached by Lowenstein, pp. 76–86.

32 B. Boyarsky, quoted in Chester *et al.*, *op. cit.*, p. 210.

33 *Ibid.*, pp. 220–1.

34 *Ibid.*, p. 302.
35 A. M. Schlesinger, Jr and F. L. Israel (eds), *History of American Presidential Elections, 1789–1968* vol IX 1960–1968, New York, 1985, p. 3716.
36 *Ibid.*, pp. 3797–3809.
37 Chester *et al.*, *op. cit.*, p. 303, p. 304, respectively.
38 Schlesinger and Israel, *op. cit.*, p. 3836.
39 Chester *et al.*, *op. cit.*, pp. 488–9.
40 Ginsberg and Shefter, in Nelson, *op. cit.*, p. 11.
41 'Political responses to the New Class', in Bruce-Briggs, *op. cit.*, p. 141.
42 Ginsberg and Shefter, in Nelson, *op. cit.*, p. 11.
43 P. Mooney and J. Bown, *Truman To Carter: A Post-War History of America*, London, 1979, p. 179. The amnesty issue focused on those who had refused to fight in Vietnam; acid, otherwise known as LSD, on the recreational use of illegal drugs.
44 *Reed v. Reed*, 404 US 71 (1971).
45 *Swann v. Charlotte-Mecklenburg Board of Education*, 402 US 1 (1971).
46 *Furman v. Georgia*, 408 US 238 (1972).
47 *Roe v. Wade*, 410 US 113 (1973).
48 See, for example, K. Luker, *Abortion And The Politics of Motherhood*, London, 1984; R. Tatalovich and B. Daynes, *The Politics of Abortion: A Study of Community Conflict in Public Policy Making, New York, 1981; E. Rubin, Abortion Politics and the Courts: Roe v. Wade and Its Aftermath*, New York, 1982; P. Conover and V. Gray, *Feminism and the New Right: Conflict Over the American Family*, New York, 1983.
49 R. Petchesky, *Abortion And Woman's Choice: The State, Sexuality, and Reproductive Freedom*, London, 1986, p. 245. Petchesky argues that the link between abortion and other New Right issues is substantive, as well as symbolic. The main substantive connection is the concept of 'corporate privatism', which allows businesses, churches and the family, for example, to regulate individual behaviour without the interference of the liberal state.
50 A. Crawford, *Thunder On The Right: The 'New Right' and the Politics of Resentment*, New York, 1980.
51 *Ibid.*, pp. 272–7
52 P. Davies and J. White, 'The New Class in Massachusetts: politics in a technocratic society', *Journal of American Studies*, XIX, 1985, pp. 225–38, 231.
53 Himmelstein, *op. cit.*, p. 104.
54 M. Hershey, 'The campaign and the media', in G. Pomper *et al.*, *The Election of 1988: Reports and Interpretations*, Chatham, N.J., 1989, p. 82. (emphasis added).
55 *Ibid.*, p. 95.
56 *Ibid.*
57 G. Pomper, 'The presidential election', in Pomper *et al. op. cit.*, p. 147 (emphasis added).
58 *Ibid.*, p. 142.
59 *Ibid.*
60 *Ibid.*, p. 148 (emphasis added).
61 R. McKeever, 'Obituary for the "Living Constitution"? Policy making and the constitutional framework two hundred years on', in R. Maidment and J. Zvesper, *Reflections On The Constitution*, Manchester, 1989, pp. 198–222.
62 W. Lunch, *The Nationalisation of American Politics*, Berkeley, 1987, p. 3.
63 *Ibid.*, p. 5.
64 The convention among the nine Justices is that a majority of them must vote to grant review before a case can be taken. If, however, four Justices wish to take a case the practice is that a fifth Justice will supply the necessary vote, even if s/he disagrees with the desirability of doing so.
65 *Marbury v. Madison*, 1 Cranch 137 (1803).
66 Nixon appointed Chief Justice Warren Burger (1969) and Associate Justices Harry

Blackmun (1970), Lewis Powell (1971) and William Rehnquist (1971). President Ford appointed Associate Justice John Paul Stevens (1975). R. Funston, *Constitutional Counter-Revolution?*, New York, 1977; V. Blasi (ed.), *The Burger Court: The Counter-Revolution That Wasn't*, New Haven, 1983.

67 V. Blasi, 'The rootless activism of the Burger Court', in Blasi, *op. cit.*, pp. 198–9.

68 N. Glazer, 'Toward an imperial judiciary', *The Public Interest*, XLI, 1975, pp. 104–23, 108.

69 M. Silverstein and B. Ginsberg, 'The Supreme Court and the New Politics of judicial power', *Political Science Quarterly*, CII, 1987, pp. 371–88, 377–8; K. Orren, 'Standing to Sue: Interest Group Conflict in the federal courts', *American Political Science Review*, LXX, 1976, pp. 723–41.

70 347 US 483 (1954).

71 410 US 113 (1973).

72 Silverstein and Ginsberg, *op. cit.*, pp. 379–80.

73 Abraham, *op. cit.*, p. 371, n. 13.

74 Silverstein and Ginsberg, *op. cit.*, p. 382.

75 381 US 479.

76 *Eisenstadt v. Baird*, 405 US 438 (1972).

77 *Roe v. Wade* 410 U.S. 113 (1973).

78 Glazer, *op. cit.*, p. 112.

79 A discussion of substantive due process follows in the next chapter. In brief, however, it is used when the Court reads into the Due Process Clause of the Fifth or Fourteenth Amendment a new substantive right, such as liberty of contract or the right to use contraceptives. These substantive rights are different from procedural rights, such as the right to arraignment and trial.

80 410 US 113, 168 (1973).

81 Blasi, *op. cit.*, pp. 208–9.

82 Glazer, *op. cit.*, p. 116.

83 S. C. Halpern, 'On the imperial judiciary and comparative institutional development and power in America', in S. C. Halpern and C. M. Lamb, *Supreme Court Activism and Restraint*, Lexington, 1982, p. 223. See also Blasi, *op. cit.*, who emphasises '. . . the rampant growth of government bureaucracy, at the state as well as the federal level.', p. 209.

84 E. Nordlinger, *On The Autonomy of the Democratic State*, Cambridge, 1981; R. Miliband, *Class Power and State Power*, London, 1983.

85 'By 1964, just two percent of the black children in the South attended integrated schools, and none at all in the two southern counties involved in the *Brown* decision; H. Sitkoff, *The Struggle For Black Equality 1954–1980*, New York, 1981, p. 38.

86 J. Roelofs, 'Judicial activism as social engineering: a Marxist interpretation of the Warren Court', in Halpern and Lamb, *op. cit.*, pp. 256–7.

87 A. Miller, *Toward Increased Judicial Activism:The Political Role of the Supreme Court*, London, 1982, p. 31.

88 *Ibid.*, p. 36.

89 *Ibid.*, p. 47.

90 *Ibid.*, p. 107.

91 Glazer, *op. cit.*, p. 119.

92 *Ibid.*, p. 119. Glazer appears, however, to have overlooked the activities of the American Civil Liberties Union see, for example, S. Krislov, 'The amicus curiae brief: from friendship to advocacy', *Yale Law Journal*, LXXII, 1963, pp. 694–721, 709.

93 A. Neier, *Only Judgement: The Limits of Litigation in Social Change*, Middletown, 1982, p. 233.

94 C. Vose, *Caucasians Only*, Berkeley, 1959.

95 M. Meltsner, *Cruel and Unusual: The Supreme Court and Capital Punishment*, New York, 1973.

THE RISE OF THE 'SOCIAL ISSUE'   27

96 Krislov, *op. cit.*, p. 703.

97 K. O'Connor and L. Epstein, 'Amicus curiae participation in U.S. Supreme Court litigation', *Law and Society*, XVI, 1981–2, pp. 311–20, Table 1, p. 316.

98 *Ibid.*, Table i, p. 316.

99 *Ibid.*, Table 2, p. 316.

100 *Ibid.*, p. 317.

101 *Ibid.*, p. 318.

102 *Ibid.*, pp. 119–20.

103 K. O'Connor and L. Epstein, 'Court rules and workload: a case study of rules governing *amicus curiae* participation', *The Justice System Journal*, VIII, 1983, pp. 35–45, 37.

104 *Ibid.*, p. 40.

105 R. Cortner, 'Strategies and tactics of litigants in constitutional cases', *Journal of Public Law*, XVII, 1968, pp. 287–307.

106 D. Horowitz, *The Courts And Social Policy*, Washington, D.C., 1977, p. 10.

107 K. O'Connor and L. Epstein, 'Beyond legislative lobbying: women's rights groups and the Supreme Court', *Judicature*, LXVII, 1983, pp. 134–43.

108 See the discussion which follows in chapter two.

109 Krislov, *op. cit.*, p. 721, (emphasis added).

110 R. Dahl, 'Decision-making in a democracy: the Supreme Court as a national policy-maker', *Journal of Public Law*, VI, 1957, pp. 279–95; R. McCloskey, *The American Supreme Court*, Chicago, 1960. For a somewhat different and more updated view, see J. Casper, 'The Supreme Court and national policy making', *American Political Science Review*, LXX, 1976, pp. 50–63.

111 Silverstein and Ginsberg, *op. cit.*, p. 379. R. Scigliano, *The Supreme Court and the Presidency*, New York, 1971.

112 For a discussion of Robert Bork's critique of modern judicial review, see Ch. 2. For an analysis of his nomination and rejection by the Senate, see E. Bronner, *Battle for Justice*, New York, 1989; R. Hodder-Williams, 'The strange story of Judge Robert Bork and a vacancy on the United States Supreme Court', *Political Studies*, XXXVI, 1988, pp. 613–37. Of course, the alliance is not sufficiently powerful to defeat all Supreme Court nominees it dislikes, as subsequent nominations have shown: R. McKeever, 'Courting the Congress: President Bush and the nomination of David H. Souter', *Politics*, XI, 1991, pp. 26–33.

113 C. Clayton and C. McMahon, 'The new judicial politics and dealignment: the impact on the government legal bureaucracy', p. 6. Paper presented to the Annual Conference of the American Politics Group, Bristol, UK, January 1991.

114 *Ibid.*, p. 18. See also, C. Fried, *Order and Law*, New York, 1991; L. Caplan, *The Tenth Justice*, New York, 1987.

115 *Ibid.*, p. 19.

116 S. Wasby, *The Supreme Court in the Federal Judicial System* (3rd ed.), Chicago, 1988, p. 313. Donald Horowitz, *op. cit.*, makes the same point, adding that some legislative acts actually have judicial review procedures written into them, p. 5.

117 *Supra*, p. 11.

118 492 US – , 109 SCt 3040 (1989).

119 'Bush takes new tack in debate on abortion', *International Herald Tribune*, 9 November, 1989, p. 3.

120 J. Ely, 'The wages of crying wolf: a comment on *Roe v. Wade*, *Yale Law Journal*, LXXXII, 1973, pp. 920–49, 947.

121 W. Lasser, *The Limits of Judicial Power: The Supreme Court in American Politics*, Chapel Hill, 1988, p. 4.

122 Horowitz, *op. cit.*, p. 12.

Two—The Court and constitutional interpretation

> The Supreme Court has become a major and unpredictable source of innovation in the political system; its political significance is greater now than ever before.[1]

As we saw in the previous chapter, it is generally recognised that the Supreme Court today plays a role in American politics quite different from that which it has played throughout most of its history. One of the main reasons for this is that the concept of constitutional interpretation has undergone a fundamental change in recent years. Many take the emergence of the Warren Court as the critical moment in this transformation, in particular its decision in *Brown v. Board of Education* in 1954. From *Brown* onwards, the Warren Court resuscitated judicial activism, after the passivity which followed the Court's losing struggle against the New Deal, but did so for a purpose previously absent from the Court's history: it took the initiative in pursuing social reform. The record of liberal activism during the Warren era is too well documented to require lengthy repetition here: suffice to say that the Court put an end to *de jure* segregation in the South and elsewhere, ended the gross malapportionment of legislatures, tried to eliminate police malpractice by strengthening the legal rights of the accused and restricted the power of government to curtail First Amendment freedoms. These decisions were highly controversial and, as we saw in the last chapter, came under attack from conservative politicians who accused the Court of usurping the power of elected legislatures, thereby undermining democracy in the United States. One consequence of this was a debate within the country's law schools as to whether the Warren Court's interpretation of the Constitution could be justified according to accepted canons of judicial practice.

Yet this debate was essentially a new phase in an old argument: should the Supreme Court practise judicial activism or judicial restraint? Although there are various aspects to both doctrines, the difference between them boils down to two basic questions. First, should the Justices interpret the clauses of the Constitution narrowly or expansively? Second, should the Justices show maximum deference to legislatures when evaluating the constitutionality of laws, or confidently and frequently assert their own judgement of what the Constitution permits? Judicial restraint and activism were viewed as opposite ends of a continuum of the practice of judicial review and, while the debate generated considerable heat, it is important to stress that both were held by their supporters, as well as by some of their opponents, to be genuine methods of constitutional interpretation.

To be sure, there were those who argued that both judicial restraint and judicial activism were little more than the preferred fig-leaves of judges who, in fact, simply read their own ideological and policy preferences into the vague and accommodating phrases of the Constitution.[2] Nevertheless, most legal scholars and Supreme Court Justices took the debate seriously. The reason for doing so is not hard to see. The power of judicial review is counter-majoritarian and, therefore, to the extent that it determines public policy, is undemocratic. Although in theory subject to reversal by constitutional amendment, in practice a decision of the Supreme Court is almost always final: yet the Justices are neither elected by nor answerable to any public constituency. In a representative democracy, then, the power of judicial review requires special justification and this is where the concept of constitutional interpretation comes in. Since 1803, when Chief Justice Marshall expounded a new version of judicial review,[3] the power of the Supreme Court to declare laws unconstitutional has been deemed acceptable only because, through constitutional interpretation, the Justices enforce the will of the framers rather than their own. There may be disputes about what the will of the framers actually was in any given case, just as there may be disputes about the methodology to be employed in ascertaining the will of the framers. Moreover, interpretation might inescapably require the Justices to bring to bear some elements of their own constitutional theories. Nevertheless, constitutional interpretation was viewed as a meaningful exercise through which the Justices could enforce the supreme law of the Constitution, without imposing their own political preferences on an unwilling majority. Even judicial activists argued that it was the Constitution which defined the ends: judicial discretion was confined to evaluating the means. For much of its life, then, the controversy over the liberal activism of the Warren Court was debated in language and concepts long familiar in American judicial history.

This debate, however, no longer holds centre stage in the argument over the proper role of the Supreme Court in the American political system. The question of *how* the Court should interpret the Con-

stitution has been replaced by that of *whether* the Court should interpret the Constitution at all. In academic circles, this is known as the
debate between interpretivists and non-interpretivists.[4]

Interpretivism encompasses a wide range of approaches to constitutional interpretation. Paul Brest identifies three main schools of interpretivism, or originalism as he prefers to call it: textualism,
intentionalism and inferentialism.[5] Textualism and intentionalism
have much in common, primarily that judges must conduct a historical
enquiry into the origins of the relevant constitutional clause in order to
ascertain its meaning. Nevertheless, says Brest, there is an important
distinction between the two. The textualist places primary emphasis
upon the words of the clause and attempts to identify their 'plain
meaning'; that is, the meaning that would have been given to the clause
by 'the normal speaker of English' at the time of its adoption. In this
view, the subjective intention of those who framed the constitutional
clause is, at best, of only secondary importance. By contrast, the
intentionalist places this element at the centre of the constitutional
enquiry. The intentionalist acknowledges that the constitutional text is
a valuable guide to the framers' intent, but other sources are equally as
important: for example, the speeches made by the framers when the
clause was enacted.

Strict textualists and strict intentionalists are advocates of judicial
restraint. Their method of reasoning places the Justices of the
Supreme Court under the obligation to subordinate their own values to
those of an external authority whose values have received super-
majoritarian approval. They see their duty as being to enforce the views
of the framers and their society, no matter how far back in history such
views were prevalent. Only by such a method, they argue, can the
inherently undemocratic nature of judicial review be rendered
compatible with the principles of a democratic society.

Inferentialists would allow somewhat greater scope for creative
interpretation. In this interpretive method, the Court may infer powers
and rights from the structures and relationships created by the Constitution. Citing the work of Charles Black, Brest argues that this is
what happened in the famous case of *McCulloch v. Maryland* in 1819,[6]
when the Court held that Congress had the power to create a national
bank and that states had no power to tax such a bank. The decision
rested neither on textualism nor intentionalism, but rather '. . . on
inferences from the structure of the federal system . . .'[7] Nevertheless,
inferentialists, like other interpretivists, are bound by a search for some
kind of original meaning in the Constitution.

There is, however, a less restrictive form of interpretivism, which Brest calls moderate originalism: 'A moderate textualist takes account of the open-textured quality of language and reads the language of provisions in their social and linguistic contexts. A moderate intentionalist applies a provision consistent with the adopters' intent at a relatively high level of generality, consistent with what is sometimes called the "purpose of the provision". Where the strict intentionalist tries to determine the adopters' actual subjective purposes, the moderate intentionalist attempts to understand what the adopters' purposes might plausibly have been, an aim far more readily achieved than a precise understanding of the adopters' intentions.'[8] This form of moderate originalism has been used to justify judicial activism. Indeed, it was employed by Chief Justice Earl Warren in his opinion in *Brown*. Warren argued that there was conflicting evidence as to whether the framers of the Fourteenth Amendment intended to outlaw racially segregated schools.[9] And since public schooling was in its infancy in 1868, it was equally difficult, he claimed, to apply the strict textualist test of 'plain meaning'. Inevitably, then, the Court was required to give the Equal Protection Clause a plausible application to the issue of segregated public schooling in the light of modern conditions and knowledge.[10] The *Brown* decision was thus an example of judicial activism, but also one which proclaimed itself to be interpretivist. It is also defended as such by many of its supporters. Archibald Cox, for example, acknowledged that there was more to the criticism of *Brown* than crude racism. After all, in order to reach its verdict in *Brown*, the Court had to overrule the long-standing precedent of *Plessy v. Ferguson*[11] and to disregard considerable historical evidence that the Fourteenth Amendment was not intended to disbar segregated schooling.[12]

Nevertheless, Cox remains convinced that the decision was rooted in an interpretation of the Fourteenth Amendment, rather than in the personal policy predilections of the Justices. An enquiry into the intent of the framers must define their broad purpose which, he claims, was to secure all individuals a right to human dignity and equal standing before government, regardless of race. Furthermore, that purpose must be applied in the light of contemporary conditions. He concludes:

> In my view, therefore, the Desegregation Cases of the 1950s faithfully projected the general intent of the sponsors of the Equal Protection Clause upon a more particular set of circumstances as to which the sponsors left no adequate record of their particular intent. In my view, too, a court that on great occasions applies this historically grounded general intent in a

manner consistent with traditional national ideals decides in accordance
with the judge's antinomous duty to decide in a manner that invokes the
authority of an overshadowing past yet discovers some composition with
the dominant needs and aspirations of its times. The decision leans toward
the creative branch of the antinomy *but is in accordance with law* even though
it requires the overruling of precedent and the abandonment of familiar,
specific practices that fail to meet the historical ideal and general constitutional purpose.[13]

Here is revealed the ultimate importance of having a justification based
in some interpretivist method: interpretation is *law*, not *politics*. It
squares the circle of an undemocratic judiciary wielding policy-making
power in a democracy. It legitimates the exercise of the power of
judicial review.

For this reason above all, supporters of the Warren Court clung to
the defence of judicial activism as one of several permissible theories of
interpretation. However, as Warren Court jurisprudence grew ever
more distant from plausible originalist readings of the Constitution and
as conservative critics of judicial policy making gained greater
credibility, liberal supporters of judicial activism began to turn away
from interpretivism altogether. Instead, they sought to construct
justifications based on criteria which they openly conceded had nothing to do with the Constitution as originally conceived. Since the early
1970s, therefore, the academic and political battle over the legitimacy
of activist judicial review has been dominated by, on the one hand,
conservatives who demand a return to strict originalism and, on the
other, liberals who urge the Court to adopt new rationales for judicial
review. It is to that battle that we must now turn.

The interpretivists

The leading campaigners for a return to strict originalism have been
Robert Bork, Raoul Berger and Edwin Meese. They have been joined
by many others,[14] but these three have made the most important and
distinctive contributions to their side of the debate.

Bork threw down the challenge to judicial activists with his 1971
article, 'Neutral principles and some First Amendment problems',[15] in
which he contended that contemporary constitutional law lacked any
principled theory. Moreover, the debate launched in 1959 by Herbert
Wechsler over the need to discover neutral principles in constitutional
law[16] was inadequate to supply such a theory, as it concerned merely
the neutral *application* of constitutional principles rather their

derivation. If the aim and justification of judicial review was that it was free of judges' personal values, then clearly both neutral derivation and application of principles were required. Bork noted that Supreme Court Justices professed such neutrality, though he attributed this to their perception of what the public demanded of them, rather than any serious attempt to achieve it: 'The Supreme Court regularly insists that its results, and most particularly its controversial results, do not spring from the mere will of the Justices in the majority but are supported, indeed compelled, by a proper understanding of the Constitution of the United States. Value choices are attributed to the Founding Fathers, not to the Court. The way an institution advertises tells you what it thinks its customers demand.'[17]

He proceeded to dissect several of the Warren Court's leading decisions in order to demonstrate the weakness of their constitutional reasoning and the enlargement of the Court's power which resulted.[18] In *Griswold v. Connecticut*[19] in 1965, the Court revived 'substantive due process', a concept which had supposedly been jettisoned by the Court in 1937 when it ceased to employ it to invalidate New Deal legislation.[20] Substantive due process allows Justices to go beyond requiring simply that government can only deprive a citizen of life, liberty and property when it does so through established procedures of legal process, such as arraignment and trial: Justices may also require that unwritten substantive rights are observed, such as freedom of contract, which may not be infringed even by legal process. Because substantive due process inevitably requires the Justices to consult non-constitutional sources, especially their own personal values, in order to identify these new rights, none will openly confess to using it. Thus, in *Griswold*, the Court struck down a Connecticut statute forbidding married couples to use contraceptives, but in the absence of any clear constitutional basis for doing so and needing to avoid the taint of substantive due process, it squarely invented a new constitutional right altogether: the right to privacy. This was achieved by what Bork calls '. . . a miracle of transubstantiation'.[21] The opinion of Justice William O. Douglas for the Court stated that various clauses of the Constitution have penumbras which contain ancillary rights which need protection if the specified right is to be upheld. Thus, government may not require a political organisation to hand over its membership list because to do so would chill the exercise of the rights of assembly guaranteed by the First Amendment.[22] Douglas, however, then asserted that several of these penumbras created a separate and distinct right to privacy. Bork notes the evident weaknesses in Douglas' opinion. What authority

exists to explain how several penumbras are converted into a
self-standing right? Even if that existed, why should the invoked
penumbra of the First Amendment lead to a *privacy* right when it
protects activity conducted in both public and private? Is the right of
privacy indeterminate and, if not, what are its limitations? Bork concludes: 'The *Griswold* opinion fails every test of neutrality. The
derivation of the principle was utterly specious, and so was its
definition. In fact, we are left with no idea of what the principle really
forbids.'[23] For interpretivists, then, *Griswold* stands as an egregious
example of judge-made law. This is not because they approve of
restrictions on the use of contraceptives: some, like Justice Potter
Stewart, who dissented in *Griswold*, thought the Connecticut statute to
be 'uncommonly silly'.[24] It is rather because of their belief that where
the Constitution is silent on the protection to be awarded to any given
value, the elected branches of government must be left free to act as
they wish:

> Where the Constitution does not embody the ethical or moral choice, the
> judge has no basis other than his own values upon which to set aside the
> community judgement embodied in the statute. That, by definition, is an
> inadequate basis for judicial supremacy. The issue of the community's
> moral and ethical values, the issue of the degree of pain an activity causes,
> are matters concluded by the passage and enforcement of the laws in
> question. The judiciary has no role to play other than that of applying the
> statutes in a fair and impartial manner.[25]

Just as Bork is not concerned with getting the right policy outcome in
any case, neither is he impressed by a decision which could have been
justified by an originalist method, but which was actually reached by a
non-originalist method. The reason why is once again that non-
originalism leads to an unwarranted expansion of judicial power at the
expense of democracy. He demonstrates the point with a critique of
two of the Warren Court's greatest cases: *Brown v. Board of Education*,[26]
which held unconstitutional the *de jure* segregation by race of state
schools, and *Baker v. Carr*,[27] which broke with recent precedent to
order a state to reapportion its legislature. In both cases the Court's
decision was based on the Equal Protection Clause of the Fourteenth
Amendment. Bork, however, believes that the actual rationale was the
illegitimate notion of 'substantive equal protection'. This occurs when
the Court uses the Equal Protection Clause to strike down statutes
which discriminate between categories of people or things, even where
the basis of this categorisation is not explicitly forbidden by the Fourteenth Amendment. The Equal Protection Clause, says Bork, is

actually quite limited in scope: 'The equal protection clause has two legitimate meanings. It can require formal procedural equality, and, because of its historical origins, it does require that government not discriminate along racial lines. But much more than that cannot properly be read into the clause. The bare concept of equality provides no guide for courts. All law discriminates and thereby creates inequality. The Supreme Court has no principled way of saying which non-racial inequalities are impermissible.'[28]

In neither *Brown* nor *Baker*, says Bork, did the Court apply this limited concept of equal protection. The Court's decision in *Brown* was based rather on the value judgement of the Justices that '. . . government may not employ race as a classification . . .',[29] as a later series of rulings against both private and public racial discrimination demonstrated. As there is no originalist basis for interpreting the Equal Protection Clause in this way, the underlying rationale in *Brown* is illegitimate. Ironically, Bork argues, the result in *Brown* was not only correct, but it could have been justified on the originalist ground that there must be no state-enforced discrimination.[30] However, he notes, neither the Court nor most legal scholars believed that *Brown* could be sustained by an originalist principle. Yet since the result achieved by non-originalism was so manifestly right, the Court's reasoning was defended: 'It was accepted by law professors as inconsistent with the original understanding of the equal protection clause. That fact was crucial. The end of state-mandated segregation was the greatest moral triumph constitutional law had ever produced. It is not surprising that academic lawyers were unwilling to give it up; it *had* to be right. Thus, *Brown* has become the high ground of constitutional theory.'[31] Along with it went the acceptance, tacit or otherwise, of the legitimacy of judicial legislation, with the Equal Protection Clause as the constitutional instrument for the imposition of the Justices' own substantive notions of equality. And as Lino Graglia, among others, observed: 'The result was to enable the Court to move from its historic role as a brake on social change to a very different role as the primary engine of such change.'[32]

The reapportionment cases followed a similar pattern, says Bork. *Baker* could have been justified on an originalist interpretation of Article IV, Section 4 of the Constitution which states that 'The United States shall guarantee to every State in this Union a Republican Form of Government . . .' The Tennessee legislature at issue in *Baker* had not been reapportioned since 1901 and legislative districts were so uneven in population that the principle of majority rule was clearly being frustrated. This, says Bork, could reasonably be interpreted as a denial of what was intended by Article IV – a representative government.[33]

The Court, however, relied on the Equal Protection Clause, with the inevitable result that the Justices would be called upon to define equality in legislative apportionment. Two years later, in *Reynolds v. Sims*,[34] it produced that definition: one man, one vote (*sic*). The problem with the judicial imposition of such a standard on the States is not that it is a bad standard, but rather that it is one which the Constitution itself rejects in the structure of the United States Senate. It is also true that throughout their history, States have frequently mirrored the federal apportionment design by having only the lower legislative chamber apportioned according to population. It is difficult to see, therefore, why the Justices should enforce the *Reynolds* standard to the exclusion of all others, save that they thought it the most desirable and equitable basis for apportionment.

In both *Baker* and *Brown*, Bork concedes, the Court achieved a result that was justified by the Constitution. For interpretivists, however, the essence of law, constitutional or otherwise, is not results, but process. Unless judges decide according to a process of law rather than of politics, their power is incompatible with democracy. Interpretivism is an attribute of law because it involves the application of values selected by others; non-interpretivism is an attribute of politics because it involves the primary selection of values.

An inevitable consequence of interpretivism is that the Supreme Court will sometimes, perhaps frequently, make decisions that are repugnant to contemporary sensibilities. To his credit, Bork does not shrink from the policy consequences of his constitutional theory: it would entail, for example, allowing states to sterilise robbers and to ban the use of contraceptives, as well as tolerating a wide range of governmental sex discrimination and non-governmental racial discrimination.[35] However, it is important to stress that interpretivism does not *require* such policies: it rather permits elected legislatures to adopt them, leaving it to the electorate to vote for change as it sees fit.

This is very much the position of Raoul Berger, whose historical enquiries into the original intent of the Fourteenth Amendment did so much to undermine any interpretivist defence of the Warren and Burger Courts.[36] Based on analysis of the full transcript of what was said in Congress during the framing of the Fourteenth Amendment, Berger demonstrates the unfortunate fact that it was never intended to end school desegregation, to allow federal courts to order state legislative reapportionment or to incorporate the rights protected against federal government invasion by the Bill of Rights. Rather, the Fourteenth Amendment was intended to constitutionalise the rights recently protected in statute law by the Civil Rights Act of 1866.[37] These rights were limited to such things as the right to own property, to make and enforce contracts, to travel freely and to personal security.[38] As Berger concludes, 'This was a limited – tragically limited – response to the needs of blacks newly released from slavery; it reflected the hagridden racism that held both North and South in thrall; nonetheless, it was all the sovereign people were prepared to do in 1868.'[39]

Berger's analysis highlights the principal reason for the modern trend away from strict intentionalism: in the case of the Fourteenth Amendment, for example, it means constitutional toleration of barbaric racism where state legislatures are content to practise it. In a First Amendment context, as Leonard Levy has demonstrated, it would allow imprisonment for those who dared to criticise the government.[40] The simple fact is that prior to the twentieth century, and particularly its second half, American society had little notion of what are today regarded as vital civil liberties. Interpretivism, therefore, may well be more in tune with *democratic process* than non-interpretivism, but it yields results which may be out of tune with *civilised values*. Interpretivism recommends itself strongly as political theory in a social vacuum, but provides cold comfort when faced with the realities of what some states even recently have been prepared to adopt as public policy.

A further argument against interpretivism is that it is espoused by those who are at least as interested in the policy results it yields, as they are in restoring the integrity of the democratic process. Whereas both Robert Bork and Raoul Berger may be absolved of this accusation,[41] the same may not be said of the Nixon and Reagan administrations. Both were indifferent, if not hostile, to much of the substance of Warren and Burger Court liberalism and their assaults on judicial activism were simply one facet of their social and political agenda. The Reagan administration, for example, gave early evidence that it was not prepared to continue supporting efforts to eliminate even the most egregious racial discrimination. As Charles Fried, Reagan's second Solicitor-General, conceded, the administration '. . . got off to a bad start . . .'[42] In the legislative arena, it opposed re-enactment of the 1965 Voting Rights Act when it fell due for renewal in 1982, a position shared by only a few members of Congress. In the legal arena, the administration sent the Solicitor-General into bat for Bob Jones

University, a fundamentalist Christian institution in South Carolina, which, although it had admitted some black students since 1975, also had a rule against interracial dating. Such racism had caused the Internal Revenue Service under President Carter to refuse Bob Jones a charitable-status tax exemption. Now, however, the Reagan Administration went before the Supreme Court to argue for a reversal of that policy.[43] Fried also recalls that the head of the Civil Rights Division of the Attorney-General's Office, William Bradford Reynolds, '. . . proposed a constant stream of suicidally radical and unconvincing projects . . .'[44] aimed at severely curtailing legal protections against racial discrimination. On a broader level, says Fried, the views of unreconstructed Southerners were informing administration policy: 'Some Southerners never completely accepted (the) passing of the old, segregated order, and they too became part of the remarkable 1980 Republican sweep of the South. The currents of their influence also flowed into what was to become the Reagan civil-rights agenda.'[45]

It is not without reason, then, that one may be sceptical of some demands for a return to the doctrine of original intent. Edwin Meese, President Reagan's second Attorney-General, decided to lead this campaign on behalf of the administration. In a series of speeches during Reagan's second term, Meese argued for a return to 'a jurisprudence of original intention'.[46] He warned against

> . . . seeing the Constitution as an empty vessel into which each generation may pour its passion and prejudice . . . Our own time has its own fashions and passions. In recent decades, many have come to view the Constitution – more accurately, part of the Constitution, provisions of the Bill of Rights, and the Fourteenth Amendment – as a charter for judicial activism on behalf of various constituencies. Those who hold this view often have lacked demonstrable textual or historical support for their conclusions. Instead they have 'grounded' their rulings in appeals to social theories, to moral philosophies or personal notions of human dignity, or to 'penumbras,' somehow emanating ghostlike from various provisions – identified and not identified – in the Bill of Rights. The problem with this approach . . . is not that it is bad constitutional law, but that it is not constitutional law in any meaningful sense at all.[47]

While the argument was no different from that put forward by other originalists, it took on a particular resonance coming from the chief legal officer of an administration identified with the New Right social agenda.

Similarly, a later speech by Meese questioned whether the framers had intended to permit regulatory agencies, such as the Interstate

Commerce Commission and the Federal Reserve Board, which were not entirely under the control of the president. Were Meese's position to be accepted by the Supreme Court, it would result in a massive shift in power to the presidency, something to which his boss would unlikely have been adverse.[48] As with Meese's other speeches on the subject, it raised the suspicion that originalism was no less result-oriented that the non-interpretivism it excoriated.

Whatever Meese's true motivations, they helped turn a lively scholarly argument into an acrimonious political conflict. Unsurprisingly, this reached fever pitch when the scholarly and political debate became fused in 1987, with the nomination of Robert Bork to the Supreme Court of the United States. The failed Bork nomination gave rise to a massive narrative and analytical literature and does not require extensive discussion here.[49] The important point from the perspective of this discussion is that Bork's opponents – a great coalition of politicians, interest groups, academics and elements of the media – succeeded in portraying the nominee and his originalism as being 'outside the mainstream' of contemporary American jurisprudence. This outcome, like so much else in the whole episode, was at least as important for its symbolism as for its impact on future Court decisions. As the voting record of the eventual successful nominee, Anthony Kennedy, reveals, a Supreme Court Justice may reach conservative conclusions without earning the reputation of a high-profile proselytiser on behalf of originalism.[50] Nevertheless, the defeat of the Bork nomination has given additional respectability and long-term hope to non-interpretivism. Robert Bork's uncompromising exposition of originalist thinking was once, not so long ago, accepted as the orthodoxy in American jurisprudence. If indeed it now lies outside the American mainstream, it follows that the most important constraint on judicial policy making, the pre-selection of primary constitutional values by the framers, has effectively been jettisoned. There is, in fact, a vacuum in constitutional theory. The recent outpouring of non-interpretivist articles and books has been an attempt to fill that vacuum.

Before examining some of the most prominent of these works, however, it is necessary to return for a moment to the concept of Brest's 'moderate originalism'. As we saw with Archibald Cox's defence of the *Brown* decision, this allows the Justices to go so far beyond the original meaning of constitutional clauses in so many areas of law that it defies the term originalism in most respects. As Brest himself argues, moderate originalists may define the 'broad purpose' of a clause at a high level of generality. For example, the purpose of the First Amend-

ment may be '. . . to promote a free marketplace of ideas or individual
autonomy . . .' and that of the Equal Protection Clause of the Fourteenth Amendment to protect '. . . discrete and insular minorities
. . .'[51] One may reasonably ask where the Justices are to go to discover
what 'individual autonomy' requires of the law. Once the specificity of
originalism is removed, the Justices are free to decide for themselves
the source of the values they are required to read into the Constitution,
be it public opinion, legislative opinion or enlightened opinion. They
are inevitably required to select primary constitutional values, a task at
odds with democratic concepts of law. Admittedly there may be some
limits to judicial innovation imposed by moderate originalism: Brest
cites the probable inability to encompass the incorporation of the Bill of
Rights into the Due Process Clause of the Fourteenth Amendment as
one of several examples. Even here, however, there is doubt: 'Although
these doctrines strain or go beyond the text of the Constitution . . . one
cannot say with certainty that they are not authorised by the original
understanding.'[52] Moderate originalism may therefore urge judicial
restraint, but it does not command it. Neither does it provide a
coherent explanation of what the Court has actually been doing in
recent times, as different levels of generality have been selected in
different cases and by different Justices. No wonder, then, that many
scholars appear to have lost patience with it and sought an entirely new
basis for the justification of judicial review.

The non-interpretivists

Advocates of non-interpretivism often assert that the modern Supreme
Court does not operate on the basis of any form of interpretivism. Lief
Carter, for example, introduced his thesis as follows: 'This book offers
a straightforward explanation for why the conventional criteria of legal
analysis – *stare decisis*, consistency with canons of legal reasoning,
discovery of the intent of those who adopt legal rules, judicial self-
restraint, and, so forth – mix the reader up: The Supreme Court has
never paid much attention to them.'[53] Michael J. Perry is equally
sweeping: 'The decisions in virtually all modern constitutional cases of
consequence . . . cannot plausibly be explained except in terms of
non-interpretive review, because in virtually no such case can it plausibly be maintained that the framers constitutionalised the determinative
value judgement.'[54]

In this respect, of course, they differ little from the conservative
critics of the Court whose views we have just examined. However, the

radical departure of the non-interpretivists is that they approve of non-interpretivism and expend considerable effort in attempting to justify it on a principled basis. The result has been the publication of numerous works seeking to persuade scholars and judges that liberal judicial activism is legitimate, despite its flagrant inconsistency with traditional concepts of democracy and law.

Some non-interpretivists are quick to acknowledge the problematic nature of the task they have set themselves. Jesse Choper concedes that non-interpretive prescriptions '. . . either strike at the very heart of majoritarianism or pose dilemmas for democracy that demand exceedingly wise resolution.'[55] Ely lists numerous objections that may reasonably be made to a non-interpretivist approach, including that it may lead judges to decide in a highly subjective manner: '. . . vague and untethered standards inevitably lend themselves to the virtually irresistible temptation to intervene when one's political or moral sensitivities are sufficiently affronted.'[56] Thus, as Perry observes, 'The legitimacy of non-interpretive review is the central problem of contemporary constitutional theory.'[57]

Yet despite these reservations, each goes on to elaborate a non-interpretive rationale for judicial review. Perry follows Choper in arguing a functional justification:

> There is no plausible textual or historical justification for constitutional policymaking by the judiciary – no way to avoid the conclusion that non-interpretive review, whether of state or federal action, cannot be justified by reference either to the text or the intentions of the framers of the Constitution. The justification for the practice, if there is one, must be functional. If non-interpretive review serves a crucial governmental function that no other practice can reasonably be expected to serve, and if it serves that function in a manner that somehow accommodates the principle of electorally accountable policymaking, then that function constitutes the justification for non-interpretive review.[58]

It is important to note that Perry's non-interpretivist model is selective, restricting judicial power to areas where the judiciary has a unique competence to perform a particular function. Thus, he would preclude virtually all judicial review of federalism and separation of powers cases because the branches of government involved in these are more capable than the judiciary of determining between them the best arrangements.[59] In human rights cases, however, he believes that the judiciary has developed an expertise that exists nowhere else in the political system: 'Over time, the practice of non-interpretive review has evolved as a way of remedying what would otherwise be a serious defect in American government – the absence of any policymaking institution that *regularly* deals with fundamental political-moral problems other than by mechanical reference to established moral conventions.'[60] Americans are open to moral leadership, Perry argues, but other branches which must follow the logic of the electoral process are largely incapable of providing it. Thus:

> As a matter of comparative institutional competence, the politically insulated federal judiciary is more likely, when the human rights issue is a deeply controversial one, to move us in the direction of a right answer (assuming there is such a thing) than is the political process left to its own devices, which tends to resolve such issues by reflexive, mechanical reference to established moral conventions.[61]

Whether Perry is correct in either his empirical or prescriptive points is something that will be considered in the final chapter. For present purposes, it is sufficient to note that his model frees the Court from all constraint by the Constitution. This is true both in the sense that the Constitution never envisaged such a role for the judiciary and also in that the moral values on which the Court must adjudicate need not be drawn from that document. It is a frank appeal for the Court to be assessed on its performance and results. Perry believes that its performance to date is encouraging: 'My own view is that non-interpretive review in most substantive due process cases, specifically those in which the judiciary has sought to establish freedom of intimate association as a human right, consists, in the main, of right answers . . .'[62]

There remains then, for Perry, only the question of how such judicial review can be squared with democracy: in what sense does it produce electorally accountable policy making? The answer, he argues, is already in place. At any time it chooses, Congress may withdraw the Court's appellate jurisdiction over a given area of law. The fact that this has frequently been attempted since the 1950s, but never once successfully achieved, indicates to him that there is considerable support for what the Court has been doing.[63]

John Hart Ely's prescription for non-interpretivist review is directed more towards achieving the best political process than the most desirable policy results. In fact, Ely is deeply troubled by the fact that several provisions of the Constitution, by their vagueness, actually invite the Court to look elsewhere for the substantive values that it should enforce. The First, Eighth, Ninth and Fourteenth Amendments all invite judicial 'freelancing',[64] with the undemocratic result that courts, not legislatures, make fundamental value and policy choices. He proposes that the Court steer clear of making such choices and, instead, adopt '. . . a participation, representative-reinforcing approach to judicial review.'[65] Three main factors are cited to justify this approach, only the first of which is related to the text of the Constitution. This is that the Constitution is preoccupied with procedural fairness in regard to individual disputes and with ensuring broad participation in the processes of government. The Court should therefore take its cue from this asserted preoccupation and ensure a maximum of participation and representation.[66] The second merit of this scheme is said to be that, unlike the judicial determination of fundamental value choices, it supports the principles of representative democracy rather than undermining them.[67] Third, it is an approach to which judges are particularly suited, since they are '. . . experts on process and (more important) . . . political outsiders'.[68] This last argument echoes the functionalism of Perry and Choper, though it adds political process to moral philosophy as areas in which judges are said to have particular expertise.

Other non-interpretivists offer still further rationalisations. Lief Carter argues that the Supreme Court's decisions should be assessed not according to traditional canons of legal interpretation but '. . . employ instead aesthetic criteria of good performance.'[69] *Brown* was thus decided well because the Court produced a coherent, though not necessarily correct, syllogism: 'I believe the opinion persuasively harmonised the basic principle of equality of opportunity with the evidence that racial segregation unequalises the opportunities of racial minorities, but my point is that goodness depends not on the rightness of the principle of equality of opportunity or the scientific accuracy of the factual evidence, but on the nature of the fit the opinion claimed to create.'[70]

For his part, Paul Brest has a broad proposal which encompasses concern for both process and results:

> Having abandoned both consent and fidelity to the text and original understanding as the touchstones of constitutional decision making, let me propose a designedly vague criterion: How well, compared to possible alternatives, does the practice contribute to the well-being of our society – or, more narrowly, to the ends of constitutional government? Among other things, the practice should (1) foster democratic government; (2) protect individuals against arbitrary, unfair, and intrusive official action; (3) conduce to a political order that is stable but which also responds to changing conditions, values, and needs; (4) not readily lend itself to arbitrary decisions or abuses; and (5) be acceptable to the populace.[71]

Such a sweeping delegation of authority to the Court would clearly represent a radical break with the past and suggests very few limits to judicial power other than those imposed by a rebellious polity. Whatever merits it may possess, it undeniably challenges the very concept of an elective democracy and calls to mind Judge Learned Hand's oft-quoted comment that 'Even if I knew how to choose them, I would find it extremely irksome to be governed by a bevy of Platonic Guardians.'[72]

One last approach deserves mention here, because it claims to be neither interpretivist nor non-interpretivist, though, in fact, it clearly belongs with the latter set of models. (If it requires a distinctive name, it should perhaps be 'intentionalist non-interpretivist', but that would hardly be helpful!) This approach takes issue with the interpretivists' theory of the Framers' theory of interpretation. It argues that the framers did not intend successive generations of Americans to interpret the Constitution according to the intentions or values of their predecessors, including the Framers themselves. David A. J. Richards has recently produced a complex elaboration of this thesis, which begins with a basic challenge to advocates of original intent: '. . . strict constructionism can give no adequate answer to a fundamental question of political legitimacy: why should a contemporary generation be bound to the will of a generation long dead?'[73] A detailed examination of the framers' uses of history and political theory persuades Richards that they regarded such 'historicist patriarchalism' as 'morally and politically corrupt'.[74] In short, the Framers never intended to bind future generations to their will. On the other hand, he berates non-interpretivists for urging that the judiciary be given an '. . . unchecked political power with no interpretive obligations to make sense of history and tradition.'[75] However, Richards' detailed exposition raises the suspicion that the judicial obligation to interpret constitutional clauses in their historical contexts, both present and past, boils down to little more than the right of the Justices to abandon original intent wherever contemporary morality suggests it is reasonable to do so. For example, he says of the Equal Protection Clause of the Fourteenth Amendment:

> The factual and normative premises underlying the consensus of the 1868 'founders' are no longer reasonable interpretations of the abstract value of equal dignity that they respected, and the attempt to limit the interpretive scope of equal protection by adopting these premises insults the intelligence and morality of a community of principle that does find and should find this interpretation reasonable.[76]

A rough summary would be that times and values have changed and if the Fourteenth Amendment were to be enacted today, it would disbar many of the practices thought reasonable in 1868. This is unexceptional apart from one major fact: the Supreme Court has never been conceded the power to revise the Constitution – the procedure for doing that is laid out in Article V. Richards appears to be doing little more than continuing one strand of non-interpretivism which would concede the power of constitutional amendment to the Court, if for no other reason than that Article V procedures are too impractical to meet society's changing needs. Leonard Levy advocated this some twenty years ago when he wrote that '. . . the Supreme Court is and must be for all practical purposes a "continuing constitutional convention" in the sense that it must keep updating the original charter by reinterpretation – and in the sense that it cannot decide cases on the basis of what the Constitution says.'[77]

Richards' non-interpretivism is even clearer in his discussion of unenumerated rights, especially the Court's privacy rights relating to marriage, contraception, abortion and so on. These fundamental rights may only be abridged by the state when justified by a goal that is free of sectarian disagreement, so that all persons, regardless of sect or philosophy, could reasonably agree that the law protects the general good. Thus the right to an abortion must be constitutionally protected because,

> The nature of the moral debate over abortion is as profoundly sectarian as the comparable debate over contraception. In both cases, condemnation derives from a traditional conception of both sexuality and gender roles, one in which value in living is viewed through the sectarian prism of exclusively procreational sexuality and women's ordained role as selflessly devoted mother with no other aims or aspirations.[78]

In effect, this allows the Supreme Court first to choose which values are fundamental according to contemporary values and then to permit their abridgement only where there is universal support for doing so. This turns on its head the traditional relationship held to exist between the judiciary and the unelected branches of government: namely, majority rule is permitted, except where there is super-majoritarian support for restricting it, as when two-thirds of the Congress and three-quarters of the state legislatures approve a constitutional amendment. Richards, however, at least in some cases, would redefine majority views as 'factionalised prejudices' which unconstitutionally oppress women and homosexuals, for example.[79] Legislative distinctions between these groups and others ought to be regarded as 'suspect classifications' under the Equal Protection Clause, along with distinc-

tions based on race. The poor might also be brought in under the same
constitutional umbrella: 'We might . . . come to see the traditional
republican view of the slavish poor as reflecting an unquestioned
natural hierarchy that insults the capacity for reasonable freedom due
all persons under republican constitutionalism.'[80]

Many will share Richards' moral and political philosophy, but as
constitutional theory it has little in common with any other type of
intentionalism and much in common with the other non-interpretive
theories discussed here.

What is clear from this survey of contemporary constitutional theory
is that a new phase has been reached in thinking about judicial policy
making. As interpretivism, the orthodox approach until recently,
becomes increasingly incapable of yielding decisions that deal
authoritatively with contemporary social issues, many in America's law
schools are urging the Court to abandon the Constitution, rather than
the issues. A frank call is being made for political judging, something
which its critics regard as a heresy which has taken over in important
legal and political circles. As Robert Bork writes: '. . . the heresy of
political judging is systemic. A great many judges subscribe to it, a large
number of left-wing activist groups promote it, many senators insist
upon it, and in the legal academy this heresy is dominant.'[81] For many
of the 'heretics', however, interpretivist criticism simply has no sting –
it is not so much wrong, as simply irrelevant. In their view, interpretivism is based on a concept of the judicial function that belongs to
the past, when neither contemporary views of law and judges nor the
contemporary social agenda were apparent. Non-interpretivism is by
contrast held to be an approach which best serves society's contemporary needs. An important agenda of social issues does exist and the
federal judiciary is the institution best suited to address it.

The extent to which Supreme Court Justices have been affected by
non-interpretivist thought will be examined empirically in subsequent
chapters. As most commentators agree, however, federal judges are
very open to influence by law school theorists. Nor is this a recent
development, as Henry Abraham observed: 'Articles that appear in law
reviews and other legal periodicals undoubtedly have exerted a
formative influence on the law for some time. This is only natural,
because the best legal thinking finds expression in these periodicals . . .
The jurists are part of the legal process and are quite naturally
generally familiar with the thinking that presents itself in the pages of
the reviews; indeed, they must be familiar with it if they wish to keep
their fingers on the pulse of the profession and, as Justice Holmes put it

so cogently, "the felt necessities of the times".'[82] Robert Bork agrees, pointing out that judges are both members of the legal community and of the intellectual community: 'Like most people, judges tend to accept the assumptions of the culture that surrounds them, often without fully understanding the foundations of those assumptions or their implications. If they can be persuaded to abandon the idea of original understanding, they are quite likely to frame constitutional rules that reflect the assumptions of modern liberal culture.'[83]

In practice, non-interpretivism has developed in tandem with the appearance on the political scene of the Social Issue and the systemic changes in the political and judicial process outlined in the previous chapter. Whatever the causal relationship between them, these three factors have been mutually reinforcing developments that go a long way in explaining the modern Supreme Court. As we now turn to a detailed examination of the Court's decisions on prominent aspects of the Social Issue, we will see how each has played a vital role in determining constitutional outcomes.

Notes

1 Lunch, *op. cit.*, p. 2.
2 See, for example, the work of the 'judicial behaviourist', Glendon Scubert: *Judicial Policy Making: The Political Role of the Courts* (rev. ed.), Glenview, 1974.
3 *Marbury v. Madison*, 1 Cranch 137. For a thorough discussion of Marshall's innovations in judicial review, see S. Snowiss, *Judicial Review And The Law of the Constitution*, New Haven, 1990.
4 J. Hart Ely, 'Constitutional interpretivism: its allure and impossibility', *Indiana Law Journal*, XIII, 1978, pp. 399–448. Ronald Dworkin also acknowledges the current centrality of this debate, but he dislikes its terms. All judges are interpretivists, he argues, because all law is inherently interpretivist. Judges who are labelled interpretivists, he says, would be better described as 'historicists': *Law's Empire*, Cambridge, 1986, pp. 359–60. Dworkin's critique is not very helpful, however. Apart from adding to an already overcrowded field of terminology, it also ignores the point made by Ely and Bork alike that non-interpretivism is not law at all.
5 P. Brest, 'The misconceived quest for the original understanding', *Boston University Law Review*, LX, 1980, pp. 204–38.
6 4 Wheat. 316.
7 Brest, *op. cit.*, p. 217.
8 *Ibid.*, p. 223.
9 347 US 483.
10 *Ibid.*, p. 489–90. I do not wish to imply that I find this argument convincing, nor that it was the only method employed by the Chief Justice in this case.
11 163 US 537 (1896).
12 See, for example, R. Berger, *Government By Judiciary*, Cambridge, 1977.
13 A. Cox, *The Court And The Constitution*, Boston, 1987, p. 260 (emphasis added).
14 I would include here, for example, L. Graglia, *Disaster By Decree: The Supreme Court's Decisions on Race and Schools*, Ithaca, 1976; N. Glazer, 'Towards an imperial judiciary?', *The Public Interest*, XV, 1975, pp. 104–23; C. Wolfe, *The Rise of Modern Judicial Review:*

From Constitutional Interpretation to Judge-Made Law, New York, 1986.
15 *Indiana Law Journal*, XLVll, 1971, pp. 1–35. This has recently been reprinted, along with other relevant, useful articles in J. N. Rakove (ed.), *Interpreting The Constitution: The Debate Over Original Intent*, Boston, 1990.
16 'Towards neutral principles of constitutional law', *Harvard Law Review*, LXXVI, 1959, pp. 1–35.
17 Bork, *op. cit.*, pp. 3–4.
18 It is important to note that Bork does not believe that the Warren Court alone has been guilty of unprincipled jurisprudence. As his more recent work shows, the trend started long before 1954 and continued into the Burger and Rehnquist Courts: *The Tempting of America: The Political Seduction Of The Law*, New York, 1990.
19 381 US 479 (1965).
20 See, for example, R. McCloskey, 'Economic due process and the Supreme Court: an exhumation and reburial', in P. Kurland (ed.), *The Supreme Court and the Judicial Function*, Chicago, 1975.
21 Bork, 1971, *op. cit.*, p. 8.
22 *NAACP v. Alabama*, 357 US 449 (1958).
23 Bork, 1971, *op. cit.*, p. 9. Imprecision remains a serious flaw in the right to privacy. As we shall see later, the Court held in 1973 that it protected the right to choose to have an abortion, even though such a medical procedure is not a wholly private act. The right to choose is better described as an act of personal autonomy, than as an act of privacy. On the other hand, in 1986 the Court refused to grant privacy protection to consenting adult homosexuals engaging in sex in their own homes, perhaps the most private activity of all.
24 381 US 479, 527 (1965). Justice Hugo Black, a leading liberal on the Court, also dissented, citing the fact that the text of the Constitution simply contained no right to privacy.
25 Bork, 1971, *op. cit.*, p. 10.
26 347 US 483 (1954).
27 369 US 186 (1962).
28 Bork, 1971, *op. cit.*, p. 11.
29 Bork, 1990, *op. cit.*, p. 79.
30 Bork, 1971, *op. cit.*, p. 15. I am not entirely convinced that Bork's rationale is in fact originalist, since he says that it is based in part on the fact that the framers of the Fourteenth Amendment 'did not understand' that the equality they desired and the segregation they permitted '. . .' were mutually inconsistent . . .' (1990), p. 82. This sounds an awful lot like the judicial practice of 'keeping the Constitution in tune with the times' which Bork so roundly condemns.
31 Bork, 1990, *op. cit.*, p. 77.
32 'How the constitution disappeared', in J. Rakove, *Interpreting the Constitution: The Debate over Original Intent*, Boston, 1990, p. 36.
33 Bork, 1971, *op. cit.*, p. 19; 1990, *op. cit.*, p. 85.
34 377 US 533 (1964).
35 Bork, 1971, *op. cit.*, pp. 12–15. To be fair, he also believes that interpretivism would have avoided such monstrous decisions as *Dred Scott v. Sandford*, 60 US 693 (1857).
36 *Government By Judiciary: The Transformation of the Fourteenth Amendment*, Cambridge, Mass., 1977. See also *Death Penalties*, Cambridge, Mass.,1982. The defence against Berger's charges concentrate less on disputing his history – although some partial rebuttal is attempted – than on the interpretivist method he advances. See, for example, W. F. Murphy, 'Constitutional interpretation: the art of the historian, magician, or statesman', *Yale Law Journal*, LXXXVII, 1978, pp. 1752–71.
37 *Ibid.*, p. 23.
38 *Ibid.*, pp. 24–36.
39 *Ibid.*, p. 407.

40 'Liberty and the First Amendment', in *Constitutional Opinions*, New York, 1986, p. 162.
41 The works of both seem to me to be more inspired by a particular concept of law than by a specific policy agenda.
42 C. Fried, *Order & Law: Arguing The Reagan Revolution – A Firsthand Account*, New York, 1991, p. 102.
43 *Bob Jones University v. US*, 461 US 574 (1983).
44 Fried, *op. cit.*, p. 41.
45 *Ibid.*, p. 102.
46 Address before the American Bar Association, Washington, D.C., 9 July, 1985, reprinted in Rakove, *op. cit.*, pp. 13–21.
47 *Ibid.*, p. 18.
48 B. Schwartz, *The New Right And The Constitution: Turning Back The Legal Clock*, Boston, 1990, p. 200. See also Fried, *op. cit.*, p. 50.
49 See, for example, Bonner, *op. cit.*; Hodder-Williams, *op. cit*; Bork, 1990, *op. cit.*, Part III.
50 For example, in the Court's 1989 Term, Justice Kennedy voted in ways very similar to the Court's other conservatives: *Harvard Law Review*, CIV, 1991, p. 360.
51 Brest, *op. cit.*, pp. 223–4.
52 *Ibid.*, p. 224.
53 *Contemporary Constitutional Lawmaking: The Supreme Court and the Art of Politics*, New York, 1985, p. 1.
54 *The Constitution, The Courts, and Human Rights: An Inquiry into the Legitimacy of Constitutional Policymaking by the Judiciary*, New Haven, 1982, p. 11.
55 *Judicial Review and the National Political Process*, Chicago, 1980, p. 75.
56 Ely, *op. cit.*, p. 403.
57 Perry, *op. cit.*, p. 10.
58 *Ibid.*, p. 24.
59 *Ibid.*, Chapter 2. Perry draws heavily on Choper, *op. cit.*, for these arguments.
60 *Ibid.*, p. 101.
61 *Ibid.*, p. 102.
62 *Ibid.*, p. 118.
63 *Ibid.*, p. 134.
64 Ely, *op. cit.*, p. 413.
65 *Democracy and Distrust: A Theory of Judicial Review*, Cambridge, Mass., 1980, p. 87.
66 *Ibid.*, p. 87.
67 *Ibid.*, p. 88.
68 *Ibid.*.
69 *Ibid.*, p. 1.
70 *Ibid.*, p. 2.
71 *Ibid.*, p. 226.
72 L. Hand, *The Bill of Rights*, Cambridge, 1958, p. 73. So radical is Brest's proposal that it has been used to illustrate the critique of conventional legal theories by the Critical Legal Studies Movement, even though he is not formally a part of the movement: M. Kelman, *A Guide To Critical Legal Studies*, Cambridge, 1987, p. 213. The CLS Movement not only asserts that law is politics, but also that the Rule of Law itself is primarily a means of codifying social inequality: H. Stumpf, *American Judicial Politics*, San Diego, 1988, Chapter 2.
73 *Foundations of American Constitutionalism*, Oxford, 1989, p. 11.
74 *Ibid.* p. 143.
75 *Ibid.*, p. 144.
76 *Ibid.*, p. 271.
77 'Judicial activism and strict construction', in Levy, *op. cit.*, p. 235.
78 Richards, *op. cit.*, p. 234.
79 *Ibid.*, p. 285.
80 *Ibid.*.

81 Bork, *op. cit.*, p. 7.
82 H. Abraham, *The Judicial Process* (5th ed.), New York, 1986, p. 243.
83 Bork, *op. cit.*, p. 8.

Three—Capital punishment

> It should be remembered that until 1963, no one really gave a second
> thought to the idea of attacking capital punishment through the judicial
> system.[1]

In 1972, in the case of *Furman v. Georgia*,[2] the Supreme Court produced one of the greatest constitutional surprises in its entire history: it
struck down every death penalty statute in the land on the grounds that
they violated the Eighth Amendment's ban on 'cruel and unusual
punishments'. Just four years later, in *Gregg v. Georgia*,[3] the Court beat
a hasty retreat in the face of a 'post-*Furman* legislative frenzy'[4] and
upheld the constitutionality of capital punishment *per se*. Since then,
the Court has been deeply mired in the endless struggle between the
forces of abolition and retention, as it has tried to find a formula which
retains the integrity of the principles of both *Furman* and *Gregg*.

The Supreme Court's embroilment in the death penalty issue
involves virtually every judicial and political factor discussed in the two
previous chapters. The Court in *Furman* in effect employed a non-
interpretive method to impose an enlightened policy on an
unsympathetic majority, over a question which lay at the heart of the
Social Issue. In so doing, it was responding to the campaign of a
pressure group which cleverly exploited recent developments in the
use of litigation as an instrument of social reform. The *Furman* decision
generated a popular and legislative backlash, partly because most
Americans believe that the death penalty is an important weapon in the
war against crime, but also because the issue symbolises a broader
moral and social conflict which pits traditionalists against progressives.
Indeed, given the lack of any compelling evidence that the death
penalty actually deters criminals, and the relative infrequency with
which those sentenced to death are executed, the death penalty in the
United States should be viewed as primarily a moral issue. In reaching
out to provide a strong lead on capital punishment, the Court found
that, as with other moral controversies, mounting the tiger's back was
far easier than descending unscathed.

The *Furman* decision came as a great surprise even to those who had campaigned for it. Michael Meltsner, a lawyer for the Legal Defence and Educational Fund, Inc. (LDF) of the National Association for the Advancement of Coloured People, which led the fight for judicial abolition, said the *Furman* decision came 'against every expectation'.[5] The reasons why are not hard to see. In the first place, the text of the Constitution explicitly allows for the imposition of the death penalty. Most obviously, the Fifth and Fourteenth Amendments permit 'the deprivation of life' provided it is done according to due process of law. In this context, the Eighth Amendment's ban on 'cruel and unusual punishments' was clearly not intended to encompass capital punishment, but rather barbaric punishments, such as burning at the stake or crucifixion.[6] No originalist-interpretivist basis for abolition was therefore available.

Worse still, however, was that despite the recent injection of a non-interpretivist standard into Eighth Amendment jurisprudence, no less a liberal activist than Chief Justice Earl Warren had specifically dismissed the idea that the death penalty was constitutionally cruel and unusual. In 1958, in *Trop v. Dulles*, Warren wrote the Court's opinion which held that the meaning of the Eighth Amendment was not immutably fixed at the time of its adoption: rather, it '. . . must draw its meaning from from the evolving standards of decency that mark the progress of a maturing society.'[7] The 'evolving standards' criterion clearly opened wide the door to a non-interpretivist application of the Eighth Amendment to capital punishment, yet Warren closed it firmly: 'At the outset, let us put to one side the death penalty as an index of the constitutional limit on punishment. Whatever the arguments may be against corporal punishment – and they are forceful – the death penalty has been employed throughout our history, and, in a day when it is still widely accepted, it cannot be said to violate the constitutional concept of cruelty.'[8]

Right up until the eve of the decision in *Furman*, the Court continued to give abolitionists little hope. In May 1971, in *McGautha v. California*, a 6–3 majority of the Justices turned down a claim that, in capital cases, the absence of jury sentencing standards and the failure to provide separate trial and sentencing hearings violated the Due Process clause of the Fourteenth Amendment.[9] If the Court was unwilling to entertain a partial and relatively low-key attack on the death penalty, it was highly unlikely that it would uphold a frontal assault through the Eighth Amendment.

A third reason for judicial caution was simply that the vast majority of states, as well as the federal government, retained a death penalty statute. At the time of the *Furman* decision, thirty-nine states plus the District of Columbia had capital punishment.[10] These figures hardly seemed conducive to a showing that the death penalty was cruel *and* unusual. Furthermore, the tide of public opinion was running against abolitionism and, by inference, against the notion that capital punishment was unacceptably cruel. Public opposition to the death penalty had been growing steadily in the first half of the 1960s, in line with the general development of liberal thinking. In May 1966, for the first (and only) time, an opinion poll showed a majority of Americans, 47 per cent–42 per cent, opposed the death penalty for murder.[11] Thereafter, however, support for abolition fell away and by the time of the *Furman* decision, retentionists had a 15 per cent lead over abolitionists.[12] The reversal of the abolitionist trend was almost certainly related to a fearsome rise in violent crime which took place in the late 1960s: between 1967 and 1971, the number of murders rose by 61 per cent and other violent crimes by 80 per cent.[13] Combined with the general conservative trend in politics in the late 1960s, heightened public fear of crime made a bold strike against capital punishment by the Supreme Court seem untimely.

In short, the Constitution, the Court's own recent precedents, the views of the elected branches of government and public opinion all appeared to militate against the decision that was eventually reached in *Furman*. What then impelled the Court to take such a politically rash step?

Hugo Bedau, perhaps the most prolific abolitionist author, attributes great importance to the '. . . indispensable role of moral elites.'[14] Three such elites were centrally involved in the campaign to abolish the death penalty. First, '. . . the self-appointed guardians of civil rights and civil liberties in the United States, notably the NAACP Legal Defence and Educational Fund, Inc. (LDF) and the American Civil Liberties Union (ACLU).'[15] As we shall see below, the LDF mounted a brilliant legal campaign which led first to a *de facto* moratorium on executions and then to the *Furman* decision itself. The role of the ACLU was secondary in this campaign, in part because its national leaders could not be sure of the support of its regional affiliates or its rank and file membership. It is a mark of the political weakness of abolitionism that the ACLU only took a formal position of opposition to the death penalty in 1965.[16] As Bedau concedes, even with these and other interest groups who played a role in the abolitionist movement, it was the leaders, the elite of the elites, who committed themselves to abolition: '. . . opposition to the death penalty as such is not and has never been *vox populi*.'[17]

It was precisely because of this lack of determined public support that it was necessary for the abolitionist campaign to address itself to the governmental elite that is furthest from popular control, the federal judiciary. As others have pointed out, successful campaigns for the abolition of capital punishment in Western nations have never relied upon the approval of the general public. Rather, legislators have taken the responsibility of the decision upon themselves, usually in the teeth of strong public disapproval.[18] In the United States, however, with its profound populist traditions, legislators are rarely so bold. It is then left to the federal judiciary, if anyone, to exploit its insulation from the electorate to make principled, though unpopular, decisions.

The third elite cited by Bedau consists of those who, in chapter one, were identified as New Class members: 'These moral and judicial elites have had continuing support from the highly educated academic and professional elites (social scientists, physicians, lawyers, humanists) from whom they are drawn.'[19] However, support from such people has been by no means complete. The American Bar Association, for example, has never come out against capital punishment and in 1978 its House of Delegates heavily defeated a motion calling upon the states to abolish the death penalty by 168 votes to 69.[20] The American Law Institute's Model Penal Code only went so far as to recommend a more systematic approach to capital punishment: two-stage trial/sentencing processes, with the second hearing weighing aggravating and mitigating circumstances.[21] Bedau also points out that of twelve *amicus* briefs filed in support of abolition in *Furman*, none came from concerned professional organisations such as the American Sociological Organisation, the American Psychiatric Association or the American Philosophical Association.[22]

On the other hand, he says, individual members of important elites do provide key support for the LDF's activities. LDF lawyers have access to every major law school in the country, most of whose faculty members, he believes, are sympathetic to abolition; the support of some of the nation's most influential newspapers, such as the *New York Times*, *Washington Post* and *Boston Globe*; and 'The annual receptions held by the LDF in New York, Boston and other major cities for its benefactors and supporters represent every elite in American society: social, financial, political, academic, intellectual, and professional'.[23] It is important to stress that these are '. . . disinterested moral elites . . .'[24] in that they derive no direct, personal benefit from abolition of the death penalty: they are simply not of the class to whom it is usually meted out. Their motivation is their commitment to certain moral values which seem to derive, at least in part, from their professional and educational backgrounds. Demographic analysis of opinion on the death penalty does not yield many clear explanatory factors, though those with a college education are significantly more likely to oppose the death penalty than those with only high school or grade school education.[25]

As noted above, one of these elites, the LDF, played a central role in preparing the ground for the *Furman* decision. As an off-shoot of the NAACP, the LDF had originally become interested in the death penalty issue because of the racially discriminatory pattern of its use.[26] Given the difficulty of proving discrimination in individual cases, however, the LDF by the mid-1960s had adopted the strategy of appealing every single death sentence in the country, in the hope of establishing a *de facto* moratorium on executions.[27] The number of executions actually carried out had already fallen drastically, from forty-seven in 1962 to seven in 1965.[28] If they could be stopped altogether for a long enough period, hundreds, if not thousands, of prisoners would be on death row and, hopefully, the prospect of restarting executions on a wholesale basis would be too repugnant to contemplate. However, in 1966, Ronald Reagan and Claude Kirk were elected Governor of California and Florida, respectively. These states had the highest death row populations in the country, but the new Governors began signing death warrants in unprecedented numbers.[29]

The sheer number of individual appeals generated by this development threatened to overwhelm LDF resources and defeat its moratorium strategy. It was therefore obliged to attempt an innovation in legal doctrine: to seek to apply the concept of the class action to criminal, as opposed to civil, cases, something which had never been attempted successfully.[30] In April, 1967, however, a Florida District Judge issued a temporary stay order on all executions in the state. In July, a California judge did the same. The net effect of these decisions was to halt executions in the two states until the constitutionality of the death penalty was itself resolved.[31] Even LDF lawyers had little confidence in the outcome of these hearings and discouraged the class action strategy in other states. Anthony Amsterdam, the LDF's leading counsel in the campaign, advised a colleague: 'I would . . . approach the thought of a class suit in the way in which porcupines are said to make love – *very* gingerly'.[32]

Amsterdam was equally unconfident about the chances of the

Supreme Court declaring that the death penalty violated the Eighth Amendment's ban on cruel and unusual punishments. At a 1968 LDF national conference, he recommended a collateral attack on the death penalty through the Due Process and Equal Protection clauses of the Fourteenth Amendment.[33] This could encompass such issues as racially discriminatory sentencing; the use of 'death-qualified juries', where prosecutors had successfully challenged any prospective juror who voiced doubts about the death penalty; single verdict trials, where guilt and sentence were determined at the same hearing, thereby obliging an accused who wished to plead for leniency to undermine the chances of a not-guilty verdict; and unfettered jury sentencing discretion, which, in the absence of clear guidelines, could lead to arbitrary or random imposition of the the death sentence. Amsterdam described the Eighth Amendment, on the other hand, has having 'limited value' as a legal argument.[34]

The LDF campaign for a moratorium was successful. No one was executed in the United States between 1968 and 1976 inclusive. It was broken only by Gary Gilmore's own insistence that he be executed by firing squad in Utah in January, 1977. The first involuntary execution after the moratorium did not take place until May 1979, when John Spenkelink was electrocuted in Florida.[35] Thus, by the time the Supreme Court came to consider the death penalty head-on in 1972, there were over six hundred death row prisoners whose fate depended on the outcome.[36] As intended, this fact is said to have put at least some of the Justices under considerable pressure to declare the current death penalty statutes unconstitutional.[37] This is hardly surprising. The personal feelings and philosophy of a Justice can be influential or even decisive in determining his or her vote in any given case. When the vote is literally a matter of life and death for hundreds of human beings, and when Justices personally find capital punishment repugnant, the urge to vote one's policy predilection is inevitably intense.[38] The LDF had certainly created a moral, as well as judicial, dilemma for the Court.

On the other hand, the Justices were undoubtedly aware of the potential controversy of their decision. 1972 was a presidential election year and '. . . capital punishment was now a hot political issue. Nixon had made the death penalty a foot soldier in his war on crime.'[39] Moreover, the Court was currently also contemplating a decision on another hot political issue – abortion. As Justice White is reported to have said in case conference, 'If the Court struck down the death penalty and at the same time allowed abortion . . . the public reaction would be awful. The Court would be portrayed as allowing convicted killers to live, and sentencing unborn babies to die.'[40] The Justices were in an unenviable position.

We come then to the Supreme Court's decision in *Furman v. Georgia*. It was not, to say the least, entirely clear. A 5–4 majority voted to strike down all existing death penalty statutes, but there was no agreed rationale for so doing. Of the majority Justices, Brennan and Marshall argued that the death penalty *per se* violated the Eighth Amendment, but Stewart, Douglas and White only went so far as to say that the infrequent and random pattern of its imposition made current laws unconstitutional. All four dissenting Justices argued that the majority had failed to demonstrate that the death penalty was indeed deemed cruel and unusual in contemporary society.

At the heart of the legal issues lay the interpretation and application of the formula delineated by Chief Justice Warren in his *Trop* opinion in 1958, that the Eighth Amendment '. . . must draw its meaning from the evolving standards of decency that mark the progress of a maturing society.'[41] Even the dissenting Justices accepted that this was the correct judicial formula for deciding the case: hence none argued for an originalist-interpretivist approach which would have held unconstitutional only those punishments deemed cruel and unusual at the time of its adoption in 1791, or when the Fourteenth Amendment was adopted in 1868.[42] Thus, Chief Justice Burger agreed that while the constitutional criterion of 'cruel' remained constant, '. . . its applicability must change as the basic mores of society change.'[43]

'Evolving standards of decency' is not a precise concept and it leaves the Justices considerable discretion in defining it. Whose standards should be followed? Public opinion, legislative opinion, 'enlightened' opinion and the Justices' own moral sense are all possible touchstones. And if 'social consensus' is the key to what evolving standards are at any given moment, how is that consensus to be ascertained and interpreted? The confusion in *Furman* resulted primarily from the fact that there was wide disagreement on these issues, rather than from disagreement on the morality of capital punishment. In other words, the interpretive method of the Court was in dispute and along with it, inevitably, the political role of the Court in a system of separation of powers.

Justice Brennan elaborated a cumulative four-point test of the constitutionality of a punishment under the Eighth Amendment:

> If a punishment is unusually severe, if there is a strong probability that it is inflicted arbitrarily, if it is substantially rejected by contemporary society,

and if there is no reason to believe that it serves any penal purpose more effectively than some less severe punishment, then the continued infliction of that punishment violates the command of the Clause that the state may not inflict inhuman and uncivilised punishments upon those convicted of crimes.[44]

The problem with each of the four points is, however, that there simply is no agreement on whether they are true of the death penalty. With opinion so divided, the Justices have only two basic choices: to defer to the views of others, such as the elected representatives of the states, or to follow their own inclinations and assert the power of the Court. Brennan and Marshall chose the latter route, despite some rhetoric to the contrary.

On the key question of whether the death penalty was acceptable to contemporary society, Justice Brennan paid lip-service to the need to avoid judicial subjectivity, arguing that the Court must seek 'objective indicators' of acceptability.[45] He proceeded, however, to dismiss as insufficient the most obvious such indicators – the existence of death penalty statutes in the large majority of states and the public approval of the death penalty in referenda and opinion polls. The decisive factor, rather, is the steadily declining imposition and implementation of the death penalty: the sheer infrequency of executions demonstrates the contemporary unacceptability of capital punishment. With consider-able ingenuity, Brennan asserts that the evidence of polls, referenda and numerous statutes actually supports his conclusion: it '. . . simply underscores the extent to which our society has in fact rejected this punishment. When an unusually severe punishment is authorised for widespread application but not, because of society's refusal, inflicted save in a few instances, the inference is compelling that there is a deep-seated reluctance to inflict it. Indeed, the likelihood is great that the punishment is tolerated only because of its disuse.'[46] This is a highly selective inference from what is already highly selective evi-dence: after all, as Chief Justice Burger pointed out, if juries are assumed to display civilised values when they *refuse* to impose the death penalty, why should they not be assumed to display the same values when they *do* impose it?[47]

Only Justice Marshall shared Brennan's belief that the death penalty was repugnant to contemporary American society and his rationale was perhaps even more contentious. Marshall argued that the decisive question for the Court was not what people actually believed, but '. . . whether people who were fully informed as to the purposes of the penalty and its liabilities would find the penalty shocking, unjust, and unacceptable.'[48] The American public, he said, was largely ignorant about the death penalty, but the relevant information '. . . would almost surely convince the average citizen that the death penalty was unwise . . .'[49] He concedes that this might still not completely negate the public desire for retribution, but then makes a further, highly dubious assertion:

> I cannot believe that at this stage in our history, the American people would ever knowingly support purposeless vengeance. Thus, I believe that the great mass of citizens would conclude on the basis of the material already considered that the death penalty is immoral and therefore uncon-stitutional.[50]

Both Brennan and Marshall cited moral, philosophical and social scientific evidence to buttress their conclusions, but this could not mask the weaknesses in their constitutional argument. The text and history of the Constitution and the legislation of thirty-nine states and the federal government all indicated the moral acceptability of the death penalty. Furthermore, all the judicial precedents, including *McGautha* decided just fourteenth months earlier, had without exception upheld its constitutionality. There was, as Burger argued, no evidence that an 'instant evolution' in societal standards had taken place.[51] Indeed, as we shall see, all the evidence from *Furman* until this day suggests the very opposite. It is likely that Brennan and Marshall aimed to lead the social consensus, rather than follow it, and did so more in hope than in expectation of success. After all, Justice Brennan did tell his clerks after the case conference 'Boys, it's a surprise to me, but the death cases seem to be coming out 5 to 4 against the death penalty.'[52]

The critical votes in *Furman*, however, came not from those who accepted the Brennan-Marshall position on the inherent uncon-stitutionality of capital punishment. Justice Douglas declined to address that issue, focusing instead upon the fact that the imposition of the death sentence was arbitrary and discriminatory, falling almost wholly on members of racial minorities and the poor:

> A law that stated that anyone making more than $50,000 would be exempt from the death penalty would plainly fall, as would a law that in terms said that blacks, those who never went beyond the fifth grade in school, those who made less than $3,000 a year, or those who were unpopular or unstable should be the only people executed. A law which in the overall view reaches that result in practice has no more sanctity than a law which in terms provides the same.[53]

Justices Stewart and White elaborated upon different aspects of the
arbitrariness which characterised the imposition of the death penalty.
For Stewart, the death penalty appeared to be inflicted in a random,
wholly unreasonable manner:

> These death sentences are cruel and unusual in the same way that being
> struck by lightning is cruel and unusual . . . The Eighth and Fourteenth
> Amendments cannot tolerate the infliction of a sentence of death under
> legal systems that permit this unique penalty to be so wantonly and so
> freakishly imposed.[54]

White's main concern was that the infrequency of the use of the death
penalty made it impossible to believe that it served any valid policy goal,
be it deterrence or retribution. As implemented, the death penalty
statutes amounted to '. . . the pointless and needless extinction of life
with only marginal contributions to any discernible social or public
purposes.'[55]

It is worth emphasising that Douglas, Stewart and White did not
hold that the death penalty *per se* was unconstitutional. Their problem
was the unreasonable way in which juries inflicted it. That Justice
Douglas should take this position came as no surprise: fourteen
months earlier, in *McGautha*, he, along with Brennan and Marshall,
had dissented from the Court's decision that due process of law did not
require the states to draw up standards to guide jury sentencing in
capital cases. Justices Stewart and White, however, had voted with the
majority in that case, a stand that seemed incompatible with their
Furman opinions. This paradox was underlined by the fact that Justice
Harlan's majority opinion in *McGautha* stated not merely that
sentencing standards were unnecessary for due process purposes, but
that it was beyond human ability to devise standards in language which
would ensure their fair and consistent application.[56] Justices Stewart
and White were now in the position of having voted both that standards
were unnecessary and unfeasible *and* that standardless sentencing was
arbitrary to the point of unconstitutionality. Three main inferences
were possible. First, that Stewart and White had concluded that, for all
practical purposes, the death penalty was unconstitutional but did not
want to say so in an abrupt, provocative decision. Justice White,
however, had gone out of his way to discourage this inference, saying at
the outset of his *Furman* opinion that it should not be read as implying
that '. . . the death penalty is unconstitutional *per se* or that there is no
system of capital punishment that would comport with the Eighth
Amendment.'[57] The second possible inference, and an ominous one

for abolitionists, was that the two Justices would be prepared to uphold *mandatory* death sentences. This would resolve the apparent contradiction between their *McGautha* and *Furman* votes, though at the cost of reverting to a practice abandoned long ago as unfair and unworkable.[58] It would also, of course, lead to a greatly increased number of executions, something which, as noted above, might trouble Justice Stewart at least. The third possibility was that Justices Stewart and White had simply changed their minds and decided that they had made the wrong decision in *McGautha*. If so, the obligation to give clear guidance to state legislators might have led them to say so openly, their judicial obligation for consistency notwithstanding. Neither one, however, addressed the issue in their *Furman* opinions. Moreover, Woodward and Armstrong report that *McGautha* was a touchy subject for Justice White: when one of his law clerks told him that his *Furman* reasoning overruled *McGautha sub silentio*, 'White scowled. The other two clerks, out of White's line of vision, frantically motioned to their colleague to drop the point.'[59]

Taken as a whole, the five opinions of the majority Justices were unclear as to what form of capital punishment statute, if any, would pass constitutional muster. This factor was to contribute considerably to the Court's future entanglement with the issue. For the dissenting Justices, however, this was secondary to their conviction that the Court had greatly exceeded its legitimate authority in striking down the nation's death penalty statutes. All four of them – Chief Justice Burger and Justices Blackmun, Powell and Rehnquist – had been nominated by President Nixon to practise judicial self-restraint and all four now excoriated the majority Justices for their usurpation of legislative power. They argued that the first measure of acceptable societal standards in a democracy must be the laws passed by the democratically-elected representatives of the people. As Chief Justice Burger put it: '. . . in a democracy the legislative judgement is presumed to embody the basic standards of decency prevailing in the society. This presumption can only be negated by unambiguous and compelling evidence of legislative default.'[60] No such evidence existed. State and federal legislation, referenda and opinion polls pointed in the opposite direction. On the question of deterrence, said Burger, there was an 'empirical stalemate'.[61] Furthermore, the question of whether the death penalty was socially useful was a policy question to be determined by legislatures, not judges: 'The constitutional provision is not addressed to social utility and does not command that enlightened principles of penology always be followed.'[62] Justice Blackmun, who declared himself personally opposed to the death penalty, was blunt, if sorrowful, about the majority decision: 'I fear the Court has over-stepped. It has sought and achieved an end.'[63] Justice Powell was more vehement: the decision would have a 'shattering effect' on '. . . the root principles of *stare decisis*, federalism, judicial restraint and – most importantly – separation of powers . . . I can recall no case in which, in the name of deciding constitutional questions, this Court has sub-ordinated national and democratic processes to such an extent.'[64]

The majority had a powerful moral case, but constitutionally it took the Court out on a limb. Since the constitutional issue revolved around 'societal standards', the state of public and legislative opinion was particularly important. Yet all the evidence suggested that the Court was now way ahead of that opinion. Of course, the Warren Court had frequently aroused public and legislative ire with its activist decisions – and got away with it. On this issue, however, there was an important difference. Normally, the only way to reverse a Supreme Court decision is by constitutional amendment, a rare and difficult process. In *Furman*, however, the majority had based its decision on assump-tions, or assertions, about what the American public deemed civilised standards of punishment to be. Should the public react to *Furman* in a manner which showed clearly that it considered executing murderers to be civilised, then the Court would have great difficulty in main-taining its constitutional position.

Despite the somewhat fragile nature of the majority vote, 'To many observers, *Furman* had, for all practical purposes, ended the practice of executions in America.'[65] Even Chief Justice Burger predicted that 'There will never be another execution in this country.'[66] The *Furman* decision, combined with the moratorium and potential difficulties over both sentencing standards and mandatory sentences, established con-siderable practical barriers to any return to executing criminals.

The states reject *Furman*

Yet the legislative backlash to *Furman* proved too ferocious for the Court to withstand. All across the country, states whose death penalty statutes had been invalidated by the decision moved to enact new legislation. Some fifteen states introduced mandatory death sentences for specified crimes and in North Carolina, the state Supreme Court ruled that the state's existing statute need not fall, but rather should henceforth be applied in a manner compatible with *Furman*. Some twenty other states passed new statutes providing varying degrees of guidance for juries who retained discretion in imposing the death penalty.

Another blow to abolitionist hopes occurred in California where, prior to *Furman*, the State Supreme Court had ruled that the death penalty violated the California Constitution's ban on 'cruel or unusual punishments'. The necessary signatures to force a referendum on a constitutional amendment to reinstate the death penalty were rapidly collected and in November, Proposition 17 was overwhelmingly approved by the California electorate.[67] Such actions exposed the fallacy that the death penalty was considered cruel and unusual by American society. As John Hart Ely, an abolitionist himself, commented: 'Such claims always have a good chance of being nonsense, and this one was, as the post-*Furman* spate of reenactments tragically testifies.'[68]

The new legislation, of course, would inevitably be appealed all the way to the Supreme Court. By early 1976, the Court was faced with some fifty petitions for review.[69] Five cases were chosen as representative of the range of new laws: *Gregg v. Georgia*, *Proffitt v. Florida*, *Jurek v. Texas*, *Woodson v. North Carolina* and *Roberts v. Louisiana*.[70] The Georgia, Florida and Texas statutes all provided some detailed sentencing guidance for jurors. In Georgia, for example, the jury must identify in writing which of ten specified aggravating circumstances it found present, before it could impose the death penalty. It further attempted to ensure consistency in sentencing by requiring an automatic appeal to the state Supreme Court, which, in turn, had to identify other similar cases in which it had upheld the death sentence before it could affirm a jury's capital sentence. Gregg had been convicted on two counts of murder and sentenced to death, with armed robbery identified as the aggravating circumstance. The Georgia Supreme Court had affirmed the sentence.

The North Carolina and Louisiana laws, on the other hand, enacted mandatory death sentences for anyone convicted of first degree murder. The Louisiana statute did, however, require that in any first degree murder trial the jury must be instructed on the charges of first degree murder, second degree murder and manslaughter. The jury was also allowed to return verdicts of guilty of second degree murder and manslaughter, instead of guilty on the first degree charge.

The Supreme Court was again badly divided and no opinion commanded majority support. The voting was as follows: seven Justices agreed that the death penalty did not in itself violate the Eighth Amendment – Brennan and Marshall dissented. The same seven

Justices then upheld the constitutionality of the Georgia, Florida and Texas statutes. A majority of five, however, also voted to strike down the two mandatory laws over the objections of Chief Justice Burger and Justices White, Rehnquist and Blackmun. The key role in the case fell, therefore, to Justices Stewart, Powell and Stevens[71] who entered a joint 'plurality' opinion.

Their first major point signalled a retreat from *Furman*. They maintained that the constitutional criterion in Eighth Amendment cases was the *Trop* evolving standards test, but conceded that the post-*Furman* evidence made clear that the death penalty did not invariably violate contemporary standards of decency.[72] While the Court could still invalidate punishments which were excessive, either because they were disproportionate to the crime or because they inflicted unnecessary pain, it owed considerable deference to legislative opinion in assessing which punishments were permissible. Moreover,

> . . . it is now evident that a large proportion of American society continues to regard (the death penalty) as an appropriate and necessary criminal sanction. The most marked indication of society's endorsement of the death penalty for murder is the legislative response to *Furman*. The legislatures of at least 35 states have enacted new statutes that provide for the death penalty for at least some crimes that result in the death of another person.[73]

They also pointed out that Congress had shown its approval of capital punishment in 1974 by enacting the death penalty as punishment for air piracy which resulted in loss of life. The public, too, had clearly signalled its approval: since the end of 1974, juries had sentenced some 254 defendants to death under the new laws.[74] By any objective measurement, it could not be argued that Americans thought the death penalty for murder to be uncivilised.

Justice Marshall's dissent conceded as much, but then countered with his *Furman* argument about the public's ignorance of the realities of the death penalty:

> I would be less than candid if I did not acknowledge that these developments have a significant bearing on a realistic assessment of the moral acceptability of the death penalty to the American people. But if the constitutionality of the death penalty turns, as I have urged, on the opinion of an *informed* citizenry, then even the enactment of new death statutes cannot be viewed as conclusive.[75]

The sincerity of Justice Marshall's argument cannot mask its weakness. Apart from being a highly speculative basis on which to

declare a common practice unconstitutional, it is not usual in a democracy to heed only the policy preferences of those who are 'informed'.

For his part, Justice Brennan effectively asserted an extreme activist
view of the Court's power and duty in deciding cases which turn on
notions of morality: namely, that the Justices should rely on their own
values: 'This Court inescapably has the duty, as the ultimate arbiter of
the meaning of our Constitution, to say whether, when individuals
condemned to death stand before our Bar, "moral concepts" require us
to hold that the law has progressed to the point where we should
declare that the punishment of death . . . is no longer morally tolerable
in our civilised society.'[76] This statement clearly illustrates the capacity
of non-interpretivism to augment the policy-making power of the
judiciary.

Having declared the death penalty constitutional in principle, the
plurality now turned to the issue of its arbitrary imposition. On this,
they cited three main improvements in the new law compared with that
invalidated in *Furman*: the bifurcated trial, with a separate hearing for
sentencing, which allowed the defendant to plead mitigating circumstances without self-incrimination; the specific statutory list of aggravating circumstances which channel death sentences; and automatic
appeals to the State Supreme Court, which should ensure evenness of
sentencing. The plurality wrote that 'On their face these procedures
seem to satisfy the concerns of *Furman*.'[77]

The plurality, however, did not intend to abdicate all judicial
authority over this issue. With the supporting votes of Brennan and
Marshall, they held that the two mandatory laws did fail the evolving
standards test. They cited the history of such laws prior to the *Furman*
case in support of this conclusion, noting that a gradual process from
the mid-nineteenth century onward, had seen the elimination of the
mandatory death sentence from all US jurisdictions. To a considerable
extent, this had been forced by the reluctance of juries to return guilty
verdicts where they felt the death sentence would be excessive. Thus,
'. . . the practice of sentencing to death all persons convicted of a
particular offence has been rejected as unduly harsh and unworkably
rigid. The two crucial indicators of evolving standards of decency
respecting the imposition of punishment in our society – jury determinations and legislative enactments – both point conclusively to the
repudiation of automatic death sentences.'[78]

Justice Rehnquist, in dissent, disputed this interpretation of history,
but he also pointed out that a significant number of states had enacted
mandatory laws since *Furman*. This showed that such laws were not

considered uncivilised by contemporary society.

The plurality, however, 'second-guessed' the real wishes of the North Carolina legislature and others who had passed similar legislation, by asserting that these laws '. . . reflect attempts by the States to retain the death penalty in a form consistent with the Constitution, rather than a renewed societal acceptance of mandatory death sentencing. The fact that some States have adopted mandatory measures following *Furman* while others have legislated standards to guide jury discretion appears attributable to diverse readings of this Court's multi-opinioned decision in that case.'[79] Rehnquist, in turn, described this as 'glib' and said the plurality were trying 'to save the people from themselves'.[80] He further argued that they had exceeded the bounds of their legitimate authority, violating precedent in the process: 'What the plurality opinion has actually done is to import into the Due Process Clause of the Fourteenth Amendment what it considers to be desirable procedural guarantees where the punishment of death, concededly not cruel and unusual for the crime of which the defendant was convicted, is to be imposed. This is squarely contrary to *McGautha*, and unsupported by any other decision of this Court.'[81] Surprisingly, the plurality came close to admitting as much: '. . . the prevailing practice of individualising sentencing determinations generally reflects simply enlightened policy rather than a constitutional imperative . . .',[82] but, they added, the qualitative distinctiveness of the death penalty compared to any other punishment makes it indispensable.

The 1976 decisions took some of the heat out of the capital punishment issue by producing a compromise: the states could impose and carry out death sentences, but not with the near-total autonomy of the pre-*Furman* days. The Supreme Court would oversee death penalty practices in order to ensure that 'evolving standards' were adhered to by the states. This oversight would be exercised in two broad ways: first, to ensure that the penalty itself was not excessive and second, to ensure that the defendant had been given ample opportunity to demonstrate that the imposition of the death penalty was inappropriate in the particular case. The following Court Term was to throw up important cases of both types and demonstrate that the Court had by no means fully capitulated to conservative political pressures.

In June 1977, in *Coker v. Georgia*, a 7–2 majority of the Justices declared the death penalty for rape to be unconstitutional.[83] Again, there was no agreement on the rationale for the decision, but Justice White wrote a plurality opinion joined by Justices Stewart, Blackmun and Stevens. As was to become their unvarying practice, Justices Brennan and Marshall continued to insist that the death penalty was inherently unconstitutional and could never be sustained. Chief Justice Burger's dissent was joined by Justice Rehnquist.

The details of the case were particularly important to the constitutional dispute. In 1974, Erlich Coker had escaped from the Ware Correctional Institution in Georgia, where he was serving consecutive life sentences for murder, rape and kidnapping. He entered the home of Allen and Elnita Carver, tied up Mr Carver and raped Mrs Carver at knifepoint. He then fled, taking money, the Carver's car and Mrs. Carver with him. He was later arrested, still holding Mrs Carver, who had not been subjected to further harm. Coker pleaded guilty to rape, kidnapping and armed robbery. Under the Georgia law recently upheld in *Gregg*, the death sentence could be imposed for rape either if committed by someone previously convicted of another capital felony or if committed during the course of another capital felony, which included armed robbery. The jury found both aggravating circumstances present and sentenced Coker to death. The Georgia Supreme Court upheld the verdict.

Despite Coker's past record, Justice White argued that '. . . a sentence of death is grossly disproportionate and excessive punishment for the crime of rape . . .'[84] In line with the *Gregg* rationale, his major reference point for this conclusion is the tendency of state legislative practice. White noted that prior to *Furman*, sixteen states had the death penalty for rape, but only three had attempted to reinstate it afterwards. As of June, 1977, Georgia was the sole state that retained the death penalty for rape of an adult woman. He further noted that of sixty-three rape cases reviewed by the Georgia Supreme Court since 1973, juries had imposed the death sentence in only six. He concluded:

> These recent events evidencing the attitude of state legislatures and sentencing juries do not wholly determine this controversy, for the Constitution contemplates that in the end our own judgement will be brought to bear on the question of the acceptability of the death penalty under the Eighth Amendment. Nevertheless, the legislative rejection of capital punishment for rape strongly confirms our own judgement, which is that death is indeed a disproportionate penalty for the crime of raping an adult woman.[85]

He added that Coker's previous criminal record does not alter the fact that, in this case, no life was taken. Yet it was precisely this previous record that vexed Chief Justice Burger and he framed the constitutional question accordingly: does the Eighth Amendment '. . . prohibit the State of Georgia from executing a person who has, within the space of three years, raped three separate women, killing one and attempting to kill another, who is serving prison sentences exceeding his probable lifetime and who has not hesitated to escape confinement at the first opportunity?'[86] He added that, without the right to impose the death penalty, Georgia can impose no sentence on Coker which he has not already received and hence can offer no deterrent to his committing further rapes.

The second major case that Term involved another issue guaranteed to set conservative pulses racing – the murder of a police officer. The case was *Roberts v. Louisiana* and a 5–4 majority quashed a mandatory death sentence because it did not allow for individualised sentencing.[87] For the majority, this case was governed by the previous Term's decisions on mandatory death sentences, but the four dissenters there insisted that the present case was different precisely because the victim was a police officer. For Justice Rehnquist, for example, '. . . the arguments in favour of society's determination to impose a mandatory sentence for the murder of a police officer in the line of duty are far stronger than in the case of an ordinary homicide.'[88] In an intense opinion, he went on to describe police officers as 'the foot soldiers of society's defence of ordered liberty' and 'both symbols and outriders of our order of society'.[89] He heaped scorn on the majority's list of possible mitigating circumstances that needed to be considered even when the victim was a police officer, especially their point that the perpetrator might genuinely have believed his action was necessary: 'John Wilkes Booth may well have thought he was morally justified in murdering Abraham Lincoln, whom, while fleeing from the stage of Ford's Theatre, he characterised as a "tyrant"; I am appalled to believe that the Constitution would have *required* the Government to allow him to argue that as a "mitigating factor" before it could sentence him to death if he were found guilty.'[90]

Nothing in the majority's opinion, of course, prevented Louisiana from executing every police killer, if that was the decision of the juries. All it insisted upon was that the defendant have an opportunity to plead mitigating circumstances. Justice Rehnquist and the other dissenters could hardly have believed that Louisiana jurors would lightly accept a cop killer's self-justification as mitigation – though what they might have done in the case of John Wilkes Booth is a quite different matter! The issue here then was essentially a symbolic one. Nevertheless, the symbols involved were sufficiently powerful to persuade four Justices of the Supreme Court to defer to public sentiment.

The following year, the Court attempted to clarify its view of the sentencing procedures required by the Constitution in capital cases. Sandra Lockett had helped to plan the robbery of a pawnshop in Ohio. While she was seated in the escape car, an accomplice had shot the pawnbroker dead in his shop. Lockett was sentenced to death under Ohio's law which required the death penalty for aggravated murder unless the victim had induced the crime, the offender was under strong duress or if the crime was the product of the perpetrator's mental deficiency. Lockett claimed that the law did not permit the sentencing judge to consider a wide range of potentially mitigating factors, including her previous character, her young age, her lack of intent to cause death and her relatively minor part in the crime. In *Lockett v. Ohio*, seven of the eight participating Justices agreed that her death sentence could not stand, though only six approved the sentencing procedures outlined in Chief Justice Burger's plurality opinion.[91]

Burger conceded that, since *McGautha*, the Court had not been giving the states clear guidance and that '. . . we have an obligation to reconcile previously differing views in order to provide that guidance.'[92] The Ohio law, he said, does allow some mitigating factors to be taken into consideration; but given the unique finality of the death penalty, that will not satisfy constitutional requirements. Henceforth, the sentencer must not be precluded from considering as mitigation anything at all about the defendant's history or crime that he or she wishes to put forward. Justice White, who deemed Lockett's sentence unconstitutional on other grounds, found this new position unacceptable: 'The Court has now completed its about-face since *Furman v. Georgia* . . .'[93] In that case it had outlawed unfettered discretion for the sentencer; then in *Woodson*, it had outlawed mandatory sentences which precisely eliminated such discretion; now, it holds that the sentencer must once again be allowed unfettered discretion, at least in considering mitigating circumstances.

Justice Rehnquist, the sole vote to sustain Lockett's sentence, made the same point about the lack of consistency and clarity in the Court's Eighth Amendment jurisprudence: '. . . the Court has gone from pillar to post, with the result that the sort of reasonable predictability upon which legislatures, trial courts and appellate courts must of necessity rely has been all but completely sacrificed.'[94] *Furman* was undercut by the return of unfettered discretion to the sentencer, for 'By encouraging defendants in capital cases, and presumably sentencing judges and juries, to take into consideration anything under the sun as a "mitigating circumstance", it will not guide sentencing discretion but will totally unleash it.'[95]

The lack of consistency from *McGautha* to *Lockett* cannot be denied. The most obvious reason for it was that the Court had no constitutional principle to guide it. Beyond deciding whether or not the Eighth Amendment permitted capital punishment, the Court was inevitably deciding questions of policy on which the Constitution was silent. In effect, the Court was engaging in a 'debate' over penal policy with the states and was prepared to change tack if enough states demanded it. That most of the Justices up until *Lockett* leaned toward a humane policy does not alter that stark fact: it may be evidence in support of a *functional* justification of judicial review, but it cannot be defended as interpretivism in any meaningful sense of the term.

Lockett did settle the position on mitigating factors: defendants could proffer and sentencers consider anything they wanted to. The same was not true of aggravating factors, however, the Court still requiring that these be specified in writing in capital punishment laws. Neither was it settled whether states were free from all constitutional restraint in deciding what factors to include as aggravation. An interesting development along these lines came in *Godfrey v. Georgia*, in 1980.[96] Robert Godfrey had been convicted of shooting to death his wife and mother-in-law. As one of its aggravating circumstances allowing the imposition of the death penalty, the Georgia law included a murder which was 'outrageously or wantonly vile, horrible or inhumane in that it involved torture, depravity of mind, or an aggravated battery'. Godfrey alleged that this clause was unconstitutionally vague. Six of the Justices agreed that Godfrey's death sentence should be quashed, but once again there was no rationale which could command the support of a majority. Justice Stewart, joined by Justices Blackmun, Powell and Stevens, entered a plurality opinion.

Stewart noted that the Court had decided in *Gregg* that this clause was not unconstitutionally vague on its face. The Georgia Supreme Court had since upheld death sentences under it, giving it more precise definition in the process: those cases had clearly involved the kind of torture and depravity at which the clause was aimed. Here, however, no such actions were involved – Godfrey, said Stewart, had simply shot his victims once in the head after a simmering domestic dispute. Thus, in this case, the Georgia Supreme Court's *construction* of the clause was vague, even though the clause itself was not.

In dissent, both Chief Justice Burger and Justice White seized on the fact that the Court's decision implied an even greater involvement in death penalty cases than before and, inevitably, another increase in the

Court's power. Burger disagreed with Stewart's characterisation of the murder, but 'More troubling . . . is the new responsibility that it assumes with today's decision – the task of determining on a case-by-case basis whether a defendant's conduct is egregious enough to warrant a death sentence . . . (It is not the Court's role) to second-guess the jury's judgement or to tell the States which of their "hideous" intentional murderers may be given the ultimate penalty.'[97] Justice White, having first recounted the details of the murder in somewhat gory fashion, wrote: 'Our mandate does not extend to interfering with factfinders in state criminal proceedings or with state courts that are responsibly and consistently interpreting state law.'[98]

Justice Marshall, who concurred in the plurality's decision to overturn Godfrey's sentence, launched a powerful argument from quite the opposite direction. He focused on the fact that the Georgia Supreme Court had failed to identify Godfrey's sentence as an arbitrary one and that other state appellate courts had done likewise in cases which were arbitrary.[99] Such cases '. . . strongly suggest that appellate courts are incapable of guaranteeing the kind of objectivity and even-handedness that the Court contemplated and hoped for in *Gregg*. The disgraceful distorting effects of racial discrimination and poverty continue to be painfully visible in the imposition of the death sentence.'[100] He pointed out that as of 20 April, 1980, blacks constituted fully 40 per cent of all those put on death row since *Gregg*.[101] He concluded that 'The task of eliminating arbitrariness in the infliction of capital punishment is proving to be one which our criminal system – and perhaps any criminal system – is unable to perform.'[102]

Justice Marshall has a powerful argument. However, it raises a point which does not appear decisive to a majority of the American people, the state legislatures or the Justices of the Supreme Court. As long as they are satisfied that the decision to impose the death sentence is fitting to the particular crime and criminal involved, they are not prepared to forgo the sentence on the grounds that similar crimes and criminals are not similarly punished. It is hard to see how it could be otherwise in a system where only a small percentage of those convicted of homicide actually receive the death sentence and, of those, only a small percentage are actually executed. As Zimring and Hawkins noted, 'There have been, in the past decade, more than 20,000 criminal homicides per year in America. An estimated current annual rate of twenty to thirty executions per year represents less than 0.2 per cent of the homicide rate.'[103] In the period from the *Gregg* decision in 1976 to August 1990, only 136 death sentences have actually been carried out. The highest number in any one year was 25, in 1987.[104]

The paradox of the death penalty issue in the United States is that while there is no great demand for executions, both politicians and the public continue to clamour for retention of the death penalty in ever greater numbers. A 1988 Gallup poll found, for example, that 79 per cent of Americans supported the death penalty, with only 16 per cent opposed.[105] While George Bush's 'Willie Horton' campaign may have boosted support to a new high, more recent polls still register support at 72 per cent.[106] Even politicians who used to oppose the death penalty, like Andrew Young, the former Mayor of Atlanta, have been converted.[107] Rational or not, the evidence could not be clearer that at the present time, the arbitrary and discriminatory imposition of the death penalty has done nothing to convince Americans that it violates standards of decency.

Executing minors and the mentally retarded

The Court's more recent decisions reflect this societal consensus, although they also reflect, of course, the fact that conservative presidents have been able to appoint new Justices who are opposed to liberal judicial activism on this and every other subject. Nothing confirms the present judicial deference to popular notions of civilised penal standards more than two highly controversial cases decided the same day in 1989. In *Penry v. Lynaugh*, the Court ruled 5–4 that the Eighth Amendment does not preclude the execution of mentally retarded persons who have been convicted of murder.[108] In *Stanford v. Kentucky*, and its companion case, *Heath v. Wilkins*, the Court ruled 5–4 that the Eighth Amendment also does not preclude the execution of juvenile murderers.[109] In both cases the majority consisted of the three Reagan appointees, Justices O'Connor, Scalia and Kennedy, Chief Justice Rehnquist, who had been promoted by President Reagan, and Justice White.

Johnny Paul Penry had been convicted in 1980 of the rape and murder of Pamela Carpenter in her home in Livingston, Texas. He also had a previous conviction for rape. Before the trial itself, there was a hearing to decide whether Penry's mental retardation made him incompetent to stand trial. Penry had suffered organic brain damage as a child and had an IQ of between 50 and 63, which indicated mild to moderate retardation. A clinical psychologist testified that Penry, aged twenty-two at the time of the murder, had the mental age of a six-and-a-half year old and the social maturity of a nine or ten year old. The jury nevertheless, found him competent to stand trial. At trial, conflicting psychiatric evidence was introduced as to Penry's insanity plea. However, although state psychiatric witnesses testified that Penry was legally sane, they acknowledged that Penry's mental ability was extremely limited and that he seemed unable to learn from his mistakes. The jury rejected the insanity plea and sentenced Penry, who had confessed to the crimes, to death.[110] Although the Supreme Court reversed Penry's sentence on a technicality,[111] the decision on the main constitutional issue marked a new level of judicial deference to legislative will in Eighth Amendment cases.

Justice O'Connor maintained that *Trop's* evolving standards was still the relevant test and that the best indicator of such standards was legislative and jury behaviour. On the issue of the death penalty for the mentally retarded, as opposed to the insane or 'idiots', however, these were mostly silent. The Federal Anti-Drug Abuse Act of 1988 bans the execution of the retarded but, O'Connor found, only one state explicitly does the same. Therefore, 'In our view, the single State statute prohibiting execution of the mentally retarded, even when added to the 14 States that have rejected capital punishment completely, does not provide sufficient evidence at present of a national consensus.'[112]

She further noted that Penry offered no evidence of jury attitudes on the question, although she did acknowledge that the evidence of public opinion polls showed overwhelming opposition to the execution of the mentally retarded. She also conceded that the American Association on Mental Retardation, the country's leading professional association dealing with the subject and which had filed an *amicus* brief, had formally passed a resolution opposing such executions. However, rather than resolve the uncertainty by reference to her own notions of civilised standards, Justice O'Connor said the resolution must await further legislative developments: 'The public sentiment expressed in these and other polls and resolutions may ultimately find expression in legislation, which is an objective indicator of contemporary values upon which we can rely. But at present, there is insufficient evidence of a national consensus against executing mentally retarded people convicted of capital offenses for us to conclude that it is categorically prohibited by the Eighth Amendment'.[113] The clear implication is that anything the states do not explicitly and overwhelmingly forbid, the current Court will allow.

The decisions in *Stanford* and *Wilkins* reinforce this impression. Kevin Stanford was seventeen years and four months old when he and an accomplice had robbed a gas station, repeatedly raped and sodomised the twenty-year-old station attendant and then shot her to prevent her from identifying them. Wilkins was sixteen years and six months old when he robbed a store in Avondale, Missouri, and repeatedly stabbed the owner, leaving her to die. In deciding whether the Eighth Amendment would permit the execution of such young murderers, Justice Scalia's majority opinion reviewed previous cases in such a manner as to indicate the numerical point at which state legislative behaviour might induce a constitutional prohibition. In *Coker*, where the Court outlawed the death penalty for rape, only one state authorised such a punishment. In *Enmund v. Florida*, where the Eighth Amendment was held to prevent the execution of a 'non-triggerman' without further proof of intent, only eight states allowed the practice.[114] And in *Ford v. Wainwright*, where the execution of the insane was held impermissible, no state authorised it.[115] On the other hand, in *Tison v. Arizona*, the Court had upheld the death penalty for participation in a major felony with reckless indifference to human life, observing that only eleven states who had the death penalty at all prohibited it in those circumstances.[116] On the question of the execution of juveniles, said Scalia, the legislative situation is more like *Tison* than *Ford*, *Enmund* or *Coker*: 'Of the 37 States whose laws permit capital punishment, 15 decline to impose it upon 16-year-old offenders and 12 decline to impose it on 17-year-old offenders. This does not establish the degree of national consensus this Court has previously thought sufficient to label a particular punishment cruel and unusual.'[117]

Furthermore, the States have no obligation to demonstrate that there is a national consensus *in favour of* their punishment practice; rather, petitioners bear a heavy burden of establishing that there is a national consensus *against* it.[118] And the primacy of state law over all other indicators of national consensus was emphasised when Scalia downgraded the weight of opinion polls and professional and interest group attitudes: 'We decline the invitation to rest constitutional law upon such uncertain foundations. A revised national consensus so broad, so clear and so enduring as to justify a permanent prohibition upon all units of democratic government must appear in the operative acts (laws and application of laws) that the people have approved.'[119] For those who oppose the death penalty for any reason, the unmistakable invitation is to take their campaign to the state legislatures, not the federal courts.

The retirement of the two staunchest opponents of the death

penalty, Justices Brennan and Marshall, can only confirm the abandonment of judicial activism on the question in the 1990s and probably beyond. In 1991, Justice Souter joined Rehnquist, O'Connor, Scalia and Kennedy in ruling for the first time ever in a criminal case, never mind a capital case, that the concededly wrongful use of an involuntary confession in a trial was 'harmless error' and did not require reversal of the verdict.[120] In the debate over progressive versus traditional attitudes to crime and punishment, the traditionalists have won out on the Court just as surely as they have elsewhere in the American political system.

Notes

1 R. Schwed, *Abolition And Capital Punishment: The United States' Judicial, Political and Moral Barometer*, New York, 1983, p. 176.
2 408 US 238.
3 428 US 153 (1976).
4 F. Zimring and G. Hawkins, *Capital Punishment and the American Agenda*, Cambridge, 1986, p. 41.
5 M. Meltsner, *Cruel and Unusual: The Supreme Court and Capital Punishment*, New York, 1973, p. 289.
6 R. Berger, *Death Penalties: The Supreme Court's Obstacle Course*, Cambridge, Mass., 1982, p. 49. As Berger points out, even ardent abolitionists, such as Hugo Bedau, acknowledge this historical point.
7 356 US 86, 101.
8 *Ibid.*, p. 99.
9 402 US 183 (1971).
10 Zimring and Hawkins, *op. cit.*, Table 2.8, p. 43.
11 Schwed, *op. cit.*, p. 69.
12 Zimring and Hawkins, *op. cit.*, Table 2.7, p. 39. Their figures of 58 per cent–43 per cent reflect the rounding up of decimal points and the elimination of non-committal answers.
13 Schwed, *op. cit.*, p. 103.
14 H. Bedau, *Death Is Different*, Boston, 1987, p. 135.
15 *Ibid.*, p. 134.
16 Schwed, *op. cit.*, p. 113.
17 Bedau, *op. cit.*, p. 135.
18 Zimring and Hawkins, *op. cit.*, Chapter 1.
19 Bedau, *op. cit.*, p. 135.
20 *Ibid.*, p. 138.
21 *Ibid.*.
22 *Ibid.*, p. 142.
23 *Ibid.*, p. 136.
24 *Ibid.*, p. 137.
25 In the 1972 Gallup poll, 47 per cent of college graduates opposed the death penalty, compared with 39 per cent of high school graduates. N. Vidmar and P. Ellsworth, 'Public opinion on the death penalty', in H. Bedau and C. Pierce, *Capital Punishment in the United States*, New York, 1976, p. 144, n. 38. The clearest predictor of attitude on the subject is race: in 1972, 58 per cent of whites supported the death penalty, compared with 29 per cent of non-whites. The figures in 1977 were 70–46 per cent. H. Bedau (ed.), *The Death Penalty in America*, (3rd ed.), New York, 1982, p. 85.

26 The clearest evidence for this are the statistics on the imposition of the death sentence
   for convicted rapists in Southern states. Between 1945 and 1965, 36 per cent of blacks
   convicted of raping whites were sentenced to death; this compared with just 2 per cent of
   all other defendant/victim race combinations: Schwed, *op. cit.*, p. 57.
27 Meltsner, *op. cit.*, Chapter 6.
28 Zimring and Hawkins, *op. cit.*, p. 35.
29 Schwed, *op. cit.*, p. 109.
30 *Ibid.*, p. 110.
31 *Ibid.*, pp. 110–11; Zimring and Hawkins, *op. cit.*, p. 34.
32 Schwed, *op. cit.*, p. 111.
33 *Ibid.*, p. 114.
34 *Ibid.*, p. 118.
35 *Ibid.*, p. 165.
36 Meltsner, *op. cit.*, p. 292.
37 Justice Stewart, in particular, allegedly suffered in this way: B. Woodward and S.
   Armstrong, *The Brethren: Inside The Supreme Court*, New York, 1979, p. 209.
38 Despite this, however, it is clear from their *Furman* opinions that two of the four Justices
   who voted to uphold the death penalty, Chief Justice Burger and Justice Blackmun,
   were personally opposed to it. On the other hand, Justice White, who voted to strike the
   capital punishment laws, did not appear to find it morally reprehensible.
39 Woodward and Armstrong, *op. cit.*, p. 207.
40 *Ibid.*, p. 218.
41 *Supra*, n. 7.
42 For such an argument, see Berger, *op. cit.*, pp. 116–27.
43 408 US 238, 382.
44 *Ibid.*, p. 282.
45 *Ibid.*, pp. 277–8.
46 *Ibid.*, p. 300.
47 *Ibid.*, p. 437.
48 *Ibid.*, p. 361.
49 *Ibid.*, p. 363.
50 *Ibid.*.
51 *Ibid.*, p. 382.
52 Woodward and Armstrong, *op. cit.*, p. 211.
53 408 US 238, 256.
54 *Ibid*, pp. 309–10.
55 *Ibid.*, p. 312.
56 402 US 183, 204.
57 408 US 238, 311.
58 Berger, *op. cit.*, pp. 142–4.
59 *Ibid.*, p. 218.
60 408 US 238, 384.
61 *Ibid.*, p. 395.
62 *Ibid.*, p. 394.
63 *Ibid.*, p. 414.
64 *Ibid.*, pp. 417–18.
65 Zimring and Hawkins, *op. cit.*, p. 64.
66 Woodward and Armstrong, *op. cit.*, p. 219.
67 Schwed, *op. cit.*, pp. 144–5.
68 Ely, *op. cit.*, p. 173.
69 Woodward and Armstrong, *op. cit.*, p. 431.
70 428 US 153 (1976); 428 US 242 (1976); 428 US 262 (1976); 428 US 280 (1976); 428
   US 325 (1976), respectively.
71 John Paul Stevens had been nominated by President Ford in 1975 to replace Justice

Douglas, who had retired through ill-health.

72 Of the three Justices, only Stewart had doubted this in *Furman*.

73 *Gregg*, pp. 179–80.

74 *Ibid.*, p. 182.

75 *Ibid.*, p. 232 (emphasis in original).

76 *Ibid.*, p.229.

77 *Ibid.* p. 198.

78 *Woodson*, pp. 292–3.

79 *Ibid.*, pp. 298–9.

80 *Ibid.*, p. 313.

81 *Ibid.*, p. 324.

82 *Ibid.*, p. 304.

83 433 US 584 (1977).

84 *Ibid.*, p. 592.

85 *Ibid.*, p. 597.

86 *Ibid.*, p. 607.

87 431 US 633 (1977). This case should not be confused with the 1976 *Roberts v. Louisiana* case, which involved an entirely different Mr Roberts.

88 *Ibid.*, p. 643.

89 *Ibid.*, p. 647.

90 *Ibid.*, p. 649.

91 438 US 586 (1978). Justice Brennan did not participate.

92 *Ibid.*, p. 602.

93 *Ibid.*, p. 622. White believed Lockett's sentence was unconstitutional because it hadn't been shown that she had intended the death of the victim, p. 624.

94 *Ibid.*, p. 629.

95 *Ibid.*, p. 631.

96 446 US 420 (1980).

97 *Ibid.*, p. 443–4.

98 *Ibid.*, p. 451.

99 Marshall had made the same objection in *Lockett*, for example.

100 *Godfrey*, p. 439.

101 *Ibid.*, p. 439, n. 7.

102 *Ibid.*, p. 440.

103 *Ibid.*, p. 70.

104 *International Herald Tribune*, 23 August 1990, p. 3.

105 *International Herald Tribune*, 19–20 May 1990, p. 3.

106 *New York Times*/CBS News Poll, April 1990, reported in the *International Herald Tribune*, 5 April 1990, p. 3.

107 *Ibid.*

108 109 SCt 2934 (1989).

109 492 US – , 106 L Ed 2d 306, 109 S Ct –.

110 *Penry*, pp. 2941–2.

111 In yet another complex voting pattern, Justice O'Connor was supported by Justices Marshall, Blackmun, Brennan and Stevens, in her holding that, in this particular case, technicalities of the Texas statute had prevented the jury from giving full consideration to the mitigating effect of Penry's retardation. Penry's death sentence was reversed and the issue remanded to Texas for reconsideration in the light of this aspect of the Court's opinion, pp. 2947–52.

112 Ibid., p. 2955.

113 *Ibid.*

114 458 US 782 (1982).

115 477 US 399 (1986).

116 481 US 137 (1987).

117 106 L Ed 2d 306, 318–19.
118 *Ibid.*, p. 320.
119 *Ibid.*, p. 323.
120 *Fulminante v. Arizona*, 499 US – , 113 L Ed 2d 302, 111 S Ct – , (1991). Fulminante had 'confessed' to the murder of his eleven year old stepdaughter to a 'fellow prisoner' who, in return for a confession, offered him protection from other prisoners who had threatened him with violence. The 'fellow prisoner' was, in fact, a paid FBI informant.

Four—Abortion

There is little evidence that the United States was on the verge of emerging, in the early 1970s, from the long shadow of shame that had branded women as blameworthy for extramarital sex and nonprocreative sex and that condemned them for choosing abortion even when the choice was a painful and profoundly reluctant one.[1]

Of all the social issues on the agenda of American politics in the last twenty years, none has remotely matched abortion for its political intensity and bitterness. Almost twenty years after the Supreme Court's landmark decision in *Roe v. Wade*[2] created a constitutional right to have an abortion, the campaign to overturn it shows no sign of running out of steam. On the anti-abortion, or pro-life, side of the conflict, Operation Rescue is conducting a campaign of civil disobedience on a scale not seen since the heyday of civil rights protest. In 1991, Wichita, Kansas, was chosen by the organisation as the site of its 'Summer of Mercy', an attempt to prevent all abortions at the city's three providing clinics by blocking access to them. By the middle of August, over two thousand anti-abortion demonstrators had been arrested and more than half-a-million dollars spent by the city in containing the protest. And when a federal judge called in United States marshals to help protect the clinics, President Bush's Justice Department sent the Deputy Solicitor-General into court to argue that the judge's order should be overturned.[3] Meanwhile, the pro-abortion, or pro-choice, activists are stepping up their own activities in state and federal politics in anticipation of unsympathetic decisions by the 'Reagan-Bush' Supreme Court. A significant recent development here is the introduction into Congress in 1991 of the Freedom of Choice Act. This bill would effectively give federal statutory protection to the abortion rights granted in *Roe* and would thus protect these rights from attack by the states should *Roe* be overturned. Despite significant support for the bill in Congress,[4] it is unlikely to become law if only because President Bush will veto it should it pass through Congress.[5] It may succeed, however, in putting the President's pro-life policy into the electoral spotlight at a time when there are increasing signs of rebellion within the Republican Party over its formal hostility to abortion rights. Linda Chavez, a prominent Republican and former White House aide, has argued that the overwhelming majority of young Republican women are pro-choice and that in the run-up to the 1992 election, 'The best thing for the party is for this issue to disappear.'[6] Pro-choice groups will try to ensure that it doesn't, as will pro-life organisations. However, whatever role abortion plays in the 1992 election, it will remain the most controversial of all the social issues principally because it has come to epitomise the wider clash of traditional and modern social values. As groups on both sides of the conflict have sought to appropriate values and symbols that are central to American culture – individual freedom, equality, the family, God – abortion has become a metaphor in the struggle for control over the future of that culture.

It would be an exaggeration to say that this modern political conflict began with the Court's decision in 1973, but *Roe* did transform the issue by nationalising it and by politicising it to an unprecedented degree. A movement to reform abortion laws in the United States was well under way by the mid-1960s, but it was essentially a movement of concerned professionals with a liberal approach to the subject. Kristin Luker traced the process of reform in California which, in 1967, became one of the first states to liberalise its abortion law.[7] As with most states, California law dated back to the mid-nineteenth century and banned all abortions except those necessary to save the mother's life. Physicians differed, however, in their interpretation of the statute and in 1961, following the lead of the American Law Institute's 1959 Model Law, a bill was introduced in the state legislature to clarify the law. Doctors and lawyers were concerned about the horrors of illegal abortion, as well as legal uncertainties, and the bill represented an attempt at liberalisation as well as clarification.

In 1962, support for the bill was generated by the Sherri Finkbine case. Like many other women, Finkbine had been prescribed the sleeping pill Thalidomide during her pregnancy. When evidence began to appear that 'Thalidomide children' were being born with terrible physical deformities, Finkbine's doctor recommended an abortion, to which she agreed. The hospital, however, was unsure of the legal position and delayed the abortion and Finkbine eventually flew to Sweden for her abortion. The fetus was indeed severely deformed and would not have lived, according to the Swedish doctors. Further sympathy for abortion reform came in 1964–65 when California experienced an epidemic of rubella, an infection long identified as a cause of fetal abnormalities.

Nevertheless, neither the 1961 bill, nor another introduced in 1964, made it out of committee, for most politicians remained cautious on the subject. What finally triggered legislative action was the decision of the State Board of Medical Examiners to prosecute three reputable physicians who had performed an abortion on a woman with rubella. The medical profession generally rallied to the defence of the physicians and lobbied the legislature for a clarification and liberalisation of the law. Such was the consensus behind it, that Governor Ronald Reagan, an opponent of liberalised abortion, felt constrained to sign the new bill.

The campaign in California bore little resemblance to abortion politics today. It was essentially a dialogue of professional elites, mostly men, a majority of whom wanted a more enlightened and humane approach to abortion. That they succeeded in persuading the legislature and Governor to support them was due in part to the fact that the reformers were not radicals at all. The major force behind reform identified by Luker was the California Committee on Therapeutic Abortions, which she describes as follows: 'The members of CCTA resembled those of a typical "blue-ribbon" group. It included lawyers who would later be judges, physicians who were and would become heads of departments in major universities, and representatives from many of the local colleges and universities, law schools, and medical schools. Most had advanced degrees, and most had attended Ivy League universities or their West Coast equivalents.'[8]

They had their opponents within the professions, but neither side attempted to mobilise the public on its behalf. There was opposition from the Catholic Church, but this was understood as essentially sectarian rather than political. There was no 'Right To Life' movement at the time, and neither, on the other side, was the women's movement closely involved. This absence of grass-roots fervour made compromise on a liberalised abortion law possible.

What is also extremely important, however, is that the new law was perceived by most people as being inspired by medical rather than ideological concerns. The 1967 statute made no mention of women's right to an abortion, did not broach the issue of when life begins and certainly did not create 'abortion on demand'. What it did, rather, was to allow physicians to perform abortions where they deemed the mother would otherwise suffer serious physical or mental harm. As such, the California law did not appear to raise the most contentious political issues that were to be present in the Supreme Court's *Roe* decision.

The political pace did pick up between 1967 and 1973. The National Organisation for Women (NOW), which had been formed in 1966, decided to make reproductive freedom part of its Women's Bill of Rights the following year.[9] In 1969, the National Abortion Rights Action League (NARAL) was founded as a single-issue pressure group.[10] In 1970, Hawaii and New York passed new laws which went much further than the reformed California statute. The New York statute, for example, destined to be the only abortion law to survive the *Roe* decision, allowed abortion for any reason during the first three months of pregnancy. Despite this, it was endorsed as a model law by both the US Commission on Population Growth and by the American Bar Association.[11] Significantly, 'The contest over the repeal of New York's criminal abortion law was particularly fierce. The battle lines were drawn for the first time in the way that has become so familiar to us all in the years since *Roe*.'[12] In particular, feminists had played a role in the campaign to the extent that Governor Rockefeller credited women's groups for the success of the repeal effort.[13] There was a negative side to this feminist achievement, however: according to Luker, the campaign by women's groups to have abortion recognised as a women's right upset the liberal consensus that viewed abortion as progressive medical and social policy. Abortion reform now appeared as part of a radical political agenda that did not appeal to all amongst the professional elites.[14]

The early 1970s also saw the beginnings of an effective anti-abortion campaign. The 1970 New York statute was itself only saved from partial repeal in 1972 by Governor Rockefeller's veto and that year also saw the defeat of abortion reform referenda in Michigan and North Dakota.[15] John C. Willke, the founder of the National Right To Life Committee, played a prominent role in the Michigan campaign by distributing anti-abortion brochures to most homes in the state. While the financial and organisational support of the Catholic Church was important here as elsewhere in the pro-life movement, sentiment against abortion was clearly not confined to one sectarian group.[16]

Despite these conflicts over policy in particular states, the abortion issue was not yet one of *national* political prominence. The principal reason for this was that abortion policy, like capital punishment, was deemed by most Americans to be a question for the states, not the federal government. Furthermore, when the Supreme Court had nationalised capital punishment policy in *Furman*, it had at least been able to point to the Eighth Amendment as a specific place in the text of the Constitution where the issue arose. While the Eighth Amendment originally restricted only the powers of the federal government, it was relatively easy for the Court to maintain that it had been made applicable to the states through the subsequent passage of the Fourteenth Amendment. Other guarantees in the Bill of Rights had already been subjected to this process of 'incorporation' by the Supreme Court.[17] On abortion, however, there was no such clear invitation to the Court to intervene.

Nevertheless, it was not long before the abortion issue made its appearance in the federal courts. As one writer put it, 'During the 1970 term, the Court found itself literally bombarded with appeals and petitions for certiorari concerning abortion law decisions.'[18] But the Court showed no inclination to tackle the abortion question head-on and it dealt with most of the cases on a technical basis. Only one case was selected for a full hearing on its merits and that, significantly, was an appeal from a federal jurisdiction, the District of Columbia. Moreover, in that case, *U.S. v. Vuitch*,[19] the Court reversed a lower court decision declaring the District's criminal abortion law to be unconstitutional on grounds of vagueness.

Woodward and Armstrong report the same diffidence on the part of the Justices towards the abortion issue. They note that while the Court agreed in the 1971 Term to take two abortion appeals from Texas and Georgia, this had been done to settle the question of federal jurisdiction over state abortion cases. Furthermore, it seemed that the vote was likely to go against granting federal jurisdiction, ensuring that the substance of the abortion issue would not be settled in the Supreme Court.[20] As it turned out, however, the jurisdiction issue went the other way, due to a decision in a quite separate case; thus, 'Suddenly, unexpectedly, the Court found itself faced with the underlying constitutional issue in the abortion cases. Did women have the right to obtain abortions?'[21]

The case was put over for reargument in order to allow the new Nixon appointees, Powell and Rehnquist, to participate in the case. *Roe v. Wade*[22] and its companion case, *Doe v. Bolton*,[23] were eventually decided on 22 January, 1973. The outcome was unexpected and controversial: 'The Supreme Court's 1973 decision to void the abortion laws of 49 states surprised both opponents and proponents. Less than half the states had even liberalised their laws by that time.'[24] But there was more to the surprise than the mere impact on existing state legislation. The decision to strike the laws was taken by a vote of seven to two, with three of President Nixon's four appointees in the majority and one of whom, Justice Blackmun, actually wrote the opinion.[25] Moreover, Blackmun's opinion was based on constitutional reasoning that was to strike many, including some of the majority Justices,[26] as tenuous. As Justice Blackmun's constitutional rationale became a prime source of vulnerability in the backlash against the *Roe* decision, it is necessary to explore it in some depth.

The facts of the two cases with which he had to deal were as follows: Jane Roe[27] was an unmarried, pregnant Texan, who had been denied an abortion under the state law which permitted abortions only where necessary to save the mother's life. She asserted that the Texas statute, which dated from 1854, violated her constitutional right to privacy and that of all other women similarly situated. The *Doe* case raised similar issues, though it was different in two important respects. First, Mary Doe was married.[28] Second, the Georgia statute under which she had been denied an abortion was a modern, 'liberalised' law, passed in 1968. Both cases were class actions and had been organised and financed by pro-choice interest groups. By the time the cases reached the Supreme Court, of course, neither woman was still pregnant and the decision of the Justices could not affect them personally. In short, *Roe v. Wade* and *Doe v. Bolton* were calculated attempts to bring about a major social reform by persuading the Court to constitutionalise and radicalise abortion law.

Justice Blackmun began his opinion for the Court by acknowledging that the controversy over abortion was an emotive one, informed by deep convictions on both sides. Personal philosophy and experience, religion and moral values all affected one's view of abortion. Policy issues such as poverty and population growth were also complicating considerations. He then, however, set himself a tall order: 'Our task, of course, is to resolve the issue by constitutional measurement, free of emotion and of predilection.'[29]

The problem was that the Constitution provided little, if any, guide that would allow the Justices to reason in the disinterested fashion desired. There was nothing explicit in the text or history of the Constitution to indicate that the framers had intended to protect the right to an abortion. However, just eight years before *Roe*, the Court had taken the unique step of declaring the existence of a new, independent right – the right to privacy. That case, *Griswold v. Connecticut*,[30] involved an anachronistic state statute that prohibited the use of contraceptives by married couples. A seven-to-two majority of the Justices had voted to strike the law and five subcribed to the reasoning in Justice Douglas' opinion. This argued that specific guarantees in the Bill of Rights which exhibited a concern with privacy had 'penumbras', 'emanations' from which create 'zones of privacy'.[31] Douglas cited, for example, the Third Amendment's prohibition against the quartering of soldiers in a private house in time of peace without the owners' consent; and the Fourth Amendment's protection against unreasonable searches and seizures by government officers. He also pointed out that the Court had, in a series of cases, recognised penumbral privacy rights. Up to this point, Douglas' argument was unexceptional. The pioneering step came when he asserted that these penumbral rights combined to create a separate, self-standing constitutional right to privacy.[32]

Justices Black and Stewart dissented on the grounds that there was no constitutional basis to this right of privacy. While both made clear their belief that the Connecticut statute was unwise, they also insisted that that was no basis for the Court to strike it down. Black wrote that 'I like my privacy as well as the next one, but I am nevertheless compelled to admit that government has a right to invade it unless prohibited by some specific constitutional provision.'[33] Stewart made the rather telling point that Douglas had failed to identify even one of the explicit guarantees of the Bill of Rights which could be said to relate to the Connecticut law. He appeared to take mischievous delight in enumerating their irrelevance, pointing out, for example, that in this case no soldiers had been quartered in any house.[34]

There was, however, no great outcry over the *Griswold* decision, even though it contained the potential for a considerable expansion of federal judicial power over the states. Justice Black accused the majority of falling prey to the misconception that it was '. . . the duty of this Court to keep the Constitution in tune with the times.'[35] Yet few people seemed willing to attack the Court for adopting that role when the law was, in Justice Stewart's own words, 'uncommonly silly'.[36]

The right to privacy was next used in 1972, in *Eisenstadt v. Baird.*[37] For all the rhetoric in *Griswold* about the sanctity of the marriage relationship, a majority of the Justices decided that a ban on the distribution of contraceptives to unmarried persons also violated the new right. It seemed, then, that the right to privacy was not destined to protect revered social institutions, such as marriage and the family, but the privacy of individuals engaging in certain sexual and, perhaps, other related activities.

In *Roe*, Justice Blackmun simply asserted, rather than argued, that, 'This right of privacy . . . is broad enough to encompass a woman's decision whether or not to terminate her pregnancy.'[38] He was able to point to past decisions of the Court which had protected certain procreative rights, but he was not able to demonstrate convincingly why the right to choose an abortion should be joined to them. In this respect, there were three main difficulties. First, as Blackmun himself argued, the Court's past decisions '. . . make it clear that only personal rights that can be deemed "fundamental" or "implicit in the concept of ordered liberty" . . . are included in this guarantee of personal privacy.'[39] While there is no difficulty in making a *political* argument that abortion should be seen as a fundamental right of women, a *constitutional* demonstration of fundamentality requires that a right be shown to be '. . . so rooted in the traditions and conscience of our people as to be ranked as fundamental.'[40] Yet Justice Blackmun's own extensive review of the history of attitudes towards abortion, both in the United States and elsewhere, demonstrates precisely that opinion on abortion has always been divided. Furthermore, the variation in the existing state laws emphasised the fact that there was no consensus behind abortion rights such as there was behind the right to marry and have children.

Abortion was also different from other privacy rights that the Court had previously protected because it involved not only government and the individual, but also a third entity – the fetus. As we shall see below, the majority opinion did acknowledge this complicating factor and tried to deal with it in a reasonable manner: the fact remains, however, that the existence of the fetus makes the right to an abortion qualitatively different from other privacy rights because it requires a determination of what rights and duties both government and individual have towards that third party.

The third problem involved in connecting abortion rights to previous privacy decisions stemmed from the fact that the Court had never really defined its concept of privacy. On the one hand, it seemed to be a physical concept, protecting the private home from soldiers and government officials, or, as Justice Douglas put it in *Griswold*, forbidding '. . . the police to search the sacred precincts of marital bedrooms for telltale signs of the use of contraceptives.'[41] On the other, there was a suggestion that the Court was seeking to establish a privacy, or autonomy, of decision making in matters which were no business of government. Either way, however, the argument for abortion rights was not straightforward. The physical concept of privacy did not apply, since the woman went to a public facility for her abortion. Autonomy of decision making was therefore the point, but it ran into the two other problems outlined above – how could the Supreme Court know when a decision was no business of government, especially when third party interests had to be considered?

Most commentators, whatever their position on abortion, agreed that the *Roe* decision went well beyond *Griswold* in its use of privacy doctrine.[42] Most of them agreed, in fact, that there was no convincing interpretive basis to *Roe* at all. The impression that the majority Justices were impelled by policy considerations was reinforced by the legislative style of Justice Blackmun's opinion, which, in its concern for the detailed balancing of what it perceived as the different interests involved, resembled the product of compromise and bargaining so typical of American legislation.

Justice Blackmun addressed the interests and rights of the three parties concerned as follows. First, as already noted, the constitutional privacy right did give women the right to choose to have an abortion. This was justified by a consideration of the detriment to a woman's life that would result if she were deprived of that right: physical and mental harm, the distressful life and future associated with an unwanted pregnancy, difficulties for the family and existing children and the stigma of unwed motherhood.[43] However, Blackmun then specifically rejected the feminist contention that a woman has a right to total control over her reproductive capacity: '. . . appellant and some amici argue that the woman's right is absolute and that she is entitled to terminate her pregnancy at whatever time, in whatever way, and for whatever reason she alone chooses. With this we do not agree.'[44] The woman's privacy right cannot be absolute, argued Justice Blackmun, because her privacy itself is not absolute: she is carrying an embryo or fetus. This makes the situation inherently different from the privacy of marriage, procreation and the like protected in previous cases such as *Griswold* and *Eisenstadt*. Therefore, 'The woman's privacy is no longer sole and any right of privacy she possesses must be measured accordingly.'[45] In other words, the decision to have an abortion is sufficiently like the decision to use contraceptives to warrant constitutional privacy protection, but is also 'inherently different' from it and therefore precludes the same degree of protection.

Although the existence of the fetus conditions the mother's privacy right, it does not itself have any constitutional rights. This is because a fetus is not a person in the legal sense of the word and Justice Blackmun is able to cite many precedents in support of this.[46] He emphasises, however, that this does not represent a judgement as to when life begins in a biological or philosophical sense. Indeed, he argues that this is an issue that the Court could not and should not decide: 'We need not resolve the difficult question of when life begins.

When those trained in the respective disciplines of medicine, philosophy, and theology are unable to arrive at any consensus, the judiciary, at this point in the development of man's knowledge, is not in a position to speculate as to the answer.'[47] The desire to avoid this aspect of the abortion issue is understandable, given the controversy which surrounds it. Nevertheless, *any* policy on abortion carries an implicit judgement on the question of when life begins and, as the post-*Roe* history of the abortion conflict testifies, it is quite unavoidable.[48]

The Court decided that for protection of any interests it has, the fetus must rely upon the state. The state was deemed to have an important and legitimate interest in protecting potential life, as well as a second, distinct interest in protecting women's health.[49] However, since the woman's right to have an abortion was fundamental in constitutional terms, the State could only act on its interests, and regulate or ban abortions, when it had a compelling reason for doing so.[50] In effect, the Court required the mother's rights and interests to be balanced against those of the state, in a manner which gave due recognition to both. Apparently pursuing his belief that such a compromise was possible on a non-ideological basis, Justice Blackmun turned to medical evidence to effect the necessary balance.

With regard to the state's right to intervene on the basis of its interest in protecting maternal health, the compelling point came at the end of the first trimester, or three months, of pregnancy: 'This is so because of the now-established medical fact . . . that until the end of the first trimester mortality in abortion may be less than mortality in normal childbirth.'[51] During the first three months of pregnancy, then, abortion poses an even lesser threat to maternal health than does continuing pregnancy, so the state has no health interest to assert and may not interfere in the decision of the woman and her physician to opt for abortion. After the first trimester, when the relative health risks of abortion and continuing pregnancy are reversed, the state's interest in maternal health becomes compelling. It may regulate abortion '. . . to the extent that the regulation reasonably relates to the preservation and protection of maternal health.'[52] Such regulation would be the licensing of abortion physicians and facilities, for example.

With regard to the state's interest in protecting potential life, the Court held that the compelling point was fetal viability, that is, the point at which the fetus could survive outside the womb, with or without artificial means of support: 'This is so because the fetus then presumably has the capability of meaningful life outside the mother's womb.'[53] As viability may occur at twenty-four weeks (though more often at twenty-eight),[54] the state's interest in protecting potential life becomes compelling at the end of the second trimester. During the third trimester, therefore, the state '. . . may go so far as to proscribe abortion . . . except when it is necessary to preserve the life or health of the mother.'[55]

Here, then, was the Court's so-called 'trimester system' of abortion rights. Justice Blackmun summed up the scheme as follows:

> This holding, we feel, is consistent with the relative weights of the res-
> pective interests involved, with the lessons and examples of medical and
> legal history, with the lenity of the common law, and with the demands of
> the profound problems of the present day. The decision leaves the State
> free to place increasing restrictions on abortion, so long as those restric-
> tions are tailored to the recognised state interests. The decision vindicates
> the right of the physician to administer medical treatment according to his
> professional judgement up to the points where important state interests
> provide compelling justifications for intervention. Up to those points, the
> abortion decision in all its aspects is inherently, and primarily, a medical
> decision, and basic responsibility for it must rest with the physician.[56]

This passage provides considerable insight into the non-interpretive bases of the Court's decision. In the first place, it omits any mention of the constitutional justification of the decision. Instead, it seeks to demonstrate that it has achieved a reasonable compromise between the interests it believes to exist. That reasonableness lies in a consideration of the profound contemporary problems involved in abortion issues in the light of medical and statutory history. This is exactly the approach a reasonable *legislator* might take, but interpretivism does not permit a *judge* to settle issues simply because they involve profound social problems or because medical evidence suggests a solution.[57] The judge is required to identify a constitutional problem and a constitutional solution to it. Blackmun's reliance upon medical and other professional opinion, however, is central to the decision in *Roe*. This is in part evident from the fact that he spends considerable time in his opinion discussing the views on abortion of the American Medical Association, the American Public Health Association and the American Bar Association.[58] He also emphasises his belief that abortion is primarily a medical issue, at least during the first six months of pregnancy. Most important of all in this respect, however, is the fact that the passage above omits any mention of women's rights while making much of physicians' rights. As Rosalind Petchesky has pointed out, by predicating the right to an abortion on medical considerations and judgements, *Roe* '. . . makes the physician the final arbiter of the abortion decision.'[59] Chief Justice Burger, in his concurring opinion, also stressed the fact, though with approval, that the Court's decision should not be read as vindicating a feminist concept of abortion: 'Plainly, the Court today rejects any claim that the Constitution requires abortion on demand.'[60]

Only two Justices, White and Rehnquist, dissented. Justice White's opinion was short though hardly sweet. He wrote that the majority's claim was that '. . . the Constitution of the United States values the convenience, whim, or caprice of the putative mother more than the life of the fetus.'[61] But, he continued, there was nothing in the history or language of the Constitution to support that judgement. Moreover, the majority had scarcely attempted to provide any constitutional reason or authority for the new right to have an abortion. In taking the right to decide abortion policy away from the states in such a manner, he argued, the Court had behaved illegitimately: 'As an act of raw judicial power, the Court perhaps has authority to do what it does today; but in my view its judgement is an improvident and extravagant exercise of the power of judicial review that the Constitution extends to this Court.'[62] On a sensitive issue over which reasonable people will differ, and on which there is no constitutional mandate, the decision '. . . should be left with the people and to the political processes the people have devised to govern their affairs.'[63]

Many scholars expounded on White's blunt critique. John Hart Ely supports abortion rights and also defends the judicial activism of the Warren Court. Nevertheless, he concluded that *Roe* was a bad decision: 'It is bad because it is bad constitutional law, or rather because it is *not* constitutional law and gives almost no sense of an obligation to try to be.'[64] What concerns Ely is the lack of any plausible relationship to the Constitution of the new right to an abortion, especially as the right is given unusually strong constitutional protection by the Court:

> What is frightening about *Roe* is that this super-protected right is not inferable from the language of the Constitution, the framers' thinking respecting the specific problem in issue, any general value derivable from the provisions they included, or the nation's governmental structure. Nor is it explainable in terms of the unusual political impotence of the group judicially protected vis-à-vis the interest that legally prevailed over it. And that, I believe . . . is a charge that can responsibly be leveled at no other decision of the past twenty years. At times the inferences the Court has drawn from the values the Constitution marks for special protection have been controversial, even shaky, but never before has its sense of an obligation to draw one been so obviously lacking.[65]

What Ely and other critics agreed was that the Court had effectively employed substantive due process in *Roe*. In other words, the majority Justices had read into the Constitution their own view that the right to an abortion was fundamental to the liberty of women. Their unwillingness to say so openly stemmed from the fact that substantive due process was used by a succession of conservative Courts in the late nineteenth and early twentieth century to outlaw progressive socio-economic legislation that interfered with the 'liberty of contract' of employers. Those Courts took the concept of 'liberty' protected by the Due Process Clause of the Fourteenth Amendment and read laissez-faire economic principles into it. The most infamous example was probably *Lochner v. New York*,[66] where the Court ruled that due process requirements outlawed maximum hours legislation for bakery workers. Although the political orientation of the *Roe* majority is quite different from that of the earlier Court, Ely is convinced that the *Roe* decision is nevertheless an example of 'Lochnering'.[67] Richard Epstein came to a similar conclusion[68] as, intriguingly, did Justice Stewart in his con-curring opinion in *Roe*. Stewart, it will be recalled, dissented in *Griswold* because he could find no basis in the Constitution for a right of privacy and therefore concluded that the Court had resurrected substantive due process but was too embarrassed to say so. In *Roe*, however, he accepts the liberal version of substantive due process as a *fait accompli* and goes on to hold that the liberty it protects includes the right to abortion: '. . . the *Griswold* decision can be rationally under-stood only as a holding that the Connecticut statute substantively invaded the "liberty" that is protected by the Due Process Clause of the Fourteenth Amendment. As so understood, *Griswold* stands as one in a long line of . . . cases decided under the doctrine of substantive due process, and I now accept it as such.'[69]

Substantive due process is not necessarily, however, a crude process in which the Justices scour the Constitution for a convenient hook on which to hang their most cherished policy preference. While it might be plausible to so depict some conservative Justices of the early twentieth century or some liberal members of the Warren Court, it is not convincing in the case of, say, Blackmun, Powell or Stewart. For as Vincent Blasi pointed out, they appear to have practised an ideologically 'rootless activism'.[70] It is necessary, therefore, to look for other reasons which, apart from or in conjunction with personal ideology, explain why the *Roe* majority took it upon themselves to attempt to resolve the abortion issue.

It is said that when mountaineers are asked why they wish to climb

Mount Everest, they answer 'Because it's there'. The same may be true of the Supreme Court and the abortion issue. There were several factors which combined to make abortion a 'judicial Everest'. As noted above, there were by 1973 the beginnings of an abortion controversy in the United States. A number of states had liberalised or repealed their criminal abortion statutes, though the majority had not. Women's rights groups had emerged as strong proponents of abortion rights, while the Catholic Church was co-ordinating a mass anti-abortion movement. Public opinion was generally favourable on 'therapeutic' abortions, that is, those deemed medically necessary. For example, approval of abortion on the grounds that the mother's health would otherwise be seriously endangered stood at 83 per cent in 1972.[71] Approval of 'non-therapeutic' (or 'elective') abortions, however, was much less, though even here the trend was liberal: whereas in 1968 only 11 per cent of the public approved of elective abortions, the figure for 1972 was 27 per cent.[72] And as the Court recognised explicitly in *Roe*, medical and legal professionals were generally in favour of more liberal abortion rights. Finally, the Court was being asked to rule on numerous aspects of state abortion laws and the denial of jurisdiction or a decision that the matter was one for the states would have the substantive effect of allowing some women free access to abortion, while denying it almost completely to others.

This can be considered the classic combination of factors which invites non-interpretive review by the Court. Here is an important and sensitive question of individual rights which, although not addressed in the Constitution, cries out for resolution. Why not use the expertise and freedom of the Justices from immediate electoral pressures to find an answer to such a vexed question? The invitation is perhaps doubly alluring if the judicial will exists to find a resolution based on compromise and the knowledge of supposedly dispassionate experts.

This certainly appears to be the spirit of the *Roe* decision. Robert Burt has argued that '*Roe v. Wade* is perhaps the most egregious instance of the Court's desire to stifle conflict . . .', but also that it is part of a wider '. . . authoritarian impulse in cases involving family relations.'[73] Vincent Blasi focused on the pragmatic approach adopted by the Court in *Roe*: '. . . even so fundamental an issue as abortion was treated by this Court as a conflict of particularised material interests – a conflict that could be resolved by accommodating those interests in the spirit of compromise.'[74]

Ideology did, of course, affect the compromise that the Court struck in *Roe*. It was not the ideology of the crusader, however, so much as that of the class and profession from which the centrist Justices were drawn. Indeed, both Justices Blackmun and Powell had close connections with the medical as well as legal professions: Blackmun had spent ten years as general counsel to the Mayo Clinic in Minnesota and much of his *Roe* opinion was researched and written in the Clinic's library.[75] Powell had married into a family of obstetricians and '. . . had heard all the horrifying stories of unsanitary butchers and coat-hanger abortions.'[76] Beyond such personal factors lies the statistical evidence that upper-class, well-educated Americans generally, and the legal elite in particular hold opinions on abortion that are more liberal than the mass public. One study, for example, showed the legal elite approving a woman's unfettered autonomy in choosing an early term abortion 65 per cent–22 per cent, compared with the mass public's approval by 48 per cent–40 per cent.[77] Another showed the college educated approving of first trimester abortions by 71 per cent–29 per cent, compared with high school educated *disapproval* by 49 per cent–51 per cent.[78] When the personal beliefs of Justices coincide with predominant professional beliefs about social issues like abortion, it is not surprising that these should be reflected strongly in a non-interpretive decision.

Roe and the pro-life movement

The Court's attempt to impose a compromise on the issue of abortion was a complete failure. *Roe* galvanised a fledgling anti-abortion movement, which in turn fuelled the broader New Right movement. With the benefit of hindsight, the reasons why are not hard to see. First, as with its 1972 decision on the death penalty, part of the provocation was that the Court had abruptly taken away the power of the states to decide the fundamentals of abortion policy. States whose legislatures and citizens did not agree with the new policy would inevitably resent this transgression of a traditional boundary line of federalism.

Second, the Court transformed abortion from a medical issue into a political issue. As we saw above, in states like California, where laws had been liberalised to take fuller account of health factors, abortion reform had been a consensual process. Where, as in New York, new laws aimed to give women the right to choose an abortion for any reason, there had been bitter conflict. The Court's decision in *Roe* was closer to the New York law in this respect. Women were in effect free to choose an abortion in the first six months under the *Roe* trimester scheme, provided they could find a physician willing to perform it.

Even in the final trimester, a woman could have an abortion on health grounds, with health being given a broad definition. Despite the rhetorical and practical limitations on abortion as a political right of women, *Roe* was nevertheless an obvious gain in the battle for reproductive freedom. As the *Christian Science Monitor* wrote in reaction to the *Roe* decision, 'No victory for women's rights since enactment of the 19th Amendment has been greater than the one achieved Monday in the Supreme Court'.[79] Those who were hostile to abortion, or who at least had grave doubts about it, now perceived abortion not so much a medical procedure approved by doctors, as a victory for a group of radicals who despised traditional values.

Luker reported that more people joined the anti-abortion movement in 1973 than in any year before or since. Moreover, the new activists were significantly different from the largely Catholic males who dominated the movement up until *Roe*: 'The new group of people brought into active participation in the anti-abortion movement were predominantly women with high-school educations (and occasionally some college) who were married, had children, and were not employed outside the home. They were, as the earlier pro-life activists called them, "the housewives".'[80]

There is no doubt that the significance of abortion in American politics goes well beyond the comparatively narrow issue of whether or not it is morally permissible to abort a fetus. Abortion rights connect directly to the social institution of the family and through that to the role and status of women in society. For many feminists, abortion is the key to the freedom and equality they seek:

> Abortion is not simply an aspect of social welfare; it is above all a condition of women's liberation, and by the turn of the seventies had become recognised by advocates and foes as deeply symbolic of feminist aspirations for sexual autonomy, as a paradigmatic feminist demand. Although often unarticulated even by feminists, the meanings resonating from abortion politics have more to do with compulsory heterosexuality, family structure, the relationship between men and women and parents and children, and women's employment, than they do with the fetus.[81]

Others have drawn attention to the class element in abortion politics. Peter Skerry argued that abortion coincided with the values of educated, upper-middle-class women for whom the family was a constraint on their career and other ambitions. For working-class women, for whom satisfying careers were unlikely, the family represented positive values, with motherhood being an avenue of status achievement.[82] For Conover and Gray, picking up on Ladd's concept of the

New Bourgeoisie,[83] abortion and the *Roe* decision brought home to lower-class Americans the extent to which the traditional values they still cherished were under threat: '. . . the time was ripe to organise against the perceived sources of those threats: modernism, relativism, humanism, individualism, intellectualism, professionalism, and feminism.'[84]

And Faye Ginsberg, a social anthropologist who decided to observe the abortion conflict in the mundane location of Fargo, North Dakota (pop. 62,000), found the same broad cultural divisions operative there as in New York or California; 'For the local pro-life proponents, the availability of abortion in their own community represented the intrusion of secularism, narcissism, and materialism, the reshaping of women into "structural men". Pro-choice activists reacted to right-to-life protesters as the forces of narrow-minded intolerance who would deny women access to a choice that they see as fundamental to women's freedom and ability to overcome sexual discrimination.'[85]

Even allowing for the fact that the passions generated by the subject may have led to a certain overstatement in academic writing, it is clear that the abortion issue carries an extraordinary burden of political and cultural conflict. Not surprisingly, then, it has provoked street demonstrations, bombings of abortion clinics and running battles in state legislatures, the United States Congress and, of course, in the Supreme Court itself.

For most of the post-*Roe* era, the pro-life movement has held the initiative. The pro-choice movement took up a defensive position and was perhaps even complacent in its belief that abortion was firmly established as a constitutional right and there was little its opponents could do about it. This belief was not without foundation, especially as public opinion surveys consistently showed majority approval for the Court's decision. For example, a Harris poll of 1973 showed support for *Roe* by 52 per cent to 41 per cent.[86] However, pro-life groups had little difficulty finding sympathetic state and federal legislators willing to lead the attempt to restrict or reverse outright the Court's decision in *Roe*.

The anti-*Roe* campaign had various strands. One was to seek a constitutional amendment that would either make abortions illegal in most circumstances or that would give the states and Congress ultimate authority to make abortion policy. According to one count, between 1973 and 1986, there were two hundred and seventy-five bills introduced into Congress proposing constitutional amendments that would effectively overturn *Roe*.[87] All were unsuccessful. Congressional approval of a constitutional amendment requires a two-thirds majority of both chambers: the nearest a pro-life amendment came to achieving that was in 1982, when the Hatch Amendment, giving power over abortion to legislatures, received the approval of the Senate Judiciary Committee by ten votes to seven, but was then defeated the following year by 50 votes to 49 by the full Senate.[88] A quasi-constitutional amendment was attempted by Senator Jesse Helms in the so-called Helms Human Life Statute. It sought to avoid the two-thirds requirement for constitutional amendments by having a statute declare an embryo to be a person within the protection of the Fourteenth Amendment. The effect would have been to make abortion murder, but it was probably the implication that Congress could change the meaning of the Constitution by statute which prevented the Helms bill from ever being put to a vote.[89]

A second tack taken by the pro-life movement was to have state legislatures and Congress pass statutes which would test their powers to regulate abortions under the *Roe* trimester scheme. Such regulation was almost always intended to restrict, not regulate abortions, but some of these efforts proved very successful none the less. Nancy Ford recounted events in Rhode Island, Pennsylvania and Illinois as illustrative of this legislative reaction.[90] Rhode Island indicated its 'compliance' with *Roe* by passing a law which stated that human life began at conception, that a fetus was a person within the meaning of the Fourteenth Amendment and imposed criminal penalties for performing abortions not necessary to save the mother's life.[91] The 1974 Pennsylvania Abortion Control Act required a woman to obtain her spouse's consent before she could have an abortion and threatened physicians with a charge of second-degree murder if they failed to use special care to preserve the life of a potentially viable fetus.[92] Illinois at first complied with *Roe* but then, in 1975, passed a law which declared the state's opposition to all abortions except those necessary to save the mother's life, required spousal consent for adult women and parental consent for minors and mandated a veritable host of detailed informed consent, record-keeping and medical procedures prior to the performance of any abortion.[93] As we shall see below, many of these attempts to restrict abortion rights eventually found their way on to the Supreme Court's docket.

A third goal was to influence the appointment of judges, especially federal judges, so that the judiciary would be less favourable to abortion rights. This has been highly successful, largely through the influence which the movement has gained in the Republican Party during the presidencies of Ronald Reagan and George Bush. The anti-abortion movement, along with other parts of the New Right, provided important elements of the social agenda of the Republican Party in the late 1970s and 1980s. One reflection of this was the increasingly clear anti-abortion language of the Republican Party platform for presidential elections during those years. Whereas President Nixon had used the abortion issue in 1972 to try to attract the votes of Catholic voters, it was not until 1976 that the issue appeared in the Republican platform. In an obvious response to the *Roe* decision, it called for a constitutional amendment to restore the right to life of 'unborn children'. The 1980 platform went further by adding a clause calling for '. . . the appointment of judges at all levels of the judiciary who respect traditional family values and the sanctity of innocent human life.'[94]

Upon taking office, President Reagan began implementing this policy with great enthusiasm. All potential Reagan nominees were subjected to a strict process of ideological screening by the new President's Committee on Federal Judicial Selection.[95] It soon became obvious that opposition to *Roe* was a critical factor in passing this test, not only for members of the President's Committee but even more so for hard-line anti-abortion Senators on the Senate Judiciary Committee. Senators Jeremiah Denton, Orrin Hatch and John East, for example, handed one nominee to a federal judgeship a questionnaire on various social issues. The first four questions were all about abortion and asked the nominee to give details of his views on the constitutional validity of the right to privacy, whether or not he agreed that *Roe* was an exercise of raw judicial power, whether or not he believed the *Roe* trimester system had any constitutional basis and whether or not a viable fetus was a person within the meaning of the Fourteenth Amendment.[96] And, as we shall see, as members of the *Roe* Court were gradually replaced by Reagan appointees, the constitutional right to an abortion became increasingly fragile.

The pro-life movement has also tried to influence judicial decision making on abortion by stepping up the number and range of *amicus curiae* briefs submitted in Supreme Court cases. In *Roe v. Wade*, pro-choice briefs were more numerous and represented a wider range of interests than pro-life briefs. Pro-choice briefs in *Roe* included those by professional medical organisations, such as the American College of Obstetricians and Gynecologists, the American Psychiatric Association and the New York Academy of Medicine; groups concerned with poverty and population, such as Planned Parenthood of America, the

National Legal Programme on Health Problems of the Poor and the American Public Health Association; ethical and religious groups such as the American Ethical Union, the American Jewish Congress and the United Church of Christ; and women's groups, including the American Association of University Women, NOW, the Professional Women's Caucus and the National Board of the Young Women's Christian Association of America. Against these were pro-life briefs from relatively new, small and unprestigious groups: Americans United for Life, Women for the Unborn, the National Right to Life Committee and the League for Infants, Fetuses, and the Elderly (LIFE). No major political, professional, religious or ethical organisation filed a pro-life brief.[97] Neither were the Justices likely to have been too impressed by the opening comments in oral argument before them of Jay Floyd, the attorney representing Texas: referring to the women lawyers representing Jane Roe, he said 'It's an old joke, but when a man argues against two beautiful ladies like this, they're going to have the last word.'[98] The pro-life effort in *Roe* had a rather small-scale, old-fashioned look about it.

By the time of the *Webster* case in 1989, the pro-life *amicus* effort had become much more impressive. That case saw a new record in the number of *amicus* briefs filed in a Supreme Court case: seventy-eight, surpassing by twenty the previous record established in the affirmative action *Bakke* case. Remarkably, the pro-life briefs outnumbered the pro-choice briefs by forty-seven to thirty-one, although the latter actually represented more organisations.[99] Not only the quantity but the quality of pro-life briefs had improved considerably since the time of *Roe*, particularly in the sophistication of legal and historical arguments advanced.[100] Whether either the quality or quantity of *amicus* briefs ever actually changes a Justice's mind once made up is highly debatable, though both sides claim that they do affect decisions indirectly, if not directly.[101] The point here, however, is simply that the pro-life legal campaign can now match that of the pro-choice groups who once held a clear ascendancy. The turning point was probably the decision by the Catholic Church in November 1975, to launch its Pastoral Plan for Pro-Life Activities, which included a strategy of lobbying all branches of government, including the judiciary.[102]

The fifth and final major tactic of the anti-abortion movement has been direct action in the form of public protest, civil disobedience and criminal violence. Most famously, every 22 January, the anniversary of the *Roe* decision, pro-life supporters hold a mass March for Life protest rally on the steps of the Supreme Court building in

Washington. Most infamously, the mid-1980s saw the onset of a bombing campaign against abortion clinics by religiously-inspired anti-abortion zealots. One group who carried out bombings called themselves the Army of God. A group of four young fundamentalist Christians who bombed an abortion clinic in Pensacola, Florida, on Christmas Day 1984, said their bombs were a 'gift to Jesus for his birthday'.[103] In an attempt to find an effective, but more respectable, form of direct action, some activists have moved from picketing abortion clinics to physically trying to block access to them. As noted above, this form of action is particularly associated with Operation Rescue and its leader, Randall Terry. Operation Rescue was founded in 1987 and by mid-1989, it claimed 35,000 adherents.[104] It achieved prominence in 1988 when it besieged the Democratic Party Convention in Atlanta, and has carried out hundreds of 'rescue operations', consisting of blocking access to abortion clinics by having hundreds of protesters lie down in front of the doors. When arrested, they try to overload the law enforcement system by refusing to pay the small administrative fees involved in their arrest and spend the weekend in jail.[105] Other Operation Rescue efforts at publicity include displaying an aborted fetus in a coffin lined with white satin at press conferences and showing a video which has shots of aborted fetuses intercut with scenes from Nazi concentration camps.[106]

This, then, is the hostile climate in which the Court had to deal with a never-ending series of challenges to its decision in *Roe* and it was not long before the Court appeared to be in retreat. Some of the first post-*Roe* cases saw the Court strengthen women's autonomy over abortion. For example, in *Planned Parenthood v. Danforth*,[107] a 6–3 majority of the Justices held unconstitutional a requirement of Missouri's 1974 abortion statute that a woman seeking an abortion obtain her spouse's consent. And a 5–4 majority also struck the requirement that a minor obtain parental consent to an abortion. While the Court upheld provisions of the statute that required the woman's informed consent to an abortion and certain record-keeping and reporting procedures, it made it clear that such regulations must not significantly interfere with the woman's basic right of decision.[108]

Abortion and public funding

In 1977, however, the anti-abortion movement achieved its first great success in the Supreme Court. At issue in *Maher v. Roe*,[109] was the question of whether states were obliged to provide funds for the non-therapeutic abortions of indigent women, if they also provided funds to meet the childbirth costs of indigent women. The Welfare Department of the State of Connecticut decided to limit state Medicaid benefits to medically necessary (therapeutic) abortions during the first trimester of pregnancy. Thus, poor women who were otherwise entitled to Medicaid benefits were required to obtain a physician's certificate of medical necessity before the costs of any abortion would be met by public funds. It was claimed in *Maher* that this differential treatment of childbirth and abortion involved discrimination prohibited by the Equal Protection clause of the Fourteenth Amendment and interfered unconstitutionally with a woman's right to have an abortion. The Court dismissed the claim by a vote of 6–3, with Chief Justice Burger and Justices Powell and Stewart of the *Roe* majority also in the majority here.[110] In an opinion by Justice Powell, the Court ruled that the right to opt for an abortion established in *Roe* was not absolute; rather it protected a woman from '... unduly burdensome interference with her freedom to decide whether to terminate her pregnancy. It implies no limitation on the authority of a State to make a value judgement favouring childbirth over abortion, and to implement that judgement by the allocation of public funds.'[111] He further argued that Connecticut's decision not to fund an indigent woman's non-therapeutic abortion, but to provide money for her if she chose childbirth, placed no obstacle in the path of her choosing an abortion: 'The State may have made childbirth a more attractive alternative, thereby influencing the woman's decision, but it has imposed no restriction on access to abortions that was not already there. The indigency that may make it difficult – and in some cases, perhaps, impossible – for some women to have abortions is neither created nor in any way affected by the Connecticut regulation.'[112] Finally, in a passage that was to be of key importance in future cases, Powell wrote: 'Our conclusion signals no retreat from *Roe* or the cases applying it. There is a basic difference between direct state interference with a protected activity and state encouragement of an alternative activity consonant with legislative policy.'[113]

Justice Brennan, in dissent, thought this distinction to be illusory. The Connecticut regulation invaded the *Roe* abortion right '... by bringing financial pressures on indigent women that force them to bear children they would otherwise not have.'[114] And the fact that the withholding of funds does not constitute an *absolute* barrier to having an abortion does not save it from unconstitutionality. In numerous previous cases where a fundamental right was involved, the Court had struck down forms of state interference which were far from abso-lute.[115] The state is only permitted to intervene in the exercise of a fundamental right when it can demonstrate that it has a compelling interest to advance: yet *Roe* declared that the state had no compelling interest in abortion that was operative during the first trimester. Brennan, then, did not believe that anyone would take seriously the majority's claim that it was not retreating from *Roe v. Wade*.[116]

The question of whether the Court retreated in *Maher* is an intriguing one. As is often the case with Supreme Court opinions, there is a certain amount of plausibility in both majority and dissenting opinions in *Maher*. However, aside from the relative merits of the legal arguments in *Maher*, there is other evidence to suggest that a partial judicial retreat was indeed involved. Most importantly, there is a striking difference between the judicial activism of *Roe v. Wade* and the judicial restraint of *Maher v. Roe*. As noted above, virtually all com-mentators agree that *Roe* was a bold, innovative decision that rode roughshod over the abortion policy preferences of state legislatures to create a right which had, at best, a tenuous constitutional basis. Now, in *Maher*, the Court had to decide whether to extend its activism. To be sure, the Court has never held that government must fund all constitu-tional rights, but it has ruled that some fundamental rights require public funding. The most famous instance, perhaps, is the case of *Gideon v. Wainwright*, where the Court held that indigents charged with committing a serious crime must be provided with lawyers at public expense.[117] Other Supreme Court decisions, such as those requiring the reapportionment of legislatures or the busing of schoolchildren to achieve racially integrated education involved incalculable expenditure of public funds.

Furthermore, in order to conclude in *Maher* that the Connecticut regulation placed no obstacle in the path of an indigent woman seeking an abortion, the Court had to turn a blind eye to the fact that that was precisely what the regulation was intended to do. The Court was as aware as anyone of what many states had attempted by way of under-mining *Roe*. Indeed, Justice Powell acknowledged this implicitly in *Maher* when he wrote: 'The decision whether to expend state funds for non-therapeutic abortions is fraught with judgements of policy and value over which opinions are sharply divided . . . Indeed, when an issue involves policy choices as sensitive as those implicated by public funding of non-therapeutic abortions, the appropriate forum for their resolution in a democracy is the legislature.'[118] It is ironic that this passage is so reminiscent of the dissenting opinions in *Roe* itself.

Important as they were, however, the key to the Court's rediscovery of judicial restraint in *Maher* is to be found less in the activities of State legislatures, than it is in events in Congress. In June 1976, that is, six months before oral argument in *Maher* and a year before the Court actually decided it, the Hyde Amendment was introduced into the House of Representatives. The original amendment to the Health, Education and Welfare Appropriation Bill for fiscal 1977 prohibited the use of public funds for all abortions, therapeutic or non-therapeutic, and without any exceptions. The amendment was passed by the House 206–167. The Senate rejected it, but in September, 1976, a compromise amendment was passed by both chambers allowing an exception for abortions where the mother's life would otherwise be endangered.[119]

Every year since then, the Hyde Amendment has been readopted, though with certain variations in the exceptions allowed. For example, the 1977 version allowed a further exception for where the mother's health would otherwise be severely damaged and where the pregnancy had resulted from rape or incest.[120] Whatever the exceptions in any particular year, however, Congress has made it clear that it wishes virtually no Medicaid funds to be spent on abortions. Although the Supreme Court did not decide upon the constitutionality of the Hyde Amendment until 1980, in the case of *Harris v. McRae*,[121] it was well aware of its import while it was deliberating in *Maher*. Indeed, the very day the Court announced its decision in *Maher*, it also vacated the decision of a federal district court judge who had earlier enjoined enforcement of the 1976 Hyde Amendment.[122]

Furthermore, an examination of the Court's opinion in *Harris*, which upheld the validity of the Hyde Amendment by a vote of 5–4,[123] shows that it closely follows the reasoning laid down in *Maher*. There was a serious material difference between the two cases: *Maher* was concerned with whether health care funds should be spent on abortions which were not deemed medically necessary, but *Harris* with abortions that were indisputably medically necessary. The Court, however, saw no constitutional distinction between the two. Justice Stewart's majority opinion acknowledges that health concerns may lie at the core of a woman's desire to choose an abortion, but '. . . it simply does not follow that a woman's freedom of choice carries with it a constitutional entitlement to the financial resources to avail herself of the full range of protective choices. The reason why was explained in *Maher*: although government may not place obstacles in the path of a woman's exercise of her freedom of choice, it need not remove those not of its own creation. Indigency falls into the latter category.'[124] He added that just because the Constitution protected the right to use contraceptives, that didn't mean government was obliged to pay for them.[125] Most of the rest of the opinion reiterates the central points of the *Maher* decision, particularly that government may express a value judgement in favour of childbirth by offering financial 'incentives' to encourage it.[126]

Justice Brennan's dissent attacked the majority's reasoning as unrealistic. First, the principle of *Roe* was not that the state is obliged to ensure access to abortion, but that the state must not wield its power to burden the woman's freedom to choose.[127] Yet this is what the Hyde Amendment does in practice, if not in abstract theory. It is not merely the woman's poverty which interferes with her freedom of choice, but the combination of her poverty and government subsidy of childbirth but not abortion. In reality, 'By funding all of the expenses associated with childbirth and none of the expenses incurred in terminating pregnancy, the Government literally makes an offer that the indigent woman cannot refuse. It matters not that in this instance the Government has used the carrot rather than the stick.'[128]

Brennan also raised an issue which the majority opinion chose to ignore: the real purpose behind the Hyde Amendment. It was, he said, nothing less than an attempt to undermine *Roe* by indirect means:

> ... the Hyde Amendment is a transparent attempt by the Legislative Branch to impose the political majority's judgement of the morally acceptable and socially desirable preference on a sensitive and intimate decision that the Constitution entrusts to the individual. Worse yet, the Hyde Amendment does not foist that majoritarian viewpoint with equal measure upon everyone in our Nation, rich and poor alike; rather, it imposes that viewpoint only upon that segment of our society which, because of its position of political powerlessness, is least able to defend its privacy rights from the encroachments of state-mandated morality.[129]

There was no doubt that Brennan was absolutely correct in his judgement of legislative intent. Congressman Henry Hyde himself made it clear that the goal of his amendment was to stop as many abortions as possible. Apologising to members of Congress for using an appropriation bill to deal with the abortion issue, he said 'Constitutional amendments which prohibit abortion stay languishing in subcommittee ... and so the only vehicle where Members may work their will, unfortunately, is an appropriation bill.'[130] On the question of his amendment's discrimination against the poor, Hyde said that he would like to prevent all women from having abortions, but, 'Unfortunately, the only vehicle available is the HEW Medicaid Bill. A life is a life. The life of a little ghetto kid is just as important as the life of a rich person.'[131]

It is clear, then, that the Court in both *Maher* and *Harris* was aware that the public funding instrument was an attempt to prevent poor women from having abortions. Furthermore, it was clear by the late 1970s that the Hyde Amendment was having the impact its proponents desired: the number of Medicaid abortions fell from 295,000 in 1977 to just 2,000 in 1978.[132] The Court also knew, however, that if it struck down this particular strategy for stopping abortions, it would face the wrath of not merely the states, but of its coequal branch in the federal government, the Congress. Indeed, Congress had rammed home the point in *Harris* when 238 members of Congress, led by Congressman Jim Wright of Texas, entered an *amicus* brief which reminded the Court in very strong terms that the Constitution gives Congress alone 'the power of the purse'. Moreover, the present case did not concern a federal judicial enforcement against a *state* legislature, as in busing cases: rather, 'This is a case where there is an express constitutional provision protecting a co-ordinate branch of the federal government.'[133] It acknowledged that the Supreme Court could strike an actual appropriation if it was judged to violate the Constitution, but 'What it has not power to do is to make a non-existent appropriation into an appropriation.'[134] The brief concluded with an admonition to the Justices not to allow politics to influence their decision: 'No doubt members of the federal judiciary have strong views as to what the right outcome of the political contest should be. A number of these judges have not concealed their opinions. Members of the judiciary are called, not to further the political cause they think is right, but to respect the foundations of our government of separate and limited powers, of which the power of the purse is democratically entrusted to the Congress.'[135] The Court has always shown far greater deference to the federal legislature than it has to state legislatures. One recent empirical study found that the Court is 'highly likely' to defer to federal policy makers, whether the law is supported by public opinion or not.[136] The same study found that the Court was far less deferential when it came to overturning state and local laws.[137]

That Congress should feel so strongly on the subject as to take these steps is not wholly surprising: like other American political institutions, it is jealous of its powers. But it also reflects the heat that Congress was feeling from the anti-abortion movement. In fact, the 1976 decision to attach the Hyde Amendment to an appropriations bill was a reversal of the position it had adopted in 1974. Then, a similar amendment had been rejected by both House and Senate on the grounds that an appropriations bill was an improper vehicle for substantive legislation on such an issue as abortion. According to one observer, 'The fact that Congress changed its tack in 1976 is partially attributable to the changes that took place in the political atmosphere of that period. Between 1974 and 1976 anti-abortion pressure groups increased in size and strength and mobilised their energies in the direction of Capitol Hill. By 1976 politicians had become aware that abortion was a very sensitive issue that could no longer be ignored.'[138]

Many observers agreed with the dissenting Justices in *Maher* and *Harris* that the Court had effectively retreated from its promotion of abortion rights in the face of pro-life pressure.[139] The extent of that retreat was not, however, very clear. Anti-abortion forces throughout the country now knew that at least some forms of abortion 'regulation' which had the practical effect of stopping abortions for some women, would be found constitutionally acceptable to the Supreme Court. On the other hand, the Court in *Maher* and *Harris* had reaffirmed that legislatures could not put a direct burden on women's right to choose an abortion, as established by *Roe*. The invitation to anti-abortion legislatures was now to test at what point regulations ceased to be regulations.

Abortion and state 'regulation'

In 1983 and again in 1986, the Court considered this question in some detail. In *Akron v. Akron Centre For Reproductive Health*[140] and *Thornburgh v. American College of Obstetricians*,[141] the Court struck down a raft of local and state regulations on the grounds that they did not regulate the choice to have an abortion but rather seriously discouraged it. Moreover, a majority of the Justices in both cases were quite clear that the regulations constituted a deliberate attempt to prevent women from exercising their freedom of choice.

In 1978, the city council of Akron, Ohio, had narrowly voted to adopt an abortion ordinance that had been devised by an attorney for the Ohio Right To Life Society. This came in the wake of a public controversy over the opening of several abortion clinics in the city as a result of the *Roe* decision.[142] The ordinance had seventeen provisions, five of which were challenged before the Supreme Court. The first required all second and third trimester abortions to be performed in a hospital (as opposed to a specialist clinic). The second required physicians intending to perform abortions on minors below the age of eighteen to give at least twenty-four hours notice to one of her parents; and in the case of minors below the age of fifteen, the physician was to obtain the informed, written consent of one parent. The third ordered the physician to ensure that a woman gave her informed consent to an abortion. The fourth required a twenty-four hour delay between the signing of the consent form and the operation. The fifth required that fetal remains be disposed of 'in a humane and sanitary manner'.[143]

In an opinion by Justice Powell for the Court's majority of six, all five provisions were struck down. In so doing, Justice Powell rendered a firm restatement of the validity of the *Roe* trimester system and displayed a willingness to probe both legislative intent and effect that was notably absent from *Maher* and *Harris*. On the hospitalisation requirement, for example, Powell reasoned that it could effectively double the cost of the abortion and therefore '. . . it placed a significant obstacle in the path of women seeking abortions.'[144] Furthermore, although *Roe* acknowleged the state's interest in health regulation after the first trimester, such regulation needed to be reasonably related to that interest. In this case, medical evidence suggested the regulation was not reasonable. At the time of *Roe*, medical opinion was that second and third trimester abortions should be performed in hospitals where there were full acute-care facilities. Since 1973, however, the development of Dilation and Evacuation (D & E) procedures made second trimester abortions much easier and safer and suitable for performance in clinics. Powell explicitly cites the views of the American Public Health Association and the American College of Obstetricians and Gynecologists that all second trimester abortions need no longer be performed in hospital.[145] Justice Powell concluded that '. . . Akron has imposed a heavy, and unnecessary, burden on women's access to a relatively inexpensive, otherwise accessible, and safe abortion procedure.'[146]

The part of Justice Powell's opinion dealing with the informed consent provision is also an important feature of the *Akron* case, since it is here that he most openly questions the professed motives behind the statute. He recalls that in *Planned Parenthood v. Danforth*,[147] the Court had upheld the principle of the State's power to require the woman's informed consent to her abortion. This was in the woman's own interest. Akron's provision, however, went well beyond what the Justices deemed necessary, in the nature and detail of the information which the physician was obliged to relay to the woman. For example, the physician had to describe the fetus as to '. . . appearance, mobility, tactile sensitivity, including pain, perception or response, brain and heart function, the presence of internal organs and the presence of external members.'[148] There was also a mandatory passage on the dangers of abortion: '. . . abortion is a major surgical procedure which can result in serious complications, including hemorrage (*sic*), perforated uterus, infection, menstrual disturbances, sterility and miscarriage and prematurity in subsequent pregnancies . . . abortion may leave essentially unaffected or may worsen any existing psychological problems she may have, and can result in severe emotional disturbances.'[149] Not unreasonably, Justice Powell concluded that '. . . much of the information required is designed not to inform the woman's consent but rather to persuade her to withhold it altogether.'[150] And he descibed the passage on the dangers of abortion as 'a parade of horribles'.[151]

The mandatory twenty-four hour delay furthered no legitimate state interest, according to Justice Powell, being arbitrary and inflexible, and it burdened the woman's choice by increasing the cost of the abortion through requiring her to make two trips to the abortion facility.[152] And the provision requiring the humane disposal of fetal remains was unconstitutionally vague: although Akron claimed that the purpose of this clause was to prevent 'the mindless dumping of aborted fetuses on to garbage piles', Powell openly doubted this and thought that the city was trying to require some sort of 'decent burial' for fetuses.[153]

The scepticism of the Court's majority in *Akron* was again evident in *Thornburgh*, three years later. Justice Blackmun opened his opinion for the Court by noting that Pennsylvania's 1982 Abortion Control Act '. . . was not the Commonwealth's first attempt, after this Court's 1973 decisions . . . to impose abortion restraints.'[154] He then briefly listed the various attempts at anti-abortion legislation in the state. He also noted that since *Roe*, many other states and municipalities had tried to undermine the rights granted there by adopting measures designed to prevent women from exercising their freedom of choice. He then bluntly reminded these legislatures, and Pennsylvania in particular, that the Court would not tolerate such disingenuous attacks on *Roe*:

> The States are not free, under the guise of protecting maternal health or potential life, to intimidate women into continuing pregnancies. Appellants claim that the statutory provisions before us today further legitimate compelling interests of the Commonwealth. *Close analysis* of these provisions, however, shows that they wholly subordinate constitutional privacy interests and concerns with maternal health in an effort to deter a woman from making a decision that, with her physician, is hers to make.[155]

thus, Pennsylvania's informed consent provision, although not explicitly 'a parade of horribles', was '. . . nothing less than an outright attempt to wedge the Commonwealth's message discouraging abortion into the privacy of the informed consent dialogue between the woman and her physician.'[156] Other information about State financial assistance for childbirth costs and possible financial support from the father were '. . . poorly disguised elements of discouragement for the abortion decision.'[157]

The Pennsylvania statute also required certain record-keeping and reporting procedures, but Justice Blackmun found that 'The scope of the information required and its availability to the public belie any assertions by the Commonwealth that it is advancing any legitimate interest.'[158] Blackmun noted that the statute claimed that the identity of the women having abortions would not be revealed even though the records would be made public. In his view, however, the amount of information required would likely lead to identification. Moreover, the state was again being disingenuous: 'Identification is the obvious purpose of these extreme reporting requirements.'[159]

Justice Blackmun closed his opinion with a reminder that the Justices of the Supreme Court have a duty to uphold constitutional rights even when they are unpopular and give rise to bitter controversy. This is because the Constitution protects a private sphere of individual liberty that extends to women, as well as to men. He continued, 'Few decisions are more personal and intimate, more properly private, or more basic to individual dignity and autonomy, than a woman's decision – with the guidance of her physician and within the limits specified in *Roe* – whether to end her pregnancy. A woman's right to make that choice freely is fundamental.'[160]

Such a ringing reaffirmation of the *Roe* decision, combined with the willingness of the Court openly to confront the subterfuges of anti-abortion legislatures, encouraged the belief that abortion rights were now safe. Several commentators thought that the tone of the Court's decisions in *Akron* and *Thornburgh* recalled the commitment of *Roe* rather than the retreat of *Maher* and *Harris*.[161]

However, other aspects of *Akron* and *Thornburgh* pointed in a different direction. Whereas *Roe* had been supported by seven of the nine Justices, only six supported the *Akron* decision and just five the decision in *Thornburgh*. In *Akron*, President Reagan's first appointee, Sandra Day O'Connor, had joined the two *Roe* dissenters, White and Rehnquist. Moreover, her dissenting opinion, while passing on the issue of whether there was any constitutional right to an abortion, included a powerful attack on the trimester system elaborated by the Court. First, developments in medical science were blurring the lines between the three trimesters. On the one hand, advances in D & E procedures had pushed back the state's interest in the mother's health well into the second trimester. On the other, advances in support for fetal life were bringing viability, and therefore the state's interest in potential life, earlier than the third trimester. She concluded that 'The *Roe* framework, then, is clearly on a collision course with itself.'[162] Beyond this practical consideration, however, was a more fundamental criticism. Justice O'Connor argued that the two legitimate state interests in abortion, protecting maternal health and potential life, were present throughout pregnancy. For example, '. . . *potential* life is no less potential in the first weeks of pregnancy than it is at viability or afterward . . . The choice of viability as the point at which the state interest in *potential* life becomes compelling is no less arbitrary than choosing any point before viability or any point afterward.'[163] The implications of Justice O'Connor's view that states may regulate abortion throughout the entire period of pregnancy are great, especially as she simultaneously suggested a weakening of the standard of review that the Court should apply in such cases. Rather than evaluate legislation according to whether it advanced a compelling state interest, O'Connor suggested that the Court should evaluate whether the legislation imposed an undue burden on the woman's choice.[164] Given her belief that the *Akron* ordinance was not unduly burdensome to the woman's right of choice, Justice O'Connor's approach would greatly expand state control over abortion policy, even if the state were still precluded from banning abortions outright.

Justice O'Connor's vote and opinion in *Akron* was a reminder of how the power of appointment can change the Court's jurisprudence, and, in that respect, President Reagan had struck his first blow. In *Thornburgh*, however, a less common factor was at work: a Justice of the Supreme Court changed his mind. Chief Justice Burger had never been terribly happy with the Court's decision in *Roe* and had apparently argued strongly for upholding the state laws at issue when that case had first been argued.[165] He had entered a concurring opinion in *Roe* which tried to emphasise the relative narrowness of the decision, as he saw it. Now, in *Thornburgh*, he dissented, arguing that the Court now outlawed state regulation of the sort he believed *Roe* permitted. He concluded his opinion by calling for a re-examination of *Roe*.[166]

The right to an abortion was now highly vulnerable to a change in the Court's personnel. There were five votes to uphold abortion as a fundamental right: Justices Brennan, Marshall, Blackmun, Powell and Stevens. Four seemed willing to review and, perhaps overturn *Roe*: Chief Justice Burger and Justices White, Rehnquist and O'Connor. The first of these to leave the Court was a member of the minority: shortly after the *Thornburgh* decision, Chief Justice Burger announced his retirement. President Reagan nominated Justice Rehnquist to become Chief Justice and nominated Appeals Court Judge Antonin Scalia to the vacant seat. Scalia was noted as a conservative with a sharp intellect and there was little doubt that he would vote to overturn *Roe*. Nevertheless, the five-four split still stood. In the summer of 1987, however, Justice Powell took his retirement. He had been a critical vote in abortion cases, being part of the majority in *Roe*, but also in *Maher*, *Harris*, *Akron* and *Thornburgh*. His replacement would probably swing the Court one way or the other on abortion: when President Reagan nominated the outspoken conservative judge, Robert Bork, to the seat vacated by Powell, there was no doubt in anyone's mind as to which direction the swing would take.

The uproar over the Bork nomination is well documented and need not be repeated here. As it turned out, the Senate rejected his nomination, although the seat eventually went to the equally conservative, if more obscure, Anthony Kennedy.[167] Everyone supposed that Kennedy would vote to overturn *Roe* and so the scene was set for what could prove the final showdown on abortion. The first case to come before the Court after Justice Kennedy's appointment was *Webster v. Reproductive Health Services*,[168] argued before the Court in April 1989, and decided in July of that year.

At issue in *Webster* was the constitutionality of Missouri's 1986 abortion statute. The Missouri law did not explicitly challenge the fundamental right of abortion, but several of its provisions were unmistakably hostile to it; and in presenting its case, the state asked the Court to reconsider and overrule *Roe v. Wade*.[169] Furthermore, as had happened in both *Akron* and *Thornburgh* under President Reagan, the Bush administration added its voice to this request.[170] In its *amicus* brief, the Solicitor-General's Office repeated the essence of the dissenting opinions in *Roe* and *Akron* before concluding: 'We therefore believe that the time has come for the Court to abandon its efforts to impose a comprehensive solution to the abortion question.'[171]

Even the prospect of *Roe* being overruled was enough to spur abortion activists on both sides into unprecedented action. As noted above, the record for the number of *amicus* briefs filed in a Supreme Court case was easily surpassed, and demonstration and counter-demonstration filled the streets in the months prior to the Court's decision. In April, just before the Court was due to hear oral argument in the case, one pro-choice demonstration in Washington attracted some 300,000 participants.[172]

Webster, however, turned out to be something of an anti-climax. The Court, or more precisely, Justice O'Connor, declined to reconsider *Roe v. Wade*. And in dealing with the merits of the Missouri statute, five Justices upheld its constitutionality, but they split three ways on the rationale and implications of their decision. The result was a set-back for pro-choice advocates, but one which left constitutional abortion law more uncertain than ever.

Three provisions of the Missouri statute were challenged before the Court. First, there was a preamble that unmistakably proclaimed its pro-life philosophy; for example, it stated that 'The life of each human being begins at conception' and 'The natural parents of unborn children have protectable interests in the life, health, and well-being of their unborn child'.[173] Second, there was a clause prohibiting both public employees and public facilities from any participation in abortions which were not necessary to save the mother's life. Third, and most controversially, a clause required physicians to perform certain viability tests:

> Before a physician performs an abortion on a woman he has reason to believe is carrying an unborn child of twenty or more weeks gestational stage, the physician shall first determine if the unborn child is viable by using and exercising that degree of care, skill, and proficiency, commonly exercised by the ordinary, skilful, careful, and prudent physician engaged in similar practice under the same or similar conditions. In making this determination of viability, the physician shall perform or cause to be performed such medical examinations and tests as are necessary to make a finding of the gestational age, weight, and lung maturity of the unborn child and shall enter such findings and determination of viability in the medical record of the mother.[174]

Chief Justice Rehnquist wrote an opinion on behalf of himself and Justices White, O'Connor, Scalia and Kennedy with regard to the first and second provisions; and an opinion for himself and Justices White and Kennedy with regard to the third. Justices O'Connor and Scalia each wrote separate opinions with regard to the viability tests, and these differed significantly from each other, as well as from the opinion of Chief Justice Rehnquist, even though all five voted to uphold the provision.

The preamble was upheld partly because *Maher* and *Harris*

permitted states to make a value judgement favouring childbirth over abortion and partly because it actually regulated nothing. Although all state laws had to be interpreted in line with the preamble, except where constitutional law dictated otherwise, Chief Justice Rehnquist thought the Court would have to wait and see what impact, if any, the profession of pro-life philosophy would have in practice.[175]

The ban on the participation of public employees and facilities in abortions not necessary to save the mother's life, was, said Rehnquist, in line with the Court's decisions in *Maher* and *Harris*. Just as the Court there permitted states to express their preference for childbirth by withholding public funds for abortion, here Missouri may do the same by the allocation of other public resources.[176] Logical as that appeared, Justice Blackmun's dissent drew attention to the fact that a majority of the Court was once again willing to ignore the realities of what was involved. Missouri had defined the term 'public facility' so broadly that it included any private facility that even rented land from the state or any other political authority within the state. Justice Blackmun cited the example of the Truman Medical Centre in Kansas City which, in 1985, had performed virtually all Missouri hospital abortions beyond sixteen weeks gestation. The Centre was administered by a private corporation and staffed primarily by private doctors. It was located, however, on land leased from a subdivision of the state. Here again, then, state 'regulation' of abortion was being used to try to put an effective block on abortions.[177]

The real heat in *Webster*, however, was generated by the viability tests provision. The ostensible issues it raised were how its language was to be interpreted and whether it infringed the *Roe* trimester system. The underlying issue was whether it furnished an occasion to overturn *Roe* completely. As already noted, Rehnquist, White, O'Connor, Scalia and Kennedy rejected the argument that the provision was unconstitutional. Unlike the dissenters, they did not read its language as mandating certain viability tests whatever the patient's circumstances, but only those tests which were counselled by normal medical prudence on the part of the physician. Thus, the tests were not arbitrary but reasonably related to the state's interest in protecting potential life.[178]

More significant was the fact that by mandating tests to be carried out at twenty weeks, the state had exercised its interest in potential life during the second trimester: *Roe*, it will be recalled, determined that this particular state interest did not become compelling, and therefore operative, until the third trimester. Here, then, seemed to be a flat

contradiction of a significant aspect of *Roe*. The choice for the Court
seemed to be between finding the provision unconstitutional under
Roe, or overturning *Roe* in part or in whole.

Justice O'Connor, however, surprised her colleagues by finding a
third way. She argued that while viability normally occurs around
twenty-four weeks, difficulty in the precise determination of gestational stage makes a margin of error of four weeks not unreasonable.
And since the Court had never held that the State may not pursue its
interest in protecting potential life where viability is possible, she
concluded that the provision in no way conflicted with *Roe* or its
progeny.[179] She did concede that the performance of the tests would
increase the financial costs of the abortion to the mother, but did not
believe that this fell foul of the *Akron* ruling where increased cost had
been an important factor in striking down the hospitalisation
requirement. Here, the increased cost was marginal and could not be
considered an undue burden on the woman's freedom of choice.[180]

The most intriguing aspect of Justice O'Connor's opinion was its
lengthy discourse on the merits of judicial self-restraint and its refusal
to acknowledge the implications for *Roe* which every other Justice,
including the four dissenters, thought *Webster* must have. She left her
colleagues, and indeed, everyone else, in suspense as to her position on
Roe, writing, 'When the constitutional invalidity of a State's abortion
statute actually turns on the constitutional validity of *Roe v. Wade*, there
will be time enough to reexamine *Roe*. And to do so carefully.'[181]

At the very least, one could surmise that Justice O'Connor was in no
hurry to overrule *Roe*. In the case of Justice Scalia, nothing could be
further from the truth. He attacked Justice O'Connor's argument for
restraint in dealing with *Roe* as one that '. . . cannot be taken
seriously.'[182] The most important argument in favour of reconsidering
Roe now, he said, was the political and constitutional chaos which
currently reigned over the abortion issue:

> Alone sufficient to justify a broad holding is the fact that our retaining
> control, through *Roe*, of what I believe to be, and many of our citizens
> recognise to be, a political issue, continually distorts the public perception
> of the role of this Court. We can now look forward to at least another Term
> with carts full of mail from the public, and streets full of demonstrators,
> urging us – their unelected and life-tenured judges who have been awarded
> those extraordinary, undemocratic characteristics precisely in order that
> we may follow the law despite the popular will – to follow the popular will.
> Indeed, I expect that we can look forward to even more of that than before,
> given our indecisive decision today.'[183]

The barb in the final sentence was aimed as much at Chief Justice Rehnquist's plurality opinion as it was at Justice O'Connor. Although Rehnquist and White had opposed *Roe* from the very start, they (and presumably Justice Kennedy) perhaps deemed it impolitic in this case to break decisively with Justice O'Connor. It is possible that they hoped to garner her vote when the right case came along for her to reconsider *Roe* and they were thus willing to go half-way in meeting her call for restraint in *Webster*. Rehnquist's opinion, therefore, looked like a compromise between the positions adopted by O'Connor and Scalia and appeared all the more strained for being so. Although it held that the viability tests provision was constitutional, it pointed out that the state did superimpose some regulation of the physician's medical determinations during the second trimester and that the tests did have financial implications for the mother: both aspects seemed in tension with previous cases, according to the Chief Justice. He then seized upon this tension to attack the *Roe* trimester system: 'We think that the doubt cast upon the Missouri statute by these cases is not so much a flaw in the statute as it is a reflection of the fact that the rigid trimester analysis of the course of a pregnancy enunciated in *Roe* has resulted in subsequent cases . . . making constitutional law in this area a virtual Procrustean bed.'[184] The opinion went on to argue that the trimester system had no basis in constitutional reasoning and there was no reason why the state should not pursue its interest in potential life throughout the entire period of pregnancy.[185] He concluded that *Webster* afforded no opportunity to re-examine *Roe* and, therefore, that it was left 'undisturbed'. However, in the light of the comments on the trimester system, '. . . we would modify and narrow *Roe* . . .'[186]

The *Webster* decision was a real mess. As Justice Scalia pointed out, the Court's lack of clarity gave no clear lead on the constitutional parameters of abortion rights: 'Of the four courses we might have chosen today – to reaffirm *Roe*, to overrule it explicitly, to overrule it *sub silentio*, or to avoid the question – the last is the least responsible.'[187] And Justice Blackmun, in dissent, attacked the Court's lack of clarity from a different angle: he wrote of the plurality's 'feigned restraint' and its claim to leave *Roe* undisturbed as 'meaningless'. Worst of all, it was an implicit invitation to state legislatures to pass laws contradicting *Roe*: the plurality opinion, he said, was 'filled with winks, nods, and knowing glances to those who would do away with *Roe* explicitly.[188]

The next significant abortion case after *Webster*, *Hodgson v. Minnesota*,[189] did little to clear up this judicial confusion. Justice O'Connor joined Justices Stevens, Blackmun, Brennan, and Marshall in declaring unconstitutional Minnesota's requirement that a woman under eighteen years of age who wished to have an abortion must wait for the operation until at least forty-eight hours after both her parents had been notified. She did so, however, not because it was, as she herself acknowledged, the most stringent notification statute in the country,[190] but because it provided no alternative means for the minor to demonstrate either that she was mature enough to make the decision for herself or that it was in her best interests to have an abortion. Minnesota had foreseen this objection and included a provision saying that if its first notification clause were struck down, then a second should become operative: this included the alternative to parental notification of a 'judicial bypass', whereby a court could determine that the parents of a particular minor need not be informed. Justice O'Connor joined Chief Justice Rehnquist and Justices White, Scalia and Kennedy in upholding this.[191]

Events took a further turn after *Hodgson*, however. First, Justices Brennan and Marshall retired and were replaced by David Souter and Clarence Thomas. When these two Bush nominees appeared before the Senate in confirmation hearings, they were clearly under instructions not to give away their views on *Roe v. Wade*. For example, one journalist reported that Thomas was asked for his views on abortion on no less than seventy occasions, yet he still managed to avoid giving a straight answer.[192]

Then, in June 1992, the Court gave its clearest ruling on abortion in many years. In *Planned Parenthood of Southeastern Pennsylvania v. Casey*,[193] three distinct blocs amongst the Justices emerged. The Court had been asked to consider the constitutionality of several provisions of the Pennsylvania Abortion Control Act. Among these were a twenty-four hour waiting period and an informed consent provision, similar to those that the Court had struck down in *Akron* and *Thornburgh*. There was also a provision requiring a married woman to give her husband notice of her intention to undergo an abortion. Once again, the Bush Administration effectively asked the Court to overrule *Roe*, by arguing that it should abandon strict scrutiny and employ instead the rational basis test to the review of abortion statutes. This went even further than the state's position, which argued instead for the adoption of Justice O'Connor's preferred intermediate standard of review: namely, that any abortion regulation would be held constitutional if it did not impose an undue burden on the woman's freedom to choose an abortion.[194]

Although there was a distinct possibility that the recent addition to the Court of Justices Souter and Thomas would provide the votes for an outright reversal of *Roe*, this failed to materialise. Four of the Justices – Rehnquist, White, Scalia and Thomas – did indeed argue for *Roe*'s demise, as well as the constitutionality of all the provisions of the Pennsylvania statute. However, a group of three other Reagan-Bush appointees – O'Connor, Kennedy and Souter – did not go along with them. They did agree that, with the exception of the spousal notification provision, the Pennsylvania law was constitutionally valid. But they joined the two other members of the Court, Blackmun and Stevens, in holding that *Roe* must be preserved. In so doing, this 'centrist' group of three argued that *Roe* should be upheld, not necessarily because it had been decided correctly in 1973, but rather because it deserved respect as a major decisional precedent. In turn, such respect for precedent was a critical factor in maintaining respect for the Court and preserving the legitimacy of the judicial power:

> A decision to overrrule *Roe*'s essential holding under the existing circumstances would address error, if error there was, at the cost of both profound and unnecessary damage to the Court's legitimacy, and to the Nation's commitment to the rule of law. It is therefore imperative to adhere to the essence of *Roe*'s original decision, and we do so today.[195]

Moreover, the 'circumstances' uppermost in the three Justices' minds appeared to be the political campaign waged against *Roe*. The opinion stressed that if the Court overturned *Roe* while 'under fire', it would be seen as a decision 'to surrender to political pressure' and thus create the impression that the Court was no different from any other political institution.[196]

If the coalition of five Justices declined to overrule *Roe*, however, the coalition of seven did severely undermine it. Most importantly, strict scrutiny was removed as the judicial standard by which to measure the constitutionality of abortion regulations. Thus, legislation need no longer be justified by a compelling state interest, but only avoid creating an undue burden on a woman's choice. Moreover, the decisions in *Akron* and *Thornburgh* were effectively reversed, since regulations of the type deemed unconstitutional there as hostile to the basic principles of *Roe*, were considered not to be unduly burdensome in *Casey*.

Beyond that, however, it is by no means certain that *Casey* will be of importance in the long term. After all, the appointment of one new Justice could be enough to tip the balance in favour of *Roe*'s political and judicial opponents. In this respect, the ultimate survival of national abortion rights will be decided as much in the political arena, as in the Supreme Court.

While there is now almost certainly a majority of Justices on the Court who believe that *Roe* was wrongly decided, that does not automatically translate into a majority willing to overturn it explicitly. Some of those Justices may feel cross-pressured, since the judicial restraint which demands the reversal of *Roe* also counsels respect for precedent. The Supreme Court has never felt itself bound absolutely by the principle of *stare decisis*, but many Justices have counselled against creating the impression that constitutional interpretation tacks with the political wind. On the other hand, abortion has become such a thoroughly politicised issue since *Roe v. Wade* that the Justices may decide that the Court has nothing else to lose by returning to the days when abortion was a matter for legislatures.

Notes

1 L. Tribe, *Abortion: The Clash of Absolutes*, New York, 1990, p. 51.
2 410 US 113 (1973).
3 *Newsweek*, 19 August 1991, pp. 24–6.
4 H.R. 3700 and S. 1912 were co-sponsored on introduction by ninety members of the House of Representatives and twenty-one Senators: *National Abortion Rights Action League Factsheet*, 'Freedom of Choice Act', 1991.
5 President Bush has previously vetoed pro-abortion legislation. For example, in 1989 he vetoed a version of the Hyde Amendment which, for the first time since 1981, allowed federal funds for Medicaid abortions where the pregnancy had been caused by rape or incest: *International Herald Tribune*, 13 October 1989, p. 3.
6 *Newsweek*, 19 August 1991, p. 26.
7 *Abortion and the Politics of Motherhood*, London, 1984.
8 *Ibid.*, p. 84.
9 Tribe, *op. cit.*, p. 45.
10 *Ibid.*, p. 46. The original name of the group was the National Association for the Repeal of Abortion Laws, but it changed its name following the *Roe* decision.
11 P. Conover and V. Gray, *Feminism and the New Right: Conflict Over The American Family*, New York, 1983, p. 5.
12 Tribe, *op. cit.*, p. 47.
13 *Ibid.*, p. 141.
14 Luker, *op. cit.*, p. 99.
15 Tribe, *op. cit.*, p. 50.
16 *Ibid.*
17 The chief proponent of the argument that the framers of the fourteenth Amendment had intended it to make the Bill of Rights applicable to the States, as well as the federal government, was Justice Hugo Black. He explained his reasons in *Adamson v. California*, 332 US 46 (1947). The Court has, however, never accepted Black's position and, instead, has 'selectively incorporated' only parts of the Bill of Rights into the Fourteenth Amendment.
18 H. Sigworth, 'Abortion laws in the federal courts – the Supreme Court as supreme platonic guardian', *Indiana Legal Forum*, v, 1971, pp. 130–42, 132.

19 402 US 62 (1971).
20 *Ibid.*, p. 165. At this time, there were only seven sitting Justices, the newly appointed Powell and Rehnquist not having yet been sworn in. The vote on the jurisdiction issue appeared to be 4–3 against expanding the Court's reach: Burger, White, Stewart and Blackmun on one side, Douglas, Brennan and Marshall on the other.
21 *Ibid.*, p. 169.
22 410 US 113 (1973).
23 410 US 179 (1973).
24 Conover and Gray, *op. cit.*, p. 6.
25 Those in the majority with Blackmun were Chief Justice Burger and Justices Powell, Stewart, Douglas, Brennan and Marshall: Justices White and Rehnquist dissented.
26 Woodward and Armstrong, *op. cit.*, pp. 230–6 for the reservations of Powell, Brennan and Stewart, for example.
27 This was a pseudonym for Norma McCorvey, who originally did not wish to reveal her true identity. McCorvey originally claimed that her pregnancy had resulted from a gang rape, though she later retracted this. She herself described her predicament as that of '. . . some little old Texas girl who got in trouble.': Tribe, *op. cit.*, p. 4. As Tribe points out, the initial shame felt by McCorvey properly belongs with the society that would condemn an unmarried mother.
28 This was also a pseudonym, for Sandra Race Cano. Cano eventually gave birth to a daughter who she put up for adoption – Melissa Able. In a remarkable instance of the complexities of feelings on the abortion issue, Cano now opposes abortion and is active in the pro-life movement, while Able is pro-choice: Tribe, *op. cit.*, pp. 5–6.
29 *Roe*, p. 116.
30 381 US 479 (1965).
31 *Ibid.*, p. 484.
32 *Ibid.*
33 *Ibid.*, p. 510.
34 *Ibid.*, p. 529.
35 *Ibid.*, p. 522.
36 *Ibid.*, p. 527.
37 405 US 438 (1972).
38 *Roe*, p. 153.
39 *Ibid.*, p. 152.
40 *Roe*, p. 174, dissenting opinion of Justice Rehnquist, quoting *Snyder v. Massachusetts* (1934).
41 *Griswold*, pp. 485–6.
42 See, for example, R. Y. Funston, *Constitutional Counter-Revolution?*, New York, 1977, p. 341; V. Blasi, 'The rootless activism of the Burger Court', in V. Blasi (ed.), *The Burger Court*, New Haven, 1983, p. 212; J. Ely, 'The wages of crying wolf: a comment on *Roe v. Wade*', *Yale Law Journal*, LXXXII, 1973, pp. 920–49, 930; R. Epstein, 'Substantive due process by any other name: the abortion cases', *The Supreme Court Review 1973*, pp. 159–85, 170. Laurence Tribe, on the other hand, mounts what he calls an interpretive defence of the *Roe* decision. However, on the critical questions of why the abortion right should be deemed fundamental and why *Roe*'s trimester system should be imposed on all the States, Tribe only offers convincing political arguments, as opposed to constitutional ones. In effect, he offers a convincing *non-interpretive* justification of *Roe*: *op. cit.*, n.1, Chapter 5.
43 *Roe* p. 153.
44 *Ibid*
45 *Ibid.*, p. 159.
46 *Ibid.*, pp. 161–2.
47 *Ibid.*, p. 159.
48 If the fetus-embryo is a life, then abortion is murder except where necessary to save the

mother's life. If, however, it is not a life but only potential life, it should not be accorded the same moral or legal status as a human being and, hence, abortion can be justified in the interests of the mother. This was, in fact, the theory of when life begins that was implicit in the *Roe* majority opinion.

49 *Roe*, pp. 148–50.
50 *Ibid.*, pp. 162–3.
51 *Ibid.*, p. 163.
52 *Ibid.*
53 *Ibid.*
54 *Ibid.*, p. 160.
55 *Ibid.*, pp. 163–4.
56 *Ibid.*, pp. 165–6.
57 Chief Justice Burger, although concurring in the Court's decision, said he was '. . . somewhat troubled that the Court has taken notice of various scientific and medical data in reaching its conclusion . . .' *Roe*, p. 208.
58 *Roe*, pp. 141–7.
69 R. Petchesky, *Abortion and Women's Choice*, London, 1986, p. 289.
60 *Roe*, p. 208.
61 *Ibid.*, p. 221.
62 *Ibid.*, p. 222.
63 *Ibid.*
64 op. cit., n. 42, p. 947.
65 *Ibid.*, pp. 935–7. On the question of the 'political impotence' of women, Ely readily agrees that women are politically weak compared with men, but they are not politically weak when compared with fetuses. *Ibid.*, pp. 933–4.
66 198 US 45 (1905).
67 *op. cit.*, pp. 937–43.
68 *op. cit.*, n. 42, p. 148.
69 *Roe*, p. 168.
70 *op. cit.*, n. 42.
71 National Opinion Research Center data, quoted in R. Tatalovich and B. Daynes, *Social Regulatory Policy: Moral Controversies in American Politics*, Boulder, 1988, p. 188.
72 Gallup surveys, quoted in J. Blake, 'The Supreme Court's abortion decisions and public opinion in the United States', *Population and Development Review*, III, 1977, pp. 45–62, 49.
73 R. Burt, 'The Burger Court and the family', in Blasi, *op. cit.*, p. 109.
74 V. Blasi, 'The Rootless Activism of the Burger Court', in *Ibid.*, p. 213.
75 Woodward and Armstrong, *op. cit.*, pp. 86–7 and 229. The authors also write '. . . as a former counsel to the Mayo Clinic, he sympathised with the doctor who was interrupted in his medical practice by the state, and told how he could or could not treat his patients. On the other hand, Blackmun generally felt the states should have the right to enforce their legislative will.' *Ibid.*, p. 167.
76 *Ibid.*, p. 230. Woodward and Armstrong also recount that 'Nevertheless, Powell came quickly to the conclusion that the Constitution did not provide meaningful guidance. The right to privacy was tenuous; at best it was implied. If there was no way to find an answer in the Constitution, Powell felt he would just have to vote his "gut". He had been critical of Justices for doing exactly that; but in abortion, there seemed no choice.', *Ibid.*, p. 230.
77 H. McClosky and A. Brill, *Dimensions of Tolerance: What Americans Believe About Civil Liberties*, New York, 1983, p. 218, Table 5.16.
78 P. Skerry, 'The class conflict over abortion', *The Public Interest*, pp. 69–84, 75, Table V.
79 R. Tatalovich and B. Daynes, *Social Regulatory Policy*, Boulder, 1988, p. 182.
80 *Ibid.*, p. 138.
81 R. Petchesky, 'Antiabortion, antifeminism, and the rise of the new right', *Feminist*

Studies, VII, 1981, pp. 206–46, 210.
82 *Ibid.*, p. 82.
83 *supra.*, Chapter 1, p. 4.
84 *Ibid.*, p. 69.
85 F. Ginsberg, *Contested Lives: The Abortion Debate In An American Community*, Berkeley, 1989, pp. 1–2.
86 Tatalovich and Daynes, *op. cit.*, p. 189. As the authors note, however, public opinion on abortion rights is not entirely clear and the wording of the question in surveys seems to have a marked effect upon the public's response. Thus, other polls indicate majority support only for therapeutic abortions, *Ibid.*, p. 187.
87 Tatalovich and Daynes, *op. cit.*, p. 201.
88 Tribe, *op. cit.*, pp. 163–4.
89 *Ibid.*, p. 162–4.
90 N. Ford, 'The evolution of a constitutional right to an abortion', *The Journal of Legal Medicine*, IV, 1983, pp. 271–322.
91 *Ibid.*, p. 279.
92 *Ibid.*, pp. 279–80.
93 *Ibid.*, pp. 280–1.
94 Tatalovich and Daynes, *op. cit.*, pp. 197–8.
95 H. Schwartz, *Packing The Courts: The Conservative Campaign To Rewrite The Constitution*, New York, 1988, pp. 60–1. See also E. Witt, *A Different Justice: Reagan and the Supreme Court*, Oxford, 1988; T. Tomasi and J. Velona, 'All The President's Men? A study of Ronald Reagan's appointments to the US Court of Appeals', *Columbia Law Review*, LXXXVII, 1987, pp. 766–93.
96 *Ibid.*, p. 201.
97 *Supreme Court of the United States: Transcriptions of Records and File Copies of Briefs*, 1972, vols 3–5 (hereafter referred to as *Records and Transcripts of Briefs*), available at the Supreme Court Library, Washington, D.C.
98 *Supreme Court, US, Oral Arguments*, October Term 1971, vol. 2, p. 30.
99 K. Kolbert *et al.*, 'The *Webster Amicus Curiae* briefs: perspectives on the abortion controversy and the role of the Supreme Court', *American Journal of Law and Medicine*, XV, 1989, pp. 153–243, 154.
100 See, for example, the summaries of pro-life briefs in Kolbert, *op. cit.*, pp. 204–33.
101 *Ibid.*, pp. 155 and 237.
102 Tatalovich and Daynes, *op. cit.*, p. 193.
103 *International Herald Tribune*, 7 January, 1985, p. 3.
104 *Newsweek*, 1 May, 1989, p. 48.
105 *Newsweek*, 3 April, 1989, p. 38.
106 *Newsweek*, 1 May, 1989, p. 48.
107 428 US 52 (1976).
108 *Ibid.*, p. 79–81.
109 432 US 464 (1977).
110 Justice Stevens had replaced Justice Douglas in 1975 and he too voted to dismiss the claim.
111 *Maher*, p. 474.
112 *Ibid.*
113 *Ibid.*, p. 475.
114 *Ibid.*, p. 484.
115 *Ibid.*, pp. 487–9.
116 *Ibid.*, p. 483.
117 372 US 335 (1963).
118 *Maher*, p. 479.
119 K. Petersen, 'The public funding of abortion services: comparative developments in the United States and Australia', *International and Comparative Law Quarterly*, XXXIII,

1984, pp. 158–80, 160.
120 *Ibid.*, p. 161.
121 448 US 297 (1980).
122 R. Lincoln *et al.*, 'The Court, the Congress and the President: turning back the clock on the pregnant poor', *Family Planning Perspectives*, IX, 1977, pp. 207–14, 207–8.
123 Only Justice Stevens changed his position from the *Maher* case – he saw a constitutionally significant difference in the fact that the Hyde Amendment applied to medically necessary abortions, not just the elective abortions at issue in *Maher*.
124 *Harris*, p. 316.
125 *Ibid.*, p. 318.
126 *Ibid.*, p. 325.
127 *Ibid.*, p. 330.
128 *Ibid.*, pp. 333–4.
129 *Ibid.*,, p. 332.
130 Petersen, *op. cit.*, p. 163.
131 *Ibid.*, p. 165.
132 Petersen, *op. cit.*, p. 170.
133 Brief of Rep. Jim Wright *et al.* as *Amici Curiae, Transcripts of Records and Briefs 1979*, CCXX, p. 15.
134 *Ibid.*, p. 23.
135 *Ibid.*, p. 31.
136 T. Marshall, *Public Opinion and the Supreme Court*, Boston, 1989, p. 83.
137 *Ibid.*, p. 85.
138 Petersen, *op. cit.*, pp. 162–3.
139 'The Supreme Court, 1979 Term', *Harvard Law Review*, LXXXXIV, 1990, pp. 77–295, p. 107; V. Brock, '*Harris v. McRae*: the court retreats from Roe v. Wade', *Loyola Law Review*, XXVI, 1980, pp. 749–60; Ford, *op. cit.*, p. 299; J. Nicholson and D. Stewart, 'The Supreme Court, abortion policy, and state response: a preliminary analysis', *Publius*, XIV, 1978, pp. 159–78; Lincoln *et al.*, *op. cit.*
140 462 US 416 (1983). There were two companion cases: *Planned Parenthood Association v. Ashcroft*, 462 US 476 (1983), reviewing abortion regulations from Missouri and *Simopoulos v. Virginia*, 462 US 506 (1983).
141 476 US 747 (1986).
142 Ford, *op. cit.*, p. 308.
143 *Akron*, pp. 422–4.
144 *Ibid.* pp. 434–4.
145 *Ibid.*, p. 436.
146 *Ibid.*, p. 438.
147 428 US 52 (1976).
148 *Akron*, n.34, p. 444.
149 *Ibid*, n. 36, p. 445.
150 *Ibid.*, p. 444.
151 *Ibid.*, p. 445.
152 *Ibid.*, p. 450.
153 *Ibid.*, p. 451. The fifth provision, on parental consent for minors' abortions, was struck down because it did not permit a minor an alternative means of demonstrating her maturity and need for an abortion, p. 441.
154 *Thornburgh*, p. 2173.
155 *Ibid.*, p. 2178 (emphasis added).
156 *Ibid*, p. 2179. This part of the statute mandated certain information to be related, though in more general terms than the Akron provision, for example, 'the probable gestational stage' and the 'fact that there may be detrimental physical and psychological effects which are not accurately foreseeable'. However, the woman was also to be told that more information was available, if wanted, and this was more explicit, pp. 2178–9.

157 *Ibid.*, p. 2180.

158 *Ibid.*, p. 2181.

159 *Ibid.*, p. 2182. Recorded information made public included the name of the physician and the abortion facility, the woman's political subdivision and state of residence, her age, race, marital status, her number of previous pregnancies, the date of her last menstrual period and probable gestational stage, p. 2181.

160 *Ibid.*, p. 2185.

161 Ford, *op. cit;* D. Fernandez, '*Thornburgh v. American College of Obstetricians*: return to *Roe*?', *Harvard Journal of Law and Public Policy*, X, 1987, pp. 711–27; P. Prieto, '*City of Akron v. Akron Centre for Reproductive Health, Inc.*: stare decisis prevails, but for how long?', *University of Miami Law Review*, XXXVIII, 1984, pp. 921–38.

162 *Akron*, p. 458.

163 *Ibid.*, p. 461.

164 *Ibid.*, p. 453.

165 Woodward and Armstrong, *op. cit.*, p. 169.

166 *Thornburgh*, p. 2192.

167 Bronner, *op. cit;* Hodder–Williams, *op. cit.*

168 492 US – , 106 L Ed 2d 410, 109 SCt 3055.

169 According to one source, the State did this after the intervention by the extremely conservative William Bradford Reynolds, head of the Justice Department's Civil Rights Division under President Reagan: Kolbert *et al.*, *op. cit.*, n. 4, p. 154.

170 Brief For The United States As Amicus Curiae Supporting Appellants, *Transcripts of Records and Briefs*, CCCII, 1988, p. 1.

171 *Ibid.*, p. 7.

172 *International Herald Tribune*, 11 April 1989, p. 3.

173 *Webster*, n. 4, p. 427 (emphasis added).

174 *Ibid.*, p. 432. A fourth provision restricting public support for abortion counselling was declared moot by the Court, p. 432.

175 *Ibid.*, pp. 426–8 LEd.

176 *Ibid.*, p. 430 LEd.

177 *Ibid.*, n. 1 p. 450.

178 *Ibid.*, p. 433.

179 *Ibid.*, pp. 440–2.

180 *Ibid.*, p. 443.

181 *Ibid.*, p. 441.

182 *Ibid.*, p. 445.

183 *Ibid.*, p. 447.

184 *Ibid.*, p. 435.

185 *Ibid.*, pp. 436–7.

186 *Ibid.*, p. 438.

187 *Ibid.*, p. 448.

188 *Ibid.*, p. 449.

189 110 SCt 2926 (1990).

190 *Ibid.*, p. 2950. Only Arkansas also required that both parents be notified and it provided numerous exceptions to the requirement.

191 *Ibid.*, p. 2951.

192 *The Guardian*, 16 September 1991, p. 8. On the Souter nomination, see R. McKeever, 'Courting The Congress', *Politics*, XI, 1991, pp. 26–33.

193 Docket No. 91–744.

194 *The Washington Post*, 23 April 1992, p. A.12.

195 *Casey*, Slip Opinion, joint opinion of Justices O'Connor, Kennedy and Souter, p. 27.

196 *Ibid.*, p. 25.

Five—Race and affirmative action

> By 1981, many forces within the civil rights movement had abandoned their
> moral dedication to equality for all and instead had embraced the concept
> of so-called 'benign' discrimination. After spending decades seeking to
> forge a national consensus upon the principle of nondiscrimination, most
> civil rights advocates stood ready as the Reagan Administration took office
> to flout not only that moral imperative, but also the American economic
> system and, on behalf of special interests, many of our traditional moral
> values. Their method was no longer an appeal to the conscience of all
> Americans, but rather a call to guilt for some, a promise of preference for
> others, and a reliance on the raw power of the three institutions that are
> least responsive to democratic forces – academia, the media, and especially
> the courts – to herd along a confused and reluctant population.[1]

Thus wrote William Bradford Reynolds, Assistant Attorney General in
the Civil Rights Division of the Justice Department during almost the
whole of the Reagan Administration. His aggressive assault on the
integrity of liberals who support affirmative action, as well as on the
policy itself, grossly distorts the aims and motivations of the contemporary civil rights movement. It does, however, accurately reflect the
intensity, and, indeed, bitterness generated since the 1960s by the
attempt to promote greater racial equality through policies which give
racial minorities certain advantages over non-minorities in matters
such as education and employment opportunities. Reynolds' statement
also reinforces the view that, as with capital punishment and abortion,
affirmative action must be seen as part of the network of social and
moral issues over which liberals and conservatives have struggled in the
last twenty-five years. Moreover, according to Reynolds, it is the courts
once again who have played the leading role in undermining traditional
values, using their 'raw power' to impose novel practices on a
bewildered population. Above all, however, the controversy over
affirmative action is a leading indicator of the breakdown of the social
consensus that prevailed until the 1960s.

Before analysing the Supreme Court's affirmative action jurisprudence, it is important to note the origins of the concept: for
parallel to the controversy over policy, there has been a struggle, rather

like that in the abortion debate, over the appropriate words with which to define it. What is 'affirmative action' or 'benign discrimination' to some, is simply 'reverse discrimination' or 'racial quotas' to others.

Ironically, the term 'affirmative action' was a product of the very 1960s consensus on civil rights that William Bradford Reynolds laments. It was used as early as 1961 in President Kennedy's Executive Order 10925. This created the Presidential Commission on Equal Employment Opportunity and called on government contractors to take affirmative action to recruit and promote members of minority groups.[2] The 1964 Civil Rights Act banned many forms of discrimination on grounds of race, colour, sex and national origin. Of greatest relevance here were Title VI and Title VII of the Act. Title VI reads 'No person in the United States shall, on the ground of race, colour, or national origin, be excluded from participation in, or be denied the benefits of, or be subjected to discrimination under any programme or activity receiving Federal financial assistance.'[3] Title VII, in essence, bans discrimination in employment on grounds of race, colour, national origin *and* sex. The Act also made the Equal Employment Opportunity Commission (EEOC) permanent. In 1965, President Johnson issued Executive Order 11246 which *required* federal contractors to take affirmative action to hire and promote racial minorities.[4] The Department of Labour was given responsibility for enforcing the Order and it in turn established the Office of Federal Contract Compliance (OFCC), later renamed the Office of Federal Contract Compliance Programmes.[5]

At this stage, there was little controversy over affirmative action, largely because it was understood as involving remedial measures to help minorities – advertising, recruiting, training, back pay – rather than a policy which would directly disadvantage non-minorities.[6] Most people, it seemed, were willing to lend a helping hand to black Americans who had suffered appalling discrimination, as long as white Americans had to bear no burden other than a small percentage of tax dollars.

What transformed affirmative action as a political issue was the introduction of statistical evidence as a means of both *identifying* past discrimination and *rectifying* that discrimination. The initiative in bringing about that transformation was taken not by the courts, but rather by the federal bureaucracy. In May, 1968, the OFCC issued new guidelines instituting numerical goals and timetables in pursuit of equal employment opportunity. The logic of this step was completed when further guidelines were issued in December 1971, requiring the greater 'utilisation' of minorities and women in various job classifications. Statistical analysis of the work-force would reveal if they were currently 'under-utilised'.[7] For example, if blacks constituted only 2 per cent of a company's work-force of electricians, but 20 per cent of all electricians in the local labour pool, this would indicate discrimination. Steps would have to be taken to eliminate such discrimination and hiring practices adopted which would result in minorities constituting 20 per cent of the company's electricians. Another such test held that there was a *prima facie* case of discrimination by a company when it hired a percentage of minority applicants that was significantly below the percentage of non-minority applicants hired.[8] This new emphasis on statistical evidence to identify discrimination and to mandate remedial action, together with the use of numerical goals to measure progress towards the elimination of racial discrimination, convinced conservatives that affirmative action now meant 'racial quotas'. Thomas Sowell wrote that ' "Affirmative action" was now decisively transformed into a numerical concept, whether called "goals" or "quotas".'[9] Nathan Glazer argued that '. . . since the 1970s affirmative action means quotas and goals and timetables.'[10]

The OFCC was by no means alone, however, in advancing 'statistical affirmative action'. In 1972, Congress passed the Equal Employment Opportunity Act, which extended the coverage of the Civil Rights Act of 1964 to cover state and local government employees and also private employers and unions with at least fifteen employees or members (originally twenty-five). In addition, it strengthened the powers of the EEOC. Most importantly, the EEOC could now sue parties who violated anti-discrimination laws and guidelines. Such was the vigour with which the EEOC exercised its new powers that '. . . firms became increasingly sensitive to the threat of litigation, and many adopted and even implemented affirmative action programmes as a hedge against lawsuits.'[11]

Surprisingly, perhaps, even the Nixon Administration expanded the use of statistical affirmative action.[12] In 1969, it promulgated the so-called Philadelphia Plan, by which bidders for federally-assisted construction projects in the Philadelphia area were required to set numerical goals for increasing the participation of blacks and other minorities in building trades. Some in the administration doubted the Plan's legality and the Attorney-General was asked for a written opinion on the question: his response would be legally binding on the executive branch until a court ruled otherwise. The responsibility for drafting the opinion was assigned to Assistant Attorney-General (now

Chief Justice) William Rehnquist, who pronounced the Plan lawful under the Civil Rights Act. It was duly implemented to considerable effect:

> The adoption of the Philadelphia Plan by the Department of Labour and support for the Plan from the Attorney-General, the President and the courts had far reaching results. Regional plans like the Philadelphia Plan were adopted by the Department of Labour for building trades in most large metropolitan areas. More significantly, numerical goals and time-tables were incorporated into the obligations of industrial and other federal procurement contractors and subcontractors in 1970 by 'Order No. 4', which later became a regulation issued by the Secretary of Labour.[13]

Opposition to affirmative action based on the notion of statistical proportionality of minority group representation stems from three major objections. First, it is allegedly unfair to the white (or male) who has never discriminated against minorities, but who is passed over for a promotion or a place in college in favour of a black who may well have less experience or credentials, and who may not have been an indivi-dual victim of discrimination. Such a policy is deemed to sacrifice meritocracy on the altar of substantive equality. Secondly, to prefer one person over another purely on grounds of race or sex is to replace individualism with a society based on group rights, something which runs against the grain of Americanism. Robert Bork expressed these objections thus:

> It makes little sense, or justice, to sacrifice a white or a male who did not inflict discrimination to advance the interests of a black or female who did not suffer discrimination. No old injustice is undone, but a new injustice is inflicted. If it is impossible to understand what rational or defensible purpose such a policy serves, it is possible to see the state of society toward which the policy moves us. It is one of quotas for groups, regardless of individual merit . . . This is radical social policy, one that sacrifices both individuals and the ideal of merit to the new fashion of group entitlements.[14]

The third objection is that this kind of affirmative action simply violates both statute law and the Equal Protection Clause of the Fourteenth Amendment to the Constitution. Indeed, it is argued, the whole pur-pose of the Civil Rights Act of 1964 and the Equal Protection Clause was to prevent assigning preference on the basis of race or sex, regardless of who were to be the beneficiaries of such preference. Equality means that, once discriminatory practices have been elimin-ated, race and sex are irrelevant factors in educational or employment opportunities. The first Justice Harlan expressed this idea in his lone dissent in *Plessy v. Ferguson* by declaring that the Constitution must be 'colour-blind'.[15] Moreover, it was this concept of racial equality that was upheld in *Brown* and its progeny.[16]

The 1964 Civil Rights Act reaffirmed the colour-blind principle. Some members of Congress who were basically sympathetic to the Act were worried lest its anti-discrimination proposals might later be deemed to have authorised group quotas. The Act's legislative sponsors repeatedly denied this. Senator Hubert Humphrey described the fear of quotas as a 'non-existent bugaboo', and said the Act was simply intended to eliminate race as a factor in employment decisions.[17] Senator Joseph Clark was even more explicit, saying that 'Quotas are themselves discriminatory'.[18] Yet such was the suspicion that a quota system might emerge that the Act's proponents eventually agreed to add Section 703(j) to the original bill: this stated that nothing in the Act should be interpreted to require employers to give preference to any individual or group on account of a numerical imbalance between the percentage of the group in the work-force and the percentage of that group in the local population.[19] As we shall see, the Justices of the Supreme Court were to disagree over the interpretation of both the Civil Rights Act and the Equal Protection Clause. However, it is at least clear that in the mid-1960s, the civil rights consensus rested on a widespread belief that racial equality meant ending discriminatory practices that worked against minorities, rather than instituting programmes which required the proportional representation in the work-force of minority groups in the relevant population.

For those who defend the use of statistical concepts of affirmative action, the justification is essentially a practical one: they are the most effective means of remedying generations of racism and discrimination that violated all notions of equality. Racial discrimination has been so deep-rooted and widespread in American society that its lingering effects can be seen everywhere, even in those places where discriminatory practices have now been eliminated. The end of formal discrimination does not suddenly elevate blacks or women to a point where they can compete with white males on an equal footing. The economist Bernard Anderson described the relative positions of blacks and whites as analogous to that of the train and its caboose: 'No matter how fast the train goes, the caboose will never catch up with the engine unless special arrangements are made to change its position'.[20] Thus the only effective way of getting more blacks or women into high places previously dominated by white males is to give them certain advantages that inevitably discriminate against that group. Some harm may thereby be done to 'innocent' white males, but priority must go to the overriding social goal of fully integrating blacks into American society. And after all, even 'innocent white males' have benefited from generations of preference based on race and sex.[21] Ultimately statistical affirmative action is seen by its proponents as an acceptable means both of identifying the effects, if not the actual practice, of racial discrimination, and of ensuring that those effects are eliminated.

This brief account of the rise of statistical affirmative action reveals the important fact that the Supreme Court initially played little part in it. Rather, the running was made by Congress and the Executive branch. To be sure, the Supreme Court had sanctioned a form of affirmative action in its school desegregation decisions and had used statistical tests and goals in the process. In particular, the Court in 1971 authorised the use of busing to achieve school integration in the South and two years later extended the practice elsewhere to overcome the effects of *de facto* school segregation.[22] As controversial as busing proved, it presented a facet of affirmative action that was significantly different from that under examination here. Quite simply, busing deprived no white pupil of an education. At worst, white parents were denied the choice of a particular school for their children, but busing was essentially a means of including blacks in public education without excluding whites. When it came to numerical goals in higher education and employment opportunities, however, the reservation of a place for a black or woman meant the concomitant exclusion of a white or male from that place. Consequently, there was some basis for the charge that there was an element of discrimination against whites in affirmative action programmes, which was absent from the busing cases.[23]

That is not to say that the Court did not become embroiled in statistical affirmative action cases or that it took no initiatives of its own in those cases. It does demonstrate, however, that not all the controversies surrounding judicial policy making on social issues owe their origins to judicial activism, pure and simple. On affirmative action, the Court was obliged to enter the field by legislation and Executive branch decisions which clearly raised problems that would call for both statutory and constitutional interpretation by the Justices. Indeed, it has been argued that this is an example of the other branches of government deliberately leaving difficult issues to be resolved by the judiciary. Most obviously, Congress made no attempt to define discrimination in the Civil Rights Act of 1964, simply leaving it up to the judiciary to decide whether or not it merely extended to private parties those constraints on the states contained in the Equal Protection

Clause. Furthermore, although the Equal Employment Opportunity Act of 1972 did increase the powers of the EEOC, attempts to make the Commission, rather than the courts, the final arbiter on affirmative action remedies were defeated. According to Gary Bryner, 'It is clear from the tortuous history of the 1972 amendments to Title VII of the 1964 act that Congress as a whole was quite willing to rely on the federal courts as the primary forum for the implementation of equal employment opportunity. For southern members of Congress, this was an attractive alternative because federal judges were residents of the area over which they presided and to some extent were screened and approved by senior members of Congress, before being appointed by the President. Thus, these judges were likely to reflect the norms and values of the communities in which they lived.'[24] Or at least they would be more likely to do so than eager EEOC personnel based in Washington, DC.

Nevertheless, it remains true that, once the Supreme Court did get involved in affirmative action cases, it exhibited many of the same characteristics that were evident in its death penalty and abortion decisions: most of all, it initially employed non-interpretive review to pursue liberal goals, while simultaneously trying to promote a consensus by incorporating some elements of opposition criticism. Eventually, however, the conservative backlash undermined many of the earlier progessive decisions to the point where it may fairly be asked whether affirmative action is still a major weapon in the struggle for racial and gender equality.

The first significant decision on affirmative action by the Supreme Court came in 1971. In *Griggs v. Duke Power Co.*,[25] the issue was whether employment criteria which on their face appeared to be non-discriminatory, could nevertheless be held to violate Title VII of the Civil Rights Act of 1964 because, in practice, they had a discriminatory impact on minorities. The Duke Power Company, of North Carolina, required those seeking its better paid, though still unskilled jobs, to possess either a high-school diploma or a pass grade in a standardised intelligence test. Although both black and white applicants were required to meet these standards, they disadvantaged blacks who, apart from anything else, had suffered generations of inferior educational opportunities due to the state's racial caste system. Several black employees brought a class action suit challenging the validity of the company's criteria. Despite the fact that a literal reading of Title VII seemed to outlaw only practices that were intended to discriminate, the Court ruled unanimously that the tests nevertheless

constituted discrimination under Title VII. It held that the tests had not
been shown by the employer to be related to ability to do the jobs at
issue, while perpetuating the discrimination of the past by ensuring
that blacks remained in the lowest paid jobs within the company. Chief
Justice Burger wrote: 'If an employment practice which operates to
exclude Negroes cannot be shown to be related to job performance, the
practice is prohibited.'[26] As the unanimity of the Justices suggests,
there was little doubt about the discriminatory nature of the company's
tests. The significance of the case lies elsewhere: it introduced the
concept of 'disparate impact' analysis. Instead of discrimination being
based on a finding of *intent*, or 'disparate treatment', it was now
expanded to encompass the effect which employment practices
actually had on rates of minority hiring and promotion. The most
obvious way of demonstrating disparate impact is, of course, through a
showing that minorities are underrepresented in the work-force, or
better-paid sections of it, as compared with their presence in the local
labour pool or in the lowest-paid jobs. Consciously or not, then, *Griggs*
gave a tremendous boost to the policy of statistical affirmative action.
And that was not all: '*Griggs* . . . did more than uncouple modern civil
rights statutes from the previous emphasis upon discriminatory intent.
Griggs also moved the focus of employment discrimination prohibitions
from the individual victims to racial or ethnic groups or women as a
whole.'[27] Affirmative action was thereby moved beyond a model based
on familiar principles of law, where the identified perpetrator of a
wrong was required to compensate, or 'make whole', the identified
victim. Now, it bore a much closer relationship to social policy, with
individuals featuring essentially as vehicles for the reordering of social
privilege between different groups.

If such a task is usually considered a legislative rather than judicial
responsibility, however, Congress took no exception to the Court's
decision in *Griggs*. Indeed, when it was considering the 1972 amendments to Title VII, it explicitly endorsed that decision and, in so doing,
approved a judicial expansion of its own original intent.[28] Non-
interpretivism, it seems, is acceptable to Congress when used to
further a policy with which it agrees. *Griggs*, therefore, did not cause
much of a stir: with all three branches of the federal government still in
broad consensus on the need to eliminate past discrimination and the
Court itself unanimous, the introduction of disparate impact analysis in
a case involving a Southern employer did not appear unreasonable.

The *Bakke* case and 'racial quotas'

When, however, affirmation action became defined as racial quotas, the consensus and inter-branch co-operation blew apart. In 1974, in *DeFunis v. Odegaard*,[29] the Court managed to circumvent the issue, but four years later it returned with a vengeance in the landmark case of *Regents of the University of California v. Bakke*.[30] In the former case, Marco DeFunis, a white resident of Seattle, had twice seen his application to study at the University of Washington Law School rejected. The most important factor in the admissions procedure was the applicant's Predicted First Year Average (PFYA), a statistic based on the applicant's performance in tests and undergraduate exams. A PFYA of over 77 virtually guaranteed admission, while one below 74.5 meant rejection. DeFunis was in the middle, with 76.23. DeFunis' complaint was that different entry standards applied to minority applicants, who were considered separately from white applicants and whose PFYA was given less weight. Thus, in 1971, all but one of the students admitted under the minorities programme had PFYA scores lower than that of DeFunis. DeFunis brought suit in a state court, asserting that the minority admissions programme violated his rights under the Civil Rights Act of 1964 and the Equal Protection Clause of the Fourteenth Amendment. As his main goal was to persuade the court to order the University of Washington to admit him, he did not bring a class action suit.[31]

DeFunis duly won his case and was admitted. Although that verdict was overturned on appeal by the Washington Supreme Court, DeFunis was allowed to continue his studies, pending the outcome of his appeal to the United States Supreme Court. However, by the time the Justices came to decide the appeal, DeFunis had already begun his last term of study. Taking the view that he would graduate regardless of the outcome of the appeal, five Justices – the four Nixon appointees and Justice Stewart – declared the case moot.

Justice Brennan dissented, warning that 'The constitutional issues which are avoided today concern vast numbers of people, organisations, and colleges and universities, as evidenced by the filing of twenty-six *amicus curiae* briefs. Few constitutional issues in recent history have stirred as much debate, and they will not disappear.'[32] Justice Brennan was certainly right about that, but the majority's caution is quite understandable given the fact that the case *was* moot, that the temperature of the issue was rising fast and that any decision would be a split one. Delay at least would give colleges and legislators the time – and responsibility – for re-evaluation of their affirmative action programmes.

If in *DeFunis* 'The Court's majority had ducked a tough issue and left the country on tenterhooks',[33] the case was by no means without interest. In particular, there were indications that those who had usually taken a liberal position on civil rights might be having difficulty with statistical affirmative action. As Justice Brennan noted, there were a large number of *amicus* briefs filed in the case; but Jewish organisations, normally found in the liberal camp, such as the Anti-Defamation League of B'nai B'rith, filed in favour of DeFunis.[34] Later cases were to confirm the opposition of Jewish interest groups to any suggestion that quotas might be permissible or that racial preference might be justified where the aim was not to oppress or denigrate the adversely affected group.[35] Coming from an ethnic group which had suffered from exclusionary quotas in the past and which had generally succeeded despite discrimination, this position is not altogether surprising.

More worrying still for liberals was the position taken by Justice Douglas in *DeFunis*. Usually an unhesitating liberal activist, Douglas dissented from the decision to declare the case moot, as did Justices Brennan, White and Marshall. He alone, however, went on to comment on the merits of the case and denounced any scheme in which preference was granted by virtue of membership of a particular ethnic group. Douglas did agree that race could be considered in assessing an individual's application where it had some bearing on that individual's ability:

> A black applicant who pulled himself out of the ghetto into a junior college may thereby demonstrate a level of motivation, perseverance, and ability that would lead a fair-minded admissions committee to conclude that he shows more promise for law study than the son of a rich alumnus who achieved better grades at Harvard. That applicant would not be offered admission because he is black, but because as an individual he has shown he has the potential, while the Harvard man may have taken less advantage of the vastly superior opportunities offered him.[36]

Douglas' dissent and the briefs of Jewish groups demonstrated that a liberalism founded on the celebration of individual merit, regardless of social origins, is not necessarily sympathetic to affirmative action. Moreover, given that many view the US Constitution as an embodiment of just such a liberalism, the decision in *DeFunis* did not bode well for the major Supreme Court case that was bound to come.[37]

When it did, in *Bakke*, it was in a form not at all helpful to proponents of statistical affirmation action. The Medical School of the University of California at Davis had created a minorities admissions programme in 1969. It had done so on the recommendation of the Association of American Medical Colleges, who, troubled by the racial violence of the late 1960s, believed that medical schools should play an active role in ending racial discrimination. Accordingly, in 1969, it suggested that schools adopt the goal of having 12 per cent black membership in first year classes by the start of the 1975 academic year. Over one hundred schools responded in the manner of Davis.[38]

By the time Allan Bakke first applied to the Davis Medical School in 1973, exactly sixteen out of one hundred places were reserved for 'disadvantaged' or minority students. Applicants for these places were considered separately from applicants for the other eighty-four places and were judged according to somewhat different criteria. For example, non-minority applicants with a Grade Point Average (GPA) of less than 2.5 were automatically turned down, but not minority 'Task Force' applicants. Thus the average GPA of Task Force applicants admitted in 1973 was 2.88, compared with 3.49 for the regular students.[39] Allan Bakke's GPA was 3.51.[40] White applicants who proclaimed themselves disadvantaged were eligible for the Task Force places, but while some had been considered, none had been admitted. As Justice Powell noted in his *Bakke* opinion, between 1971 and 1974, the Task Force had admitted twenty-one blacks, thirty Mexican-Americans and twelve Asians. In the same period, the regular programme had admitted one black, six Mexican-Americans and thirty-seven Asians.[41]

Bakke reapplied to Davis, but was again turned down. He filed suit in the Superior Court of Yolo County, claiming that the Task Force programme discriminated against him. He had better scores than almost all the Task Force students who had been admitted, but they were given preference over him purely because he was white and they were not. Like Marco DeFunis, Bakke chose not to make his case a class action, since this might complicate his overriding goal of persuading the judge to order Davis to admit him. However, the university asked the judge for a ruling not merely on Bakke's admission, but also on the validity of its Task Force programme *per se*. It was Davis, therefore, not Bakke, who gave the case its wider social and political implications.[42]

Nevertheless, at this stage, the *Bakke* case had not achieved any degree of prominence. No pressure groups were involved and virtually no one except the parties and the lawyers turned up for the trial in the Superior Court. As one account put it: 'Although the issues involved were complex, it would have taken the gift of prophecy to guess that affirmative action was about to be ambushed in the nearly empty courtroom of a small town in a relatively minor county of North California.'[43]

The Superior Court judge ruled that the Task Force programme was, in practice, a minorities programme and, as such, it violated the Equal Protection Clause. However, he also ruled that Bakke had not demonstrated that he would have been admitted but for the existence of the programme: rather than order Davis to admit him, the judge instructed the university to reconsider Bakke's application without regard to race. Since both parties had lost the thing most dear to them, both appealed to the California Supreme Court. It was when that court agreed to hear the case, in June 1975, that the *Bakke* case took off, with interest groups filing *amicus* briefs: 'As in the *DeFunis* case, the battle lines were quickly drawn. Jewish organisations such as the Anti-Defamation League and conservative unions such as the American Federation of Teachers attacked the use of race and "quotas" on behalf of Allan Bakke. Civil rights groups such as the NAACP and associations of medical and law schools joined the university's side of the fray.'[44]

The California Supreme Court had the reputation of being both activist and liberal. It was therefore a great blow to supporters of affirmative action when the Court split 6-1 in Bakke's favour. Worse still, the majority opinion was written by Judge Stanley Mosk, one of the Court's leading liberal lights. It was yet another sign that the liberal consensus, never mind the societal consensus, on racial equality was being severely strained by statistical affirmative action.

At this point, several of the interest groups supporting the university urged it not to appeal to the United States Supreme Court. The record was not a good one for their case since, as presented, it seemed clear that a rigid quota was involved and Bakke appeared to have been rejected while minorities with lesser scholastic records had been admitted as part of that quota. Furthermore, the US Supreme Court was generally less liberal than that of California, so there was little reason to expect the appeal to succeed. With no appeal, the damage to affirmative action programmes would be restricted to California – at least, for the moment. Groups taking this view included the National Conference of Black Lawyers, the NAACP Legal Defence Fund and the Mexican-American Legal Defence Fund. Despite this, the university took the view that the real damage had already been done and there was little to lose by taking the appeal to Washington.[45] In February, 1977, the US Supreme Court agreed to hear the case and the scene was set for the first really major test of the constitutionality of statistical affirmative action.

Interest groups established a new record for the number of *amicus* briefs filed – fifty-eight of them in all:

> The Court seemed less a judicial sanctum than a tug-of-war among contesting lobbyists. For *Bakke* climaxed a trend toward 'public litigation'. Supporting the university were, amongst others, the American Bar Association, the Association of American Medical Colleges, the NAACP Legal Defence and Education Fund, the American Civil Liberties Union, the Americans for Democratic Action, the National Council of Churches, the National Education Association, the prestigious private universities of Columbia, Harvard, Stanford, and Pennsylvania, and the United Auto Workers – an obligatory roll-call, in short, for America's liberal elite.[46]

Except, one might add, for the Jewish groups who, as in *DeFunis*, parted company with their liberal allies and filed for Bakke – the Anti-Defamation League of B'nai B'rith, the American Jewish Committee and the American Jewish Congress.

Yet another sign of the political heat generated by the case was the pressure that Solicitor-General Wade McCree came under from the White House. As Bernard Schwartz put it: 'In *Bakke* . . . the Government brief was prepared as much in the White House as in the Solicitor-General's office.'[47] The Carter Administration had already sought to demonstrate a strong commitment to racial justice by appointing two blacks to senior positions in the Justice Department: McCree himself and Assistant Attorney-General for Civil Rights, Drew Days, formerly a lawyer with the NAACP Legal Defence Fund.[48] The issue of statistical affirmative action, however, saw the administration in something of a quandary. For example, in June 1977, just after the Solicitor-General's office began work on its *Bakke* brief, the Secretary for Health, Education and Welfare, Joseph Califano, gave a speech endorsing the concept. He said that 'Arbitrary quotas will not be a part of our enforcement programmes; we want to rely on the good faith and special effort of all who join us in the final march against discrimination. But we will also rely – because we must rely – on numerical goals as a benchmark of progress.'[49] Jewish organisations immediately condemned the speech and took out a full-page advertisement in *The New York Times* calling for Califano's resignation. President Carter was able to smooth things over by softening

Califano's position, but the episode shows how politically sensitive the issue had become.

The first draft of the Solicitor-General's brief created worse problems still. Traditionally, the Solicitor-General is regarded as a legal expert, whose principal role is to give a non-partisan view of any legal issue on which the government wishes to take a position.[50] Sometimes the Supreme Court requests a brief from the Solicitor-General, other times the Solicitor-General decides to intervene because of the perceived importance of a case for the government. In *Bakke*, the latter applied, with Days advising McCree that he should file a brief in support of affirmative action and the Davis programme. Others in the Justice Department, however, took precisely the opposite view: this faction was led by two holdovers from the Nixon administration, Lawrence Wallace and Frank Easterbrook.[51] Days asked Easterbrook to draft a memo to McCree advising him to intervene and the memo emerged as a draft brief in support of Allan Bakke's position. The draft was leaked to the press and a row erupted in the White House. Stuart Eizenstat, Carter's chief domestic policy adviser, thought the draft 'a political disaster'.[52] And Joseph Califano wrote a memo to the President alerting him to the political danger: 'I believe you will make the most serious mistake of your administration in domestic policy to date if you permit the Justice Department to file the *Bakke* brief in the form I read it and under present circumstances.'[53] President Carter eventually took the position that the government strongly supported affirmative action but was opposed to 'rigid quotas'.[54] Whether or not White House pressure was directly responsible for the change, that too was the final position taken in the Solicitor-General's brief filed in *Bakke*, with the further recommendation that the case be remanded to the California courts.[55]

By the time the Supreme Court actually came to consider the *Bakke* case, it had become the focus of one of the hottest political debates of its time. Public opinion was overwhelmingly opposed to anything which smacked of quotas or group preferences: for example, a Gallup poll of March 1977, showed that 83 per cent of Americans opposed preferential treatment for women and minorities in both higher education and employment.[56] And the issue appeared to have the capacity to divide even those who normally found themselves in broad political agreement, as well as sharpening the usual conservative-liberal ideological oppositions. The unenviable task for the nine Justices of the Supreme Court was to find an authoritative resolution of the controversy, without sparking a political backlash of the kind which had followed *Roe*. Furthermore, this was to be achieved, theoretically, at least, by constitutional interpretation, free of political considerations.

Yet there was no easy constitutional answer to the question posed by *Bakke*. On the one hand, the Equal Protection Clause seeks to guarantee that an individual not be disadvantaged because of race; on the other, it also sought to guarantee emancipated slaves some measure of racial justice and equality with whites, an equality which was still far short of achievement. For some, the Court's decision had to accommodate both these values: 'Perhaps there never has been a case before the Supreme Court with opposing arguments of more equal legitimacy. The Court's own task in *Bakke* was to avoid a conclusive outcome. It must not, in this most decisive of cases, hoist the arms of a victorious contestant.'[57] It is an outstanding illustration of the enormous demands that the political system of the United States can place on its judges.

When the decision was eventually announced, in June 1978, the Court had certainly managed to avoid decisiveness. There were six separate opinions, none of which commanded the support of a majority of the Justices. There was a block of four Justices who subscribed to the opinion of Justice Brennan, which fully sustained affirmative action in general and the Davis scheme in particular.[58] A second group of four Justices subscribed to Justice Stevens' view that the Davis scheme was impermissible, but that the Court on this occasion need not decide the constitutionality of affirmative action *per se*.[59] That left Justice Powell with the controlling vote and opinion, but not one of the other Justices subscribed to his analysis of the case. On two critical issues, Powell reached the same result as the Stevens bloc, but on a third, and possibly most important issue, he cast his vote with the Brennan bloc.

The boldest opinion was undoubtedly that of Justice Brennan. He attempted to establish a comprehensive framework for the Court's consideration of affirmative action, present and future, and it was one which would sustain virtually any affirmative action programme. The first major point Brennan sought to make was that the Court need not treat policies that advantaged racial minorities in the same way as those which advantaged the majority. The problem he faced with this differential approach is that it appears to be at odds with both the wording of the Equal Protection Clause and the Court's recent liberal jurisprudence on race discrimination. The relevant part of the Fourteenth Amendment reads that no state shall 'deny to any person within its jurisdiction the equal protection of the laws'.[60] In the context of race, this would seem to require that each individual be treated alike in law. Moreover, that view underpinned the Court's unanimous decision in *Brown*, which had condemned the classification of citizens by race.[61] Finally, the Court's established practice in reviewing the constitutionality of laws which classified by race was to subject them to 'strict scrutiny'. This meant that the legislators were required to demonstrate that the law was enacted in pursuit of a 'compelling interest' of the state and that it was necessary to the furtherance of that interest: this, in turn, required the state to show that other means of pursuing its compelling interest, less destructive of the principle of race neutrality, were unavailable. In practice, such a test is almost impossible for a state to overcome in race cases, except where the law is intended to remedy past acts of discrimination.

Justice Brennan, however, proposed that strict scrutiny, although the correct test in such cases as the South's former segregation laws, should not be applied in affirmative action cases. This was because the segregation laws were intended to stigmatise blacks, to stamp them as inferior. By contrast, there had been no suggestion that the Davis programme had intended to so stigmatise whites as a group or Allan Bakke as an individual. Thus, he wrote: 'Unlike discrimination against racial minorities, the use of racial preferences for remedial purposes does not inflict a pervasive injury upon individual whites in the sense that wherever they go, whatever they do, there is a significant likelihood that they will be treated as second-class citizens because of their colour.'[62] Because affirmative action laws simply did not pose the same level of threat to equality, they need only be subjected to a less exacting judicial test, that is: '. . . racial classifications designed to further remedial purposes must serve important governmental objectives and must be substantially related to achievement of those objectives.'[63]

As noted above, this lowering of the constitutional barrier to legislative classification by race fell short of commanding a majority of the Court by just one vote. It was a narrow, but critical defeat for proponents of affirmative action, for success would have ensured the survival of most, if not all, affirmative action schemes. For as Justice Brennan went on to argue in *Bakke*, plans such as that operated by Davis clearly pursued a goal that was important – racial equality – and were substantially related to that end. Thus, his second and third major points were that affirmative action in general and the Davis scheme in particular were indeed constitutional. Even the fact that Davis employed a fixed quota did not condemn the plan because, unlike quotas which had earlier been used to restrict the number of minority admissions, it did not seek to put a ceiling on the number of blacks,

Hispanics, Asians or native Americans admitted to the medical school.[64] And in answer to those who opposed quotas, but who would allow the kind of system operated by Harvard, in which race was a factor in favour of a minority applicant but in which no places were set aside exclusively for minorities, Brennan intimated that the distinction was largely a matter of public relations, rather than constitutional interpretation:

> It may be that the Harvard plan is more acceptable to the public than is the Davis "quota". If it is, any State, including California, is free to adopt it in preference to a less acceptable alternative, just as it is generally free, as far as the Constitution is concerned, to abjure granting any racial preferences in its admissions programme. But there is no basis for preferring a particular preference programme simply because in achieving the same goals that the Davis Medical School is pursuing, it proceeds in a manner that is not immediately apparent to the public.[65]

Justice Brennan's opinion was non-interpretive in the sense that there was no support in either the history of the Fourteenth Amendment, the Civil Rights Act of 1964 or the Court's own precedents for the proposition that racial classifications which do not stigmatise are constitutionally more acceptable than those which do. Indeed, Justice Stevens' opinion argued that Title VI of the Civil Rights Act plainly settled the issue. Title VI, he recalled, reads as follows:

> No person in the United States shall, on the ground of race, colour, or national origin, be excluded from participation in, be denied the benefits of, or be subjected to discrimination under any progamme or activity receiving Federal financial assistance.[66]

Since the university did receive such assistance and since Allan Bakke was denied participation because of his race, the Davis plan was clearly unconstitutional. Title VI, he pointed out, contains no qualification on the ground of 'no stigmatisation'.[67] Allan Bakke must therefore be admitted to Davis. Following long-standing (but often ignored) principles of judicial restraint, Stevens said that if the issue could be resolved by statutory interpretation, there was no need at this time to consider the broader issues surrounding the use of affirmative action. Since Allan Bakke's personal case was settled by the 'crystal clear' language of Title VI, and since he had not filed a class action suit, it would be inappropriate to decide whether race could ever be used in an admissions programme.

It was left to Justice Powell, then, to break the tie. He agreed with the Brennan bloc that the Court had to reach the issues raised under the

Equal Protection Clause. Prior to the Justices' conference on the case, he had circulated a memo rejecting the argument that they dispose of the case on statutory grounds. His reasons were largely political: 'Any action by us that may be perceived as ducking this issue for the second time in three years would be viewed by many as a "self-inflicted wound" on the Court.'[68] Besides, he added, the relief would only be short-lived, as the Fourteenth Amendment issue was bound to return to the Court sooner rather than later. In his opinion, he buttressed this essentially tactical decision with a legal argument: he believed that Title VI barred precisely the same racial classifications as the Equal Protection Clause.[69] In effect, then, the statutory and constitutional challenges to the Davis plan were synonymous.

Justice Powell went on, however, to agree with the Stevens bloc both that affirmative action involving racial classifications required strict judicial scrutiny and that the Davis plan could not withstand that scrutiny. Dismissing the debate over whether the plan involved a 'goal' or a 'quota' as a semantic irrelevance, he focused on the fact that it involved a racial classification. Any such classification must be subject to strict scrutiny because 'The guarantee of equal protection cannot mean one thing when applied to one individual and something else when applied to a person of another colour. If both are not accorded the same protection, then it is not equal.'[70] To argue otherwise on the basis that discrimination against the white majority may be benign would invite a return to racial attitudes that existed prior to the passage of the Fourteenth Amendment.[71] Moreover, it would lead to instability: 'The concepts of "majority" and "minority" necessarily reflect temporary arrangements and political judgements.'[72]

At least in terms of judicial standards of review, then, Powell was reaffirming that the Constitution was indeed 'colour-blind'. Of course, that did not mean that all racial classifications were unconstitutional: but in this case, he could find no sufficient justification for the plan. First, it did not seek to remedy any past discrimination against minorities by the university. Davis itself did not claim as much, but explained rather that the plan was aimed at remedying past *societal* discrimination. Such a generalised rationale, said Powell, is insufficient to justify the burdens it imposes on individuals innocent of discrimination themselves: '. . . the purpose of helping certain groups whom the faculty of the Davis Medical School perceived as victims of "societal discrimination" does not justify a classification that imposes disadvantages upon persons like (Bakke), who bear no responsibility for whatever harm the beneficiaries of the special admissions programme are thought to have suffered.'[73]

This dismissal of societal discrimination as a sufficient justification for affirmative action was crucial. Proving specific acts of discrimination in each and every case is both difficult and time-consuming. In short, it is an ineffective method of pursuing social reform. Nevertheless, in requiring some such proof, Powell was reflecting the fact that Supreme Court adjudication is, in important ways, still very much a legal process – something that may be lost sight of in the political turmoil which surrounds the Court these days. As Kathleen Sullivan has pointed out, Powell evaluated affirmative action in terms of those most fundamental concepts of the legal process, guilt and innocence. In line with civil and criminal trials, affirmative action cases, he implied, require an identified perpetrator and victim.[74] This focus also tends to emphasise the rectification of the past over the future development of a racially just society: 'Trapped in the paradigm of sin, the Court shrinks, even in upholding affirmative action plans, from declaring that the benefits of building a racially integrated society for the future can be justification enough.'[75]

Justice Powell did, however, find one goal of the university to be sufficiently important to qualify as a 'compelling interest' which justified some kind of affirmative action on its part. This was the goal of attaining '. . . a diverse student body.'[76] This, he argued, was a substantial objective in any university's fulfilment of its educational mission. Nevertheless, any plan devised to attain that goal must be 'narrowly tailored' to its achievement. The Davis plan failed in this respect because it focused exclusively on race, something which, by discounting all the other attributes of an applicant, actually hindered the goal of diversity.[77] Ultimately, then, Powell's condemnation of the Davis plan came back to the question of the quota, the setting aside of a number of places on the basis of race. As he put it at the December 1977 case conference: '. . . the colossal blunder here was to pick a number.'[78]

Originally, it seems, Powell was inclined to leave it there and vote to affirm the decision of the California Supreme Court, along with the Stevens bloc. But since he indicated that race could be one of several factors which admissions officers could take into account in their pursuit of student diversity, Brennan persuaded him that he should affirm in part, but also reverse on the question of race as a legitimate factor in admissions decisions. Powell agreed, thereby changing the whole tenor of the Court's decision: 'Justice Brennan himself, of course, immediately saw the significance of Powell's agreement. He stressed its importance to his law clerks, pointing out to them that if the case were to come down as a partial reversal, public attention was likely to be focussed on what he saw as the positive aspect of the decision – that the principle of affirmative action was being upheld.'[79]

In the end, Justice Powell went even further by detailing the kind of affirmative action of which he believed the Constitution approved. He specifically commended the Harvard plan in which race was counted as a plus for minority applicants, though they still had to compete for places with non-minority applicants. In an echo of Justice Douglas' *DeFunis* dissent, Powell listed the kind of qualities that a minority applicant might bring to the student body: '. . . exceptional personal talents, unique work or service experience, leadership potential, maturity, demonstrated compassion, a history of overcoming disadvantage, ability to communicate with the poor, or other qualifications deemed important.'[80]

He concluded therefore, that while the numerical quota made the Davis plan unconstitutional, '. . . the State has a substantial interest that legitimately may be served by a properly devised admissions programme involving the competitive consideration of race and ethnic origin.'[81] As to the charge that such schemes would merely constitute a subterfuge for the use of quotas, Justice Powell would rely on the integrity of university staff: '. . . a court would not assume that a university, professing to employ a facially non-discriminatory admissions policy, would operate it as a cover for the functional equivalent of a quota system. In short, good faith would be presumed in the absence of a showing to the contrary . . .'[82]

Due almost wholly to Justice Powell's pivotal position, the Court's decision in the *Bakke* case was greeted by virtually everyone as a political compromise. Whether that was a good thing, however, was debated. One view of Powell's opinion was that:

> The gentleman from Virginia had written the ultimate political opinion. He had neutralised the anti-affirmative action forces by admitting Bakke and holding that quotas were illegal. And he had given his friends in the academic establishment what (they) had asked for: the freedom to continue running their business the way they pleased. It was not clear that he had given minorities anything, but he had not shut the door on them entirely. It would be possible for them to claim victory and difficult for them to say they had been ignored.[83]

Paul Brest thought it '. . . ambivalent, obfuscatory, and inconclusive',[84] but another view was that '. . . whatever its legal merits, it seemed an astute political compromise, designed to buy time in which the Court could sort out some of the troubling issues raised by affirmative action.'[85] Whether judicial statesmanship or crude political compromise, two things may be said about the *Bakke* decision. First, that in sanctioning preferences based on race, other than for narrow remedial purposes, it involved a non-interpretive approach to judicial review. Second, because of the divisions on the Court, it gave little promise of an end to the political and judicial battle over affirmative action.

In fact, *Bakke* was just the beginning. And the battle of the 1980s was to be fought on issues even more emotive than those involved in higher education – employment opportunities, including hiring, firing, promotion and seniority rights and preferential treatment for minority businesses. In politics, affirmative action in these areas posed the stark question of just how much material sacrifice white America was willing to make on behalf of racial equality. And at a time of declining economic performance and opportunity and growing political conservatism, the answer was 'not a great deal'. The Republican Party, now dominated by its conservative wing, was firmly opposed to race preference. Its platform for the 1980 elections indicated as much when it said, '. . . our fundamental answer to the economic problems of black Americans is the same answer we make to all Americans – full employment without inflation through economic growth.'[86]

For the Court, of course, things were not so straightforward. Its precedents now allowed for some affirmative action plans and since *Brown*, it had assumed great responsibilities in overcoming the United States' long history of race discrimination. Furthermore, there were influential pressure groups and a Congressional majority, particularly on House committees, urging the Court to go further and faster: 'By the 1970s, a reliable civil rights coalition emerged, consisting of a rainbow of unions, black groups, women's groups, and other public interest groups. The House Democratic leadership and the relevant committees agreed with the coalition's civil rights agenda.'[87] The Court was about to find itself in the middle of a conflict fought with equal moral conviction by the opposing factions, each of whom would control one of the other two branches of the federal government.

Hiring and firing: Title VII does not mean what it says

Soon after *Bakke*, two new cases raised the political temperature, *United Steelworkers v. Weber*, in 1979, and *Fullilove v. Klutznick*, a year later.[88] In *Weber*, the Court split five-to-two in upholding a numerical race preference scheme operated by Kaiser Aluminum at its plant in Gramercy, Louisiana.[89] Kaiser Aluminum did not concede that it had discriminated against minorities in the past,[90] but nevertheless, in 1974, it voluntarily adopted a plan to increase the number of minority workers in skilled jobs. The plan simply undertook to award places on a special training programme for skilled jobs to whites and blacks in equal numbers. Brian Weber was a white employee who had been denied a place on the programme, despite having more seniority than some of the blacks who had been awarded places. Weber alleged discrimination under Title VII of the Civil Rights Act of 1964.[91]

The problem with the plan was that, as Chief Justice Burger pointed out in dissent, it seemed to fall foul of the clear language of Section 703(d) of the Act, which states that,

> It shall be unlawful employment practice for any employer, labour organisation or joint labour-management committee controlling apprenticeship or other training or re-training, including on-the-job-training programmes, to discriminate against any individual because of his (sic) race, colour, religion, sex, or national origin in admission to, or employment in, any programme established to provide apprenticeship or other training.[92]

While Burger conceded that he personally approved of programmes like that at Kaiser Aluminum, he thought that the language of the Act spoke with 'extraordinary clarity' against its permissibility.[93] The other dissenter, Justice Rehnquist, engaged in an exhaustive examination of the legislative history of that language and established beyond doubt that Burger and he were correct. Time and again, the Act's critics demanded assurance that the Act would not require 'racial balancing' and 'preferences for blacks'; and each time its proponents gave it. Most tellingly, Rehnquist quoted at length from statements by the bi-partisan overseers of Title VII, Senators Clark and Case. For example, they had written a floor memorandum stating that an employer '. . . would not be obliged – or indeed permitted – to fire whites in order to hire Negroes, or to prefer Negroes for future vacancies, or, once Negroes are hired, to give them special seniority rights at the expense of white workers hired earlier.'[94] And Senator Humphrey, the bill's co-sponsor, had said, 'In fact, the title would prohibit preferential treatment for any particular group, and any person, whether or not a member of any minority group, would be permitted to file a complaint of discriminatory employment practices.'[95] Finally, Justice Rehnquist added, 'Not once during the eighty-three days of debate in the Senate, did a speaker, proponent or opponent, suggest that the bill would allow employers *voluntarily* to prefer racial minorities over white persons.'[96] To escape from the strictures of such language and legislative history, concluded Rehnquist, would require the skills of a Houdini rather than a Holmes.[97]

With one bound, however, the majority was free. Although Justice Brennan conceded that this 'literal interpretation' was 'not without force',[98] he argued that it was at odds with what he considered to be the purpose of the Act. This was, he said, to open up to blacks jobs from which they had previously been excluded. He conceded that the Act specified that employers could not be *required* to adopt race preference plans, but that did not rule out such plans which were adopted *voluntarily* by a private employer. Citing the House Report accompanying the Act, he noted that it had been hoped that employers would take voluntary action to eliminate discrimination in employment. Therefore, 'Given this legislative history, we cannot agree. . . that Congress prohibited the private sector from taking effective steps to accomplish the goal that Congress designed Title VII to achieve.'[99]

Even one of Brennan's colleagues in the majority, Justice Blackmun, confessed himself troubled by this reading of the legislative history.[100] This is not surprising, since it really did stand the meaning of the Act on its head. In effect, all Brennan had going for him was a generalised expression of hope by Congress that employers would take some action voluntarily. Against him was explicit language and history that strongly suggested the illegality of what he had just approved. It is hard to deny that this was a clear example of non-interpretive, result-oriented reasoning by the Court.

Viewed from a wider political perspective, however, there is also a more subtle game being played here. As Justice Blackmun pointed out, given that *Weber* involved statutory, rather than constitutional, interpretation, Congress could reverse the Court's decision by amending the statute to that effect, *if* it believed the Justices had erred.[101] The Court had indeed misinterpreted the Congressional will as it had been in 1964, bearing in mind the compromises which had to be made to ensure the Act's passage: quite simply, a statistical affirmative action plan like that operated by Kaiser Aluminum could not have been approved in 1964. Fifteen years later, however, with developments in liberal ideas on what is needed to achieve racial equality, such a plan would have greater appeal. On the other hand, the growing outcry on the right and the clear public opposition to race preferences would make the enactment of such legislation an electorally dangerous proposition. It may well be that under such circumstances, Congress preferred the Court to advance the civil rights agenda and gave tacit, if less prominent, approval to statistical affirmative action by not overturning the Court's decision. Whether this squares with formal democratic principles is debatable: but it does show the way in which Congress may encourage the Justices to behave as a legislature rather than a court.

Fullilove involved an even more obvious encouragement by Congress for the Court to uphold the constitutionality of statistical affirmative action. At issue was the Public Works Employment Act, passed by Congress in 1977. It required that 10 per cent of federal grants to state and local governments for public works should go to minority businesses. Six of the Justices voted to uphold the Act, but again there was no opinion which commanded the support of a majority. What was notable about Chief Justice Burger's opinion, joined by Justices White and Powell, was the emphasis which it placed on the very broad powers of Congress to enforce the Fourteenth Amendment. This gave Congress wider latitude than states or courts in adopting affirmative action plans, though the quota still had to be justified by a finding of past discrimination and be narrowly tailored to the elimination of its present effects. Nevertheless, he said, such plans were valid, even where they harmed 'innocent' parties: 'When effecting a limited and properly tailored remedy to cure the effects of prior discrimination, such a "sharing of the burden" by innocent parties is not impermissible.'[102]

Weber and *Fullilove* did little to clarify the uncertainties which surrounded affirmative action. Judicial precedents were being created, but their authority was undermined by a lack of cohesion among the Justices, most obviously in their inability to formulate a decisional framework to which a clear majority of them could subscribe. Such incoherence was perhaps politically sustainable as long as Congress and the presidency shared the view that affirmative action was broadly desirable and the *ad hoc* approach of the Court was reasonably in tune with that consensus. This precarious harmony was shattered by the advent of the Reagan administration. Not only were the new President and his team strongly opposed to most forms of affirmative action, but they now had the power to put people of their own persuasion on to the Court as and when vacancies occurred.

The animosity of the Reaganites toward affirmative action was deeply held. They believed that 'quotas' not only wronged innocent whites and deprived them of what their talents and efforts deserved, but also that race preferences didn't do much good for blacks either.

Charles Fried alleges that '. . . those who benefited from the racial preferences felt a strange ambiguity: it put their teeth on edge that they could not quite say to themselves that they had made it on their own. If they admitted that they had been preferred, their response was often truculence, or self-doubt, or an elaborate sense of obligation to their communities, which, though admirable, was not quite freely chosen.'[103] Furthermore, for conservatives, it counted against affirmative action that it did not help the black underclass: 'It was obvious that preferences were irrelevant to the deplorable plight of the black underclass. Preferences tend to help the black middle class and the most ambitious and ablest poor blacks – people who would not in any event sink into the ghettos of despair.'[104] (It is a sure sign of the former Solicitor-General's dislike of affirmative action that he is willing to attack it with crocodile tears for an underclass for which the Reagan administration did nothing.)

A different, but equally powerful source of conservative opposition was economics. Business groups complained that affirmative action imposed financial costs that were second only to those imposed by environmental regulations. One such group which opposes affirmative action, the somewhat misleadingly-named Equal Employment Advisory Council, estimated the cost at $1.2 billion per year.[105] And beyond the direct financial cost was the economic inefficiency allegedly involved: 'If jobs were handed out according to membership in a group that has managed to attract political power, then the private sector and private institutions are not responsible to themselves or to the market, but to politics.'[106]

For these reasons, the Reagan administration launched an onslaught against affirmative action in general and the Supreme Court in particular. At first, there were some confusing signals from the White House, due, it seems, to the initial continuation of bureaucratic efforts on behalf of affirmative action. The Justice Department, however, ignored EEOC and other agency guidelines and filed *amicus* briefs in the lower federal courts arguing that numerical goals were unlawful.[107] The administration also changed agency personnel to facilitate its campaign. For example, it appointed Clarence Thomas to head the EEOC in 1982. Although in his confirmation hearings Thomas said that numerical goals and timetables were necessary to monitor progress towards greater equality, he acted otherwise once at work: 'Thomas's views . . . were sufficient to discourage law suits either to enforce the adverse impact branch of Title VII or to prove purposeful discrimination through the use of statistics.'[108]

The Reagan administration takes on the court

It was not until 1983, however, that the Reagan Justice Department decided to do battle with the Supreme Court. The case was *Firefighters v. Stotts*.[109] Charles Fried, then a consultant to the White House task force on employment discrimination policy, describes '. . . a furious battle in 1983 between Brad Reynolds and Rex Lee regarding the position that Lee would take as Solicitor-General in the *Stotts* case.'[110] As the quotation which began this chapter shows, Reynolds took a very dim view of affirmative action and wanted Lee to argue before the Court that it was only permissible in cases involving 'victim specificity': that is, only actual individual victims of proven discrimination are entitled to remedy. Despite resistance to this position from the Solicitor-General's office and the EEOC, 'In the end, Rex Lee argued Reynold's victim-specificity position quite forcefully.'[111] Thus, the Reagan administration went into *Stotts* arguing for a radical break with some twenty years of affirmative action policy by Congress, the Executive branch and the federal judiciary.

The case raised some very difficult issues. It dated from 1977 when Carl Stotts, a black captain in the Memphis Fire Department, filed a class action suit alleging that both the department and the city discriminated against minorities in hiring and promotion decisions. Eventually, in 1980, all parties signed a 'consent decree' which included the long-term goal of having the same proportion of minority personnel in various jobs in the Fire Department, as there were in the local area labour force. In the following year, however, the city responded to a budget deficit by laying off some employees and demoting others. The basis for these decisions was seniority, or 'last hired, first fired'. It emerged that forty people would be laid off, twenty-five white and fifteen black. The inevitable result would be that the percentage of blacks in the Fire Department would be reduced, thus reversing the intention of the consent decree.[112] A federal District Court ruled, however, that the seniority principle could not be enforced where it would reduce the percentage of minority personnel. The firefighters union appealed to the Supreme Court.

The legal issue was defined as a narrow, technical one by the majority opinion of Justice White: did the District Court possess the power to modify the consent decree and enjoin the application of the seniority system?[113] The substantive political issue, however, was of the highest importance: should the aims of affirmative action be accorded priority over the seniority rights of white employees? If the answer was yes, then some white employees would not merely fail to get jobs or promotions, they would actually lose the jobs they already had. If the answer was no, then the economic recession would effectively nullify much of the progress achieved in overcoming the effects of past discrimination. *Stotts*, then, was certainly the most significant decision on affirmative action since *Bakke*, even if the legal issue involved was of a secondary order. In the event, the decision in *Stotts* was also to trigger the Reagan administration's concerted campaign to turn back the clock on affirmative action.

The Court split six-to-three to reverse the District Court's ruling that the seniority principle could not be applied. The majority opinion, written by Justice White, first had to tackle the dissenters' claim that the case was moot: all the white employees who had been laid off had been reinstated by the time the Court came to make its decision. Again, this appears as a technical legal issue, but, as the *DeFunis* case showed, mootness can provide the Court with a means of avoiding a politically delicate decision. The fact that six Justices, usually regarded as moderates and conservatives, sought to reach the merits of the case, suggests their conviction that this form of affirmative action went too far. The fact that three liberal Justices – Brennan, Marshall and Blackmun – sought to avoid the substantive issue through a finding of mootness, suggests equally that they understood the political damage that the case could do to affirmative action.

None of the opinions in the case directly addressed the substantive policy issues. Justice White said that the case was not moot, because such a finding would leave the District Court's decision unreversed and still affecting city policy. There were also outstanding issues, such as back-pay, which required a resolution of the case. Justice Blackmun, in dissent, disputed these points, saying '. . . I regret the Court's insistence upon unnecessarily reviving a past controversy.'[114]

On the legal merits, White argued that the district court, by enjoining enforcement of the seniority principle, had effectively awarded the black officers 'competitive seniority'. Such an award, however, could only be made where the beneficiary was an actual victim of discrimination:

> If individual members of a plaintiff class demonstrate that they have been actual victims of the discriminatory practice, they may be awarded competitive seniority and given their rightful place on the seniority roster . . . mere membership in a disadvantaged class is insufficient to warrant a seniority award; each individual must prove that the discriminatory practice had an impact on him.[115]

In her concurring opinion, Justice O'Connor emphasised the point in similar language: 'A court may not grant preferential treatment to any individual or group simply because the group to which they belong is adversely affected by a bona fide seniority system. Rather, a court may use its remedial powers, including its power to modify a consent decree, only to prevent future violations and to compensate identified victims of unlawful discrimination.'[116]

More than anything else about *Stotts*, this language in the White and O'Connor opinions seemed significant, especially to Rex Lee and William Bradford Reynolds. Not unreasonably, they believed that the Court had just endorsed their own forcefully-argued concept of victim specificity. Lee described what he believed was a great victory for the Reagan administration in basketball slang – *Stotts* was a 'slam-dunk'.[117] For Reynolds, the decision was the green light to seek an end to all affirmative action programmes which were not victim specific: 'Despite the narrowness of the *Stotts* holding, the Department of Justice undertook over the next two years to extract from the case a general principle that *no* racially preferential treatment could ever be afforded to "non-victims" of past discrimination – whether voluntarily or by court order.'[118] What had been overlooked was the fact that the issue of seniority was different in important ways from, say, general hiring policies. Section 703(h) of Title VII had specifically endorsed the validity of seniority systems and, in an earlier case, the Court had upheld them against a charge of discrimination.[119] Nevertheless, it was not only the Justice Department who detected the presence of serious implications in the *Stotts* decision. The *Harvard Law Review* noted that 'By finding that the case was not moot, the majority appears to have strained for an opportunity to narrow the scope of affirmative action remedies under Title VII.'[120] More serious still, it found contradictions in the majority opinion which at least suggested that the reactions of Lee and Reynolds were not unfounded: 'It is too early to tell whether the Court intends to push the logic of its opinion as far as it might go – to the point of drastically limiting the availability of all affirmative action remedies in both consent decrees and litigated cases. The Court might merely have created a limited exception, or it may have signalled a broad retrenchment.'[121]

Reynolds, however, chose not to wait for the Court to clarify the ambiguities. As well as stating publicly that the Court had endorsed the concept of victim specificity, '. . . he wrote letters to all the state and local governments that had entered into preferential schemes over the years in settlement of Justice Department discrimination suits, stating that these arrangements had now been held unlawful and would have to be revised.'[122] As subsequent events proved, Reynolds was simply wrong. But his actions raised the political temperature of affirmative action policy even higher and may have caused his subsequent rejection by the Senate when he was nominated for the post of Associate Attorney-General.[123]

The Court's decision in *Stotts* had achieved the seemingly impossible: it had created even more confusion and uncertainty in the law of affirmative action than had existed before. It was not until 1986 that the Justices had a substantial opportunity to clear things up. In early summer of that year, the Court handed down decisions in three cases: *Wygant v. Jackson Board of Education, Local 28 of the Sheet Metal Workers v. EEOC* and *Local 93 International Association of Firefighters v. Cleveland.*[124]

Wygant was the first of the cases to come down. The facts of the case were somewhat similar to those in *Stotts*. In 1972, the School Board of Jackson, Michigan, had reached a Collective Bargaining Agreement (CBA) with the local teachers' union. Article XII of the CBA stated that, in the event of teacher lay-offs, those with most seniority would be retained, except that the percentage of minority teachers laid off must not exceed the percentage of minority teachers employed at the time. When lay-offs did become necessary two years later, the Board found that adherence to Article XII would mean that tenured non-minority teachers would have to go in order for minority teachers of probationary status to be retained. The Board refused to comply with Article XII, but after protracted litigation in both the state and federal courts, non-minority teachers were laid off, while minority teachers with less seniority were retained. One of the non-minority teachers, Wendy Wygant, and other displaced colleagues, brought suit in a federal District Court, alleging that the lay-offs violated both the Equal Protection Clause and Title VII of the Civil Rights Act of 1964. That court decided that, although the School Board had not been shown to have been guilty of past discrimination, its affirmative action was permissible as an attempt to remedy past societal discrimination and to provide role models for minority schoolchildren. The Court of Appeals affirmed that decision.

As with that Term's other affirmative action cases, Reynolds and Charles Fried, the man chosen to replace Rex Lee as Solicitor-General, saw an opportunity to get the Court to confirm the victim specificity rule that they had detected in *Stotts*.[125] Fried's brief was forthright in its condemnation of the School Board's affirmative action plan, sometimes provocatively so. Thus, on the plan's rationale of providing minority role models, he wrote: 'The most powerful role models are those who have succeeded without a hint of favouritism. For example, Henry Aaron would not be regarded as the all-time home run king, and he would not be a model for youth, if the fences had been moved in whenever he came to the plate.'[126]

The part of the brief arguing against the rationale of societal discrimination and for that of victim specificity was bluntly stated:

> Because the Equal Protection Clause protects personal not group rights, a measure cannot be fairly characterised as a remedy for a violation of equal protection unless it provides relief to an individual who was personally victimised by discrimination. Nor can a measure be termed remedial if the benefit conferred is not in some way measured by the nature and extent of the prior violation. When benefits do not correspond to any identified prior wrong and are not directed to the victim of such a wrong, they cannot in any meaningful sense be termed compensatory or remedial.[127]

Through the Solicitor-General's brief, then, the Reagan administration was asking the Supreme Court to approve a fundamental shift in public policy.

Of course, the Solicitor-General's brief did not go unchallenged. *Wygant* attracted a large number of *amicus* briefs – twenty-two in all, most of which supported the minority teacher preference. The brief of the NAACP Legal and Educational Fund devoted over twenty pages to a direct rebuttal of Fried's argument. On the issue of teacher role models, it asserted that 'the Solicitor's pedagogical theories' were unsupported by any evidence from the trial records, but rather relied '. . . on a 1972 book by a California economist and a 1974 article by an Illinois law professor'.[129] More importantly, the brief cited a plethora of judicial precedents to show that victim specificity had never been the guiding principle of either legislatures or courts in framing affirmative action plans. Quite simply, it argued, it is practically impossible to frame decrees tailored to individual victims when these are numbered in their thousands:

> School desegregation orders, for example, have never attempted to identify which student would have been in which school but for the proven de jure segregation. In framing remedial decrees, federal courts act in a complex world in which it is at times impossible to precisely reconstruct the past, and must settle for doing rough justice if they are to do justice at all.[130]

The briefs offered the Justices a clear choice, but once again they were unable, or unwilling, to respond with an equally clear answer. Five

Justices found the School Board's plan to be unconstitutional, but no single opinion or rationale for the vote united them. Furthermore, even the four dissenters could not unite on a reason for upholding the plan.[131]

The plurality opinion of Justice Powell insisted that the case required strict scrutiny and therefore asked whether the plan was supported by a compelling state interest and whether it was narrowly tailored to that interest. He began his enquiry by recalling that 'This Court never has held that societal discrimination alone is sufficient to justify a racial classification. Rather, the Court has insisted upon some showing of prior discrimination by the governmental unit involved . . .'[132] If some statistical disparity is to be accepted as proof of such discrimination, it must be a disparity between the racial composition of the Board's employees and the racial composition of the qualified local work-force. However, the role model theory adopted by the Jackson School Board is based on a different disparity: that between the number of minority teachers employed by the Board and the number of minority pupils in its district. This is no proof of past discrimination by the Board: 'There are numerous explanations for a disparity between the percentage of minority students and the percentage of minority faculty, many of them completely unrelated to discrimination of any kind. In fact, there is no apparent connection between the two.'[133] In the absence of a factual determination by a court that a governmental unit such as the Board has engaged in past discrimination, no remedial action can be justified.[134]

Justice Powell then turned to the legal question of narrow tailoring which, in its political impact, involves the critical issue of exactly what burdens non-minority employees can reasonably be asked to bear under any remedial scheme. His starting point was that 'As part of this Nation's dedication to eradicating racial discrimination, innocent persons may be called upon to bear some of the burden of the remedy.'[135] However, he finds the burden of lay-offs to be of a different order to those of hiring decisions:

> In cases involving valid *hiring* goals, the burden to be borne by innocent individuals is diffused to a considerable extent among society generally. Though hiring goals may burden some innocent individuals, they simply do not impose the same kind of injury that lay-offs impose. Denial of a future employment opportunity is not as intrusive as loss of an existing job . . . (L)ayoffs impose the entire burden of achieving racial equality on particular individuals, often resulting in serious disruption of their lives. That burden is too intrusive.[136]

Justice Powell's opinion is a clear illustration of the blurred distinction between politics and law which permeates much of the Court's jurisprudence on social issues. As an exercise in political reasoning, or even common law reasoning, his differential treatment of hiring and firing decisions is not without its attractions and logic. This argument, however, purports to be *constitutional* law, a significantly different animal. In the first place, Powell offers no constitutional basis to support his conclusion.[137] He simply says that the lay-off burden is too intrusive: that is a policy judgement. Second, such a policy judgement might be thought more acceptable if it were reversible by an elected legislature: but precisely because the majority decision does present itself as constitutional law, it cannot be reversed except by constitutional amendment, a process which requires super-majoritarian votes and almost superhuman political efforts. Does this render Justice Powell's decision illegitimate? Only if one holds to an interpretive view of the Supreme Court's role in American politics. On the other hand, one may see in the *Wygant* decision a good argument for a non-interpretive, or functional, view of the Court's role. For example, one might ask whether the Michigan legislature or Congress would have dealt with the issue in a more satisfactory manner, especially in the light of the intense political pressures involved? Did not the relative detachment of the Court in this regard allow it to produce a reasonable compromise? If the Court had gone no further than deciding that the Equal Protection Clause either allowed or prohibited affirmative action and left the elected branches to act accordingly, would that have yielded better or more stable policy outcomes? The answers to these questions are difficult to discern, but the fact that they deserve to be considered illustrates just how reliant the American political system has become on policy resolutions by the Supreme Court.

Charles Fried wrote of the *Wygant* decision that 'The bottom line was ours.'[138] It wasn't. The bottom line of this particular case was not about adherence to strict scrutiny or whether affirmative action plans could legitimately include lay-offs: in those respects, the Court simply confirmed *Stotts* and earlier cases, and then none too clearly, given the lack of unanimity within an already thin majority. The bottom line, rather, was that victim specificity had been rejected. This, after all, had been the big pitch of the Reagan administration in the case. It must have been particularly galling that it was Justice O'Connor, the sole Reagan appointee at the time, who chose to emphasise that point. In a concurring opinion notable for its stress on the things which united the Court on affirmative action, she wrote:

... the Court has forged a degree of unanimity; it is agreed that a plan need not be limited to the remedying of specific instances of identified discrimination for it to be deemed sufficiently 'narrowly tailored,' or 'substantially related,' to the correction of prior discrimination by the state actor.[139]

Justice Marshall's dissent also sought to emphasise areas of agreement among his colleagues, saying that 'Despite the Court's inability to agree on a route, we have reached a common destination in sustaining affirmative action against constitutional attack.'[140] Yet the basic substantive issue in *Wygant*, the competing claims of seniority and racial equality in firing decisions, created an unbridgeable gap between the majority and dissenting Justices. Marshall argued that Powell's position was 'untenable' in as much as it held that the Constitution permitted race preference in hiring but not lay-offs: 'As a matter of logic as well as fact, a hiring policy achieves no purpose at all if it is eviscerated by layoffs.'[141] Furthermore, he challenged Powell's premise that '. . . the tradition of basing lay-off decisions on seniority is so fundamental that its modification can never be permitted.'[142] In his review of the Court's relevant precedents, however, he failed to point to any case in which abridgement of the seniority principle was upheld as applied to lay-offs.

Clearly Justice Marshall also disagreed with Powell on the reasonableness of the division of burden contained in the School Board's plan and this led to a revealing exchange between the two. Marshall believed that it allocated '. . . the impact of an inevitable burden proportionately between two racial groups. It places no absolute burden or benefit on one race . . .'[143] Justice Powell responded:

(Justice Marshall) sees this case not in terms of individual constitutional rights, but as an allocation of burdens 'between two racial groups' . . . But the petitioners before us today are not 'the white teachers as a group'. They are Wendy Wygant and other individuals who claim they were fired from their jobs because of their race . . . The Constitution does not allocate constitutional rights to be distributed like bloc grants within discrete racial groups . . .[144]

Here we appear to be presented with two alternative concepts of constitutional rights. Yet surely the post-*Brown* decisions on race and other social issues, as well as the proliferation of devices like the class action suit, have long since rendered this distinction virtually meaningless. And this is emphatically so once the individual focus of a case is deliberately discounted, as it is here, by the rejection of victim specificity. Whichever way the Justices choose to phrase it, decisions to apportion burdens between individuals *do* amount to apportioning them between groups as well – and vice versa.

The disunity in *Wygant* caused the press to hesitate in the assessment of its significance, as illustrated by the *International Herald Tribune*'s headline, 'U.S. High Court Appears to Support Plans to Fight Hiring Bias'.[145] A Justice Department spokesman, Terry Eastland, tried to make the best of it, calling the Justices' decision 'opaque', while focusing on their vindication of the white teachers' rights.[146] The conservative columnist George Will also noted the lack of clarity, but accurately picked up the central message: '. . . all nine Justices now seem opposed to the Reagan administration's position, which is that the constitutional guarantee of "equal protection" of the law requires public policy to be colour-blind, except when correcting the effects of particular acts of discrimination against identified individual victims.'[147] Will did not approve the decision at all, saying that '. . . it has carved out an exception to the central principle of liberal democracy . . . that rights inhere in individuals not in favoured groups. So the civil rights movement will continue to concentrate on constructing a racial spoils system, getting government to accord special rights to certain minorities.'[148]

The worst fears of the conservative critics of affirmative action were borne out six weeks later, when the decisions came down in *Sheet Metal Workers* and *Firefighters v. Cleveland*. Although once again there was no majority opinion on the most important substantive aspects of the two cases, Justices Powell and White joined the four *Wygant* dissenters to uphold statistical affirmative action plans under the Civil Rights Act which were not victim specific.[149] *Sheet Metal Workers* was the lead case and the facts, unlike in *Wygant*, were not in the Reagan administration's favour.[150] Local 28 of the Sheet Metal Workers International Association represents workers in the New York City metropolitan area. As far back as 1964, it had been found guilty of not so much racial discrimination against blacks, but their actual racial exclusion: the union had never had a black member or apprentice.[151] Despite a series of court orders to admit non-white members, the union continued to discriminate and to evade implementation of those court orders, even in the face of heavy fines for contempt. Set a target of achieving a 29 per cent non-white membership in 1975, the figure achieved in 1982, a year after the target date, was still only 10.8 per cent.[152] In 1983, a District Court established a new target of 29.23 per cent, based on the labour pool in the union's area. This goal was to be achieved by August 1987. This Amended Affirmative Action Plan and Order (AAAPO) required that one minority apprentice be taken on for every white apprentice indentured. Local 28 appealed this and other aspects of the court's decision, their principal claim being that the AAAPO involved race preferences for individuals not identified as actual victims of the union's discrimination. The Reagan administration filed a brief supporting the union, despite the fact that the EEOC was on the other side.[153]

The focal point of the legal dispute was Section 706(g) of Title VII of the Civil Rights Act of 1964. Although it permits a court to order '. . . such affirmative action as may be appropriate . . .' where it finds an employer guilty of intentional discrimination, it also says that 'No order of the Court shall require the admission or reinstatement of an individual as a member of a union . . . if such individual was refused admission . . . for any reason other than discrimination on account of race, colour, religion, sex, or national origin . . .'[154] The union and the Solicitor-General interpreted this as requiring victim specificity but, according to Justice Brennan, 'This reading twists the plain language of the statute.'[155] This, he said, addresses the issue of when a union has a bona fide reason for refusing membership to an individual, such as lack of qualifications. It does not say that judicial relief may only be given to actual victims of past discrimination.

Justice Brennan then rehearsed the now familiar history of the passage of the Civil Rights Act of 1964, its subsequent application by government agencies, such as the EEOC, and the Court's own precedents to establish the fact that courts have not been limited to giving race-conscious relief to identified victims only. In so doing, he stressed that *Stotts* had imposed limits on the kind of 'make-whole' relief which courts could award to particular *individuals*. The kind of scheme at issue here, however, is quite different: 'The purpose of affirmative action is not to make identified victims whole, but rather to dismantle prior patterns of employment discrimination and to prevent discrimination in the future. Such relief is provided to the class as a whole rather than to individual members; no individual is entitled to relief, and beneficiaries need not show that they were themselves victims of discrimination.'[156] In what was a crushing defeat for the Reagan administration's position, six of the Justices agreed.[157]

Although there were nuances and complications in the voting pattern in *Sheet Metal Workers* that were not dealt with by reporters, they were clear about the political significance of the case. Henry Reske, of United Press International, began his report: 'The Supreme Court gave sweeping support Wednesday to affirmative action plans and in the process handed the Reagan Administration a stinging defeat by rejecting its claim that such programmes could be used only to help victims of discrimination.'[158] And in an analytical piece two days after the decision, Robert Pear of the *New York Times* began: 'The Supreme Court's rulings on affirmative action amount to a rejection of the policies and arguments that the Reagan Administration have been advancing for six years in the field of civil rights.'[159] William Bradford Reynolds acknowledged the defeat, calling the decisions 'disappointing' and 'extremely unfortunate', though Attorney-General Edwin Meese argued rather weakly that 'The Court has accepted the general position of this administration that racial preferences are not a good thing to have.'[160] Charles Fried wrote later that he privately offered Meese his resignation.[161]

The Court, the President and the Congress

As even the administration had to accept, victim specificity was now '. . . off the table once and for all.'[162] Instead, then, the Department of Justice set out to limit earlier rulings on affirmative action. One such target was 'set-asides' for minority business enterprises (MBEs). Fried thought set-asides one of the worst forms of affirmative action: 'The preference is not remedial. It is pure social engineering – a kind of racial industrial policy. In fact, it had become a focus for corruption and evasion.'[163] However,the Court had upheld Congressional set-asides in the *Fullilove* case and there was some reluctance to ask the Court to reverse that decision, given that it could involve declaring an act of Congress unconstitutional. The administration's efforts, therefore, became focused on a case involving local government set-asides, *City of Richmond v. Croson*.[164]

A second element of the Administration's new anti-affirmative action strategy was 'taming *Griggs*',[165] the case which had introduced disparate impact analysis and authorised affirmative action to remedy discriminatory effect, rather than merely intent. By putting the burden on employers to demonstrate that practices which effectively discriminated against minorities were justified by business necessity, conservatives believed that this encouraged companies to adopt racial quotas as a means of avoiding protracted and expensive litigation. The administration's efforts in this regard were concentrated on the case of *Wards Cove Packing Co. v. Atonio*.[166]

Both *Croson* and *Wards Cove* were eventually decided in 1989 and, together with a third case decided that year, *Martin v. Wilks*,[167] they made 1989 as good a year for conservatives as 1986 had been for proponents of affirmative action. The intervening period had seen the conservative position on the Court strengthened to some degree by the replacement of two members, Burger and Powell, by Antonin Scalia and Anthony Kennedy. They proved to be as truly conservative as the Reagan administration had intended. Furthermore, Burger's retirement had given President Reagan the opportunity to elevate the most conservative member of the Court, William Rehnquist, to the position of Chief Justice. Given the rather unpredictable views of Justices White and O'Connor on affirmative action, it was not clear that these appointments had established an unassailable conservative majority on the Court. Nevertheless, the 1989 decisions would provide some support for the old saw that, eventually, the Supreme Court follows the election returns.

The *Croson* case was politically the most important one of the three, simply because, as noted above, it concerned the sort of affirmative action that conservatives regard as a racial spoils system. It was also greatly significant because many other local governments had similar schemes: one count revealed that 190 cities and 36 states operated affirmative action set-asides.[168] Indeed, seventeen states filed *amicus* briefs in support of Richmond's MBE set-asides, as did other leading organisations concerned with local government, including the National League of Cities, the US Conference of Mayors and the National Association of Counties.[169] Also supporting Richmond were leading civil rights, minority and women's organisations, including the American Civil Liberties Union, the NAACP Legal Defence and Education Fund, the National Organisation for Women Legal Defence and Education Fund and the Minority Business Legal Defence and Education Fund.[170] Ranged against them were, among others, Associated Speciality Contractors, the Equal Employment Advisory Council, the Anti-Defamation League of B'nai B'rith and conservative legal public interest groups such as the Pacific Legal Foundation and the Washington Legal Foundation. The brief of the latter indicated clearly the close connection it saw between free enterprise capitalism and opposition to Richmond's plan: 'The widespread use of minority set-asides . . . has produced a wealth of evidence that these programmes have deleterious effects on the economy and society. In addition, they are morally repugnant because they are designed to prefer certain members of society simply because of the colour of their skin. In a free, competitive, colour-blind society, there should be equality of opportunity, not equality of results.'[171] *Croson* was thus seen as a case involving substantial self-interest, as well as issues of great policy and principle.

The facts of the case were better suited to the anti-affirmative action cause, rather than its proponents: the set-asides were large, bore no direct relationship to any specifically identified level of past discrimination and the white contractor who filed the suit had clearly gone to some lengths to comply with the plan's demands. They also illustrate the way in which petty, everyday conflicts can, through the judicial process, lead to policy making of the utmost importance.

In 1983 Richmond had adopted its Minority Business Utilisation Plan. It required that 30 per cent of the dollar value of each prime city contract should go to Minority Business Enterprises, defined as those with majority ownership of blacks, Spanish-speakers, Orientals, Indians, Eskimos or Aleuts. Out-of-state businesses were entitled to benefit. Exceptions to the requirement were permitted where it could be shown that insufficient MBEs were available or willing to particpate in any contract. The plan was declared to be remedial in purpose and designed to promote wider participation by MBEs in public construction work. Public hearings on the plan had established that, between 1978 and 1983, only 0.67 per cent of the city's prime construction contracts had gone to MBEs, despite the fact that the population of Richmond was 50 per cent black. It was further established that the local contractors' associations had virtually no minority members. Testimony, though not documented evidence, was also given that there was widespread discrimination against minorities in the local construction industry.

The J. A. Croson Co., a non-minority firm, was the only bidder for a contract to equip the city's jails with stainless steel urinals and water closets. However, despite contacting several minority subcontractors, the company could not find one to supply the basic materials. It therefore applied for a waiver to the MBE requirements. At this point a minority firm indicated it could supply the materials but only at a price which would raise the overall cost of the contract by $7,663.16. Croson asked the city for permission to raise his bid by that sum. This was refused and the City further decided to re-bid the contract. Croson then asked for an appeal hearing on the waiver denial, but was told that there was no appeal from a waiver decision. Croson filed suit in a federal District Court, claiming that the plan violated the Equal Protection Clause of the Fourteenth Amendment. The District Court upheld the plan, as did the federal Circuit Court on appeal. When it first came to the Supreme Court, the Justices remanded the case back to the Circuit

Court for reconsideration in the light of their decision in *Wygant*. The Circuit Court thereupon declared the plan unconstitutional, because there was insufficient documented evidence of past discrimination by the city. It further held that the plan was not narrowly tailored, because the figure of 30 per cent bore no reasonable relationship to the number of local minority subcontractors or any other relevant number. The city then appealed the issue back to the Supreme Court.

The Justices voted six-to-three to affirm the Circuit Court's ruling, although yet again the Court's opinion, that of Justice O'Connor, could not command a majority for all of its important aspects. Two of the Justices who did not go along wholly with O'Connor were Kennedy and Scalia and they took positions even more hostile to affirmative action than she did.[172] As a result, *Croson* was a very ominous decision for those who saw affirmative action as a major weapon in the war against the legacies of racial discrimination in the United States. Justice O'Connor insisted once again on the application of strict scrutiny to all affirmative action plans which included race preferences:

> 'Classifications based on race carry a danger of stigmatic harm. Unless they are strictly reserved for remedial settings, they may in fact promote notions of racial inferiority and lead to a politics of racial hostility . . . Indeed, the purpose of strict scrutiny is to "smoke out" illegitimate uses of race by assuring that the legislative body is pursuing a goal important enough to warrant the use of a highly suspect tool.'[173]

It may be that Justice O'Connor was suspicious of the motives behind this particular plan, because she discussed at some length the fact that blacks effectively constituted the political majority in Richmond: 50 per cent of the city's population was black, as were five of the nine-person city council which had adopted the plan.[174] Although she made no assertions to the effect, she did implicitly raise the question that this could be an example of a political majority crudely pursuing racial patronage.

The Richmond plan, she went on, failed both major aspects of the strict scrutiny test. The city did not have a compelling interest in promoting minority businesses, because there was no evidence on the record to show that it was seeking to remedy either its own past discrimination or discrimination by others within its jurisdiction. Nor was the figure of 30 per cent narrowly tailored. The fact that there is a much lower percentage of minority subcontractors in Richmond than the percentage of minority individuals in the general population does not prove discrimination in the construction industry: neither does the fact that there are few minority members of contractors' associations.

Such a disparity could be explained by minorities' career choices or discrimination in the education system.[175]

The city relied in part on the evidence of nationwide discrimination in the construction industry that had buttressed the set-asides established by Congress in 1977 and which had been upheld by the Court in *Fullilove*. Justice O'Connor considered the probative value of such findings for the existence of discrimination in Richmond to be of little value: 'If all a state or local government need do is find a congressional report on the subject to enact a set-aside programme, the constraints of the Equal Protection Clause will, in effect, have been rendered a nullity.'[176] Without concrete evidence of local discrimination, Richmond was reliant upon societal discrimination to justify a 'rigid racial preference'. If this were allowed, she said, every disadvantaged group could claim 'remedial relief' and 'The dream of a nation of equal citizens in a society where race is irrelevant to personal opportunity and achievement would be lost in a mosaic of shifting preferences based on inherently unmeasurable claims of past wrongs.'[177]

Justice Scalia's concurring opinion, which endorsed victim-specificity, also dwelt on the social and political harm caused by race preferences of the type adopted by Richmond:

> The relevant proposition is not that it was blacks, or Jews, or Irish who were discriminated against, but that it was individual men and women, 'created equal', who were discriminated against. And the relevant resolve is that it should never happen again. Racial preferences appear to 'even the score' (in some small degree) only if one embraces the proposition that our society is appropriately viewed as divided into races, making it right that an injustice rendered in the past to a black man should be compensated for by discriminating against a white. Nothing is worth that embrace.[178]

This vision of a future nightmare of racial politics cut no ice with the dissenters, who recalled the fact that Richmond was a Southern city with a long history of racial politics. Justice Marshall wrote: 'I find deep irony in second-guessing Richmond's judgement on this point. As much as any municipality in the United States, Richmond knows what racial discrimination is; a century of decisions by this and other federal courts has richly documented the city's disgraceful history of public and private discrimination.'[179] Marshall also pointed to the congressional findings of nationwide discrimination in the construction industry, something from which Richmond, of all cities, could not be supposed immune. 'In sum, to suggest that the facts on which Richmond has relied do not provide a sound basis for its finding of past racial discrimination simply blinks credibility.'[180]

Towards the end of his opinion, Justice Marshall returned to the familiar battle over strict scrutiny that had been waged ever since *Bakke*. He deplored the fact that in *Croson*, for the first time ever, a majority on the Court endorsed strict scrutiny:

> In concluding that remedial classifications warrant no different standard of review under the Constitution than the most brutal and repugnant forms of state-sponsored racism, a majority of this Court signals that it regards racial discrimination as largely a phenomenon of the past, and that government bodies need no longer preoccupy themselves with rectifying racial injustice. I, however, do not believe that this nation is anywhere close to eradicating racial discrimination or its vestiges. In constitutionalising its wishful thinking, the majority today does a grave disservice not only to those victims of past discrimination in this Nation whom government has sought to assist, but also to this Court's long tradition of approaching issues of race with the utmost sensitivity.[181]

Justice Blackmun's dissent struck a similar theme, though perhaps less in anger than Marshall and more in bewilderment:

> I never thought that I would live to see the day when the city of Richmond, Virginia, the cradle of the Old Confederacy, sought on its own . . . to lessen the impact of persistent discrimination . . . Yet this Court, the supposed bastion of equality, strikes down Richmond's efforts as though discrimination had never existed or was not demonstrated in this particular litigation. Justice Marshall convincingly demonstrates the fallacy and shallowness of that approach.[182]

Marshall and Blackmun were talking about more than a defeat for affirmative action: they were signalling the end of a judicial era in which the Supreme Court had led the way in overcoming the legacy of slavery and racial segregation in the United States. In *Croson*, the Court clearly established that, in law, that past was to be put on a par with present disadvantages experienced by members of the white majority. To make such a policy in a case involving a city whose entire history was permeated with racism was indeed a bitter pill to swallow for a lifelong champion of civil rights such as Thurgood Marshall.

Indifference to racial discrimination against minorities is not, however, the explanation of the *Croson* decision.[183] Rather, a majority of the Justices insisted that judicial interpretation of the Constitution proceed along similar lines to any other legal adjudication: most important of all, there must be precise, documented evidence of the 'crime' and the 'punishment' must fit the crime. No one could seriously be disposed to believe that the construction industry in Richmond, like virtually everything else in the city, has been free of discrimination. What might be called the 'circumstantial evidence' is simply too strong

164   RAW JUDICIAL POWER?

and, for a policy-making body, sufficient to justify remedial action. But it is precisely a major goal of conservatives in the United States to have the Supreme Court behave far more like a legal body than it has in the post-*Brown* era.

That said, however, the *Croson* majority must have been aware that their demands for precise proof of local discrimination to justify local remedial measures would impose a substantially increased barrier to the availability of affirmative action. For the second major affirmative action case of 1989, *Wards Cove*, demonstrated just how difficult meeting that burden of proof could be.

The Wards Cove Packing Co. operated a fish canning business in remote areas of Alaska. Its work-force appeared to be racially segregated: those who worked in the low-paid, unskilled jobs in the cannery itself were overwhelmingly non-white, mainly Filipinos, recruited through a particular employment agency, and Alaskan natives. Those who worked in the better-paid, non-cannery jobs were overwhelmingly white. The two work-forces were recruited by separate processes and their mess halls and dormitories were quite separate. In his dissent, Justice Stevens likened arrangements to a plantation system.[184] In 1974, Atonio and some other cannery workers brought suit alleging that these employment practices violated Title VII of the Civil Rights Act of 1964. After protracted legislation, a federal Court of Appeal found in 1987 that they had established a prima facie case of disparate impact and the company now had the burden of demonstrating that its practices were required by business necessity. The company appealed the decision to the Supreme Court.

The Justices split five-four to reverse.[185] The heart of the matter was the statistical proof of disparate impact. The Appeals Court had relied on a comparison of the racial make-up of the cannery and non-cannery work-forces. The majority, however, speaking through Justice White, found this comparison utterly irrelevant:

> Measuring alleged discrimination in the selection of accountants, managers, boat captains, electricians, doctors and engineers ... by comparing the number of non-whites occupying these jobs to the number of non-whites filling cannery positions is nonsensical. If the absence of minorities holding such positions is due to a dearth of non-white applicants (for reasons that are not the petitioners' fault), petitioners' selection methods or employment practices cannot be said to have a 'disparate impact' on non-whites.[186]

A more appropriate comparison, he concluded, would be that of the percentage of qualified applicants hired from each racial group.[187]

As a consequence of that finding, White shifted the burden of proof from the employer to the employees: the latter, moreover, would have to demonstrate not merely that there was actually a disparate impact caused by the company's practices in general, but also show '. . . that each challenged practice has a significantly disparate impact on employment opportunities for whites and non-whites.'[188]

As Justice Blackmun pointed out in dissent, this departed from the *Griggs* decision on disparate impact and made it far more difficult, if not impossible, for employees to make their case.[189] Instead of employers having to justify racial disparities in their work-force, employees must now offer conclusive proof that such disparities are caused by the employer's practices. He concluded with a decidedly barbed comment: 'One wonders whether the majority still believes that race discrimination – or, more accurately, race discrimination against non-whites – is a problem in our society, or even remembers that it ever was.'[190] It seems clear, at least, that the Court's majority will, in the absence of proof of discriminatory intent, operate a strong presumption in favour of the statutory and constitutional validity of employers' hiring and promotion practices.

The third affirmative action case of 1989 dealt a different kind of blow to affirmative action. In *Martin v. Wilks*, the *Wards Cove* majority took a decision that seriously weakened the force of consent decrees, those voluntary agreements between employers and employee representatives to adopt affirmative action plans. The case began in Birmingham, Alabama, in 1974, when the NAACP and several black firefighters filed a class action suit against the city and the Jefferson County Personnel Board. They alleged racial discrimination in hiring and promotion decisions in a variety of public service jobs. Before judgement, however, consent decrees were agreed and entered in a federal District Court. The decrees set numerical goals for the hiring and promotion of blacks in the fire department. When the District Court held hearings on the decrees the Birmingham Firefighters Association (BFA) appeared as *amicus curiae* and objected to the decrees. After the hearings were over, but before the Court had finally approved the decrees, the BFA asked to be allowed to become a party to the suit, alleging that the decrees discriminated against its members. This request was denied as 'untimely', whereupon seven individual white firefighters, all members of the BFA, sought an injunction against enforcement of the decrees. That too was denied and the District Court's decisions were both upheld by the Court of Appeals.

At this point, a new group of white firefighters, including Wilks, filed a suit claiming that the decrees violated their equal protection rights, because they had been denied promotion in favour of less qualified black firefighters. A group of black firefighters, including Martin, were then given permission to intervene to defend the decrees. The District Court decided that since the promotions in question had been part of a consent decree, they could not be challenged as discriminatory. On appeal, however, that decision was overturned, because Wilks had not been a party to those consent decrees. The Supreme Court upheld that decision.

The principal issue at stake was a highly technical one: at what stage in litigation do non-parties who are affected by it lose their right to challenge the consent decree at issue? Writing for the dissenters, Justice Stevens argued that Wilks had the opportunity to join the suit before final judgement, chose not to do so and now had no right to appeal the District Court's decision.[191] The fact that Wilks and others may be harmed by that decision does not alter things: 'Just as white employees in the past were innocent beneficiaries of illegal discriminatory practices, so it is inevitable that some of the white employees will be innocent victims who must share some of the burdens resulting from the redress of past wrongs.'[192]

The majority, however, held that 'A voluntary agreement in the form of a consent decree between one group of employees and their employer cannot possibly "settle", voluntarily or otherwise, the con- flicting claims of another group of employees who do not join in that agreement.'[193] In response to the dissent's claim that this will lead to endless relitigation on consent decrees by groups affected by them, Chief Justice Rehnquist said that the parties to the consent decree could compulsorily join all affected groups to the original litigation. In other words, it was the responsibility of the parties to the consent decree, not those affected by it, to ensure the participation of all affected groups. This, of course, puts a considerable burden on parties to a consent decree, but, said Rehnquist, they are better positioned to bear it than affected groups who may not even be aware of the litigation taking place.[194]

In policy terms, the *Wilks* decision simply made final consent decrees more difficult to achieve, thus undermining one of the main weapons in the affirmative action arsenal. And along with the other 1989 decisions, it threatened to narrow the scope for affirmative action quite drastically. The decisions were interpreted as a clear victory for the Reaganite agenda on civil rights: under a heading of 'Supreme Court Ruling Lengthens Reagan Shadow', Linda Greenhouse wrote that the decisions '. . . dispelled much of any remaining doubt about whether former President Ronald Reagan accomplished his goal of moving the Court in a more conservative direction on civil rights.'[195] Not surprisingly, then, there was a sharp response from the pro-affirmative action forces in Congress and, as a result, a major political battle with Reagan's successor, President George Bush.

In February 1990, a new Civil Rights Act was introduced into Congress, with the express intention of overturning *Wards Cove* and *Wilks*, as well as seven other Supreme Court decisions adversely affecting affirmative action in various technical ways.[196] The bill passed relatively quickly and easily through Congress and was sent to President Bush for his signature in October. With mid-term elections imminent, the President would have liked to stamp himself as a supporter of civil rights: but he was determined to defend the Court's decisions in *Wards Cove* and *Wilks* because they bolstered his administration's campaign against 'quotas'. Thus, despite attempts by members of Congress and the administration to find a compromise, the President vetoed the Act on 22 October. In his veto message, he said: 'I deeply regret having to take this action . . . But when our efforts, however well intentioned, result in quotas, equal opportunity is not advanced but thwarted.'[197] Two days later, with eleven Republicans joining fifty-five Democrats, the Senate failed to override the veto by one vote.[198]

Congress responded by introducing the Civil Rights Bill of 1991 on the very first day of the next session, with the Democrats making it their top domestic priority for the year.[199] It attempted to counter President Bush's allegations that the 1990 proposal had been 'a quotas bill', by inserting a clause saying '. . . nothing in the amendments made by this Act shall be construed to require or encourage an employer to adopt hiring or promotion quotas on the basis of race, colour, religion, sex or national origin.'[200] While this would still leave the courts the task of deciding exactly what constitutes a quota, it was a significant concession by Congressional Democrats and a recognition of the political damage that the accusation of supporting quotas can do to them. According to Mary Cooper,

> Republicans' successful exploitation of Bush's 'quota bill' label of last year's civil rights measure during last fall's election campaigns demonstrated a visible shift in public attitudes toward affirmative action. And that shift has come among a key segment of the population – blue-collar and lower-middle-class whites. Because Democrats have long depended upon these groups for their own political support, Republicans are discovering

that they can use the quota issue to drive a wedge into the Democratic Party, dividing the party's black voters from much of its white constituency.[201]

After months of further negotiations, President Bush decided to sign the bill, now being able to claim that he was both a supporter of civil rights and an opponent of quotas. However, a new row erupted when the President issued an executive order in November 1991, which purported to implement the Act but which could reasonably be seen as an attempt to undermine it. The order instructed government agencies that 'Any regulation, rule or enforcement practice, or other aspect of these programmes that mandates, encourages or otherwise involves the use of quotas, preferences, set-asides or similar devices, on the basis of race, colour, religion, sex or national origin, is to be terminated as soon as is legally possible.'[202] On its face, such language would entirely eliminate most forms of affirmative action, including those previously upheld by the Supreme Court. What the outcome will be is not clear at the time of writing, but it does suggest that the political conflict over affirmative action is not about to end with the passage of the 1991 Civil Rights Act.

It would seem that the Supreme Court was by now in effective alliance with a Republican President determined to put an end to race preference and statistical affirmative action. Yet the Court was still capable of producing an occasional surprise, as it did in June, 1990, in the case of *Metro Broadcasting v. FCC*[203] In the interest of promoting broadcast diversity, the Federal Communications Commission gave certain preferences to minority-owned television and radio stations, when awarding licences. When the FCC had moved to reconsider this policy, it had been blocked by a Congressional amendment to the FCC appropriations bill for fiscal 1988, barring the agency from using any of its funds for re-examining or changing its minority preference policies. President Reagan signed the bill, though this, of course, does not mean that he supported it in all its details.[204]

When the preference policies were challenged in the Supreme Court, five of the Justices voted to uphold them.[205] In so doing, they broke new ground by explicitly ruling that in cases of Congressional race-conscious measures, the Justices need not apply strict scrutiny, even if the measures are not remedial.[206] Instead they subscribed to the test, first suggested by Justice Brennan in the *Bakke* case, that such measures need only serve an important governmental interest and be substantially related to the furtherance of that interest. The FCC scheme clearly passed the test, given its long-established mission of broadcast diversity.

Justice O'Connor wrote the main dissent, which took the familiar line of arguing the need for strict scrutiny and a remedial purpose. More dramatic, however, was the dissent of Justice Kennedy, which was joined only by Justice Scalia. Kennedy accused the majority Justices of returning to the reasoning of *Plessy*, the infamous case of 1896 which had upheld the segregation doctrine of 'separate but equal'. In particular, he attacked the notion that strict scrutiny was not required because the FCC measures were supposedly 'benign'. He pointed out that the *Plessy* majority had denied that the segregation law at stake there had a malign purpose and also that the government of South Africa had made similar disclaimers about its apartheid policy. Thus, he argued, 'The history of governmental reliance on race demonstrates that racial policies defended as benign often are not seen that way by the individuals affected by them.'[207] And he concluded: 'I regret that after a century of opinions we interpret the Constitution to do no more than move us from "separate but equal" to "unequal but benign".'[208]

It is hard to see *Metro Broadcasting* lasting long. Already two of the majority Justices have been replaced by Bush nominees: Justices Brennan and Marshall by Justices David Souter and Clarence Thomas. Only one of them needs to join the Republican nominees of the 1980s to nullify its effect and it would be a major surprise if that did not happen, given the motives which led President Bush to nominate them.

The Supreme Court has travelled a confusing and tortuous road on affirmative action. Perhaps this is in part because, unlike abortion, many of the principal initiatives have been taken by other political actors, with the Court never quite achieving a clear vision of where it wanted to go. The Court, however, could not have avoided the issue or the controversy that surrounds it. Both legislative and executive branch policies relied to a considerable extent on the courts to give them precise content and meaning. When, in the 1960s and 1970s, the other branches were urging the Court in the same direction, the Justices were prepared to engage in non-interpretivist activism. However, both the politics and the Supreme Court nominations of the Reagan and Bush presidencies have changed all that. The Court is in alliance with the presidency and is under attack from the Congress, ironically so, since the contemporary Court majority sticks much closer to the original intent behind the Civil Rights Act of 1964 than it did earlier.

As long as that political configuration remains in operation, the Court will continue to reduce the scope for affirmative action. If, on the other hand, the Democrats regain control of the White House, the Court might find itself in the same predicament as the conservative Court of the 1930s, though with one intriguing difference: on affirmative action, at least, it would be the only branch of the federal government whose position was supported by public opinion. Whether that support alone would be sufficient political resource for the Court is impossible to say.

Notes

1 W. B. Reynolds, 'The Reagan administration's civil rights policy: the challenge for the future', *Vanderbilt Law Review*, XLII, 1989, pp. 993–1001, 994.

2 B. Schwartz, *Behind Bakke: Affirmative Action and the Supreme Court*, New York, 1988, p. 13; M. Urofsky, *A Conflict of Rights: The Supreme Court and Affirmative Action*, New York, 1991, pp. 16–17.

3 *Regents of the University of California v. Bakke*, 438 US 265, 412 (1978).

4 *Ibid.*, p. 17.

5 D. Nieman, *Promises To Keep: African Americans and the Constitutional Order, 1776 to the Present*, New York, 1991, p. 205.

6 N. Glazer, *Affirmative Discrimination: Ethnic Inequality and Public Policy* (rev. ed.), Cambridge, Mass., 1987, pp. vii–xi.

7 T. Sowell, *Civil Rights: Rhetoric or Reality*, New York, 1984, p. 41.

8 The *prima facie* case was made when the minority hiring rate was 80 per cent or less of the non-minority rate. R. Maidment, 'The US Supreme Court and affirmative action: the cases of Bakke, Weber and Fullilove', *Journal of American Studies*, XV, 1981, pp. 341–56, 344.

9 Sowell, *op. cit.*, p. 41.

10 Glazer, *op. cit.*, p. xi.

11 Nieman, op. cit., p. 206.

12 I use this term with a neutral intention to distinguish between policies which involve statistical analysis and remedies from those which do not, such as recruitment drives aimed at minorities: the latter type of affirmative action is not controversial or a matter of legal dispute.

13 D. Rose, 'Twenty-five years later: where do we stand on equal employment opportunity law enforcement', *Vanderbilt Law Review*, XLII, 1989, pp. 1121–82, 1143.

14 Bork, *The Tempting of America*, p. 106.

15 163 US 537, 559 (1896).

16 Maidment, *op. cit.*, pp. 352–3.

17 Fried, *op. cit.*, p. 91.

18 Glazer, *op. cit.*, p. 45.

19 G. Bryner, 'Affirmative action: minority rights or reverse discrimination', in Tatalovich and Daynes, *op. cit.*, p. 148.

20 Quoted in Urofsky, op. cit., p. 24.

21 For useful summaries of the range of arguments for and against affirmative action, see Nieman, *op. cit.*, pp. 206–13; and Urofsky, *op. cit.*, pp. 15–35.

22 *Swann v. Charlotte-Mecklenburg Bd. of Education*, 402 US 1 (1971) and *Keyes v. School District No. 1, Denver*, 413 US 189 (1973), respectively.

23 In fact, when the Court faced the issue of whether a busing scheme could incorporate the schools of a district which was held to be innocent of past discriminatory practice, it ruled against the scheme on equal protection grounds, *Milliken v. Bradley*, 418 US 717

(1974).

24 Bryner, *op. cit.*, p. 150.
25 401 US 424 (1971).
26 *Ibid.*, p. 431.
27 D. Days, 'The Court's response to the Reagan civil rights agenda', *Vanderbilt Law Review*, XLII, 1989, pp. 1003–16, 1006.
28 W. Eskridge, 'Reneging on history? Playing the Court/Congress/President civil rights game', *California Law Review*, LXXIX, 1991, pp. 613–84, 623.
29 416 US 312 (1974).
30 438 US 265 (1978).
31 416 US 312, 317.
32 *Ibid.*, p. 350.
33 J. Wilkinson, *From Brown To Bakke: The Supreme Court and School Integration, 1954–78*, Oxford, 1979, p. 258.
34 J. Dreyfuss and C. Lawrence, *The Bakke Case: The Politics of Inequality*, New York, 1979, p. 35.
35 *Ibid.*, pp. 105–7. For a more detailed and decidedly unsympathetic analysis of the position taken by Jewish groups in affirmative action cases, see D. Bishop, 'The affirmative action cases: *Bakke, Weber*, and *Fullilove*', *Journal of Negro History*, LXVII, 1982, pp. 229–44.
36 416 US 312, 331.
37 Woodward and Armstrong report that in *DeFunis*, 'At first, all nine Justices leaned toward holding that such fixed racial quotas were unconstitutional.', *op. cit*, p. 282. They do not, however, explain how Brennan, White and Marshall came to see things differently.
38 Dreyfuss and Lawrence, *op. cit.*, p. 19.
39 *Ibid.*, p. 20.
40 *Ibid.*, p. 75.
41 438 US 265, 276–7.
42 Dreyfuss and Lawrence, *op. cit.*, p. 44.
43 *Ibid.*, p. 60.
44 *Ibid.*, p. 69.
45 *Ibid.*, p. 90; Wilkinson, *op. cit.*, pp. 259–60.
46 Wilkinson, *op. cit.*, p. 260. As noted in the previous Chapter, however, this record was beaten in the *Webster* case, n. 99.
47 Schwartz, *op. cit.*, p. 46.
48 Dreyfuss and Lawrence, *op. cit.*, p. 162.
49 *Ibid.*, p. 164.
50 See, for example, L. Caplan, *The Tenth Justice: The Solicitor General and the Rule of Law*, New York, 1987.
51 *Ibid.*, p. 43. Easterbrook is a staunch conservative who, in 1985, was made a Federal Court of Appeals Judge by President Reagan.
52 Dreyfuss and Lawrence, *op. cit.*, p. 166.
53 Caplan, *op. cit.*, p. 43.
54 *Ibid.*, p. 44.
55 Dreyfuss and Lawrence, *op. cit.*, p. 169; Caplan, *op. cit.*, p. 47. It seems that Attorney-General Griffin Bell decided to try to insulate McCree from political interference by not passing on to him the heated arguments taking place in the White House. On the other hand, the Justices of the Supreme Court were themselves aware, and disturbed, by the press reports of the brief-drafting process which kept being leaked, so McCree must have at least known the broad outlines of the controversy: Caplan, pp. 45–7; Schwartz, p. 46.
56 Bishop, *op. cit.*, pp. 232–3.
57 Wilkinson, *op. cit.*, p. 298.

58 Justices White, Marshall and Blackmun concurred in Brennan's opinion.
59 Chief Justice Burger and Justices Stewart and Rehnquist concurred in Stevens' opinion.
60 The University of California is a subdivision of the state.
61 Maidment, *op. cit.*, pp. 352–4.
62 438 US 265, 375.
63 *Ibid.*, p. 359. This is an 'intermediate' level of review, at a point mid-way between strict scrutiny and the 'rationality' test. The latter requires only that the legislation at issue pursues a legitimate governmental interest and is rationally related to that interest. In practice, all legislation bar the egregiously unconstitutional can survive rationality review.
64 *Ibid.*, p. 375.
65 *Ibid.*, p. 379.
66 *Ibid.*, p. 412.
67 *Ibid.*, p. 414.
68 Schwartz, *op. cit.*, p. 60. Powell was referring to the Court's disposition of *DeFunis* for mootness.
69 *Bakke*, pp. 283–4.
70 *Ibid.*, pp. 289–90.
71 *Ibid.*, pp. 294–5.
72 *Ibid.*, p. 295.
73 *Ibid.*, p. 310.
74 K. Sullivan, 'Sins of discrimination: last term's affirmative action cases', *Harvard Law Review*, C, 1986, pp. 78–98.
75 *Ibid.*, p. 98.
76 *Bakke*, op. cit., p. 314.
77 *Ibid.*, p. 315.
78 Schwarz, op. cit., p. 96.
79 *Ibid.*, p. 97.
80 *Bakke*, p. 317.
81 *Ibid.*, p. 320.
82 *Ibid.*, pp. 318–9.
83 Dreyfuss and Lawrence, *op. cit.*, pp. 212–3.
84 Blasi, op. cit., p. 128.
85 Urofsky, op. cit., p. 46.
86 Bryner, op. cit., p. 160.
87 Eskridge, op. cit., p. 624.
88 Respectively, 443 US 193; and 448 US 448.
89 The majority consisted of Justices Brennan, Stewart, White, Marshall and Blackmun. Chief Justice Burger and Justice Rehnquist dissented; Justices Powell and Stevens did not participate.
90 None the less, the statistical evidence pointed strongly to just such a past: less than 2 per cent of its skilled work-force was black, compared to 15 per cent of its unskilled work-force and a Gramercy area work-force that was 39 per cent black. *Weber*, p. 210. Furthermore, the OFCC had made a finding that the work-force was racially imbalanced and brought pressure on Kaiser Aluminum to do something about it: Maidment, *op. cit.*, p. 351.
91 Since Kaiser Aluminum was a private corporation, not a state agency, there was no Fourteenth Amendment issue at stake.
92 *Weber*, pp. 216–7.
93 *Ibid.*, p. 216.
94 *Ibid.*, p. 240.
95 *Ibid.*, p. 243.
96 *Ibid.*, p. 244.

97 *Ibid.*, p. 222. The latter reference is to the venerated former Justice, Oliver Wendell Holmes.
98 *Ibid.*, p. 201.
99 *Ibid.*, p. 204. Justice Brennan avoided responding to Burger's question, 'But how are judges supposed to ascertain the purpose of a statute except through the words Congress used and the legislative history of the statute's evolution?', *Ibid.*, p. 217.
100 *Ibid.*, p. 209.
101 *Ibid.*, p. 216.
102 *Fullilove*, p. 484.
103 Fried, *op. cit.*, pp. 99–100.
104 *Ibid.*, pp. 100–1.
105 Bryner, *op. cit.*, p. 161.
106 Fried, *op. cit.*, p. 100.
107 Rose, *op. cit.*, pp. 1153–4.
108 *Ibid.*, p. 1159.
109 467 US 561 (1984).
110 *Ibid.*, pp. 106–7.
111 *Ibid.*, p. 108.
112 *Stotts*, pp. 565–7.
113 *Ibid.*, pp. 572–3.
114 *Ibid.*, p. 621.
115 *Ibid.*, pp. 578–9.
116 *Ibid.*, pp. 587–8.
117 Fried, *op. cit.*, p. 109.
118 Sullivan, op. cit., p. 85.
119 *Teamsters v. US*, 431 US 324 (1977).
120 'The Supreme Court, 1983 Term', *Harvard Law Review*, IIC, 1984, pp. , 273.
121 *Ibid.*, p. 277.
122 Fried, *op. cit.*, p. 109.
123 *Ibid.*, p. 110.
124 Respectively, 476 US 267 (1986); 478 US 421 (1986); 478 US 501 (1986).
125 Fried, *op. cit.*, p. 110.
126 Brief For The United States As Amicus Curiae Supporting Petitioners, *Wygant v. Jackson Board of Education, Transcripts of Records and Briefs*, XXXIX, 1985, US Supreme Court Library, p. 23.
127 *Ibid.*, p. 26.
128 *Ibid.*, XXXIX–XL.
129 Brief Amicus Curiae For The NAACP Legal Defence and Educational Fund, *Wygant v. Jackson, Transcripts of Records and Briefs*, XL, 1985, US Supreme Court Library, pp. 24–5. The authors cited by Fried were Thomas Sowell and Richard Posner, both critics of affirmative action.
130 *Ibid.*, p. 37.
131 The majority Justices were Chief Justice Burger and Justices Powell, Rehnquist, O'Connor and White. Justice White did not join Justice Powell's plurality opinion at all and Justice O'Connor joined it only in part. Justice Marshall wrote the dissenting opinion on behalf of himself and Justices Brennan and Blackmun, but Justice Stevens did not join it, filing a separate dissent.
132 *Wygant*, p. 274.
133 *Ibid.*, p. 276.
134 *Ibid.*, p. 278.
135 *Ibid.*, pp. 280–1.
136 *Ibid.*, pp. 282–3.
137 Justice White's concurrence in the judgement seemed to be based entirely on his agreement with this distinction between lay-offs and hirings, yet he, at best, only hints at

some constitutional basis for it: 'Whatever the legitimacy of hiring goals or quotas may be, the discharge of white teachers to make room for blacks, none of whom has been shown to be a victim of any racial discrimination, is quite a different matter. I cannot believe that in order to integrate a work force, it would be permissible to discharge whites and hire blacks until the latter comprised a suitable percentage of the workforce. None of our cases suggest that this would be permissible under the Equal Protection Clause. Indeed, our cases look quite the other way. The layoff policy in this case – laying off whites who would otherwise be retained in order to keep blacks on the job – has the same effect and is equally violative of the Equal Protection Clause.', p. 295. Justice White's reasoning is clever, but is not really founded in the Constitution: he takes a more extreme example of race preference, hypothesises that it would be unconstitutional, analogises the present case to it and hypothesises the same conclusion.

138 Fried, *op. cit.*, p. 113.
139 *Wygant*, p. 287. Fried concedes that '. . . victim specificity was rejected.' *op. cit.*, p. 114.
140 *Wygant*, p. 302.
141 *Ibid.*, p. 307.
142 *Ibid.*, pp. 307–8.
143 *Ibid.*, p. 309.
144 *Ibid.*, p. 281.
145 *International Herald Tribune*, Wednesday, 21 May 1986, p. 3.
146 *Ibid.*
147 *International Herald Tribune*, Monday, 26 May 1986, p. 6.
148 *Ibid.*
149 The voting in *Sheet Metal Workers* was complicated. Brennan, Marshall, Blackmun and Stevens were together on all the main issues. Justice Powell concurred in most respects, including that of rejecting victim specificity. Justice White also agreed on that issue, but dissented because he believed that the District Court had imposed a rigid quota. Justice O'Connor concurred on several issues, but not that of victim specificity: although she had rejected it in *Wygant*, that case had involved the Equal Protection Clause. Here she thought Section 706(g) of the Civil Rights Act did require victim specificity, as laid down in *Stotts*.
150 Charles Fried acknowledges this, but implies he was duty-bound to argue for 'victim specificity' after the Justice Department's victory in *Stotts*, *op. cit.*, pp. 110–11. The *Cleveland* case turned on the narrow technical question of whether an affirmative action consent decree should be treated as a court order. If so, it fell under Section 706(g) of Title VII of the Civil Rights Act of 1964, which effectively banned preferential pro-motions, except for identified victims of discrimination. Justice Brennan's majority opinion argued that consent decrees were not like court orders, because in the former, obligations were created voluntarily by the two parties: 478 US 501, 522–3.
151 478 US 421, p. 427.
152 *Ibid.*, p. 434.
153 *Ibid.*, p. 440. See also n. 149, *supra*.
154 *Ibid.*, p. 446.
155 *Ibid.*, p. 447. Justice Brennan's view here seems somewhat at odds with the position he argued in the *Weber* case, where he disregarded plain language where it seemed to him to conflict with the legislative purpose he discerned.
156 *Ibid.*, p. 474.
157 *Supra*, n. 149.
158 *International Herald Tribune*, 3 July 1986, p. 1.
159 *International Herald Tribune*, 4 July 1986, p. 3.
160 *Ibid.*, p. 1.
161 Fried, *op. cit.*, p. 117.
162 *Ibid.*, p. 118.
163 *Ibid.*, p. 119.

164 488 US 469 (1989).
165 Fried, *op. cit.*, p. 119.
166 490 US 642 (1989).
167 490 US 755 (1989).
168 *Newsweek*, 6 February 1989, pp. 32–3.
169 *Richmond v. Croson, Transcripts of Records and Briefs*, XXX–XXXI, 1988. The states who filed briefs either individually or jointly were Maryland, Michigan, New York, California, Connecticut, Illinois, Massachusetts, Minnesota, New Jersey, Ohio, Oregon, Rhode Island, South Carolina, Washington, West Virginia, Wisconsin, Wyoming. The District of Columbia also filed.
170 *Ibid.*
171 *Ibid.*, XXXI, Brief of the Washington Legal Foundation *et al.*, p. 25.
172 As in most of the affirmative action cases, the voting pattern of the Justices was complex: Justice O'Connor's opinion was joined in all parts by Chief Justice Rehnquist and Justice White. Justice Stevens joined much of her opinion, though not that part which required strict scrutiny. Justice Kennedy joined most of her opinion, though not that part which emphasised the differential powers of federal and local government in regard to the Equal Protection Clause. His separate concurring opinion also indicated a strong sympathy for Justice Scalia's views. Scalia did not join O'Connor's opinion at all, but rather stated views almost identical to those put by Fried and Reynolds on behalf of the administration in *Wygant*. The three dissenters were Justices Marshall, Brennan and Blackmun.
173 *Croson*, p. 493.
174 *Ibid.*, pp. 494–6.
175 *Ibid.*, pp. 500–3.
176 *Ibid.* p. 504.
177 *Ibid.*, pp. 505–6.
178 *Ibid.*, p. 528.
179 *Ibid.*, p. 529.
180 *Ibid.*, p. 541.
181 *Ibid.*, pp. 552–3.
182 *Ibid.*, p. 561.
183 The opinions of O'Connor, Stevens and White, for example, are replete with acknowledgements of the country's disgraceful racist past and their support for many forms of affirmative action.
184 *Wards Cove*, n. 4, p. 663.
185 Justice White wrote for the majority, with his opinion joined by Chief Justice Rehnquist and Justices O'Connor, Scalia and Kennedy. The dissenters were Justices Blackmun, Brennan, Stevens and Marshall.
186 *Wards Cove*, pp. 651–2.
187 *Ibid.*, p. 653.
188 *Ibid.*, p. 657.
189 *Ibid.*, p. 662.
190 *Ibid.*, p. 662.
191 *Wilks*, pp. 769–70.
192 *Ibid.*, p. 792.
193 *Ibid.*, p. 768.
194 *Ibid.*, p. 767.
195 *International Herald Tribune*, 8 June 1989, p. 3.
196 The other cases were *Price Waterhouse v. Hopkins*, 490 US 228 (1989); *Patterson v. McClean Credit Union*, 491 US 164 (1989); *Lorance v. AT&T Technologies*, 490 US 900 (1989); *Flight Attendants v. Zipes*, 491 US 754 (1989); *Crawford Fitting Co. v. Gibbons*, 482 US 437 (1987); *Evans v. Jeff D.*, 475 US 717 (1986); *Library of Congress v. Shaw*, 478 US 310 (1985): Eskridge, *op. cit.*, p. 613.

197 M. Cooper, 'Racial quotas', *CQ Researcher*, 17 May 1991, pp. 279–95, 290.
198 Eskridge, *op. cit.*, p. 641, fn. 191.
199 Cooper, *op. cit.*, pp. 290–1.
200 *Ibid.*, p. 291.
201 *Ibid.*
202 *The Guardian*, 22 November 1991, p. 12.
203 497 US – , 111 L Ed 2d 445, 110 S Ct – (1990).
204 An amendment to a complex bill with numerous clauses can only be vetoed by rejecting the entire bill. If much of the bill is desirable, the President often swallows his objection to a particular amendment.
205 Justices Brennan, White, Marshall, Blackmun and Stevens.
206 *Metro Broadcasting*, pp. 462–3.
207 *Ibid.*, p. 508.
208 *Ibid.*, p. 510.

Six—Gender equality

> Despite the enlightened emancipation of women from the restrictions and
> protections of bygone years, and their entry into many parts of community
> life formerly considered to be reserved to men, woman is still regarded as
> the centre of home and family life. We cannot say that it is constitutionally
> impermissible for a State, acting in pursuit of the general welfare, to
> conclude that a woman should be relieved from the civic duty of jury service
> unless she herself determines that such service is consistent with her own
> special responsibilities.[1]

Gwendolyne Hoyt was convicted of the second degree murder of her
husband by an all-male jury in Florida. She protested that the state's
law, which automatically placed men on the jury register but required
women to come forward voluntarily, violated her equal protection
rights under the Fourteenth Amendment. In a unanimous decision,
the Supreme Court rejected her claim, citing a woman's special responsibility for home and family as a reasonable basis for distinguishing
between the sexes in respect of jury service.

Those unfamiliar with the case may well suspect that it dates from
long ago: in fact, the year was 1961 and the Justices were those of the
Warren Court, at the mid-point of their judicial trail-blazing on behalf
of civil liberties. Admittedly Chief Justice Warren and Justices Black
and Douglas entered a concurring opinion, specifying that they only
voted to sustain the law because there was no evidence that Florida was
not making a genuine effort to recruit women for jury service. However, they were surprisingly lenient in this conclusion, given that the
record showed that, of some 46,000 women registered to vote in the
county concerned, just 220 had volunteered for jury service.[2]

The Warren Court, then, for all its sensitivity to other forms of
discrimination, simply reflected the conventional wisdom of the time:
that distinctions in law based on sex were reasonable and natural, given
the biological – and therefore, it was held, social – differences between
women and men. Yet, within a few short years of the *Hoyt* decision, a
new wave of feminist political agitation smashed the traditional consensus on gender roles and relations and this in turn led the Burger

Court into a new minefield of judicial policy making.

In some respects, developments in gender politics in the 1960s appeared to make the Supreme Court's task relatively straightforward. Both the elected branches of the federal government had addressed the issue of sex discrimination and significant legislation had resulted. In 1963, for example, the Equal Pay Act was passed, forbidding employers from paying women less than men for doing the same job. The following year, Title VII of the Civil Rights Act banned sex discrimination in employment, albeit as a result of a conservative wrecking amendment which backfired.[3] The Equal Employment Opportunity Act of 1972 extended Title VII coverage to public employees and in the intervening years, President Johnson had issued a series of Executive Orders requiring employers on federal contracts to take affirmative action to eliminate discriminatory practices.[4]

Confirmation that there was a legislative tide running in favour of the elimination of at least the most blatant sex discrimination came with the resuscitation of the Equal Rights Amendment. When first introduced in 1923, the proposed Amendment to the Constitution read as follows: 'Men and women shall have equal rights throughout the United States and in every place subject to its jurisdiction. Congress shall have power to enforce this article by appropriate legislation.'[5] Despite its rhetorical fit with the core American values of formal equality and individualism, it languished for almost fifty years, although without disappearing completely from the political agenda. Thus the Republican Party included support for the ERA in its party platform for the first time in 1940 and the Democratic Party did likewise in 1944.[6]

However, while using the ERA to appeal to women voters proved irresistible to the major parties, getting legislative action on it was much more difficult. Apart from traditionalists who had little sympathy with the values underpinning the ERA, the most serious opposition came from politically active women in the labour union movement. Such women had long fought for 'protective legislation' which, for example, placed limits on the number of hours women could be required to work, barred them from some forms of night work and the lifting of heavy weights. While protective legislation breached the principle of formal equality, it was argued, it took into account the realities of women's place in the labour market, including the fact that they had less bargaining power than men. The result was that the women's movement was seriously divided over the best route to gender equality: ERA tended to win the support of professional women who were best placed to take advantage of an unprotected labour market, whereas it was opposed by individuals and organisations who represented the interests of the great mass of working women.[7]

The legislative impact of this division became concrete in 1950 and again in 1953, when the ERA was actually passed by the Senate. However, it had been amended by the so-called 'Hayden rider', stipulating that the ERA should '. . . not be construed to impair any rights, benefits, or exemptions now or hereinafter conferred by law upon persons of the female sex.' The rider was a flat contradiction of the main aims of ERA supporters and so they worked, successfully, to kill the whole bill in the House of Representatives.[8]

By the late 1960s, however, this situation had changed significantly. This was partly due to the emergence of a new generation of women's organisations, such as the National Organisation for Women (NOW), which gave passage of the ERA the highest priority. This, in turn, was linked to the growing realisation that, rather than deprive women of existing advantages over men, the ERA would more likely entail the extension of these advantages to men.[9] Long-time opponents of ERA, such as the League of Women Voters, the United Auto Workers and the US Department of Labour, decided to endorse the Amendment and by 1970 prominent women in the Nixon administration were putting the President under pressure to take action on behalf of the ERA.[10]

The head of steam building up behind the ERA appeared irresistible: on 12 October 1971, the House passed by 354 votes to 23 the following version of the Amendment: 'Equality of rights under the law shall not be denied or abridged by the United States or by any State on account of sex.' On 22 March 1972, the Senate passed it by an equally overwhelming margin of 84 votes to 8.[11] With President Nixon also endorsing the Amendment, ratification by the states appeared largely unproblematic.

These legislative developments in the decade following the *Hoyt* decision gave a clear signal to the Supreme Court that the majority of Americans were ready for a new, more enlightened approach to sex discrimination cases, particularly those brought under the Equal Protection Clause of the Fourteenth Amendment. While such an approach could never be justified by the terms of strict intentionalism or, of course, by the Court's precedents, the language of the Equal Protection Clause was at least amenable to decisions requiring greater equality in the treatment of women and men in public policy.

Moreover, the general pattern of interest group participation in

litigation spread to the women's movement in the late 1960s. Perhaps
the most critical development here was the 1971 decision of the
American Civil Liberties Union to establish the Women's Rights
Project (WRP). As Ruth Cowan has argued, sponsorship by the ACLU
brought with it key ingredients of successful interest group activity –
experience, respectability, staff, money and a communications
network.[12] The WRP adopted a long-term strategy of bringing

> . . . a series of cases, each maximally suited to a favourable court response,
> each serving as a foundation for its immediate successor and each taking
> the reasoning one step closer to constitutionally guaranteed sexual equality.
> Instrumental to this strategy was the unstated WRP preference for begin-
> ning each case in a federal district court before a three-judge panel, thereby
> assuring at least the chance of direct appeal to the Supreme Court.[13]

In other words, the WRP was counting on the Court being willing to
extend its penchant for progressive judicial policy making to the new
field of gender equality.

While there seemed to be few political barriers to the Court adopting such a position, closer inspection of the issue of gender equality
suggested the need for judicial caution. Most important of all, there
was no clear consensus, even within the women's movement, of what
gender equality required of the law. The roots of that uncertainty lay in
the old dispute over what differences there actually were between
women and men and the significance that should be attached to those
differences. Some modern feminists sought no more than exactly the
same rights and obligations as men, running from equal educational
and professional opportunities to equal participation in military
service. One prominent figure in this liberal rights movement summar-
ised the philosophy as follows: 'To want equality, a voice in the
mainstream, to be part of the action of the system, that is what the
women's movement is about.'[14] On the other hand, there was a strong
radical strand to the women's movement which sought to overthrow
the system, rather than reform it. For these activists, existing political
and social institutions were instruments of male power and male values
and women should have no part of them.[15]

This question of the true scope and significance of differences
between men and women defies consensus to this day: yet for the
Supreme Court to be able to vindicate new claims for gender equality,
the Justices would be obliged to furnish at least some semblance of a
coherent and persuasive answer to it. One way of proceeding was to
accept the analogy of sexism with racism, especially as much of the

Court's equal rights jurisprudence developed from consideration of the latter. However, the analogy simply doesn't work. In the first place, there *is* a broad consensus that racial and ethnic origin are irrelevant to an individual's innate capacity to play particular social roles. Secondly, there is no question but that the Equal Protection Clause was intended to promote some kind of equality between the different races in the country. Third, in developing its position on racial equality, the Court had relied heavily on the belief that it had a particular duty to protect the rights of 'discrete and insular minorities' who were oppressed by the majorities who controlled the electoral and legislative processes.[16] Blacks are the outstanding example of such oppressed minorities in the United States, but women, while arguably oppressed, actually constitute a majority of both the population and the electorate. For these reasons, the Court could not simply transfer its race equality jurisprudence to the field of gender equality – at least, not without explaining why these differences were irrelevant for Constitutional purposes.

The Court begins cautiously

In 1971, the Court began a new phase of its work on the constitutionality of policy distinctions predicated upon alleged gender differences. In *Reed v. Reed*,[17] a unanimous Supreme Court ruled, for the first time ever, that such a distinction violated the Fourteenth Amendment.[18] The precise issue at stake was a petty example of the routine use of sex discrimination in public policy: a provision of the Idaho Probate Code gave automatic preference to men over women, where they were otherwise equally qualified, to act as administrator of a deceased's estate. *Reed* was the first case brought to the Supreme Court by the Women's Rights Project[19] and its counsel attempted a *coup-de-grâce* by urging the Court to regard sex as a suspect classification for constitutional purposes.[20] Had the Court agreed, sex classifications would have been placed on a par with racial classifications: strict judicial scrutiny would have to be applied and, with the recent history of the Court's segregation cases in mind, the likely outcome would be the striking of virtually all laws involving such classifications.

Chief Justice Burger's opinion for the Court, however, did not even respond to the WRP's argument. Instead, it applied the lowest possible judicial hurdle, the rational basis test, without even explaining why that approach was the most appropriate. Burger framed the constitutional issue as follows: 'The question presented by this case . . . is whether a

difference in the sex of competing applicants for letters of administration bears a rational relationship to a state objective that is sought to be
advanced (by the provision).'[21] He then noted the various justifications
for the preference for men advanced by the state, which included the
elimination of time-consuming judicial hearings on competing claims
and the desire to avoid intra-family controversies. The Chief Justice
dismissed the state's claim as arbitrary, without really explaining why:
'To give a mandatory preference to members of either sex over members of the other, merely to accomplish the elimination of hearings on
the merits, is to make the very kind of arbitrary legislative choice
forbidden by the Equal Protection Clause of the Fourteenth Amendment . . .'[22]

There was a marked contrast between the Court's decision and its
opinion. As WRP counsel Ruth Bader Ginsburg wrote later, 'The terse
Reed opinion acknowledged no departure from precedent, but Court-
watchers recognised that something new was in the wind.'[23] Most
obviously, there was little point in the Court taking up sex discrimination cases, only to subject them to the deferential rational basis test.
There were still many legislators willing to claim that men and women
were fundamentally different and, therefore, that legal distinctions
based on these differences were rational. While minor regulations like
that at stake in *Reed* might fall foul of the test, it promised little in cases
involving differences linked closely to major elements of traditional
gender roles. Indeed, it is not even clear that the Idaho provision was
not rationally related to a legitimate state purpose, if one accepts the
validity of traditional gender stereotypes. The implicit message of *Reed*,
then, was that women's right to equal treatment was more important
than the state's right to base laws on crude stereotyping. If such
stereotyping is itself irrational, as the *Reed* Court seemed to be saying,
but other forms of sex-based differences are not, then the Court clearly
needed some other test to distinguish between the two. What probably
happened in *Reed* was that the Justices decided, in an 'easy case', to
strike a blow against sex discrimination but, in order to give it the force
of unanimity, put off to another day the difficult and divisive issues that
may already have surfaced.

Two years later, the Court attempted to deal much more explicitly
with this question of what level of scrutiny to apply. A major part of the
explanation for this change of approach from that evinced in *Reed* was
the intervening passage of the ERA by Congress. As noted above, 1972
saw the Senate follow the House in approving the Amendment by an
overwhelming majority. Moreover, the states seemed to be rushing

headlong to add their approval and thereby complete the ratification process: '. . . on the very day that the US Senate passed the ERA, Hawaii became the first state to ratify. Delaware, New Hampshire and Nebraska ratified the next day, and on the third day Idaho and Iowa ratified. Twenty-four more states ratified in 1972 and early 1973.'[24] Thus, by the time the Court came to decide *Frontiero v. Richardson* in May 1973,[25] ratification of the ERA seemed little more than a formality.

Incorporation of the ERA into the Constitution would remove most, if not all, the doubts surrounding the constitutionality of sex-based policy distinctions. Most importantly, it would put sex on a par with race as a suspect classification requiring strict scrutiny by the judiciary. ERA therefore became the major political factor which the Justices had to consider in *Frontiero*: should they anticipate ratification of the Amendment and declare sex a suspect classification or issue a narrow ruling, conceding policy leadership on gender equality to Congress. It was, therefore, a choice between the competing attractions of judicial activism and judicial restraint.

The narrow question of Sharron Frontiero's claim posed little difficulty for the Court. As a married Air Force lieutenant, she had requested the same enhanced benefits in accommodation and medical care that were automatically granted to male officers. She was told, however, that in order to qualify, various US statutes required a female officer to demonstrate that her husband was dependent upon her for at least half his support. When Lt. Frontiero was unable to make that demonstration, her claim for enhanced benefits was denied. She brought suit in a federal District Court, but the judge ruled that the policy did not violate the Constitution because Congress could reasonably have assumed that the male was typically the breadwinner and the female typically the dependant. In other words, the policy survived judicial scrutiny under the rational basis test.

On appeal, the Supreme Court reversed, with only Justice Rehnquist dissenting. The other eight agreed that the policy violated the 'equal protection component' of the Due Process Clause of the Fifth Amendment. The Court was obliged to address the Fifth Amendment, rather than the Fourteenth, because the latter restricts only state government, while the Fifth limits the federal government. Moreover, the Fifth Amendment contains no equal protection clause. Nevertheless, despite the fact that the Fourteenth Amendment had been passed almost eighty years after the Fifth, the Warren Court read history backwards, when convenient, and held that the Fifth had acquired an equal protection component. The most famous instance of this occurred in the school desegregation cases: the Equal Protection Clause of the Fourteenth Amendment was used to invalidate segregation policies in the states, but could not reach the segregated schools of the District of Columbia, a federal jurisdiction. So in *Bolling v. Sharpe*,[26] the Court asserted that the Due Process Clause of the Fifth Amendment contained the same equal protection requirements as the Fourteenth. The logic of this reasoning is strained, to say the least: for if the Due Process Clause of the Fifth Amendment was originally conceived as incorporating equal protection requirements, why did the framers of the Fourteenth Amendment include *both* a Due Process Clause *and* an Equal Protection Clause? Clearly a departure from interpretivism, it is a measure of how far such reasoning has become routine today that not even Justice Rehnquist dissented on this point.

With eight Justices agreeing that Air Force policy violated the Constitution, the main point of discussion became whether this specific ruling should be the occasion for a broad declaration of equal protection principles. According to Woodward and Armstrong, the majority Justices originally agreed at conference to rule in favour of Frontiero on the basis of the *Reed* precedent.[27] This would explain why Chief Justice Burger was willing to assign the opinion in the case to Justice Brennan, the Court's leading activist. On reflection, however, Brennan decided that the time was ripe for a landmark decision in sex equality jurisprudence and he crafted his opinion accordingly.

Sex-based classifications, he said, should be subjected to strict judicial scrutiny. The *Reed* case gave '. . . at least implicit support . . .'[28] for adopting that position, since it had there effectively departed from the rational basis test. This was a rather weak argument, however: for not only had the *Reed* Court not said that explicitly, but it was also a long road from there to the adoption of strict scrutiny.

The heart, then, of Brennan's opinion lay in his account of the long history of invidious discrimination against women in the United States and the similarities between sex and race discrimination. He acknowledged that the position of women had undergone marked improvement in recent times but then wrote: 'Nevertheless, it can hardly be doubted that, in part because of the high visibility of the sex characteristic, women still face pervasive, although at times more subtle, discrimination in our educational institutions, in the job market and, perhaps most conspicuously, in the political arena.'[29] This last point was an attempt to summon up the Court's recent tradition of affording special protection to the politically weak, such as racial minorities.

The history of sex discrimination also had many similar features to that of race discrimination and one similarity in particular suggested that sex, like race, should be regarded as a suspect classification: '. . . what differentiates sex from such non-suspect statuses as intelligence or physical disability, and aligns it with the recognised suspect criteria, is that the sex characteristic frequently bears no relation to ability to perform or contribute to society.'[30]

His final major point was that all the remedial legislation passed by Congress, including the ERA, merely served to reinforce his view that sex classifications were indeed invidious.

Brennan's opinion attracted the support of Justices Douglas, White and Marshall but he could not get the crucial fifth vote which would have given his reasoning the force of precedent: 'If either Earl Warren or Abe Fortas had still been on the Court, he lamented to his clerks, he would have won.'[31] Opposition to the adoption of strict scrutiny coalesced around Justice Powell. Powell did not believe that all classifications based on sex were inherently suspect and Brennan's opinion had far-reaching implications for gender law which went well beyond the *Reed* rationale.[32]

What clearly perturbed him most, however, were the political implications of Brennan's activism. This concern brought forth a strong statement of the 'compelling' necessity for judicial restraint in this case, which is worth quoting at length:

> There is another, and I find compelling, reason for deferring a general categorisation of sex classifications as invoking the strictest test of judicial scrutiny. The Equal Rights Amendment, which if adopted will resolve the substance of this precise question, has been approved by the Congress and submitted for ratification by the States. If this amendment is duly adopted, it will represent the will of the people accomplished in the manner prescribed by the Constitution. By acting prematurely and unnecessarily, as I view it, the Court has assumed a decisional responsibility at the very time when state legislatures, functioning within the traditional democratic process, are debating the proposed Amendment. It seems to me that this reaching out to pre-empt by judicial action a major political decision which is currently in process of resolution does not reflect appropriate respect for duly prescribed legislative processes.
>
> There are times when this Court, under our system, cannot avoid a constitutional decision on issues which should normally be resolved by the elected representatives of the people. But democratic institutions are weakened, and confidence in the restraint of the Court is impaired, when we appear unnecessarily to decide sensitive issues of broad social and political importance at the very time when they are under consideration by the prescribed constitutional processes.[33]

For Powell, then, it is more than the substance of Supreme Court decisions which is important: *who* makes the decision is just as important as *what* decision is made, since representative democracy is about process as well as results. There is nothing new in a Supreme Court Justice warning his colleagues against usurping legislative power: but Justice Brennan's *Frontiero* opinion is a particularly appropriate occasion for Powell's admonition. After all, it is rare for the process of constitutional amendment to be fully achieved and its worth would surely be devalued further if, when on the verge of accomplishment after decades of democratic political activity, an unelected Supreme Court arrogated the final decision to itself.

Justice Powell's opinion was joined by Chief Justice Burger and Justice Blackmun. As Justice Stewart confined himself to a laconic concurrence which said only that he found the Air Force regulations to be '. . . an invidious discrimination . . .',[34] it seemed that there were four Justices in favour of strict scrutiny and four who favoured something less demanding than this, but more substantial than the rational basis test favoured by Justice Rehnquist.

There was a strong likelihood, of course, that the ERA would be adopted and therefore compel the Court to apply strict scrutiny. This seemed to be the view of both Brennan and Powell. However, the drive for ratification slowed dramatically in the second half of 1973 and eventually stopped altogether: the result of the failure of the ERA was that the Court had to return to the issue of the appropriate level of judicial scrutiny of sex classifications, only this time in a political context which was far more confused than it had been in early 1973.

The lack of clarity in the message from the political arena was compounded by the Justices' own inability to forge a consistent approach. The 1974 case of *Kahn v. Shevin*[35] appeared to retreat from the line taken in *Reed* and *Frontiero*.[36] The case involved a Florida statute which granted widows, but not widowers, a $500 tax exemption. Six Justices, including the arch-liberal William Douglas, reversed the Florida Supreme Court's decision that this was unconstitutional discrimination under the Fourteenth Amendment. Wisely, Chief Justice Burger assigned the majority opinion to Douglas, who was invulnerable to possible charges of reactionary sentiments. He based his argument on the long history of discrimination against women in the job market, a point amply supported by his inclusion of statistical evidence supplied by the Women's Bureau of the Department of Labour. Noting that in 1972 women's median earnings were just 57.9 per cent of those earned by men, he concluded: 'Whether from overt discrimination or from the socialisation process of a male dominated culture, the job market is inhospitable to the woman seeking any but the lowest paid jobs.'[37] From this, he deduced that a widower continuing his occupation was considerably better placed to support himself than a widow continuing her occupation or seeking work. This was a real difference between men and women; and the Florida statute bore a fair and substantial relationship to the legitimate state goal of compensating for the past discrimination that had made women economically disadvantaged.

In dissent, Justice Brennan again argued for the application of strict scrutiny, in which case the Florida statute would fall because it was neither narrowly tailored nor indispensable to the achievement of the state's goal: 'The State has offered nothing to explain why the inclusion of widows of substantial economic means was necessary to advance the State's interest in ameliorating the effects of past economic discrimination against women.'[38] He suggested a means test as an alternative that would be less violative of constitutional rights. Justice White took up a similar theme in his dissent and asked why, if the state wished to remedy past discrimination, it did not extend the tax exemption to poor widowers, especially blacks, for whom poverty and discrimination often went hand-in-hand. Therefore, he wrote, 'It seems to me that the State in this case is merely conferring an economic benefit in the form of a tax exemption and has not adequately explained why women should be treated differently from men.'[39]

While of no great constitutional significance, *Kahn v. Shevin* provides an interesting illustration of the difficulties of distinguishing between 'benign' and 'invidious' discrimination in the field of gender equality. Even the Court's liberal-activist bloc could not cohere in this case.

The following year the Court confused the picture further with its decision in *Schlesinger v. Ballard*.[40] As in *Frontiero*, this case involved alleged sex discrimination in the armed forces. The career of Navy officers is governed by the principle of 'up or out', whereby the failure to achieve a promotion within a specified time period requires the officer's honourable discharge. For male officers the time limit was ten years, but for women thirteen. Lieutenant Robert C. Ballard had fallen victim of this policy and brought suit in a federal District Court alleging that he had been subjected to unconstitutional discrimination because of his sex. The *Frontiero* decision appeared to provide strong support for his claim, but five of the Justices decided otherwise. Justice Stewart, writing for the majority,[41] argued that, unlike earlier cases where differential treatment had resulted from overbroad generalisations about the sexes and a desire for administrative convenience, this regulation stemmed from '. . . the demonstrable fact that male and female line officers are *not* similarly situated with respect to opportunities for professional service.'[42] In particular, women were not permitted to serve in combat or in much sea duty and therefore had fewer opportunities to demonstrate their case for promotion.

Justice Brennan wrote for the dissenters and again insisted upon strict scrutiny as the appropriate judicial test in sex discrimination cases. Much of his opinion, however, consisted of a critique of Stewart's imputation of the legislative motive behind the regulation: '. . . the Court goes far to conjure up a legislative purpose which *may* have underlain the gender-based distinction here attacked. I find nothing in the statutory scheme or the legislative history to support the supposition that Congress intended . . . to compensate women for other forms of disadvantage visited upon them by the Navy. Thus, the gender-based classification . . . is not related, rationally or otherwise, to any legitimate legislative purpose fairly to be inferred from the statutory scheme or its history, and cannot be sustained.'[43]

The Justices had clearly divided along lines of judicial activism and self-restraint. The majority had followed the traditional rule of restraint that where there is a plausible rationale for legislation, the Court should give it the benefit of any constitutional doubt. The dissenters, on the other hand, required clear proof that such a rationale had been intended by the legislature. In *Ballard*, then, it seemed that the Court had not only rejected strict scrutiny once again, but had also shown a more powerful inclination to defer to Congress than to pursue the campaign for greater gender equality. There was indeed the suspicion that the Justices had lost their earlier enthusiasm for that campaign.

Two cases later the same Term, however, removed some of that suspicion. In *Weinberger v. Wiesenfeld*,[44] a unanimous Court overturned a 1939 provision of the Social Security Act that granted survivors' benefits to widows with young children, but not to widowers. Although the government claimed the purpose of the provision was to compensate women for economic disadvantage, Justice Brennan disputed this: rather, he argued, the original purpose had been to allow the surviving parent to stay at home and care for the children. Even Justice Rehnquist, the least sympathetic member of the Court to gender equality, declared himself wholly convinced by Brennan's analysis of the legislative history.[45] Brennan concluded that to allow this gender distinction to remain in force would be to accept the validity of 'archaic and overbroad generalisations' about the significance of women's contributions to family income. Furthermore, it would signal a failure to recognise that 'It is no less important for a child to be cared for by its sole surviving parent when that parent is male rather than female.'[46] It hardly requires extensive argument to conclude that, in respect of both points, Justice Brennan's opinion reflected quite recent progress in ideas about the role of women *and* men in society. And even at the risk of belabouring the obvious, it is worth emphasising that this small, but significant, social reform had been achieved by unelected judges using a form of constitutional interpretation which relied upon an unenumerated equal protection element of the Fifth Amendment and which declared the views of the elected government to be archaic. Desirable or not, this is undeniably a judicial power different in kind from that which had existed even twenty years earlier.

The other noteworthy gender discrimination case that Term was *Stanton v. Stanton.*[47] Under Utah law, the age of majority for women was eighteen but for men, twenty-one. Thus when James and Thelma Stanton divorced, James was willing to make support payments for his son until he reached twenty-one, but refused to do so for his daughter after her eighteenth birthday. Thelma Stanton brought suit to force her ex-husband to continue support payments to their daughter, arguing that the state's majority age statute constituted sex discrimination under the Equal Protection Clause of the Fourteenth Amendment. Two Utah courts rejected her claim, but the Supreme Court, with only Justice Rehnquist dissenting, reversed them. Justice Blackmun wrote the Court's opinion. He noted that the Utah Supreme Court had referred to the 'fact' that '. . . it is the man's primary responsibility to provide a home and that it is salutary for him to have education and training before he assumes that responsibility; that girls tend to mature earlier than boys; and that females tend to marry earlier than males.'[48] (Utah, of course, is a socially conservative state, dominated politically by the Mormon Church.) Justice Blackmun simply dismissed these rationales with the pithy conclusion that 'No longer is the female destined solely for the home and the rearing of the family, and only the male for the marketplace and the world of ideas.'[49]

The defeat of the ERA

If *Wiesenfeld* and *Stanton* tended to reaffirm the thrust of *Reed* and *Frontiero*, the intervening decisions in *Kahn* and *Ballard* had given

contradictory signals about the direction of the Court's gender discrimination jurisprudence. More important than any confusion on the
part of the Justices, however, this was due to the current state of
uncertainty in gender politics in the wider political system. Most
significantly, the Equal Rights Amendment had run into serious
trouble. After the initial rush to ratification in 1972–73, the Amendment ran into a brick wall of opposition. Only three further states
ratified in 1974, one in 1975, none in 1976: and in 1977, Indiana
became the last state to approve it, leaving the ERA three states short of
the thirty-eight necessary for ratification. Despite the decision by
Congress to extend the ratification deadline from 1979 to 1982, the
Amendment was lost.[50]

The defeat of the Equal Rights Amendment carried a double warning to the Supreme Court to proceed cautiously on sex equality. In the
first place, the Court unwittingly contributed to the failure of the ERA
by its 1973 abortion decision in *Roe v. Wade*. As discussed earlier, *Roe*
provided the critical stimulus for the pro-life movement and this in
turn became an important element within the New Right coalition.[51]
By outraging many of those opposed to the new lifestyles and social
attitudes associated with the 1960s, *Roe* sparked a conservative reaction
which took in many social issues. Thus, as Hugh Graham writes, '. . .
Roe v. Wade galvanised an anti-ERA coalition of conservatives and
traditionalist women led by Phyllis Schlafly, and the resulting stalemate
ultimately doomed the feminists' congressional triumph of 1972.'[52]
Jane Mansbridge sees an even closer connection between *Roe* and the
defeat of ERA: 'Unable to overturn the *Roe* decision directly, many
conservatives sought to turn the ERA into a referendum on that
decision. To a significant degree, they succeeded.'[53]

The second warning to the Court conveyed by the ERA battle was
one of substantive policy. Quite simply, the defeat of the ERA, like the
continuing protest over *Roe* itself, indicated that there were powerful
ideological and political limits on the willingness of many Americans to
embrace the liberal and feminist agenda on sex equality. The STOP-
ERA movement founded by Phyllis Schlafly never commanded
majority support in the country; but it did succeed in raising the level of
anxiety about the ERA to the point where a committed minority of
activists were able to persuade a minority of states to block ratification.
To a considerable degree, this was achieved by stamping the Amendment as a radical measure which would upset some of the most basic
and widely accepted practices of gender relations. One of the more
serious fears aroused was that the ERA would require women to be

drafted for military service on the same basis as men, including the duty to serve in combat. Another tactic was to present the Amendment as a homosexual rights charter that would not only legalise homosexual marriage, for example, but also bar heterosexuals from defending themselves and their children from the 'homosexual menace'. The *Phyllis Schlafly Report* once contended that gays and lesbians would use the rights extended to them as teachers and educationalists under the ERA to get control of schools and asked rhetorically: 'Surely the rights of parents to control the education of their children is a right of a higher order than any alleged right of, say, the two college-educated lesbian members of the Symbionese Liberation Army to teach our young people.'[54] Later, Schlafly's Eagle Forum sought to exploit the fear of AIDS. In a pamphlet entitled 'The ERA-GAY-AIDS-CONNECTION', it asked '. . . would police, paramedics, dentists, health personnel and morticians be permitted to take adequate precautions to defend themselves against AIDS and other homosexual diseases?'[55]

The anti-ERA movement also sought to persuade Americans that the Amendment would permit no segregation of the sexes at all, even in prisons and public toilets. Thus in New York, for example, an anti-ERA group put out a pamphlet calling the ERA the 'Common Toilet Law', whilst another in Nebraska claimed that the unisex principle would further be extended to nudity laws: 'Under the proposed Equal Rights Amendment, wherever males are accustomed to appear in public, nude above the waist, equal rights are absolutely guaranteed to females. Such places would most certainly include swimming pools, tennis courts and drive-in theatres.'[56]

Absurd as many of these attacks on the ERA were, even the Amendment's proponents concede that they were effective. As Riane Eisler said of the homosexual issue, 'It sounds – and is – ridiculous. But it seems to work.'[57] It is doubtful that many opponents of ERA really did believe that unisex toilets would be compulsory under the Amendment or even that women would be compelled to serve combat duty. The effectiveness of the anti-ERA campaign, then, lies in its power to arouse the anxieties of those disturbed by the social and cultural changes symbolised by feminism and the ERA. Jane Mansbridge wrote: 'The battle against the ERA was one of the first in which the New Right used "women's issues" to forge a coalition of the traditional Radical Right, religious activists, and that previously relatively apolitical segment of the noncosmopolitan working and middle classes that was deeply disturbed by the cultural changes – especially the changes in sexual mores – in the second half of the twentieth century.'[58]

Gelb and Palley see the ERA, along with abortion, as an issue different in degree from many others designed to achieve gender equality. Both the general public and legislatures see little to fear and oppose in policies which involve *role equity*: that is, reforms which are narrow in implication, merely extending to women rights already enjoyed by men and which do not directly detract from the rights of men.[59] An example of such legislation would be the Equal Credit Opportunity Act of 1974, passed by voice vote in the Senate and by a majority of 355–1 in the House.[60]

The ERA, however, involved not so much *role equity* as *role change*. Or more precisely, it was seen originally as an issue which primarily involved role equity, but its opponents succeeded in transforming it into one perceived as involving role change. As such, it signalled a fundamental shift in the traditional role of women as wife-mother-homemaker and required men to undergo concomitant change in their role.[61] The gay and lesbian rights issue was so potent precisely because it represents the ultimate form of confusion in traditional male-female roles.

In 1976 the Supreme Court effectively decided to mirror this 'reformist' versus 'radical' distinction emerging in the wider political arena. In *Craig v. Boren*,[62] a majority of the Justices settled upon an intermediate standard of review in sex discrimination: it eschewed the equation of racism with sexism and thus stopped short of requiring strict scrutiny. On the other hand, it demanded significantly more than the rational basis test.

Craig involved a challenge to an Oklahoma statute which prohibited the sale of 3.2 per cent 'non-intoxicating' beer to males below the age of twenty-one, but to females below the age of eighteen. Over the dissents of Chief Justice Burger and Justice Rehnquist, seven members of the Court voted to strike the law and at least five of them clearly subscribed to Justice Brennan's new test:[63] 'To withstand constitutional challenge . . . classifications by gender must serve important governmental objectives and must be substantially related to achievement of those objectives.'[64] Because there is only 'a weak congruence' between gender and the characteristics gender purportedly represents, legislatures must either make their laws gender-neutral or identify those instances where there is indeed some significant congruence.[65]

Brennan concluded that the state had failed to do either. He noted that it had relied on statistics that showed a higher instance of drunk-driving among 18–20-year-old men (2 per cent) than among women of the same age (0.18 per cent). Such a disparity was not trivial, he wrote, but neither was it sufficient to justify drawing a gender line in the law: '. . . the showing offered by the appellees does not satisfy us that sex represents a legitimate, accurate proxy for the regulation of drinking and driving.'[66]

Chief Justice Burger's dissent took the Court to task for elevating an unenumerated right to a position of special constitutional protection: '. . . even interests of such importance in our society as public education and housing do not qualify as "fundamental rights" because they have no textually independent constitutional status . . . Though today's decision does not go so far as to make gender-based classifications "suspect", it makes gender a disfavoured classification. Without an independent constitutional basis supporting the right asserted or disfavouring the classification adopted, I can justify no substantive constitutional protection other than the normal . . . protection afforded by the Equal Protection Clause.'[67] The fact that only two of the Justices sympathised with this textualist critique indicates how far from original notions of constitutional interpretation the Supreme Court had come. One may also note, however, that Burger had not always been above non-textualism himself, such as when he agreed in *Roe* that privacy and abortion were fundamental rights, despite there being no mention of them in the Constitution.

The *Craig* decision did not end division amongst the Justices in sex discrimination cases, nor did it herald a wholly consistent substantive line of sympathy towards gender equality. As we shall see shortly, for example, the Court was to experience some difficulty in gaining acceptance for its attitude to pregnancy disability. Nevertheless, the main thrust of the Court's jurisprudence was now settled: if legislatures wished to treat men and women differently, they would have to prove conclusively that such distinctions were based upon 'real' and enduring differences between men and women, rather than custom, stereotype or overbroad generalisations. To that extent, the Court was in tune with the political times, progressive but hardly radical.[68]

An interesting insight into the Court's line on 'real' differences between the sexes can be gained from examining two cases decided in March 1977. In *Califano v. Goldfarb*[69] the Court struck down a provision of the Federal Old-Age, Survivors and Disability Benefits programme because it discriminated between men and women on the basis of stereotypes. The provision automatically paid survivor's benefits to a widow, but a widower had to prove that he had been dependent on his wife for at least half his income before he could qualify. Justice Brennan found the case indistinguishable from *Wiesenfeld* and *Frontiero*: there was no evidence from the legislative history that Congress had intended to compensate women for past discrimination, but rather relied on the outdated assumption that men, but not women, were responsible for the support of their spouse and children.[70]

It seemed from *Goldfarb* that the Court had moved decisively beyond the thinking evident in *Kahn v. Shevin*, where differential treatment of widows and widowers had been upheld as 'benign discrimination'. Three weeks later, however, in *Califano v. Webster*[71] a unanimous Court upheld a provision of the Social Security Act which favoured women. Retirement benefits were calculated on the base of a person's most productive years of earnings, but women were allowed to discount three more years than men in the definition of their most productive income period. This raised the value of their base and consequently their pensions. In a *per curiam* opinion joined by the same five Justices who constituted the majority in *Goldfarb*, the Court applied the intermediate standard of review but then upheld the provision. The Court found some evidence in the legislative history that convinced them that Congress intended to compensate women for past employment discrimination and thus: 'The more favourable treatment of the female wage earner enacted here was not a result of archaic and overbroad generalisations about women . . . or of the role-typing society has long imposed upon women, such as casual assumptions that women are "the weaker sex" or are more likely to be child rearers or dependants.'[72]

The other four Justices concurred in the decision but were uneasy about the fact that the Court seemed prepared to second-guess legislatures in order to reach substantive results. Chief Justice Burger wrote: '. . . I question whether certainty in the law is promoted by hinging the validity of important statutory schemes on whether five Justices view them (as "offensive" or "benign").'[73]

As it turned out, decisions such as *Kahn and Webster* were to prove exceptions, with the Court generally insisting upon precisely the same treatment of men and women in matters of pension and unemployment benefits.[74] Of course, because of the blatant discrimination against women involved in these cases, equal treatment did achieve the substantive goal of helping women. Thus it would seem that the application of intermediate review in gender discrimination cases was sufficiently flexible to enable the liberal-moderate bloc on the Court to strike or uphold sex distinctions in the law in accordance with substantive judgements of which decision would materially benefit women.[75]

Sex-based distinctions upheld by the Court as compensatory inevitably raised the spectre of the affirmative action controversy that was rocking the Court – and the country – in race discrimination cases.[76] Although the Court had rejected the equation of sex discrimination with race discrimination, voluntary affirmative action plans intended to compensate women for past discrimination still had to withstand scrutiny under Title VII of the Civil Rights Act of 1964 and the Equal Protection Clause of the Fourteenth Amendment. Moreover, by the time affirmative action for women came before the Court in 1987, the Justices had developed a substantial jurisprudence in race cases that would be of clear relevance to gender cases. In short, affirmative action for women threatened a re-run of the battle over 'benign discrimination' and 'quotas' in racial preference plans.

Affirmative action and sex

Johnson v. Transportation Agency[77] was the first ever Supreme Court ruling on the validity of affirmative action for women. The case dated from 1979, when Paul Johnson and Diane Joyce vied for the position of dispatcher with the Santa Clara County highway department in California's Silicon Valley.[78] Both were among the final seven applicants deemed qualified to do the job, but Paul Johnson seemed to be the favourite for the job, partly because he was 'one of the boys' at the department and his boss had indicated that the job would be his one day. He had also been told following the interviews that the board members were going to recommend him for the job. Diane Joyce gained the impression that she had never had a genuine chance of the job and called in the County's affirmative action officer. The Transportation Agency's affirmative action co-ordinator then intervened with the Director, pointing out that the appointment of a woman would be an opportunity to meet the goals of the Agency's affirmative action plan. As both Johnson and Joyce were formally qualified, the Director was happy to count Joyce's sex as a positive and decisive factor and duly named her to the post.

Johnson responded by contacting a lawyer, who in turn obtained approval from the Equal Employment Opportunity Commission to bring a Title VII suit in a federal District Court. Johnson won his case there, but the decision was then reversed by the federal Appeals Court for the Ninth Circuit.

At this point, the case took on a sharper political dimension with the intervention of interest groups on both sides. Johnson had been prepared to drop the case after the Appeals Court decision, but several conservative public interest law firms were keen to take it to the Supreme Court and were willing to pay all the expenses. Johnson eventually selected the Mountain States Legal Foundation to handle the case.[79] The Solicitor-General, Charles Fried, was also keen for the Reagan Administration to join the case on Johnson's behalf. Fried wished to share time for oral argument before the Supreme Court with Connie Brooks, the Mountain States lawyer assigned to the case, but she considered him a liability. Fried's appearances before the Court in the previous Term's affirmative action cases had apparently antagonised certain of the Justices by his aggressive approach. As Melvin Urofsky put it: 'Fried had emerged as the Darth Vader of the civil rights movement, the point man for the Reagan Administration's efforts to undo thirty years of civil rights progress which the Justice Department had previously championed, a situation that the plurality opinions in several cases had commented upon critically.'[80] It was said that the mere appearance of Fried would end all hope of attracting Justice Stevens' vote, for example. In the end, the Solicitor-General had to be content with participating as an *amicus curiae*.[81]

To an unusual degree in gender equality cases, a large number of interest groups decided to get involved in *Johnson*, mostly in support of Diane Joyce. Although only eight briefs were entered on behalf of the Transportation Agency's affirmative action plan, these represented some forty groups, among them a coalition of women's organisations which included NOW, the League of Women Voters and the Women's Equity Action League.[82] This level of interest was a clear sign that the significance of the case had far transcended the personal interests of Johnson and Joyce: once again, the Court would make a decision with deep social policy implications.

The Justices split 6–3 to uphold the validity of the Transportation Agency's affirmative action plan. In so doing, they once again rehearsed the merits of their earlier decision in *Weber*,[83] which had established the basic validity of voluntary affirmative action plans under Title VII. While that discussion was vital to the votes of at least three of the Justices, more interesting from the point of view of substantive policy was the clash over the cause of the disparity between the numbers of men and women employed in certain types of work.

Justice Brennan wrote the Court's opinion and, as Charles Fried commented, '. . . more or less republished his *Weber* opinion.'[84]

Although none of the parties to the case had called for a reconsideration of that precedent,[85] the recently-appointed Justice Scalia
launched a vigorous attack on it and gave a series of reasons why the
principle of *stare decisis* should not save it.[86] This critique persuaded
Justice White, who had voted with the majority in *Weber* on the grounds
that the plan involved there had been designed to remedy the
intentional and systematic exclusion of blacks. Now, however, the
Court was validating a plan that merely sought to correct '. . . a
manifest imbalance between one identifiable group and another in an
employer's labour force.'[87] That, he said, was a perversion of Title VII.

Justices Stevens and O'Connor were not convinced that *Weber*
should be overturned, even though they believed it departed from the
original intent behind Title VII. Justice Stevens thought simply that the
value of stability and order in the law outweighed any harm caused by
that deviation.[88] Justice O'Connor was additionally reassured by the
Court's earlier decision in *Wygant*, which had ensured that *Weber* did
not validate affirmative action plans which were merely designed to
correct societal discrimination, but rather required some showing of
past or present discrimination by the employer.[89]

With the authority of *Weber* thus confirmed, the *Johnson* case turned
on whether there was any evidence to indicate that the Santa Clara
County Transportation Agency had ever engaged in discrimination
against women. The Agency did not admit to any such discrimination
for the very obvious reason that this would make them vulnerable to
numerous and expensive Title VII claims by women. The principal
question, then, was whether the statistical disparity between men and
women on the Agency's payroll should be interpreted as a product of
discrimination against women or, instead, their preference to avoid
certain types of work. In other words, the Court was dealing with a form
of the old question of whether differences between men and women
were natural.

That a great statistical disparity did exist in the Agency's work-force
was not in dispute. Women constituted 76 per cent of office and
clerical workers, but only 7.1 per cent of administrators, 8.6 per cent of
professionals and 22 per cent of service and maintenance workers.
Moreover, of the 238 skilled craft positions which included the dispatcher's job, not one was occupied by a woman.[90] Justice Brennan's
opinion never squarely stated that the Agency's affirmative action plan
was aimed at past discrimination, but rather that it was '. . . designed to
eliminate Agency work force imbalances in traditionally segregated job
categories.'[91] The obvious implication, however, is that the cause of

that segregation was discrimination.

Justice O'Connor agreed and was more explicit. She concluded that the work-force statistics were sufficiently clear to provide a *prima facie* basis for a Title VII discrimination suit brought by unsuccessful women job applicants. She noted that 5 per cent of the local work-force of skilled craft workers were women, yet the Agency did not have a single one on its books.[92]

Justice Scalia rejected this interpretation of the statistics: 'It is absurd to think that the nationwide failure of road maintenance crews, for example, to achieve the Agency's ambition of 36.4 per cent female representation is attributable primarily, if even substantially, to systematic exclusion of women eager to shoulder pick and shovel. It is a "traditionally segregated job category" *not* in the *Weber* sense, but in the sense that, because of longstanding social attitudes, it has not been regarded by *women themselves* as desirable work'.[93] Scalia recognised that some considered such social attitudes to be themselves the product of discrimination, but he not only indicated his disagreement with that, but also his belief that it was not the Court's role to try to change social attitudes:

> There are, of course, those who believe that the social attitudes which cause women themselves to avoid certain jobs and to favour others are as nefarious as conscious, exclusionary discrimination. Whether or not that is so (and there is assuredly no consensus on the point equivalent to our national consensus against intentional discrimination), the two phenomena are certainly distinct. And it is the alteration of social attitudes, rather than the elimination of discrimination, which today's decision approves as justification for state-enforced discrimination. This is an enormous expansion, undertaken without the slightest justification or analysis.[94]

Beneath the various legal issues raised in the *Johnson* case, therefore, lay an ideological debate drawn directly from the political arena and the question of the Court's role in resolving that debate. The point is not that legal issues act as camouflage for the real conflict over ideology, so much as the fact that questions of law are inextricably bound up with questions of politics.

Indeed, later in his dissent, Justice Scalia added a further political dimension when he took a populist swipe at the government, professional and interest group elites who would be likely to support the Court's decision. On the Court's insistence that approval of the Agency's plan did not mean that successful job applicants need not be qualified for the post, he commented sarcastically that this will be '. . . undoubtedly effective in reducing the effect of affirmative-action discrimination upon those in the upper-strata of society, who (unlike road maintenance workers, for example) compete for employment in professional and semi-professional fields where, for many reasons, including most notably the effects of past discrimination, the numbers of (minimally qualified) applicants from the favoured groups are substantially less.'[95] Justice Scalia then turned his aim at the other proponents of 'progressive judicial policy':

> It is unlikely that today's result will be displeasing to politically elected officials, to whom it provides the means of quickly accommodating the demands of organised groups to achieve concrete, numerical improvement in the economic status of particular constituencies. Nor will it displease the world of corporate and government employers (many of whom have filed briefs as *amici* in the present case, all on the side of Santa Clara) for whom the cost of hiring less qualified workers is often substantially less – and infinitely more predictable – than the cost of litigating Title VII cases and of seeking to convince federal agencies by non-numerical means that no discrimination exists. In fact, the only losers in the process are the Johnsons of the country, for whom Title VII has not merely been repealed but actually inverted. The irony is that these individuals – predominantly unknown, unaffluent, unorganised – suffer this injustice at the hands of a Court fond of thinking itself the champion of the politically impotent.[96]

The prose is different, but the David versus Goliath sentiments of the populist Right are unmistakable: upper-middle-class professionals, intellectuals and government bureaucrats in Washington engage in social engineering at the expense of the ordinary American Joe who has no-one in power to speak up for him.

The flaws in formal equality

Johnson was indeed a victory for the cause of gender equality, simply because '. . . the Court for the first time included women as a group eligible for affirmative action.'[97] However, the constitutionality of affirmative action, whether involving race or sex, was about to undergo renewed challenge as new appointees to the Court replaced retiring members who had been amongst the most sympathetic to the practice. For better or worse, an important facet of women's rights would stand or fall with the fate of affirmative action for ethnic minorities.[98]

The decision, however, raises another problem that neither the Court nor the women's movement has yet solved: it clearly abrogated the principle of formal equality that both, for the most part, had advanced since the 1970s.[99] As noted above, formal equality or equal rights advocates argue that the Constitution should be 'sex-blind', treating men and women identically.[100] Ironically, while the Court was beginning to implement this approach, more and more feminists became convinced of its inadequacy and, indeed, of its adverse consequences. Mary Becker has argued that formal equality, even including the exception of affirmative action, does not get to the root causes of the social and economic subordination of women. Rather, 'In the context of employment, it only opens men's jobs to women on the terms and conditions worked out for men.'[101] Moreover, some equal rights decisions actually do more harm than good, particularly to lower-class women. Citing in particular *Orr v. Orr*, the decision in which the Court held that states could not require only men to pay alimony,[102] Becker writes:

> Formal equality is likely to help most, and hurt least, professional women who either have no children or who hire other women to care for their children and are able to compete with men on men's terms. These women have tended to control the women's movement. And it is likely to hurt most mothers and wives who are not well-paid professionals.[103]

Given the ambivalence in the women's movement about the appropriate method of achieving equality, it is hardly surprising that the Court has at times appeared hesitant and stumbling. In no area of law has this been more true than in the rights of pregnant women. This issue goes right to the heart of sex equality: it involves an undeniable biological difference between men and women who are therefore not 'similarly situated' and not simply amenable to identical treatment in law. If, on the one hand, this difference is ignored, then women will continue to suffer great disadvantages in career and income opportunities: on the other hand, if 'special treatment' is required for women on biological grounds, this would appear to undermine other claims to equality based on the irrelevance of biological differences. This problem has dominated the debate among the Justices right from the start and also led to tension with Congress as to what Title VII of the Civil Rights Act of 1964 required by way of ending sex discrimination.

The first major case on the issue was *Gedulig v. Aiello*.[104] This involved a California state insurance programme which paid benefits to those temporarily unable to work through disability. Disability because of pregnancy was excluded from coverage, however, and this was challenged as a violation of the Equal Protection Clause of the Fourteenth Amendment. The women who brought the suit had the support of *amicus* briefs from a number of civil liberties, union and women's groups, as well as the EEOC. Against them were powerful corporate and business groups, including the United States Chamber of Commerce, the National Association of Manufacturers and the General Electric Company.[105] This would suggest that economics, rather than patriarchy, was the primary argument against the women's claim.

Indeed, as the Court voted six to three to reject that claim, Justice Stewart's opinion barely addressed the issue of how pregnancy disadvantages women in the work-place.[106] It was rather the costs of including pregnancy disability in the programme that seemed uppermost in his mind, along with the state's right to determine the level of its welfare expenditure: 'Particularly with respect to social welfare programmes, so long as the line drawn by the State is rationally supportable, the courts will not interpose their judgement as to the appropriate stopping point.'[107] He then explained why the exclusion of pregnancy disability involved no discrimination: 'There is no risk from which men are protected and women are not. Likewise, there is no risk from which women are protected and men are not.'[108] In other words, since men are not protected from the risk of becoming pregnant, neither are women! Herein lies the trap of formal equality: since men and women are not the same in reproductive function, the disadvantages which flow to women from that difference need not be equalised under the Fourteenth Amendment. What Justice Stewart achieves here is the separation of pregnancy from gender, though curiously he only explained his rationale in a footnote: he argued that the statute did not distinguish between men and women, but rather between '. . . pregnant women and non-pregnant persons. While the first group is exclusively female, the second includes members of both sexes. The fiscal and actuarial benefits of the programme thus accrue to members of both sexes.'[109] As the *Harvard Law Review* was to comment: 'The conclusion that pregnancy-based classifications are not in themselves sex-based suggests an exceedingly formalistic view of the problem.'[110] What it does demonstrate, however, is that the Court can employ the concept of formal equality in a narrow, specific sense and yet sanction one of the principal instruments of the subordination of women. The adoption of this approach deservedly attracted a great deal of criticism, to the point where 'Criticising *Gedulig* has since become a cottage industry.'[111] Whatever it says about the particular Justices involved, however, it says more about the limitations on the pursuit of social reform through constitutional interpretation. Not surprisingly, Justice Brennan's dissenting opinion eschewed the cramped approach of the majority and he emphasised the practical effect of the insurance plan:

... a limitation is imposed upon the disabilities for which women workers may recover, while men receive full compensation for all disabilities suffered, including those that affect only or primarily their sex, such as prostatectomies, circumcision, hemophilia, and gout. In effect, one set of rules is applied to females and another to males. Such dissimilar treatment of men and women, on the basis of physical characteristics inextricably linked to one sex, inevitably constitutes sex discrimination.[112]

Two years later, in *General Electric Co. v. Gilbert*,[113] the Court persisted in ignoring this seemingly obvious fact of life, but this time it was subjected to a swift counter-attack by women's groups and the Congress. *General Electric* involved the eponymous company's disability insurance plan which, like that in *Gedulig*, did not include pregnancy disability. The main difference from that case was that since *General Electric* involved a private rather than state plan, it had to withstand scrutiny under Title VII rather than the Constitution. As it turned out, this made little difference to the Court's decision. Justice Rehnquist relied heavily on *Gedulig* in arguing that the definition of 'sex discrimination' in Title VII had not been intended to encompass pregnancy and placed Stewart's footnote into the text of his opinion in full.[114] Rehnquist was not deterred by the fact that the EEOC had issued guidelines in 1972 saying squarely that pregnancy-related disabilities should be treated as other temporary disabilities in insurance plans. These guidelines, he noted, were not contemporaneous with the passage of Title VII and, furthermore, contradicted earlier EEOC guidelines.[115] The original intent behind Title VII thus demanded the same understanding of pregnancy disability taken by the Court in *Gedulig*.

A Supreme Court decision turning on statutory, rather than constitutional interpretation, can be reversed by Congressional legislation. That is precisely what women's groups set out to achieve in response to *General Electric*. A coalition of more than fifty organisations created the Campaign to End Discrimination Against Pregnant Workers. Less than a year after the Court's decision, the Senate passed legislation that explicitly overturned *General Electric* by a vote of 75–11. The Senate Human Resources Committee Report stated that *General Electric* '. . . threatens to undermine the central purpose of the sex discrimination prohibitions of Title VII . . . It would be difficult to overstate the importance of removing this barrier to equal employment opportunity for women.'[116] After some wrangling with the House of Representatives over an anti-abortion clause, the legislation was eventually passed by voice vote in both chambers as an amendment to the sex-discrimination prohibition of Title VII and labelled the Pregnancy Discrimination Act of 1978. The pertinent part of the statute reads:

> The terms 'because of sex' or 'on the basis of sex' include, but are not limited to, because of or on the basis of pregnancy, childbirth or related medical conditions; and women affected by pregnancy, childbirth or related medical conditions shall be treated the same for all employment-related purposes, including receipts of benefits under fringe benefit pro-grammes, as other persons not so affected but similar in their ability or inability to work . . .[117]

Whatever the original intention behind Title VII, the Court had clearly misread the mood of Congress in 1976. A majority of the Justices not only acknowledged this in later cases, but actually seem to have read the passage of the Pregnancy Discrimination Act as Congressional encouragement to pursue a more activist and liberal policy on preg-nancy disability than even that Act demanded. In the *Newport News* case in 1983,[118] seven Justices interpreted the Act's concept of sex dis-crimination to require that the pregnant spouses of employees receive the same disability benefits as pregnant employees – just as the com-pany's plan provided for other disabilities. In dissent, Justice Rehnquist demonstrated quite convincingly that 'The plain language of the Pregnancy Discrimination Act leaves little room for the Court's conclusion that the Act was intended to extend beyond female employees.'[119]

Justice Stevens, however, employed logic rather than statutory lan-guage to go beyond the original intent: '. . . since the sex of the spouse is always the opposite of the sex of the employee, it follows inexorably that discrimination against female spouses in the provision of fringe benefits is also discrimination against male employees.'[120] Thus, he concluded, 'Petitioner's plan is the mirror-image of the plan at issue in *Gilbert.*'[121] Implicitly, Justice Stevens advanced the intriguing concept of the pregnancy rights of male employees!

Newport News marked only a small step beyond the original intention of the Pregnancy Disability Act, but seven years later the Court took a giant leap. In *California Federal Savings and Loan Association v. Guerra*,[122] five Justices interpreted the language of the Pregnancy Discrimination Act to mean not that employees disabled by pregnancy must be treated *the same* as employees temporarily disabled for other reasons, but rather may be given *preferential treatment*.[123] At issue was a 1978 amendment to the California Fair Employment and Housing Act which required employers to provide up to four months unpaid pregnancy leave for female employees. There was no requirement that leave be provided for any other non-work-related temporary disability. This seemed flatly to contradict the language and intent of the Pregnancy Discrimination Act which, to repeat, said that '. . . women affected by pregnancy . . . shall be treated the same for all employment-related purposes . . . as other persons not so affected but similar in their ability or inability to work . . .'.[124]

Justice White, in dissent, hardly needed elaborate argument to conclude that 'This language leaves no room for preferential treatment of pregnant workers.'[125] Even those who most ardently approve of such preferential treatment acknowledge that the decision was in tension with the statutory language.[126]

Justice Marshall's opinion for the Court tackled this by boldly, though not convincingly, redefining Congressional intent and then citing the beneficial result of the California statute as evidence of its legality. Borrowing from the language of the Appeals Court below, Marshall claimed that '. . . Congress intended the PDA to be a floor beneath which pregnancy disability benefits may not drop – not a ceiling above which they may not rise.'[127] That is, indeed, a strange way of interpreting the phrase 'the same for all employment-related purposes'. Then, citing the common goal of Title VII, the PDA and the California statute as equal employment opportunity, Marshall concluded: '. . . California's pregnancy disability-leave statute allows women, as well as men, to have families without losing their jobs.'[128]

This reasoning is, in effect, substantive equal protection, not interpretation. Many feminists have no qualms about advocating such an approach in gender equality cases. Ann Scales has argued that judges should move away from the abstract concept of equality employed since the 1970s because, at best, it freezes the status quo: 'Feminism does not claim to be objective because objectivity is the basis for inequality. Feminism is not abstract, because abstraction when constitutionalised shields the status quo from critique. Feminism is result-oriented. It is vitally concerned with the oblivion fostered by lawyers' belief that process is what matters.'[129] Wendy Strimling made a similar point when she wrote approvingly that: '. . . *Cal Fed* suggests a more subtle approach whereby the impact of the law, rather than the mere fact it classifies by pregnancy, would determine whether it violates the equal protection guarantee.'[130]

But the 'subtlety' required here is of a legislative rather than judicial nature, given that it involves a jurisprudence of concrete results rather than one of abstract principle capable of consistent application to all pregnancy-related issues. As Mary Becker argued: 'Since it is unlikely that we will be able to imagine one abstract standard capable of providing an effective means for resolving all such problems, much change in the legal system must occur (if it is to occur at all) as a result of legislative change, often piecemeal change.'[131]

All the while that the Court was moving away from the judicial restraint of *General Electric* in Title VII cases, it remained largely silent about the force of its decision in *Geduldig*. Despite the fact that the *Geduldig* view of discrimination and pregnancy provided the basis for *General Electric*, that does not mean that it was automatically overruled when the latter was repudiated by the Pregnancy Discrimination Act. Sylvia Law noted in 1984 that the Court rarely cites *Geduldig*, indicating that its precedential weight is minimal in practice.[132] On the other hand, while it remains the Court's last formal word on the Fourteenth Amendment rights of pregnant workers, '. . . the jurisprudence of pregnancy discrimination (is) in chaos.'[133]

In that respect, nothing much has changed since Ruth Bader Ginsberg wrote in the early 1980s that the 'Burger Court decisions relating to pregnancy in the employment context display less than perfect logic and consistency.'[134] Politically, however, a Democrat-controlled Congress and the Court seemed to have reached an unspoken agreement, whereby given a choice of interpreting Congressional will on pregnancy disability in a conservative or liberal fashion, the Justices will choose the latter. Assured of Congressional support, the Court can afford to reject the exhortations of the Republican-controlled White House to cease the extension of pregnancy-disability rights.[135] The Court further observes a discreet silence on *Geduldig*, neither offending the Congress by using it to thwart statute law nor offending the White House by openly overruling it. Thus, despite the fact that *Cal Fed* and *Geduldig* are blatantly contradictory, the Court did not even address that tension. On the other hand, when, shortly before *Cal Fed*, the Court was squarely confronted with an Equal Protection as well as a Title VII challenge to a pregnancy-disability law, the Justices adroitly avoided it. They chose to decide *Cal Fed* first, on statutory grounds, and then remand the other case, *Miller-Wohl Co. v. Commissioner of Labour*,[136] for reconsideration in the light of the *Cal Fed* decision. Of course, there is no certain way of knowing exactly why the Court disposed of *Miller-Wohl* in this way: but it surely resulted in removing a thorny problem from the Court's docket.[137]

Equal rights meets fetal rights: *Johnson Controls*

Despite the uncertainties and even contradictions within the Supreme Court's sex discrimination jurisprudence, the broad picture is of an institution that has recognised a widespread demand for social reform. Not only has it incorporated many of those reformist sentiments into the nation's constitutional and statutory law, it has at times added new impetus to the process. In short, it has been cautiously progressive and innovative. Acceptance of its decisions has undoubtedly been helped by the fact that much of the political heat generated by feminism has been channelled into the issues of abortion rights and the Equal Rights Amendment. Yet with the latter defeated and the former under severe threat of reversal, it might be thought that a general backlash against feminist gains in the courts might soon prove successful. While a possibility, the evidence at this point suggests it will not happen. Most significantly, the Court recently took a case which looked to bring together the issues of equal employment rights for women and the status of fetuses, one of the key aspects of the abortion conflict. As such, it presented an opportunity for opponents of abortion and feminism to attack equal rights through a powerful political, legal and emotional framework. It was by no means clear how a Court controlled by a conservative majority, including four Reagan-Bush appointees, would respond to that challenge.

The case was *Automobile Workers v. Johnson Controls*,[138] decided in March 1991. Johnson Controls, Inc. manufactures batteries, a process which involves the use of lead and therefore exposes employees to well-documented health risks: in particular, exposure to lead increases the risks of miscarriage. Between 1979 and 1983 eight employees who became pregnant had blood lead levels higher than those recommended by the federal agency, the Occupational Safety and Health Administration (OSHA), for women intending to have children. The response of the company was to exclude all women capable of bearing children from jobs that exposed them to lead.

A number of employees and the United Auto Workers union, who organised at nine of the company's plants, brought a class action challenging Johnson Controls' fetal protection policy as a violation of Title VII of the Civil Rights Act of 1964, as amended by the Pregnancy Discrimination Act of 1978. The gravity of the implications of the company policy was illustrated by the fact that one of the plaintiff employees, Mary Craig, had opted to be sterilised rather than lose her job which exposed her to lead.

The District Court and Appeals Court had decided that the company's policy was 'facially neutral', that is, it involved discriminatory effect rather than intent; or disparate impact rather than disparate treatment. Furthermore, in the light of the recent *Wards Cove* decision,[139] the burden of persuasion lay with the *employees* to show that the policy was not justified by reasonable business necessity. If, on the other hand, the policy was taken as facially discriminatory, then the *employer* would have to demonstrate that it qualified as a Bona Fide Occupational Qualification (BFOQ) – an exception provided for in Title VII, whereby a person's sex can be regarded as debilitating to job performance.

A unanimous Supreme Court reversed the lower courts on the applicability of the 'business necessity' test and then went on to hold that the fetal protection policy could not be regarded as a BFOQ. Justice Blackmun delivered the opinion of the Court.[140] He had no doubt that the policy discriminated against women, stating bluntly that 'The bias in Johnson Controls' policy is obvious. Fertile men, but not fertile women, are given a choice as to whether they wish to risk their reproductive health for a particular job.'[141] And this despite evidence in the record that lead exposure damaged the reproductive system of men as well as women. He also dismissed the company's contention that the benign purpose of its policy, protecting fetal health, somehow mitigated the discrimination: 'Whether an employment practice involves disparate treatment through explicit facial discrimination does not depend on why the employer discriminates but rather on the explicit terms of the discrimination.'[142]

The critical question therefore became whether the discrimination could be defended as, in the language of Title VII, '. . . a bona fide occupational qualification reasonably necessary to the normal operation of that particular business or enterprise.' The Court had shown in the past, however, that this standard could work both for and against gender equality. In *Dothard v. Rawlinson*,[143] for example, a majority of the Justices struck down part of an Alabama statute that required all prison guards to be at least five feet two inches tall and weigh at least 120 pounds. Against the lone dissent of Justice White, eight Justices found no evidence that such qualifications were related to job performance. Six of the Justices then went on, however, to uphold a different part of the statute which prohibited women guards from working in 'contact positions' in men's maximum security jails. Writing for the Court, Justice Stewart argued that 'A woman's relative ability to maintain order in a male, maximum-security, unclassified penitentiary of the type Alabama now runs could be directly reduced by her womanhood. There is a basis in fact for expecting that sex offenders who have criminally assaulted women in the past would be moved to do so again if access to women were established within the prison.'[144] As well discriminating against women because they might be victims, thereby adding insult to injury, Justice Marshall pointed out in dissent that the Court seemed to be relying on stereotype: '. . . the fundamental justification for the decision is that women as guards will generate sexual assaults. With all respect, this rationale regrettably perpetuates one of the most insidious of the old myths about women – that women, wittingly or not, are seductive sexual objects.'[145] As only Justice Brennan agreed with him, however, it is not surprising that feminists have been critical of the Court's BFOQ jurisprudence.[146]

Justice Blackmun sought to distinguish *Dothard* and other cases which had upheld a BFOQ by confining them to situations where third-party interests – such as prisoners – were an essential element of the 'business'. In this way, he dealt with the problematic issue of the rights of the fetus and the vulnerability of the company to a suit brought by a child damaged as a fetus. The concurring opinion of Justice White had argued that the avoidance of risk to third parties is inherently part of the normal operation of any business: 'On the facts of this case, for example, protecting fetal safety while carrying out the duties of battery manufacturing is as much a legitimate concern as is safety to third parties in guarding prisons.'[147] From this Justice White concluded that in future cases, a fetal protection policy *might* constitute a BFOQ, something the majority were eager to dismiss. Justice Blackmun did not view fetal protection as essential to Johnson Controls' business, nor, by implication, to any other: 'No one can disregard the possibility of injury to future children; the BFOQ, however, is not so broad that it transforms this deep social concern into an essential aspect of batterymaking.'[148]

Johnson Controls was an important decision in the campaign for gender equality. Partly this was because it '. . . prohibited employers from forcing women to make impossible choices between having jobs and having families.'[149] Moreover, although there was no direct connection between this fetal protection policy and the right to choose an abortion, Justice Blackmun took the opportunity to emphasise the importance of women's autonomy in reproductive issues: 'With the PDA, Congress made clear that the decision to become pregnant or to work while becoming either pregnant or capable of becoming pregnant was reserved for each individual woman to make for herself.'[150]

When we compare the unanimous decision in *Johnson Controls* with that in *Hoyt v. Florida* in 1961, it is clear that the Court has come a long way in the intervening years. From being excused jury duty on account of her 'special responsibilities' at home, a woman can now insist on a right to a job on an equal basis with men, even where it may do far greater and more tangible harm to those 'special responsibilities' than spending a few hours or days at the courthouse. By and large, the Court has moved with the flow of broader social and political developments, uneven and imperfect as that may be. Moreover, even those who criticise the inadequacies of the Court's approach to gender equality also recognise that the task of constructing a better alternative is by no means straightforward. As Mary Becker put it recently:

> We cannot, today, know what an 'ideal' world with equality between the sexes would look like, let alone how best to get there. With race we can at least imagine a world in which blacks and whites are equal. We can imagine a world in which race is no more important than eye colour. We cannot so easily imagine a world in which women and men are equal or in which sex would matter no more than eye colour. Most of us would not want to live in a world in which sex was no more important or relevant than eye colour.[151]

To assign a leading role in such a project to the Supreme Court is already to demand more of judges than most societies would deem feasible or desirable. To expect them to do it with a jurisprudence of original intent or even meaningful interpretivism is to ask the impossible. Not surprisingly, then, the Court has resorted to non-interpretivism in this area of the law, as in others involving social issues. On the whole, it appears to have read the political signals on gender equality quite skilfully.

Notes

1 *Hoyt v. Florida*, 368 US 57, 61–2 (1961).
2 *Ibid.*, p. 64.
3 Representative Howard K. Smith of Virginia introduced the amendment in the hope that opposition to it would be sufficiently widespread to cause the entire bill to be voted down, thereby defeating the bill's primary aim of combating race discrimination.
4 R. Gatlin, *American Women Since 1945*, Basingstoke, 1987, p. 201.
5 J. Mansbridge, *Why We Lost The ERA*, Chicago, 1986, p. 8.
6 *Ibid.*, p. 9.
7 Early supporters of ERA thus included the National Association of Women Lawyers and the National Federation of Business and Professional Women's Clubs; opponents included the Women's Bureau, the National Consumer League and the League of Women Voters, as well as trade unions: D. Rhode, *Justice and Gender: Sex Discrimination and the Law*, Cambridge, Mass., 1989, pp. 34–8; Mansbridge, *op. cit.*, pp. 8–9.
8 Mansbridge, *op. cit.*, p. 9.

9 R. Eisler, *The Equal Rights Handbook*, New York, 1978, pp. 16–20; Mansbridge, *op. cit.*, p. 10.
10 H. Graham, *The Civil Rights Era*, Oxford, 1990, pp. 406–7; Mansbridge, *op. cit.*, p. 10.
11 Graham, *op. cit.*, pp. 418–19.
12 R. Cowan, 'Women's rights through litigation: an examination of the American civil liberties union women's rights project, 1971–1976', *Columbia Human Rights Law Review*, VIII, 1976, pp. 373–412, 386.
13 *Ibid.*, p. 389.
14 Betty Friedan, quoted in Rhode, *op. cit.*, p. 61.
15 Kate Millet, Catherine MacKinnon and Shulamith Firestone are considered representative of this radical strand within modern feminism.
16 This concept of the Court's role was first raised by Justice Harlan Stone's famous footnote four in the case of *US v. Carolene Products Co.* Stone left hanging in the air the question of '. . . whether prejudice against discrete and insular minorities may be a special condition, which tends seriously to curtail the operation of those political processes ordinarily to be relied upon to protect minorities, and which may call for a correspondingly more searching judicial inquiry.', 304 US 144, 152–3, n. 4 (1938).
17 404 US 71 (1971).
18 Shortly before the *Reed* decision, the Court struck its first blow against sex discrimination under Title VII of the Civil Rights Act of 1964. In *Phillips v. Martin Marietta Corporation*, 400 US 542 (1971), the Court ruled that an employer could not refuse to employ mothers of pre-school children, if it did employ similarly situated fathers.
19 Cowan, *op. cit.*, p. 373.
20 Briefs of Counsel, 30 L Ed 2d 864.
21 *Reed*, p. 76.
22 *Ibid.*, p. 76.
23 Blasi, *op. cit.*, p. 133.
24 Mansbridge, *op. cit.*, p. 12.
25 411 US 677 (1973).
26 347 US 497 (1954).
27 *Ibid.*, p. 254.
28 *Frontiero*, p. 682.
29 *Ibid.*, p. 686.
30 *Ibid.*, p. 686.
31 Woodward and Armstrong, *op. cit.*, p. 255.
32 *Reed*, p. 692.
33 *Ibid.*
34 *Ibid.*, p. 691.
35 416 US 351 (1974).
36 Between those two cases the Court had also decided *Stanley v. Illinois*, 405 US 645 (1972), which extended to widowed, unwed fathers the same right to demonstrate their fitness to have custody of their children as widowed, unwed mothers.
37 *Kahn*, p. 353.
38 *Ibid.*, p. 360.
39 *Ibid.*, p. 362.
40 419 US 498 (1975).
41 The four who joined Stewart were Chief Justice Burger and Justices Blackmun, Powell and Rehnquist.
42 *Ballard*, p. 508 (emphasis in original).
43 *Ibid.*, pp. 511–12 (emphasis in original).
44 420 US 636 (1975).
45 *Wiesenfeld*, p. 655. However, Rehnquist, Powell and Burger did not subscribe to some of the most important other features of Brennan's opinion. Powell, for example, predicated his vote not on the inequality inherent in restricting the *father's* right to stay at

home to care for the children, but on the *deceased mother's* right to have her family
protected to the same degree as a father, *Ibid.*, pp. 654–5.
46 *Ibid.*, p. 652.
47 421 US 7 (1975).
48 *Stanton*, p. 14.
49 *Ibid.*, pp. 14–15.
50 Mansbridge, *op. cit.*, p. 13.
51 See Chapter 4, *supra*.
52 Graham, *op. cit.*, p. 419.
53 Mansbridge, *op. cit.*, p. 13.
54 September 1974, p. 1. Quoted in Eisler, *op. cit.*, p. 12.
55 Mansbridge, *op. cit.*, pp.144–5.
56 *Ibid.*, p. 144.
57 Eisler, *op. cit.* p. 11.
58 Mansbridge, *op. cit.*, p. 16.
59 J. Gelb and M. Palley, *Women and Public Policies*, Princeton, 1982, p. 7.
60 *Ibid.*, p. 78.
61 *Ibid.*, p. 8.
62 429 US 190 (1976).
63 Three other Justices explicitly agreed with Brennan by joining his opinion – White,
    Marshall and Blackmun. Justice Powell did not join Brennan, but he did enter a
    concurring opinion saying that ' *Reed* and subsequent cases involving gender-based
    classifications make clear that the Court subjects such classifications to a more critical
    examination than is normally applied when "fundamental" constitutional rights and
    "suspect classes" are not present.', p. 210. Powell then went on to apply the intermediate
    standard. Justice Stevens thought all talk of different standards misleading, as under-
    lying them was really just one standard; and Justice Stewart said nothing at all on
    standards, but in declaring the Oklahoma statute to be 'irrational' he clearly applied the
    rational basis test.
64 *Craig*, p. 197.
65 *Ibid.*, p. 199.
66 *Ibid.*, p. 204.
67 *Ibid.*, pp. 216–17.
68 For a detailed critique of the Court's decisions as insufficiently radical, see A.
    Freedman, 'Sex equality, sex differences and the Supreme Court', *Yale Law Journal*,
    LXXXXII, 1983, pp. 913–68.
69 430 US 199 (1977).
70 *Goldfarb*, p. 215. Brennan's opinion was joined by Justices White, Marshall and Powell;
    and Justice Stevens also agreed that the provision was based on a traditional view of
    women's economic role, but thought that it discriminated against men rather than
    women, p. 223.
71 430 US 313 (1977).
72 *Ibid.*, p. 317.
73 *Ibid.*, p. 321.
74 See, for example, *Califano v. Westcott*, 433 US 75 (1979), in which the Court struck a
    rule that paid AFDC benefits to a family with an unemployed father but not to one with
    an unemployed mother; *Wengler v. Druggists Mutual Insurance Co.*, 446 US 142 (1980),
    striking a State law distinguishing between the sexes in survivors' benefits; and *Los
    Angeles Department of Water and Power v. Manhart*, 435 US 702 (1978) and *Arizona
    Governing Committee v. Norris*, 463 US 1073 (1983), striking rules in pensions plans that
    explicitly disfavoured women because actuarial tables showed they lived longer than
    men.
75 In some of these cases, of course, men also benefited materially. And in cases such as
    Orr v. Orr, 440 US 268 (1979), where the Court ruled unconstitutional an Alabama law

which imposed alimony obligations on men, but not women, the Justices deprived
women of narrow economic advantage in pursuit of the higher goal of gender equality.
Basically, however, the Court's line was to promote the material well-being and status of
women, rather than men.

76 See previous chapter.
77 480 US 616 (1987).
78 A very full account of the case can be found in M. I. Urofsky, *A Conflict of Rights: The
Supreme Court and Affirmative Action*, New York, 1991.
79 *Ibid.*, p. 94. Two other conservative groups also entered *amicus* briefs before the
Supreme Court: the Pacific Legal Foundation and the Mid-Atlantic Legal Foundation.
80 *Ibid.*, p. 131.
81 Fried tells a rather different story, saying that the facts of the case were not advan-
tageous to the administration's cause and he sought, in vain, to make the case 'go away',
Order & Law, p. 117.
82 *Ibid.*, p. 127.
83 443 US 193 (1979). See Chapter 5 for a detailed discussion of this case.
84 *op. cit.*, p. 118.
85 *Johnson*, p. 648.
86 *Ibid.*, pp. 671–3.
87 *Ibid.*, p. 657.
88 *Ibid.*, p. 644.
89 *Ibid.*, pp.650–1.
90 *Ibid.*, p. 621.
91 *Ibid.*, p. 637.
92 *Ibid.*, p. 656.
93 *Ibid.*, p. 668 (italics in original).
94 *Ibid.*, p. 668.
95 *Ibid.*, p. 675.
96 *Ibid.*, p. 677.
97 Urofsky, *op. cit.*, p. 178.
98 See previous chapter for a discussion of the following Term's cases and the ensuing
struggle over the Civil Rights Act of 1991.
99 M. Becker, 'Prince Charming: abstract equality' in P. Kurland, G. Casper and D.
Hutchinson (eds), *The Supreme Court Review 1987*, Chicago, 1978, pp. 201–47, 205.
100 *Ibid.*, p. 183.
101 *Ibid.*, p. 212. Other critics of formal equality include C. MacKinnon, 'Towards a
feminist jurisprudence', *Stanford Law Review*, XXXIV, 1982, pp. 703–37, and 'Reflections on sex equality under the law', *Yale Law Journal*, C, 1991, pp. 1281–328; A.
Grossman, 'Striking down fetal protection policies: a feminist victory?', *Virginia Law
Review*, LXXVII, 1991, pp. 1607–36; and Freedman, *op. cit.*
102 440 US 268 (1979).
103 Becker, *op. cit.*, p. 214.
104 417 US 484 (1974). The Court had dealt with the issue before *Gedulig*, but had avoided
treating it as an equal protection matter. See, for example, *Cleveland Board of Education v.
LaFleur*, 414 US 632 (1974), in which the Court held that a rule requiring the automatic
dismissal or leave of absence of pregnant women violated due process because it created
an 'irrebuttable presumption' that the women were unfit to work. This due process
argument had not been raised by the parties to the case, who had instead focused on the
Equal Protection issue. Ruth Bader Ginsberg interpreted the Court's side-step as '. . . a
storm warning for a case in the wings', in Blasi, *op. cit.*, p. 149. That case was *Gedulig*,
decided shortly afterwards.
105 US Supreme Court Law Reports (Lawyers' Edition), 41 L Ed 2d 256.
106 He was joined in his opinion by Chief Justice Burger and Justices White, Powell,
Blackmun and Rehnquist. The dissenters were Justices Brennan, Douglas and

Marshall.
107 *Gedulig*, p. 495.
108 *Ibid.*, pp. 496–7.
109 *Ibid.*
110 'The Supreme Court, 1976 Term', *Harvard Law Review*, XCI, 1977–78, pp. 72–294, 243, commenting upon *General Electric v. Gilbert*, infra, which employed the same rationale.
111 S. Law, 'Rethinking sex and the constitution', *University of Pennsylvania Law Review*, CXXXII, 1984, pp. 955–1040, 983.
112 *Gedulig*, p. 501.
113 429 US 125 (1976).
114 *General Electric*, pp. 134–5.
115 *Ibid.*, pp.141–2.
116 *Congressional Quarterly Almanac*, XXXIII, Washington, DC, 1977, p. 486.
117 quoted in W. Strimling, 'The constitutionality of state laws providing employment leave for pregnancy: rethinking *Gedulig* after *Cal Fed.*', *California Law Review*, LXXVII, 1989, pp. 171–221, 172 (n. 8).
118 *Newsport News Shipbuilding & Dry Dock v. EEOC*, 462 US 699 (1983).
119 *Ibid.*, pp. 688–9. Rehnquist was joined in dissent only by Justice Powell.
120 *Ibid.*, p. 684.
121 *Ibid.*, p. 685.
122 479 US 272 (1987).
123 Justice Marshall wrote the Court's opinion and was joined by Justices Brennan, Blackmun, O'Connor and, in part, by Justice Stevens. Justice Scalia voted with the majority, but only on the basis of a narrow technicality. Justice White wrote the dissenting opinion, joined by Justices Rehnquist and Powell.
124 *Supra*, n. 117.
125 *Cal Fed*, p. 297.
126 'The language of the amended statute indicates that Congress considered pregnant women similar to others who were equal in their ability or inability to work. From this perspective, the outcome in (*Cal Fed*) is inconsistent with a formal standard of equality for Title VII.' Becker, *op. cit.*, 205.
127 *Cal Fed*, p. 285.
128 *Ibid.*, p. 289.
129 A. Scales, 'The emergence of a feminist jurisprudence: an essay', *Yale Law Journal*, VC, 1986, pp. 1373–1403, 1385.
130 Strimling, *op. cit.*, p. 172.
131 *Ibid.*, p. 245.
132 *Ibid.*, p. 984.
133 *Ibid.*, p. 189.
134 In Blasi, *op. cit.*, p. 149.
135 Charles Fried, the US Solicitor-General, appeared as *amicus curiae* in *Cal Fed*, on behalf of the Reagan administration, urging the Court to strike the California statute.
136 107 S Ct 683 (1987).
137 Strimling, *op. cit.*, p. 197, n. 124.
138 499 US -, 113 L Ed 2d 158, 111 S Ct – (1991).
139 490 US 642 (1989). Shortly after the Court's decision in *Johnson Controls*, Congress reversed *Wards Cove* by the Civil Rights Act of 1991. See Chapter 5.
140 Although the Court's decision was unanimous, there were differences in rationale: Blackmun was joined by Justices Marshall, Stevens, O'Connor and Souter: Justice White wrote a concurring opinion joined by Chief Justice Rehnquist and Justice Kennedy; and Justice Scalia entered a sole concurring opinion.
141 *Johnson Controls*, p. 172 (Lawyers' Edition).
142 *Ibid.*, pp. 173–4.

143 433 US 321 (1977).
144 *Ibid.*, p. 335.
145 *Ibid.*, p. 345.
146 See, for example, Grossman, *op. cit.*, pp. 1614–17.
147 *Johnson Controls*, p. 185.
148 *Ibid.*, p. 176.
149 Statement of Kate Michelman, Executive Director, National Abortion Rights Action
       League, on the US Supreme Court Decision in *UAW v. Johnson Controls*, 20 March
       1991: NARAL Office, Washington, D.C.
150 *Johnson Controls*, p. 178. Blackmun also wrote: 'Johnson Controls' professed moral and
ethical concerns about the welfare of the next generation do not suffice to establish a
BFOQ of female sterility. Decisions about the welfare of future children must be left to
the parents who conceive, bear, support, and raise them rather than to the employers
who hire those parents.', p. 178.
151 *Ibid.*, p. 234.

Seven—Religion, sex and politics

Religion, sex, and politics: in the days of my youth, these were the subjects you were not supposed to discuss at a dinner party. Today, religion and sex and the other social issues are present in American politics in the way that automobiles are present in Los Angeles: they are all around us; they bring tears to our eyes; and we don't know what to do with them.[1]

Sexual non-conformity

No other issue illustrates the clash between traditional religious values and sexual freedom as clearly as that of gay rights. To be sure, condemnation of homosexual and lesbian love is not confined to those who profess religious faith. Yet it is also true that the disapproval of homosexuality has strong roots in the Judaeo-Christian tradition and in the Old Testament in particular: 'This contempt is rooted in such Old Testament books as Leviticus, carried forward into the Roman world by such disciples as St. Paul, and turned into law when Christianity became the state religion in A.D. 323. Homosexuality was a damnable sin, and those guilty of it could be legally murdered from that time until the days of the founding of the colonies in the New World. The bundles of wood stacked around the people burned alive were called faggots.'[2] The theological origin of anti-sodomy statutes is further confirmed by the fact that sodomy did not become a *secular*, as opposed to an *ecclesiastical*, crime in English law until 1533 and that largely as a result of the general secularisation of the law following England's break with Rome.[3]

Despite the 'sexual revolution' of recent decades, the legitimacy of homosexuality still remains to be established in most people's minds. According to one series of polls, in 1973 some 76 per cent of Americans believed homosexual sex between consenting adults to be always wrong or almost always wrong. In 1989 over 74 per cent took the same attitude, with very little variation revealed in the polls taken in the intervening years.[4] While toleration of homosexuality is more evident than approval, there is still considerable resistance to its acceptance: in 1977, opinion on whether homosexual relations between consenting adults should be legal or not divided equally, both at 43 per cent. By 1989, the number favouring legality had increased to 47 per cent and those favouring illegality had fallen to 36 per cent.[5]

The precise reasons for the persistence of the taboo against homosexuality are debatable, though it is probably linked in some degree to the understanding of what causes homosexuality in the first place. And here there has been an evolution of ideas that is supportive of the concept of gay rights. Until the late nineteenth century, the predominant belief in both popular and medical opinion was that homosexuality was a sin, a perversion wilfully engaged in by the morally depraved. It was this attitude which underpinned most of the state legislation outlawing homosexual relations. Towards the end of the century, medical opinion altered, adopting the belief that homosexuality was an illness: while still morally wrong, homosexuality was recognised as being an intrinsic part of some individuals' personalities and therefore worthy of compassion or pity, rather than brute punishment.[6] Nevertheless, the image of homosexuality remained a profoundly negative one in most people's eyes: what was necessary for the creation of a positive image was the development of a political and cultural movement by homosexuals themselves, proclaiming pride in their sexual orientation. As with so many other countercultural movements, it was the broader historical currents of the 1960s which provided a propitious context for a gay pride movement. Homosexual and lesbian organisations had existed before the 1960s – the Mattachine Society and the Daughters of Bilitis, for example – but they tended to be cautious and discreet.[7] The atmosphere of the 1960s encouraged a higher public profile: 'The women's movement's attack on traditional gender roles, increased openness and lessened taboos on sexuality, and the "culture of protest" in the 1960s all contributed to the spread of "gay liberation".'[8]

Moreover, in the changed climate of the decade, harassment of gays by the authorities produced counter-attack rather than retreat. In 1968, after a police raid on a gay bar in Los Angeles, one of the arrested began a newsletter, the *Los Angeles Advocate*, which became a national newspaper for gay Americans. Most famous of all, however, was the police raid on the gay bar, the Stonewall Inn, on Christopher Street in Greenwich Village, New York, in June 1969. When the police beat up and arrested some of the bar's patrons, other gays in and near the bar fought back and gave as good as they got. This refusal by gays to accept passively the routine harassment to which they had always been subjected marked the launch of the gay rights movement.[9] As a direct response to the Stonewall Riots, the Gay Liberation Front was formed in New York and in 1970 there occurred the first Christopher Street parade calling on all gays to come 'out of the closets and into the streets'.[10]

By the end of the 1960s, therefore, the issue of gay rights was on the political agenda in the United States. Furthermore, attitudes towards homosexuals in elite medical, legal and political circles had already begun to change. In 1962, the American Law Institute's Model Penal Code recommended the decriminalisation of consensual, adult homosexual sex.[11] Medical professionals began to see homosexuality less as an illness and more as a 'neutral difference' which required no discriminatory treatment. As a result, in 1973, the American Psychiatric Association removed homosexuality from their list of psychiatric disorders and two years later the American Public Health Association and the American Psychological Association followed suit.[12] In 1961, Illinois became the first state to legislate on the sodomy decriminalistion proposals then pending before the American Law Institute. By 1987, just over half the states had done the same.[13]

In short, the march towards gay rights was beginning to look very much like that towards abortion rights: elite professionals provided the impetus and respectability for reform from the top down and gay activists were organising and demanding recognition of their claim to civil liberties. It is not surprising, then, that gays should seek vindication of those claims in the federal courts. Moreover, the Supreme Court's invention and development of a constitutional right to privacy since 1965 seemed admirably suited to that campaign: what, after all, is more private than the sexual intimacy of two consenting adults in their own home?

In 1976, male homosexuals had challenged the constitutionality of Virginia's anti-sodomy law. In *Doe v. Commonwealth's Attorney*,[14] however, the Supreme Court summarily affirmed the lower court's dismissal of their suit, without explaining why. Three Justices – Brennan, Marshall and Stevens – dissented from this disposition of the case, but they lacked the fourth vote traditionally required for a full hearing of the arguments. That situation did not change for another ten years, until the Court decided to grant review in the case of *Bowers v. Hardwick*.[15]

This case had an unusual history, but one which appeared only to strengthen the constitutional claim to privacy of Michael Hardwick, the gay resident of Atlanta, Georgia, who filed suit. In August 1982, a police officer arrived at Hardwick's home to serve a warrant on him for public drinking. Admitted by a housemate, the officer then entered Hardwick's bedroom, where he saw him performing oral sex on another man. The officer arrested both Hardwick and his companion for violation of Georgia's anti-sodomy statute.[16]

The District Attorney, however, declined to prosecute: in fact, like most state anti-sodomy laws, Georgia's was hardly ever enforced. Indeed, in oral argument before the Court, the District Attorney testified that the last time it had been enforced where the offence was committed in a private home was probably in the 1930s or 1940s.[17]

A second notable feature of the Georgia statute was that, on its face, it applied as much to heterosexuals, married or not, as it did to homosexuals. The relevant clause defined the offence as follows: 'A person commits the offence of sodomy when he performs or submits to any sexual act involving the sex organs of one person and the mouth or anus of another ...'[18] Although Georgia's statutory proscription of sodomy dated back to 1816, this particular formulation was enacted only in 1968: non-enforcement, therefore, could not be explained simply by long-standing neglect of a statutory relic. Moreover, the 1968 reformulation seems to have been intended to be as comprehensive as possible, and specifically a response to recent state court decisions excluding lesbian sex and heterosexual cunnilingus from the ambit of the pre-1968 law.[19] What the Supreme Court was faced with in *Bowers*, then, was a statute whose true purpose was highly uncertain: on the one hand, it imposed a new blanket ban on all oral and anal sex; but on the other, the state seemed to enforce it only rarely and highly selectively.

When the District Attorney decided against prosecuting Michael Hardwick, the state presumably thought that was the end of the matter. However, in the manner now typical of 'reform litigation', an interest group stepped in: the American Civil Liberties Union persuaded Hardwick that his would make a good case with which to test the constitutionality of anti-sodomy laws.[20] Hardwick failed in the federal District Court, but the Appeals Court ruled that the Georgia statute did indeed violate his constitutional right to privacy.

The Supreme Court now reversed that decision by a 5–4 majority. Justice White's opinion for the Court was curt and failed to respond to many of the substantial points made in the dissenting opinions of Justices Blackmun and Stevens. White defined the case and its central issue in such narrow fashion that Hardwick's claim never stood a chance. In the first place, he ignored the fact that the Georgia statute applied to heterosexuals and homosexuals alike and assessed it only as it applied to the latter.[21] Then, rather than consider gays' right to privacy as a principle, he narrowed the question to '. . . whether the Federal Constitution confers a fundamental right upon homosexuals to engage in sodomy. . .'[22] Reviewing the Court's precedents, he defined privacy as little more than the sum of the actual practices approved in those cases: that is, child rearing and education, family relationships, procreation, marriage, contraception and abortion. He then simply asserted: 'No connection between family, marriage, or procreation on the one hand and homosexual activity on the other has been demonstrated . . .'[23]

This reductive approach to the Court's privacy precedents was matched by Justice White's static approach to the question of whether the right to engage in homosexual sex should be considered fundamental for constitutional purposes. Applying the test of whether the right at issue is rooted in the nation's history and tradition, he noted that until 1961, all fifty states outlawed sodomy and that twenty-four states and the District of Columbia still did. He concluded that: 'Against this background, to claim that a right to engage in such conduct is "deeply rooted in this Nation's history and tradition" . . . is, at best, facetious.'[24] Such reasoning might be plausible in isolation, but when compared to the Court's decision in *Roe v. Wade*, it is quite unpersuasive. In the case of abortion, State criminal statutes had roots going back just as far as those on sodomy and the process of decriminalisation in the contemporary period had not progressed nearly as far. Abortion rights were no more rooted in the nation's traditions than sodomy rights, yet seven Justices had voted to extend the right of privacy to encompass them in 1973.[25]

Justice White defended this approach partly on grounds of judicial restraint, arguing that the Court needed to demonstrate that the identification of unenumerated fundamental rights in the Constitution was based on more than the value preferences of the Justices.[26] Yet it is by no means clear that White's approach is any less subjective than that followed in *Roe*. In *Roe*, the Court chose to give considerable weight to the modern trend of legislation, while in *Bowers* Justice White chose to ignore that trend altogether. Such subjectivity and variation in the choice of history to be considered does nothing to promote the image or substance of judicial impartiality.[27]

Equally open to accusations of subjective bias is Justice White's definition of the privacy issue at stake. Indeed, Justice Blackmun accused him of exhibiting an '. . . almost obsessive focus on homosexual activity . . .'[28] that could be justified neither by the language of the Georgia statute nor by any valid understanding of the concept of privacy. The Court's past privacy cases, he argued, do not simply approve specific actions; rather, they acknowledge the right of individuals to be free of governmental interference in making decisions which are intimate and vital to a person's self-definition and happiness. Thus, he argued, 'We protect the decision whether to have a child because parenthood alters so dramatically an individual's self-definition, not because of demographic considerations or the Bible's command to be fruitful and multiply . . . And we protect the family because it contributes so powerfully to the happiness of individuals, not because of a preference for stereotypical households.'[29] Freedom to choose the nature of one's intimate sexual relationship with others is equally important to self-definition and happiness and is therefore fundamental in a constitutional sense. And before the state can interfere in such a decision, it should have a compelling reason for doing so. The majority Justices can only ignore this through '. . . the most wilful blindness . . .'[30] to the importance of sexual intimacy. Thus:

> The Court claims that its decision today merely refuses to recognise a fundamental right to engage in homosexual sodomy; what the Court really has refused to recognise is the fundamental interest all individuals have in controlling the nature of their intimate associations with others.[31]

There can be little doubt that the *Bowers* majority employed a highly restrictive concept of privacy that was incompatible with precedent. As the *Harvard Law Review* put it, 'Had the majority examined the regulated conduct in *Hardwick* at the same level of generality employed in previous privacy decisions, it would have found constitutional protection for private, consensual, same-sex sodomy.'[32]

Why then did the *Bowers* majority change tack to block the reform of laws on homosexual sodomy, when it had previously been prepared to stimulate and accelerate other reform efforts? Most obviously the Justices may have been motivated by a moral repugnance of homosexuality. Justice White disclaimed any such motivation,[33] but in a concurring opinion, Chief Justice Burger let his moral outrage show. Summoning up not merely the Judaeo-Christian and Roman proscriptions of sodomy, he recalled Blackstone's description of it as 'the infamous crime against nature' and 'a crime not fit to be named'. Thus, wrote the Chief Justice, 'To hold that the act of homosexual sodomy is somehow protected as a fundamental right would be to cast aside millenia of moral teaching.'[34]

Moral disapproval apart, however, the Court in *Bowers* may well have feared a political backlash on the lines of those that had followed their earlier reformist decisions on abortion and the death penalty. Justice White felt moved to remind his colleagues of past calamities that had resulted from the Court's vigorous use of substantive due process:

> The Court is most vulnerable and comes nearest to illegitimacy when it deals with judge-made constitutional law having little or no cognisable roots in the language or design of the Constitution. That this is so was painfully demonstrated by the face-off between the Executive and the Court in the 1930s, which resulted in the repudiation of the substantive gloss that the Court had placed on the Due Process Clause of the Fifth and Fourteenth Amendments. There should be, therefore, great resistance to expand (*sic*) the substantive reach of those Clauses, particularly if it requires redefining the category of rights deemed to be fundamental. Otherwise, the Judiciary necessarily takes to itself further authority to govern the country without express constitutional authority.[35]

This is not, of course, judicial restraint as an interpretive principle but rather as a political tactic. That, on the other hand, does not invalidate its use. The Supreme Court lives in a real political world and the real political climate of 1986 was hardly conducive to a highly publicised declaration of the moral and constitutional equivalence of heterosexual and homosexual activities, no matter how desirable such a declaration might be.

On the other hand, the blatant injustice of the *Bowers* decision strongly suggests that the Court should not have bowed to the prejudices of the political majority. Once an unenumerated constitutional right to privacy is acknowledged, no group has a stronger claim to protection of their sexual intimacy than gays. In the first place, they are a prime example of a 'discrete and insular minority' that it has been the Court's self-assigned mission to protect over the past forty or so years. No only have gays suffered marginalisation, vilification and physical brutality as a matter of routine, but, unlike women, for example, they are not sufficiently numerous in the electorate to ensure protection of their rights through the political process.

Furthermore, 'The burden imposed on individuals by sodomy statutes is comparable to that imposed on pregnant women in *Roe v. Wade*, and the State interests justifying the regulation of abortion are far more compelling than those justifying the regulation of sodomy.'[36] Unlike abortion, where the entity of the foetus requires consideration, there is no other party to consider in sodomy cases apart from the consenting adults involved. And as Justice Blackmun pointed out, it is not reasonable to classify sodomy along with other proscribed 'victimless crimes', such as drug-taking or possession of firearms, because at least in some circumstances, drugs and firearms *are* dangerous, but sodomy is not.[37] Ultimately, Justice White cited only one basis for the state's right to ban sodomy: '. . . the presumed belief of a majority of the electorate in Georgia that homosexual sodomy is immoral and unacceptable.'[38] However, as Laurence Tribe pointed out in oral argument on behalf of Hardwick, many Americans used to believe sincerely that interracial marriage was similarly reprehensible and numerous states legislated accordingly. That did not prevent the Supreme Court from striking down such laws in 1967 in *Loving v. Virginia*.[39] As Tribe put it, '. . . this Court did not think that the Constitution's mission was to freeze that historical vision into place.'[40] Even putting aside the fact that, like racism, homophobia is often based on ignorance and fear, White's justification is hardly convincing when the state does little or nothing actually to enforce its belief that sodomy causes social harm. In the end, the main purpose of the Georgia statute appears to be to degrade those who do not conform to majority morality. But as Justice Blackmun said, '. . . the mere knowledge that other individuals do not adhere to one's value system cannot be a legally cognisable interest . . . let alone an interest that can justify invading the houses, hearts, and minds of citizens who choose to live their lives differently.'[41]

In 1990, Justice Powell openly acknowledged that he had 'probably made a mistake' in voting with the majority in *Bowers*.[42] Had he indeed voted otherwise, the *Bowers* case would stand as yet another important victory for the use of litigation for progressive social reform. As it is, it probably marks the end of an era on the Court when the Justices were willing to play a dynamic role in developing social policy. Modern substantive due process has been the flagship of non-interpretivist judicial review; yet *Bowers* and the recent abortion decisions suggest that far from expanding it to encompass further variations in lifestyle choices, the Court may not even be willing to defend its progeny from roll-back.

In 1989 the case of *Michael H. v. Gerald D.*,[43] the Court gave credence to this interpretation of the significance of *Bowers*. The case involved a modern tale of social and sexual mores.[44] Gerald D., an oil company executive, was married to Carole D., an international model, who, in 1981, in California, gave birth to Victoria D. However, although Gerald was named as the father on the birth certificate, it later emerged after blood tests, that the father was almost certainly a neigh-bour of the couple, Michael H., with whom Carole had been having an adulterous affair.[45] During the child's first three years, she and her mother lived sometimes with Gerald, sometimes with Michael and sometimes with a third man, Scott K. Since June 1984, however, Carole and her husband had been living together continuously, with Victoria.

Michael brought an action to establish his paternity and visitation rights; Victoria, through her court-appointed guardian, filed suit to establish her right to maintain filial relations with both Michael and Gerald; and Gerald filed for summary dismissal of these suits, claiming that, under California law, there were no triable issues as to the facts of Victoria's paternity. The relevant statute created a presumption that a child born to a cohabiting married couple, where the husband is not impotent or sterile, is indeed a child of that marriage. Both the Superior Court of California and the California Court of Appeal denied that this statute violated Michael's and Victoria's procedural and substantive due process rights to maintain parent-child relations.[46]

On appeal to the Supreme Court, a 5–4 majority of the Justices affirmed the lower courts' decisions, although the voting was by no means straightforward.[47] The most interesting aspect of the case was the debate between Justice Scalia and Justice Brennan over the historical analysis to be applied in this and other substantive due process cases. For the political consequences of which of their views ultimately prevails are considerable.

As in *Bowers* and other substantive due process cases, the Court had to decide the threshold issue of whether the right asserted – Michael's interest in his relationship with Victoria – was so rooted in the nation's traditions and conscience that it merited constitutional protection. But Justice Scalia made the unprecedented argument that, when searching the nation's relevant history, the Court should focus on '. . . the most specific level at which a relevant tradition protecting, or denying protection to, the asserted right can be identified.'[48] General conceptualisation of traditions should be avoided wherever possible, because being imprecise, '. . . they permit judges to dictate rather than discern society's views . . . Although assuredly having the virtue (if it be that) of leaving judges free to decide as they think best when the unanticipated occurs, a rule of law that binds neither by text nor by any particular, identifiable tradition, is no rule of law at all.'[49]

Justice Scalia's methodology would appear to be a plea for judicial impartiality and restraint. Yet, as his concrete application of it in this case showed, it is no such thing. For Scalia does not ask whether there is a tradition of support for the parental interests of a natural father, but rather '. . . whether the States in fact award substantive parental rights to the natural father of a child *conceived within and born into an extant marital union that wishes to embrace the child*.'[50] With this formulation, Scalia was now able to balance traditions of support for the traditional family against traditions of support for the natural parent-child relationship. Unsurprisingly, he found little support for the latter where the child was born into a traditional family, whereas respect for the family was of the highest: '. . . indeed, sanctity would not be too strong a term . . .'[51] He had no problem, therefore, in finding that California was entitled to continue favouring the family over the rights of natural parents such as Michael H.

Justice Scalia's claim to judicial self-restraint in the face of the state legislature's right to favour the family over the natural parent does not, however, stand up to scrutiny. His choice of the 'most specific tradition' approach skewed the outcome of the case in two ways more typical of judicial activism. First, as a general proposition, it ran counter to the Court's previous substantive due process precedents. Not only the dissenters, but Justices O'Connor and Kennedy thought this '. . . somewhat inconsistent with our past decisions in this area . . . On occasion the Court has characterised relevant traditions protecting asserted rights at levels of generality that might not be "the most specific level" available . . . I would not foreclose the unanticipated by the prior imposition of a single mode of historical analysis.'[52]

Second, as applied here, the definition of the relevant tradition seems to have been selected partly through bias towards the unitary family and partly to avoid the force of four quite recent cases. These precedents, as Justice Brennan pointed out, argued strongly that where a natural father had established a substantial relationship with his child, his parental rights would be constitutionally protected.[53] By conditioning Michael's rights on the existence of a competing family claim, however, Justice Scalia could claim that the Court was entering new constitutional territory, where there were no controlling precedents on natural parents' rights. Thus, as the *Harvard Law Review* commented,

> Justice Scalia's bias toward the unitary family . . . led him to define Michael's relationship with Victoria in terms of Carole's marriage to Gerald and to ignore other factors that might have pointed to an alternative tradition of protecting Michael's rights. As the facts of *Michael H.* demonstrate, the plurality's approach allows judges' subjective determinations of the relevant facts effectively to predetermine the result of the inquiry into

tradition.[54]

The point, then, is not that Brennan is right and Scalia wrong, but that both employ methods of interpretation which would constitutionalise their subjective responses to cultural conflict. The Scalia-Rehnquist approach, if it ever commands a majority on the Court, heralds not so much a victory for judicial restraint over activism, as the political victory in the judicial arena of the conservative backlash to countercultural developments since the 1960s.

Politics and pornography

Along with homosexuality and adultery, public attitudes towards pornography give credence to the notions of liberal revolution and conservative counter-revolution over the last thirty or so years.[55] The liberal trend was measured by Gallup polls of 1969 and 1973 which showed a marked decline in disapproval of nudity in magazines and the theatre and topless waitresses.[56] Around the mid-1970s, however, that trend came to a halt and in some respects was reversed. For example, the number of those believing that the availability of sexual materials leads to a breakdown of morals rose steadily from a low of 51.4 per cent in 1975 to 62.5 per cent by 1989.[57]

Moreover, whatever Americans profess about pornography, there is no denying the fact that the sheer volume, variety, explicitness and violence of sexual materials has increased out of all recognition. As Hawkins and Zimring noted, whatever the precise volume of the pornographic trade, 'The most important change of the last two decades is the integration of sexually explicit communications into the mainstream of the American communications industry ... Heterosexual and homosexual materials that would have been considered hard-core pornography in 1965 were available in mainstream bookstores and newstands by 1975.'[58] One empirical study of pornographic books showed that between 1968 and 1974 the number of rape depictions doubled; and another of magazine covers showed that the use of bondage and domination imagery had increased significantly, with such displays being only second in frequency to those of couples engaged in sexual activity.[59]

The question of whether this proliferation of pornography is socially harmful or not is the central issue in the political conflict over censorship. Its importance is reflected in the fact the United States government has appointed two commissions to try to answer it in the last twenty-five years. In 1967, after holding its own hearings, Congress authorised President Johnson to set up the US Commission on Obscenity and Pornography (the Johnson Committee). The Commission issued its final report in 1970. Just fifteen years later, President Reagan instructed Attorney-General Edwin Meese to establish the Attorney-General's Commission on Pornography (the Meese Commission), which duly reported in 1986. Given the political and cultural changes in the intervening years, it is no surprise that the two Commissions reached radically different conclusions.

On the alleged connection between pornography and sex crimes, for example, the Johnson Commission reported that:

> The Commission cannot conclude that exposure to erotic materials is a factor in the causation of sex crimes.[60]

The Meese Commission found quite the reverse:

> We have reached the conclusion, unanimously and confidently, that the available evidence strongly supports the hypothesis that substantial exposure to sexually violent materials ... bears a causal relationship to antisocial acts of of sexual violence and, for some subgroups, possibly to unlawful acts of sexual violence.[61]

A similar disagreement emerged over whether pornography is detrimental to the perception and status of women. The Johnson Commission wrote:

> A recent survey shows that 41 per cent of American males and 46 per cent of females believe that 'sexual materials lead people to lose respect for women' ... Recent experiments ... suggest that such fears are probably unwarranted.[62]

Again, the Meese Commission asserted the contrary:

> To the extent that these materials create or reinforce the view that women's function is disproportionately to satisfy the sexual needs of men, then these materials will have pervasive effects on the treatment of women in society ... we feel confident in concluding that the view of women as available for sexual domination is one cause of that discrimination.[63]

The ultimate conclusion of the Johnson Commission was that all censorship of pornographic materials should cease, while the Meese Commission called for greater enforcement of existing obscenity laws and tougher regulation of what it considered harmful forms of pornography.[64]

The different conclusions of the two Commissions cannot be

explained by different evidence being available to them. Examination of that evidence demonstrates that while the Meese Commission had *more* evidence at its disposal, it was not *better* evidence in terms of its significance. Thus, 'Although many more studies were available to the Meese Commission than to the Johnson Commission fifteen years earlier, the principal differences between those commissions relate not to the nature and extent of the evidence but to how the evidence was evaluated and weighed.'[65] The Meese Report in particular showed '. . . an almost schizophrenic dissociation between the research findings and their interpretation by the Commission.'[66]

The different evaluations, then, most likely reflected the different political contexts in which they were generated. The Johnson Commission Report was a liberal document produced in liberal times and was applauded by liberals and condemned by conservatives: 'President Nixon was not pleased, but intellectuals and liberals applauded (it).'[67] The Meese Commission Report was, logically enough, condemned by liberals as a moral crusade of the Reagan counter-revolution.[68]

However, the traditional ideological divide over pornography has recently been complicated in some respects by a radical feminist movement which sees the issue as one involving not public morality, but civil rights and women's subordination to men. As defined by Catherine Mackinnon and Andrea Dworkin, it is the political relationship between men and women in pornography that makes it objectionable, not the explicitness of the sexuality displayed:

> We define pornography as a practice of sex discrimination, a violation of women's civil rights, the opposite of sexual equality . . . We define pornography as the graphic sexually explicit subordination of women through pictures or words that also includes women dehumanised as sexual objects, things, or commodities; enjoying pain or humiliation or rape; being tied up, cut up, mutilated, bruised, or physically hurt; in postures of sexual submission or servility or display . . . Erotica, defined by distinction as not this, might be sexually explicit materials premised on equality.[69]

Such a concept informed the Minneapolis and Indianapolis anti-pornography ordinances drawn up by Mackinnon and Dworkin in the 1980s. The Minneapolis ordinance sought civil, rather than criminal, redress against pornographers and enforcement would have been the responsibility of the city's civil rights and affirmative action office.[70] It defined pornography as 'the sexually explicit subordination of women', according to any one of nine specified criteria. Several of these criteria would inevitably depend upon highly subjective interpretation: for example, the first involved materials where 'women are presented as sexual objects, things, or commodities' and the seventh where 'women are presented as whores by nature'.[71] The ordinance would have reached 'mainstream' pornography, as well as 'hard-core' pornography and materials currently defined legally as obscene.[72] It would also have made producers, distributors, exhibitors and sellers of pornography liable to civil suits, since their very actions were held to constitute sex discrimination.

Clearly the Minneapolis ordinance was intended to restrict the availability of sexual materials to an even greater extent than most conservative opponents of pornography intended. Nevertheless, it was twice passed by the city council, in 1983 and 1984, though twice vetoed by Mayor Donald Fraser.

The drive for the passage of the Minneapolis ordinance had been a radical-progressive movement, but it was conservatives who invited Mackinnon to draft a similar ordinance for the city of Indianapolis. In fact, radicals kept a low profile in the Indianapolis campaign, while Mackinnon worked closely with its leader, council member Beulah Coughenor, who opposed abortion and had led Indiana's successful campaign to prevent passage of ERA.[73] The Indianapolis ordinance easily passed the city-county council but was struck down by a federal Appeals Court in 1985, a decision which the Supreme Court declined to review.[74]

What the politics of the two ordinances makes clear is that while the radical feminist contribution to the modern pornography debate stems from very different motives from those of conservatives, its goals are very similar: to reverse both the liberal conception of pornography that developed in the 1960s and the legal protection afforded to it by the courts, especially the Supreme Court, that followed in its wake. Groups such as Women Against Pornography and Women against Violence against Women may otherwise have little in common with Citizens for Decency Through Law or Morality in America; but they are equally lined up in opposition to liberal groups who defend pornography as free speech, whether it be the American Civil Liberties Union or the Feminist Anti-Censorship Task Force.[75]

As with so many contemporary social issues, then, decisions on pornography by the Supreme Court need to be viewed in the political context of 1960s liberalism and the subsequent reaction against it.

It has been well documented that, from 1957 to 1973, the Court struggled to distinguish between sexually explicit materials which are protected by the First Amendment's guarantee of free speech and those which fall within the unprotected realm of 'obscenity'. With each successive case the Justices expanded the freedom of the individual to indulge a taste for pornography. In other words, the Court implicitly recognised the force of moral relativism in society and restricted the power of majorities to impose their values on 'deviant' individuals. As noted above, this progression was in line with both the trend of public opinion and the increasing quantity and variety of explicit materials.

In *Roth v. United States*,[76] the Supreme Court gave its first modern definition of obscenity, which it accepted without argument was beyond the protection of the First Amendment:

> ... whether to the average person, applying contemporary community standards, the dominant theme of the material as a whole appeals to the prurient interest.[77]

Justice Brennan's test had been crafted with a view to protecting serious art and literature from censorship. *Roth* '. . . reflected four decades of growing liberalism and sophistication in American case law . . .',[78] but it did not solve the problem of censorship in a society increasingly polarised over sexual morality. Lower courts, for example, continued to ban works that Brennan thought the test permitted.[79] Thus, in 1959, the Justices had to overturn a decision of the New York Court of Appeals which held the movie version of D. H. Lawrence's *Lady Chatterly's Lover* obscene, because it depicted adultery as 'proper behaviour'.[80] Clearly the test did not and could not remove the decisive element of subjectivity – and, therefore, moral perspective – in defining any work as obscene, as opposed to merely pornographic or erotic.

Even the Justices themselves could not agree where, in practice, the line should be drawn. For example, according to his law clerks, Justice White would tolerate '. . . no erect penises, no intercourse, no oral or anal sodomy.'[81] Justice Brennan, on the other hand, did not object to penetration, provided no erect penis was shown: his clerks referred to this as the 'limp dick' test![82] Most famously of all, Justice Stewart wrote in *Jacobellis v. Ohio* that he couldn't define obscenity precisely, 'But I know it when I see it . . .'.[83] This caused much mirth when the Justices and their clerks subsequently viewed allegedly obscene films in the Supreme Court's basement: the clerks would call out at a particular scene, 'That's it, that's it, I know it when I see it'.[84]

In 1964, also in *Jacobellis*, Brennan added a further proviso to his *Roth* test: that a work classified as obscene must be '. . . utterly without redeeming social value.'[85] And two years later, in a case involving the novel *Fanny Hill*, Brennan reformulated the *Roth* and *Jacobellis* tests as follows:

> (a) the dominant theme of the material taken as a whole appeals to prurient interest in sex; (b) the material is patently offensive because it affronts contemporary community standards relating to the description or representation of sexual matters; and (c) the material is utterly without redeeming social value.[86]

The Justices were, however, badly divided in this and other obscenity cases decided the same day. Only two other members of the Court agreed with the new test, although three others concurred in the result. Altogether, in the three cases decided that day, there were fourteen opinions by the Justices.[87] Nevertheless, as a practical matter, the *Fanny Hill* case set the Court on a course in which only the most hard-core pornography could be banned. The key was the requirement that the work be *utterly* without redeeming social value: few works would be completely beyond such redemption, if only because pornographers could always include an episode of pseudo-social or pseudo-scientific comment to 'uplift' an otherwise obscene text. As a result, in the next few years '. . . a divided Court sputtered along the liberal path . . .'[88] Over thirty obscenity convictions were reversed without a hearing, the decisive factor being that five Justices, for whatever reason, did not believe the materials to be obscene. Furthermore, in 1969, in *Stanley v. Georgia*,[89] the Court went even further down the liberal road by ruling that States could not ban the *possession* of even concededly obscene materials in the privacy of one's home. This fusing of First Amendment and privacy doctrine implied the end of any majoritarian control over what adults may read or watch by way of sexually explicit materials in the privacy of their own homes.

The addition of four Nixon appointees to the Court between 1969 and 1971 did, on the surface, appear to stem and partially reverse, the liberal tide of obscenity decisions. The main decision came in 1973, in *Miller v. California*, when Chief Justice Burger won majority support for modifying Brennan's *Fanny Hill* test as follows:

> (a) whether the average person, applying contemporary community standards would find that the work taken as a whole, appeals to the prurient interest; (b) whether the work depicts or describes, in a patently offensive way, sexual conduct specifically defined by the applicable state law; (c) whether the work, taken as a whole, lacks serious literary, artistic, political, or scientific value.[90]

The major change from the earlier test lay in the third clause, with the switch from 'utterly without redeeming social value'. On its face, the *Miller* test requires more than minimal or tokenistic social value, but in practice, it amounted to much the same proscription of hard-core pornography as existed before.[91] Moreover, the real problem with *Miller* and all such tests is their subjectivity, for this inevitably leads to uncertainty in the minds of prosecutors, juries and judges and a consequent reluctance to bring cases and to convict. *Miller*, then, did not substantially alter the course of obscenity law.[92]

The Court had tried to balance individual choice and community control over pornography, but without any meaningful guidance from the Constitution the Justices are no more objectively placed to decide what is unfit for consumption than any other citizen or politician. As a result, from the late 1950s to the 1970s, the Court tacked with the generally liberal wind in American society, but at the cost of depriving many local communities of their power to control what they regarded as worthless and dangerous filth.

As noted above, on pornography as on other social issues, the political wind changed in a markedly more conservative direction from the mid-1970s on. Some recent cases indicate that the Court is beginning to reflect that change and strengthen community control over pornography and obscenity.

In 1989, in *Sable Communications v. FCC*,[93] the Court considered the constitutionality of a quintessentially modern form of sexual explicitness, the so-called 'dial-a-porn' business. This involves calling a telephone number and listening to a pre-recorded 'adult message' and paying a special fee for the privilege. This is big business: a message may typically last only from thirty seconds to two minutes, but may be called by up to 50,000 people using a single phone number. In one six-month period in 1985, there were some six to seven million such phone calls made in New York City alone.[94]

As Justice White noted in his opinion for the Court in *Sable Communications*, the federal government had made several attempts in the 1980s to regulate this business, with the primary aim of preventing minors from gaining access to it. In 1983 Congress had passed the Federal Communications Commission Authorisation Act making it a crime to use interstate telephone lines to provide 'obscene or indecent calls' to minors. As instructed, the Federal Communications Commission issued regulations for the implementation of the act. These included ways in which dial-a-porn companies could defend themselves against prosecution under the act: namely, by operating only between 9 p.m. and 8 a.m. and by requiring pre-payment by credit card. In 1984, a federal Court of Appeals nullified the time channelling provision and ordered the FCC to devise a more narrowly tailored provision. In 1985, the FCC added user identification codes as a means of screening out minors. In 1986, the federal Court rejected this and asked the FCC to reconsider its earlier decision to exclude 'exchange blocking' as a defence: this involves blocking certain numbers either at the customer's or the provider's premises. In 1987, the FCC again rejected exchange blocking but added a new defence: message scrambling. This required the provider to scramble its messages and only adult customers would be permitted to purchase a descrambler. In 1988, the federal court upheld the credit card and message scrambling defences, but then held that the Act was unconstitutional in so far as it applied to indecent (though not obscene) phone calls. Clearly frustrated by the persistent resistance to its will by the federal Court, Congress immediately amended the Act to ban the provision of both indecent and obscene messages to *anyone*, regardless of age.

Sable Communications, a dial-a-porn company operating out of Los Angeles and using lines provided by Pacific Bell, brought suit to challenge the Act as a violation of the First Amendment. It was supported by *amicus* briefs from major broadcasting corporations and civil liberties groups, including ABC, NBC and CBS, and the ACLU and People For The American Way. This brief opposed '. . . any regulation of non-obscene communications that significantly reduces the availability of protected communications to adults or that replaces parental supervision with a government determination of what is fit for children.'[95]

Briefs in support of the FCC included the United States Catholic Conference, the American Family Association, Minority (Republican) Members of the House of Representatives Committee on Energy and Commerce (which has oversight responsibility for the FCC) and Citizens For Decency Through Law. The brief of the latter was joined by the parents of a four-year-old girl who had been raped by a twelve-year-old boy. The brief claimed that the rapist had committed the act after listening to over two hours of dial-a-porn recordings. He had apparently gained access to them through a telephone in a church pastor's study.[96] In short, the case attracted a microcosm of the broader political groupings and arguments which have done battle over pornography in recent decades.

A unanimous Supreme Court ruled that the ban on indecent communications violated the First Amendment, but the Justices split 6–3 in upholding the ban on obscene messages. Justice White relied on *Miller* and other precedents to confirm that obscenity was not protected speech.[97] He also rejected Sable's objection that, because access to its messages was possible from anywhere in the United States through interstate lines, it would have to tailor its provision to the standards of the least tolerant community in the country. In effect White said that that was the company's problem: it would have to devise ways and pay the costs of blocking out-of-area calls or risk violating some communities' obscenity standards.[98]

The three dissenters from this aspect of the decision reiterated what might be called the 'ultra-liberal' argument that obscenity could not satisfactorily be defined as a discrete form of speech and was therefore too vague to withstand the strictures of the First Amendment. Justice Brennan, who in *Roth* and the *Fanny Hill* case had attempted just such a definition, wrote: 'In my judgement, "the concept of obscenity" cannot be defined with sufficient specificity and clarity to provide fair notice to persons who create and distribute sexually oriented materials, to prevent substantial erosion of protected speech as a byproduct of the attempt to suppress unprotected speech, and to avoid very costly institutional harms.'[99]

Nevertheless, despite the ruling on obscene phone messages, the Court in *Sable* did hold the Congress to strict standards of judicial scrutiny as far as indecent messages were concerned. Justice White recognised that Congress had a legitimate interest in protecting children from the harm of such communications. However, it must also further that interest by means narrowly tailored to their achievement. The blanket ban on all indecent calls was far from that and more like '. . . burning up the house to roast the pig.'[100]

White also rejected the FCC's argument that the Court ought to defer to the judgement of Congress that there were no other effective means of preventing minors' access to indecent calls. In so doing, he indicated that judicial deference to Congress was least warranted of all in cases involving First Amendment free speech rights.[101] As we shall see, this comment was to prove of great significance in the outcome of certain other cases involving 'nonconformist' behaviour.

Sable indicated that the more conservative Court of the 1980s would not allow legislatures to ban 'non-obscene' sexually explicit materials, but it would permit more rigorous regulation of them. This became clear in a case which captured considerable public attention in 1991, *Barnes v. Glen Theatre, Inc.*[102] This involved another popular form of sexual explicitness: nude dancing in clubs and bar-rooms, commonly known as 'go-go dancing'. JR's Kitty Kat Lounge in South Bend, Indiana, claims to provide 'the hottest show in town'.[103] But it complained that its ability to fulfil this promise was unconstitutionally restrained by Indiana's 1988 Public Indecency Act which prohibited public nudity. As a result, go-go dancers and the like were required to wear 'pasties' and a G-string to cover their nipples and genitals.[104] One of the Kitty Kat's dancers, Darlene Miller, also brought suit alleging that she would make more money if she were allowed to dance completely nude. A further party to the suit was the Glen Theatre, which owned the Chippewa Bookstore in South Bend: amongst other things, this establishment offered pay-as-you-view go-go dancing, in which customers sit in booths and put coins into a slot and watch the dancers through a glass panel.

Out of these rather sordid circumstances arose a significant constitutional issue. As one journalist wrote: 'On one level, the question presented in *Barnes v. Glen Theatre* is straightforward and seemingly trivial: whether the Constitution protects the right to dance without pasties and a G-string. But the case also presents a more fundamental clash between community control and First Amendment values.'[105] Once again, a number of commerically interested and civil liberties groups filed *amicus* briefs on behalf of the dance businesses, including the Georgia On Premise and Lounge Association, the ACLU and People For The American Way. The brief for the latter expressed the free speech argument as follows:

> Respondents' nude dancing communicates an unmistakable message – an emotive one of eroticism – that their clients clearly understand. That their message is not political or educational – and, indeed, is offensive to some individuals – does not immunise it from First Amendment protection. Not unlike the erotic message that nude dancers have purveyed on more traditional stages throughout ancient and more modern times, respondents' conduct is communicative and entertaining. It is speech protected by the First Amendment.[106]

Lined up against these groups was an array of governmental representatives, such as the US Conference of Mayors and the National League of Cities, and a by now familiar range of religious and 'family-oriented' organisations. These included Concerned Women For America, Focus On The Family and the National Coalition Against Pornography. Concerned Women For America claimed to represent 600,000 people '. . . seeking to preserve Judaeo-Christian values', while Focus On The Family describes itself as a Christian organisation

'. . . committed to protecting and strengthening families in the United States and throughout the world.'[107] Another brief, for the American Family Association and others, dismissed the free speech argument in withering manner. Saying that the performances involved movement, but not expression or communication in a constitutional sense, the brief argued: 'This movement no more involves expression than does the movement by the proverbial "dirty old man" in the park opening his trench coat to expose himself.'[108]

The Justices of the Supreme Court were required to answer two basic questions: whether non-obscene nude dancing was expression protected by the First Amendment and whether Indiana's Public Indecency Act was a permissible regulation of such dancing. The Court was badly divided in voting 'yes' to both questions. Chief Justice Rehnquist wrote an opinion, joined only by Justices O'Connor and Kennedy, in which he argued that '. . . nude dancing of the kind sought to be performed here is expressive conduct *within the outer limits* of the First Amendment, *though we view it as only marginally so.*'[109] As one commentator observed, this description relegated sexual expression to a second-class category of free speech.[110] Furthermore, as a consequence of this demotion, Rehnquist did not feel obligated to apply the strict judicial scrutiny normally appropriate to legislation regulating speech protected by the First Amendment, but rather an intermediate level of scrutiny. This he took from *US v. O'Brien*, a 1968 case involving draft card burning as a protest against the Vietnam War.[111] However, in *O'Brien* the Warren Court had rejected the contention that draft card burning was symbolic speech within the protection of the First Amendment, so the Court was now breaking new ground in applying the test developed there to activity which *was* covered.

The full import of Rehnquist's innovation became apparent when he applied the *O'Brien* test. This permitted regulation of conduct with a speech element if (i) it is within the constitutional power of the government; (ii) it furthers an important or substantial governmental interest; (iii) if that interest is unrelated to the suppression of free expression and (iv) if any incidental restriction on speech is no greater than essential to further the government's interest.[112] The Chief Justice concluded that the protection of morality and order was a sufficiently important government interest to allow regulation of this admittedly protected conduct.[113] He then went on to argue that the ban on nudity was not aimed at suppressing expression *per se*, but public nudity. Furthermore, '. . . the requirement that the dancers don pasties and a G-string does not deprive the dance of whatever erotic message it conveys; it simply makes the message slightly less graphic.'[114]

Even Justice Scalia, who otherwise had no doubts about the constitutionality of the Indiana statute, objected to Rehnquist's introduction
of intermediate level review. He pointed out that the protection of
morality was a governmental interest appropriate to the rational basis
test, the least strict standard of review that was applied when no
fundamental right was at stake. To elevate the protection of morality to
a heightened status which could justify the curtailment of fundamental
rights was a mistake. He wrote: '. . . I do not believe such a heightened
standard exists. I think we should avoid wherever possible, moreover, a
method of analysis that requires judicial assessment of the "importance" of government interests – and especially of government
interests in various aspects of morality.'[115]

Justice White dissented in an opinion joined by his colleagues
Marshall, Blackmun and Stevens. He focused on the fact that, in
practice, the Indiana statute did not impose a general ban on nudity.
The state's brief had acknowledged that it was not intended to prohibit
artistic performances such as *Salome* or *Hair*, where some larger form
of expression than go-go dancing was involved. If the state wanted to
ban some, but not all, displays of nudity, it should distinguish on the
basis of whether the general public was likely to encounter the display:

> The purpose of forbidding people from appearing nude in parks, beaches,
> hot dog stands, (*sic*) and like public places is to protect others from offence.
> But that could not possibly be the purpose of preventing nude dancing in
> theatres and bar-rooms since the viewers are exclusively consenting adults
> who pay money to see these dances.[116]

This expression of the liberal view of sexual gratifaction drew the fire of
Justice Scalia, who emphasised his interpretivist convictions in
humorous fashion:

> Perhaps the dissenters believe that 'offence to others' *ought* to be the only
> reason for restricting nudity in public places generally, but there is no basis
> for thinking that our society has ever shared that Thoreauvian 'you-may-
> do-what-you-like-so-long-as-it-does-not-injure-someone-else' beau ideal
> – much less for thinking that it was written into the Constitution. The
> purpose of Indiana's nudity law would be violated, I think, if 60,000 fully
> consenting adults crowded into the Hoosierdome to display their genitals
> to one another, even if there were not an offended innocent in the
> crowd.[117]

Justice White took Scalia's hypothetical situation and used it to point
out the illogicality of interpreting the Indiana law as a general ban on
nudity, enacted to protect morality:

We agree with Justice Scalia that the Indiana statute would not permit 60,000 Hoosiers to expose themselves to each other in the Hoosierdome. No one can doubt, however, that those same 60,000 Hoosiers would be perfectly free to drive to their respective homes all across Indiana and, once there, to parade around, cavort, and revel in the nude for hours in front of relatives and friends. It is difficult to see why the State's interest in morality is any less in that situation, especially if, as Justice Scalia seems to suggest, nudity is inherently evil.[118]

Humour aside, this exchange is significant because it brings out the inherently subjective and ideological factors which inform constitutional interpretation once intentionalism is abandoned. At the same time, the greater judicial restraint of the Scalia-Rehnquist approach, in which behaviour not explicitly protected by the Constitution is subject to the will of the legislature, may leave individuals at the whim of what one of the Kitty Kat's dancers called 'moralistic busybodies'.[119]

Exactly what the *Barnes* decision means is unclear, as yet: the plurality opinion of Rehnquist, O'Connor and Kennedy would give the Court considerable flexibility in picking and choosing between attempts to regulate morality. Where they allowed regulation, they would certainly obtain Justice Scalia's concurrence, though not necessarily that of Justice Souter.[120] However, there can be little doubt that *Barnes* is a victory for the political forces who seek to reverse what they see as the permissiveness of recent decades.

Further evidence of the end of liberalism in obscenity cases is provided by *Osborne v. Ohio.*[121] In 1989, as part of a campaign against child pornography, the Ohio state legislature had enacted a provision outlawing the possession or viewing of any materials depicting minors in a state of nudity. In an attempt to tailor the law to its goal, the legislature provided for numerous exceptions that would, for example, allow parents to have such photographs of their children. It also allowed professionals with a *bona fide* interest in such materials to view and possess them.[122] Clyde Osborne, however, had no such credentials and when police found sexually explicit photographs of naked male minors in his home, he was convicted under the 1989 law and sentenced to six months' imprisonment.

As easy as the moral question may be for most people in cases involving child pornography, the Justices' task was by no means straightforward. Most significantly, the Court had ruled in *Stanley v. Georgia* in 1969 that the First Amendment protected the right to view even constitutionally obscene materials in the privacy of one's home.[123] *Stanley* was therefore a powerful precedent arguing in

Osborne's favour. A 6-3 majority of the Court, however, agreed to both narrow and distinguish *Stanley* from the present case. Justice White cautioned that '*Stanley* should not be read too broadly.'[124] And while he was willing to accept, for the sake of argument, that there might be some minimal constitutional protection for the viewing of child pornography, he found that it was far outweighed by the state's interest in combating the evils of the trade in such materials. In *Stanley*, he said, the state law had been designed to protect the public's mind from contamination by obscenity – but 'The difference here is obvious: the State does not rely on a paternalistic interest in regulating Osborne's mind. Rather, Ohio has enacted (this law) in order to protect the victims of child pornography; it hopes to destroy a market for the exploitative use of children.'[125]

As Justice Brennan pointed out in dissent, however, the question was not whether the state could outlaw child pornography and punish those engaged in its production and trade, just as in *Stanley* the Court had not questioned the state's power to criminalise the trade in obscenity. The issue, rather, was mere possession of materials at home. Thus, said Brennan, Ohio could pursue its campaign against child pornographers without prosecuting the likes of Osborne: 'Indeed, the State has already enacted a panoply of laws prohibiting the creation, sale, and distribution of child pornography and obscenity involving minors . . . Ohio has not demonstrated why these laws are inadequate and why the State must forbid mere possession as well.'[126]

Justice White responded to this by stressing the sheer 'importance' and 'gravity' of the state's interest in eliminating child pornography.[127] He also cited practical problems in combating a trade which had largely gone underground,[128] and drew on findings of the Meese Commission to conclude that '. . . encouraging the destruction of these materials is also desirable because evidence suggests that pedophiles use child pornography to seduce other children into sexual activity.'[129] But again, as Brennan pointed out, the Court had heard the same arguments in *Stanley* as to why punishing possession was necessary to the elimination of the trade in obscenity and had rejected them.[130]

There can be little doubt that the *Osborne* majority failed to follow the precedent established by *Stanley*. Justice Brennan was right, then, when he wrote: 'At bottom, the Court today is so disquieted by the possible exploitation of children in the *production* of pornography that it is willing to tolerate the imposition of criminal penalties for simple *possession*.'[131] To put it another way, when the Court has to balance the freedom of the individual against the community's determination to eliminate serious social harm resulting from egregious forms of pornography, it no longer sees the First Amendment as a trump card on behalf of the former.

For God and country

As already noted, there are clear signs that the Court today does not regard pornography as a form of speech deserving the full protection of the First Amendment. Political speech, however, is accepted by even conservatives as lying at the heart of First Amendment free speech protections.[132] Such is the force of this conviction that the Rehnquist Court recently bucked its generally conservative trend and upheld the right to burn publicly the Stars and Stripes as an act of political protest. In so doing, it had to withstand considerable pressure from the other branches of the federal government.

Americans are a people much given to public expressions of their patriotism: the national anthem is played routinely at sports matches, the front lawns of private homes frequently contain a large American flag and car stickers invite those who do not love America to leave. And every year, the creation of the Stars and Stripes is officially celebrated on Flag Day, 14 June. As the popular expression says, 'the Flag' is a core symbol of American values along with 'mother' and 'apple pie'. Not surprisingly, politicians often seek to benefit from this super-patriotism by 'wrapping themselves in the flag' and trying to impugn their opponent's patriotic ardour. In 1988, candidate George Bush did just this by visiting a flag-making factory and using the occasion to attack Michael Dukakis' decision as Governor of Massachussets to veto a state law requiring public school teachers to lead their children in a daily Pledge of Allegiance to the flag.[133] Bush quite cynically ignored the fact that Dukakis had vetoed the act because it was patently unconstitutional under the Supreme Court's 1943 decision in *West Virginia State Board of Education v. Barnette*.[134]

Of course, the very power of the flag as a symbol of patriotism makes it an equally attractive target for those who wish to criticise the country or the actions of its leaders. Gregory Lee Johnson was one such protester. When the 1984 Republican National Convention came to Dallas, Johnson and others organised a demonstration march through the city. Activities on the march included a 'die-in', involving the simulation of a nuclear attack with the demonstrators falling to the ground screaming and moaning for several minutes.[135] Numerous chants were taken up, including 'Reagan, Mondale, which will it be?

Either one means World War Three' and 'Reagan, Reagan, killer of the hour, Perfect symbol of U.S. power.'[136] The demonstration culminated in the burning of the Stars and Stripes before Dallas City Hall, accompanied by the chant of 'America, the red, white, and blue, we spit on you.' Johnson was arrested and later convicted for violation of a state statute forbidding desecration of the American flag. He was sentenced to a year in prison and fined $2,000. Johnson appealed his conviction on the grounds that the Texas statute was an unconstitutional infringement upon his freedom of expression, as guaranteed by the First Amendment. The Texas Court of Criminal Appeals upheld his claim and the state in turn appealed to the Supreme Court.

In June 1989, in *Texas v. Johnson*,[137] the Justices split along unusual lines in affirming the state court's decision. Three liberals, Brennan, Marshall and Blackmun, were joined by two Reagan appointees, Scalia and Kennedy, in striking down the flag desecration act. Of the dissenters, it was Justice Stevens, normally to be found voting with the liberals, who seemed most upset by the decision: on the day the decision was announced, he took the unusual step of reading his opinion from the bench, his voice cracking with emotion.[138] With Chief Justice Rehnquist's dissenting opinion replete with quotations from patriotic poems and songs, it is clear that the emotions generated by the flag-burning issue were strongly felt even in the most sober setting of the United States Supreme Court. As the *Harvard Law Review* noted, 'Although relatively straightforward from a doctrinal perspective, the decision nevertheless elicited emotional responses both within and outside the Court.'[139]

Justice Brennan argued that Johnson's actions were 'expressive conduct' or 'symbolic speech' and therefore liable to some level of protection under the First Amendment. He also acknowledged, however, that this level of protection was not as great as in instances involving government suppression of the written or spoken word *per se*. Nevertheless, in order to withstand First Amendment scrutiny, a state must show that the interest it seeks to further by the legislation is unrelated to the suppression of the expressive element of the conduct involved. Here, Texas asserted two interests: preventing a breach of the peace and preserving the flag as a symbol of national unity.

Justice Brennan had little difficulty dismissing the first justification for the statute. No actual breach of the peace had taken place as a result of Johnson's actions, nor did testimony suggest that one had threatened to occur. More importantly, Brennan was able to cite precedents to the effect that it is precisely when expression is controversial and offensive that the constitutional protection of free speech is most valuable. Those precedents, he wrote, '. . . recognise that a principal function of free speech under our system of government is to invite dispute. It may indeed best serve its high purpose when it induces a condition of unrest, creates dissatisfaction with conditions as they are, or even stirs people to anger.'[140]

Brennan also had little difficulty showing that the state's desire to preserve the flag as a symbol of national unity was directly aimed at the suppression of ideas. As he pointed out, the state's concern could only be triggered when someone indicated, as Johnson had done, that the flag stood for other, less laudable values: '. . . the State's claim is that it has an interest in preserving the flag as a symbol of *nationhood* and *national unity*, a symbol with a determinate range of meanings. According to Texas, if one physically treats the flag in a way that would tend to cast doubt on either the idea that nationhood and national unity are the flag's referents or that national unity actually exists, the message thereby is a harmful one and therefore maybe prohibited.'[141] However, a whole raft of precedents, including several cases involving the flag, demonstrate beyond question that government in the United States may not suppress an idea merely because it is offensive or disagreeable.

To the state's and the dissenting Justices' argument that the flag is unique as a national symbol and therefore uniquely deserving of protection, Brennan responded by reminding them that there is no originalist or intentionalist support for such a view: 'There is . . . no indication – either in the text of the Constitution or in our cases interpreting it – that a separate judicial category exists for the American flag alone. Indeed, we would not be surprised to learn that the persons who framed our Constitution and wrote the Amendment that we now construe were not known for their reverence for the Union Jack.'[142] And in a final flourish, Justice Brennan claimed the values symbolised by the Stars and Stripes were in fact upheld by the majority's decision on Johnson's rights:

> Our decision is a reaffirmation of the principles of freedom and inclusiveness that the flag best reflects, and of the conviction that our toleration of criticism such as Johnson's is a sign and source of strength. Indeed, one of the proudest images of our flag, the one immortalised in our own national anthem, is of the bombardment it survived at Fort McHenry. It is the Nation's resilience, not its rigidity, that Texas sees reflected in the flag – and it is that resilience that we reassert today.[143]

The dissenting opinion of Chief Justice Rehnquist, joined by Justices White and O'Connor, was charged with patriotic emotions, but weak in constitutional argument. In order to establish the point that the flag was unique as a national symbol, Rehnquist quoted Emerson's Concord Hymn, the national anthem and Whittier's Barbara Frietchie. Historical references included the War of Independence, the War of 1812, the Civil War, the First and Second World Wars and the Korean and Vietnam Wars. He also cited numerous public rituals involving the flag and the fact that forty-eight states and the Congress, in 1967, had proscribed desecration of the flag. Ignoring the fact that some of the wars cited involved deep divisions precisely over what the national flag did represent, Rehnquist concluded:

> The American flag, then, throughout more than two hundred years of our history, has come to be the visible symbol embodying our nation. It does not represent the views of any particular party, and it does not represent any particular political philosophy. The flag is not simply another 'idea' or 'point of view' competing for recognition in the marketplace of ideas. Millions and millions of Americans regard it with an almost mystical reverence regardless of what sort of social, political, or philosophical beliefs they may have.[144]

The powerful rhetoric, however, could not be supported by precedent: the Chief Justice could only argue that the precise issue of the constitutionality of flag-desecration statutes had never been explicitly decided by the Court; and quote from dissenting opinions in recent cases that had *quashed* the convictions of individuals who had been prosecuted under such legislation. Not surprisingly, therefore, Rehnquist moved on to suggest an implicit balancing test: the high status of the flag to most Americans against the prohibition of just one form of political protest. He pointed out that even without the right to burn the flag, Johnson was still free to condemn the United States or its government in words or by other symbolic deeds. He described Brennan's argument that the First Amendment was intended to protect even those who professed the most offensive ideas as 'a regrettably patronising civics lecture'[145] and concluded: 'Surely one of the high purposes of a democratic society is to legislate against conduct that is regarded as evil and profoundly offensive to the majority of people – whether it be murder, embezzlement, pollution, or flag burning.'[146]

The Chief Justice's analogy of flag burning to murder encapsulates the power of this issue to overcome reason and sense of proportion.[147] It thus came as no surprise when politicians reacted to the decision with patriotic frenzy. Within one week of the Court's decision in *Texas v. Johnson*, members of Congress introduced over forty constitutional

amendments designed to reverse it. One was actually passed by the
Senate, 51–48, but fell short of the required two-thirds majority.[148]
However, if Congress baulked somewhat at a constitutional amendment, there was no such reluctance to enact a law that would assert the
legitimacy of flag-burning legislation. In October, 1989, both House
and Senate approved the Flag Protection Act by huge majorities:
380–38 and 91–9, respectively.[149] The statute made it a crime to
mutilate, deface, defile, burn or trample on the flag. The House had
debated the bill on the floor for just one hour, the Senate for eight
hours.[150]

Ironically, in passing the Flag Protection Act of 1989, Congress was
engaging in symbolic politics itself. For there could be no doubt that
the Act would be declared unconstitutional, as indeed a number of
witnesses called by Congress had advised. Robert Bork, for example,
told the Senate Judiciary Committee: 'At this very moment, we are
making a record that the proposed statute is designed to evade the
Johnson ruling, and that is enough to guarantee the statute will be
struck down.'[151]

President Bush was fully aware of this but nevertheless sought to
milk the situation for political gain. First he said that he was opposed to
flag burning: 'I have to give you my personal, emotional response. Flag
burning is wrong – dead wrong.'[152] He also said that he approved the
Act and allowed it to become law, but declined to sign it on the grounds
that he seriously doubted its constitutionality.

As anticipated, the Flag Protection Act was declared unconstitutional by the Court in 1990, in *US v. Eichman*.[153] The Justices split
exactly as they had done in *Johnson*. While it was clear, however, that
the legal issues in the two cases were essentially the same, the Court did
nevertheless have to withstand an unusually strong attempt to
intimidate it by the elected branches of government. The Democratic
Party leadership of the House filed an *amicus* brief urging the Court to
uphold the Act, as did Mario Cuomo, the Democratic Governor of
New York, and Senator Joseph Biden, Democratic Chairman of the
Senate Judiciary Committee and sponsor of the Act.[154] Moreover, the
brief for the United States as appellant in the case argued forcefully
that the Court should defer to the will of the elected branches:

> Regardless of whether the Court regards flag burning as presenting . . .
> serious dangers, the Article III branch should, we believe, defer to the
> considered judgement of the elected branches on the question of how
> important it is to the Nation to protect the flag from physical attack and
> destruction. With all respect to the Court, that is a judgement that the

elected branches are particularly well-suited to make. Of course, the Court must decide, as is its duty, whether the Act is constitutional – but in so doing it should not, we believe, gainsay the compelling governmental interest reflected in the passage of the Act in *Johnson's* wake.[155]

This passage comes perilously close to saying 'we want this so badly that you'd better give it to us, whatever you think of its constitutionality'. However, perhaps anticipating such application of political muscle, many other groups joined *amicus* briefs which urged the Court to stand firm. None was more telling than that submitted by the American Bar Association. After noting the background to the Act's passage, it said: 'The entire exercise was . . . an attempt to get around the First Amendment barrier identified by the Court in *Texas v. Johnson* . . . We submit that for the Court to accept such a subterfuge would make a mockery of reason and experience, and create a dangerous precedent for restriction of the Bill of Rights, and seriously weaken the guarantees of the First Amendment.'[156] The support of the legal establishment must have provided some comfort to the majority Justices as they stood up to the political establishment.

Indeed, having shown that the Act possessed the same flaws as the Texas statute struck down in *Johnson*, Justice Brennan dealt directly with the assertion that it should nevertheless be upheld because the elected branches felt very strongly about it: 'We decline the Government's invitation to reassess this conclusion in light of Congress' recent recognition of a purported "national consensus" favouring a prohibition on flag burning. Even assuming such a consensus exists, any suggestion that the Government's interest in suppressing speech becomes more weighty as popular opposition to that speech grows is foreign to the First Amendment.'[157]

The tone of the dissent, written by Justice Stevens, was considerably more low-key that that of the Chief Justice, and even his own, in *Johnson*. All the same, Stevens concluded that just as the majority had effectively restated its *Johnson* reasoning, he too remained convinced by his dissent there. The Justices, then, were largely going through the motions in *Eichman*, having been forced to do so by politicians anxious to wrap themselves in the flag.

In spite of the *Eichman* decision, however, the politicians were not yet ready to let go of the issue. The strength of public opinion on the issue suggested there was further political mileage in it. A *New York Times*/CBS poll in May showed 83 per cent of respondents agreeing that flag burning should be illegal and 59 per cent supporting a constitutional amendment to that effect. A USA Today poll, taken immediately after *Eichman* was announced, reported 69 per cent in favour of a constitutional amendment. Just ten days after the decision was announced, therefore, the House decided to vote on the constitutional amendment that had failed to gain a two-thirds majority in the Senate the previous year. It passed by 254 votes to 177, 34 votes short of the necessary majority. Although the amendment was now dead, the Senate nevertheless decided to go on the record again and, five days after the House, re-passed the amendment by 58–42, nine votes short.[158]

It was left to Senator Jesse Helms to try the last option: removing the Court's jurisdiction over flag-burning cases. That proposal was resoundingly defeated by 90 votes to 10 in the Senate on the same day that the Senate failed to approve the constitutional amendment. To all intents and purposes, the issue was now dead. It had, however, provided many elected politicians the opportunity to parade their patriotic credentials in public. It had also provided the Court with an opportunity to demonstrate the moral and political strength of counter-majoritarian decisions which are firmly grounded in the text of the Constitution and a long history of judicial interpretation.

We have seen that many of the cases examined here engage an underlying social conflict over traditional morality and values. It seems appropriate, then, to end with a look at how the Supreme Court has responded when that conflict has taken its most explicit constitutional form: the place of religious belief and practice in American life, in the light of the First Amendment's stricture that 'Congress shall make no law respecting an establishment of religion, or prohibiting the free exercise thereof . . .'

Until the mid-twentieth century, these religion clauses gave rise to little controversy. Congress did not attempt an establishment of religion, that is, the creation of an official Church for the United States; and most legislation which impinged on an individual's right to practise religion freely was enacted by the states and was therefore beyond the reach of the First Amendment. However, in the 1940s, the Supreme Court held that both the Free Exercise Clause and the Establishment Clause would henceforth be applicable to the states, as well as to the federal government.[159]

The ensuing decades saw a whole series of decisions by the Court which, because of their perceived hostility to religious values, generated considerable public anger and opposition.[160] Most controversial of all were cases decided under the Establishment Clause, involving the place of religion in the nation's public schools. In 1948, in *McCollum v. Illinois*,[161] the Court struck down a released-time programme, in which students were allowed time free from other studies to have religious education on school premises. Such was the outcry against the decision that when, four years later,[162] the Court upheld a released-time programme where the children left school for the religion classes, the dissenting Justices accused the majority of having bowed to public pressures.[163]

In 1962, however, the Court returned to its controversial path. In *Engel v. Vitale*,[164] the Court declared unconstitutional the reading of a non-sectarian prayer at the beginning of the school day in New York. The following year, in *Abington School District v. Schempp*,[165] the Court struck down a Pennsylvania statute which required a Bible reading at the start of the school day. In 1968, in *Epperson v. Arkansas*,[166] the Court unanimously declared unconstitutional the Arkansas 'Monkey Law', which made it illegal to teach the theory of evolution as applied to human beings.

These decisions have provoked over two hundred constitutional amendments to reverse them, though all unsuccessful.[167] Typical was that introduced in Congress in 1982 and publicly supported by President Reagan, which read: 'Nothing in this Constitution shall be construed to prohibit individual or group prayer in public schools or other public institutions. No person shall be required by the United States or by any State to participate in prayer.'[168] Senator Jesse Helms has also tried his usual method of reversing Supreme Court decisions – withdrawing the Court's jurisdiction over religious issues – but that too has failed.[169] There has also been widespread non-compliance with these decisions, as well as continuing attempts by State legislatures 'to put prayer back in the schools'.[170]

There are several major factors which explain the public and political opposition to the school prayer decisions. First, Americans are a notably religious people: studies from the 1980s show that 95 per cent of Americans believe in God, 60 per cent belong to a religious organisation and 40 per cent are regular church-goers.[171] On the specific issue of permitting prayer in public schools, surveys show a clear majority in favour: for example, the American National Election Study of 1980 reported 72 per cent in favour,[172] while a *Time*/CNN poll of 1991 put the figure at 78 per cent.[173]

Second, at the core of this support for religion lies a militant, well-organised and well-financed New Christian Right movement, which is driving the political and legal campaign against the Court's decisions. While there is no clear indication of exactly what percentage of the population supports the political agenda of the New Christian Right,[174] it did achieve a high political profile in the late 1970s and 1980s and was an important element within the electoral coalition that supported Ronald Reagan.[175] While President Reagan did not always satisfy his New Christian Right supporters, he did try seriously to get the Supreme Court to change tack, as we shall see shortly.

Third, the Court's decisions on the Establishment Clause seemed to many to be in conflict with the Free Exercise Clause. This perhaps was inevitable, since there is an inherent tension between the former, which appears to bar government support for religion, and the latter, which appears to require government to accommodate religion. The problem is compounded, however, by the fact that '. . . the outcome of cases may often depend on whether a particular dispute is charac- terised as an establishment or free exercise claim. For example, the regular use of public university facilities for student religious services may be characterised either as government advancement of religion or an accommodation to religious students, required by the Free Exercise Clause.'[176] The result has been a significant level of confusion in religion cases, as the Justices have themselves acknowleged.[177] To the lay person who may not appreciate the subtleties of close judicial reasoning, the outlawing of traditional practices like school prayer may be perceived as outright hostility to religion.

All these factors help explain why the issue of church-state relations in the Supreme Court has refused to die down, even though it is now some forty-five years since the Court's first controversial decision in the *McCollum* case. But most important of all is the same underlying cultural conflict that has underpinned other aspects of the Social Issue: conservative Protestants, or fundamentalists, have particularly felt threatened by the growth of secular, liberal and cosmopolitan values which have been advanced by the national state. As Steve Bruce put it, the conditions for the rise of the New Christian Right in the 1970s were created partly because '. . . an increasingly liberal state, committed to promoting interests (such as those of blacks, women, and homosexuals) which fundamentalists opposed, was intervening more and more in the sub-societies and sub-cultures of conservative Protes- tant America.'[178] The Supreme Court, in particular, was depriving fundamentalists of their 'right' to have their beliefs promulgated in the critical public forum of local school systems. The public aspect of the church-state conflict is central: what fundamentalists – and, indeed, other religious and cultural activists – want is symbolic and official

248 RAW JUDICIAL POWER?

endorsement of their values:

> Conservative Protestants were not impressed with the right to say prayers at
> home with their own families, or in church with other believers; they
> wanted the right to have their prayers said in public places, by large
> numbers of people outside their own church fellowship. To put it bluntly,
> they wished to see their culture in a position of pre-eminence and the
> Court's decisions thwarted that desire.[179]

As noted above, however, opposition to the Court's decisions on
religion was by no means limited to fundamentalist Protestants.
Catholics are about as likely to support school prayer as Protestants,
though Jews much less so.[180] The leading determinant of support is,
unsurprisingly, religiosity: but education, a key factor in the cleavage
on other socio-cultural issues, is the second most important determinant. Thus, in the American National Election Study of 1980, 91
per cent of those with less than eight years of education supported
school prayer; this compared with 71 per cent of those with nine to
twelve years education and only 60 per cent of those with thirteen or
more years education.[181] There is also a positive link between support
for school prayer and support for conservative positions on other social
issues. Thus, 'Advocates of school prayer, in addition to being
theologically conservative and religiously active, tend to be less educated, to disapprove of the Equal Rights Amendment, are politically
conservative, and are slightly older than those who believe that religion
does not belong in the schools.'[182] In short, there is a familiar element
of lower-class conservatism and upper-class liberalism in the conflict
over church-state relations.

The Warren Court had by no means been as hostile to religion as its
critics appeared to believe: for example, in 1968, in *Board of Education v.
Allen*,[183] it upheld a law which required school districts to lend textbooks to private and parochial school pupils. Nevertheless, the Burger
Court soon instituted a new test to apply in religion cases, which
seemed to be less hostile to religion. In 1971, in *Lemon v. Kurtzman*,[184]
Chief Justice Burger reviewed the history of the Court's decisions on
religion since *Everson*, in 1947. In some respects, his rhetoric suggested
a more 'accommodationist' approach to state support for private,
religious schools. For example, he rejected the notion, argued by
Thomas Jefferson and employed by the Court in previous cases, that
the First Amendment had erected 'a wall' separating church from
state. Instead, he wrote, '. . . the line of separation, far from being a
"wall", is a blurred, indistinct, and variable barrier depending on all the

circumstances of a particular relationship.'[185]

Burger argued, therefore, that legislation raising issues under the Establishment Clause could be constitutional provided it could meet a three-pronged test: 'First, the statute must have a secular legislative purpose; second, its principal or primary effect must be one that neither advances nor inhibits religion; finally, the statute must not foster an excessive entanglement with religion.'[186] Applying that test, however, the Court declared over the lone, partial dissent of Justice White, that the two state statutes before it were unconstitutional. Rhode Island and Pennsylvania had both enacted schemes which, among other things, contributed state funds to supplement the salaries of parochial school teachers, provided such teachers worked only in secular courses of the school curriculum and provided that accounts were kept of the expenditure of such monies and made available to state inspection. Chief Justice Burger argued that, although the statutes clearly had a secular purpose, they fostered a level of church-state entanglement that was forbidden by the First Amendment. He was particularly concerned by the fact that state officials would have to monitor continuously both the teachers and the financial accounts to ensure that they were indeed being used only for secular purposes.

Once again, then, the Burger Court failed to bring about the constitutional counter-revolution against Warren Court liberal-activism that many had anticipated. Moreover, the *Lemon* test, as it became known, commanded the near unanimity of the Court. To be sure, the Burger Court was by no means always unanimous when it applied the *Lemon* test to particular circumstances.[187] It was, however, only in the 1980s, when the political activities of the New Christian Right and their conservative allies reached their peak, that the Court became seriously split over basic Religion Clause issues and the validity of the *Lemon* test.

Recent Establishment Clause litigation may usefully be divided into three categories: first, those cases which involve attempts squarely to install religious practice and values in educational institutions; second, those which involve the use of religious symbolism in public life; and third, cases where social policy has allegedly been designed to advance the values of religious organisations. On the whole, the Court today looks with disfavour only upon policies in the first category; and even here, there are signs that the Court may be moving towards far greater toleration for the promotion of religion by the states than at any time since the Second World War.

The Reagan administration had frequently stated its support for allowing prayer in public schools and, in 1985, in *Wallace v. Jafree*,[188] it had the opportunity to persuade the Court likewise. The case involved an Alabama statute which required schools to observe a daily 'period of silence not to exceed one minute in duration . . . for meditation or voluntary prayer'. About half the states had passed similar measures in order to circumvent the Court's earlier rulings outlawing school prayer.[189] The Justice Department decided to intervene in the case, urging the Court to uphold the Alabama law. However, 'hard-liners', such as Assistant Attorney-General William Bradford Reynolds, wanted to go further and ask the Court to overrule its major precedents on the Establishment Clause, including the *Everson* decision which had first made it applicable to the states. The Solicitor-General Rex Lee and his Deputy, Paul Bator, both opposed this confrontational approach, the latter arguing that '. . . we would jeopardise our other religion cases if we just said to the Court, "Throw out your jurisprudence about the wall of separation between church and state." We would have lost nine to zip.'[190] Instead, then, the administration urged the Court to distinguish between spoken prayer and a moment of silence.

The Court, however, rejected this by a vote of 6-3. As Justice Stevens noted, the whole history of the Alabama statute made it clear that it would have have to fall under the first prong of the *Lemon* test, which required the law to have a valid secular purpose. The statute had in fact amended a previous measure which allowed for a moment of silence, though without the specification that it could be used for prayer: thus, its only purpose was to elevate prayer as a preferred activity, rather than merely accommodate it in line with the Free Exercise Clause. Furthermore, the state had a notable recent history of a policy and practice of mandatory spoken prayer in its schools and, read in this light, the statute had both a religious purpose and a coercive character.[191] Nevertheless, the fact that Chief Justice Burger and Justices White and Rehnquist voted to uphold the statute and that Justice O'Connor's concurrence said that other moment of silence laws might be constitutional, indicates how close the Court came to allowing prayer back into the public schools, albeit indirectly.

The boldest challenge to the Court's Establishment Clause doctrine, however, came two years later in *Edwards v. Aguillard*.[192] The case explicitly linked the fundamentalist Protestant crusade of the 1970s and 1980s with an oft-ridiculed past, by resurrecting the issue of the teaching of Darwin's theory of evolution in schools. As has been noted, the Supreme Court had only in the 1968 *Epperson* case finally

declared laws banning the teaching of evolution to be unconstitutional.[193] The assault on such laws dates back, however, at least to
1925 and the Scopes Trial, when a high-school biology teacher in
Tennessee was convicted under the state's law forbidding the teaching
of evolution. Such was the derision heaped upon Tennessee that other
states' anti-evolution laws remained largely unenforced.[194]

The objection of fundamentalist Christians to Darwinian theory was
that it contradicted the literal truth of the divine theory of creation
contained in the book of Genesis. Thus the clash was one between
secular science and scripture. When the Court in *Epperson* declared the
Genesis story of the creation to be a sectarian doctrine which states
could not advance in schools, anti-evolutionists responded by simply
stealing their opponents' clothes and inventing 'creation science' or
'creationism'. In 1970, the Creation Science Research Centre was
founded to promote Creationism as a legitimate field of scientific
enquiry, followed two years later by the Institute for Creation
Research. The latter developed a legal arm, the Christian Legal
Defence Fund, later the Creation Science Legal Defence Fund
(CSLDF).[195] Proponents of creation science argue that there is
scientific evidence to support the theory that all things were created out
of nothing by God.[196] They also attack the status of evolution as
scientifically-proven truth.

In 1981, pursuant to such beliefs, Louisiana passed the Balanced
Treatment for Creation-Science and Evolution Science in Public
School Instruction Act, otherwise known as the Creationism Act or
Balanced Treatment Act. This neither banned the teaching of evolution nor mandated the teaching of creation science: rather, it required
that if one of these were taught in school, so must be the other. The
avowed purpose of the act was secular, namely, to ensure academic
freedom.

Interest groups on both sides became involved immediately.
CSLDF lawyers were deputised by the Attorney-General of Louisiana
to represent the state in any challenges to the new law and shortly
afterwards, the American Civil Liberties Union filed suit alleging that
the Act was unconstitutional.[197] Both the federal District Court and
the Court of Appeals found the act unconstitutional under the Establishment Clause. Not surprisingly in view of its precedents and the
facts of the case, the Supreme Court affirmed these decisions by a vote
of 7-2. However, the dissenting opinion of Justice Scalia, joined by
Chief Justice Rehnquist, together with the rather grudging concurrence of Justice White, could point the way to a very different

outcome at some future date.

Writing for the majority, Justice Brennan found the Act's alleged secular purpose of ensuring academic freedom to be 'a sham',[198] agreeing with the Appeals Court that '. . . the Act does not serve to protect academic freedom, but has the distinctly different purpose of discrediting evolution by counterbalancing its teaching at every turn with the teaching of creationism'.[199] Furthermore, an examination of the legislative history of the Act persuaded Brennan that creation science was a religious rather than scientific doctrine: for example, creation scientists called as witnesses and the bill's sponsor all made clear that belief in God was the source of their 'science'. One of the bill's supporters in the state legislature went so far as to proclaim the existence of God to be a scientific fact.[200] Justice Powell's concurring opinion delved even deeper into the nature of creation science and he found no evidence to negate the view that its purpose is to promote a particular religious viewpoint.[201] Given the weight of the factual evidence about the nature of creation science, therefore, it was straightforward for Justice Brennan to conclude that, 'The Louisiana Creationism Act advances a religious doctrine by requiring either the banishment of the theory of evolution from public school classrooms or the presentation of a religious viewpoint that rejects evolution in its entirety. The Act violates the Establishment Clause of the First Amendment because it seeks to employ the symbolic and financial support of government to achieve a religious purpose.'[202]

Justice White concurred, but indicated that he might reach a different result if the Court were willing to reconsider its Establishment Clause jurisprudence. White had dissented in *Lemon v. Kurtzman* and had never accepted the test that had been fashioned there.

A much more swingeing attack on both the Court's decision and the *Lemon* test came from Justice Scalia. He disputed the contention that the Act had no valid secular purpose. He quoted at length from the legislative history to argue that the Act's supporters appeared genuinely to believe that there was a body of scientific knowledge which supported the Genesis story of the creation and that such knowledge could be taught without reference to religious doctrine or materials: 'The vast majority of them voted to approve a bill which explicitly stated a secular purpose; what is crucial is not their *wisdom* in believing that purpose would be achieved by the bill, but their *sincerity* in believing it would.'[203] Furthermore, there was insufficient evidence on the record, he said, to disprove that their belief was indeed wrong.[204]

Thus, Justice Scalia said, he was 'astonished' by the Court's willingness to conclude that the professed secular motive behind the Act was disingenuous. Such scepticism could only be attributed to

> . . . an intellectual predisposition created by the facts and legend of (the Scopes trial) – an instinctive reaction that any governmentally imposed requirements bearing upon the teaching of evolution must be a manifestation of Christian fundamentalist repression. In this case, however, it seems to me the Court's position is the repressive one. The people of Louisiana, including those who are Christian fundamentalists, are quite entitled, as a secular matter, to have whatever scientific evidence there may be against evolution presented in their schools, just as Mr. Scopes was entitled to present whatever scientific evidence there was for it.[205]

The Court's decision, he said, was 'Scopes-in-Reverse'.[206]

Justice Scalia's dissent is, to say the least, an extreme example of judicial deference to legislative will. It stretches credulity to breaking point to insist that the Creationism Act was motivated by anything other than religious belief and that it would have been implemented without any suggestion of religious evidence and argument. It barely amounts to more than a requirement of a plausible constitutional motive, rather than a convincing one.

As it turned out, however, Scalia was essentially going through the motions in his discussion of the purpose behind the enactment of the Louisiana statute. For the remainder of the opinion is devoted to demonstrating that the secular purpose prong of the *Lemon* test is but the worst feature of '. . . our embarrassing Establishment Clause jurisprudence . . .',[207] which had sacrificed clarity for flexibility. Given the variety and combination of reasons that may induce a legislator to support a bill, he argued, the subjective intent behind legislation is impossible to ascertain.[208] Moreover, it is not required by the Establishment Clause. Contrary to some forty years of Court decisions, Justice Scalia argued that it is '. . . far from an inevitable reading of the Establishment Clause that it forbids all governmental action intended to advance religion.'[209] Therefore, he said, a good place to start the process of bringing clarity to Establishment Clause law would be the abandonment of the secular purpose prong of the *Lemon* test.

The importance of the dissent in *Edwards v. Aguillard* is that it highlights the extreme results which could be reached if the *Lemon* test and other aspects of post-Everson law are reversed. Yet some such development seems possible, indeed, probable, given the willingness of the Court to accommodate religion in more mainstream policy contexts. Thus we come to the second category of Establishment Clause cases mentioned above, those involving the use of religious symbolism in public life. That the Reagan administration attached great importance to this issue became clear when it decided to use a seemingly trivial case to ask the Court to abandon the *Lemon* test.[210] The trivial issue was whether the city of Pawtucket, Rhode Island, had violated the Establishment Clause by erecting a traditional Christmas display which included a crèche featuring Jesus, Mary and Joseph, angels, shepherds and animals, as well as a Christmas tree, a Santa Claus and other traditional images of Christmas. The American Civil Liberties Union thought so and brought suit to that effect. The federal District Court and the Court of Appeals agreed. In 1984, however, the Supreme Court handed a partial victory to the Reagan administration by reversing the lower courts in *Lynch v. Donnelly*.[211]

Chief Justice Burger's opinion for the majority of five was hardly a model of clarity. He quoted and paraphrased his *Lemon* opinion, restated the usefulness of its three prong test, but then appeared to undercut it by saying that the Court would not '. . . be confined to any single test or criterion in this sensitive area.'[212] However, after further undermining the *Lemon* test by discussing at some length the two cases where it had not been employed, he then proceeded to apply it to the Pawtucket Christmas display! Whether Burger's purpose was to placate members of the majority who did not subscribe to the *Lemon* test[213] or to retain total flexibility in handling religion cases, or both, his approach makes Justice Scalia's *Edwards* appeal for greater certainty in the Court's jurisprudence difficult to reject.

The Chief Justice found that the Pawtucket crèche survived the first prong of the *Lemon* test, because it had the secular purpose of celebrating the Christmas holiday, which is a national holiday for all Americans.[214] He also rejected the argument that the display had the primary effect of advancing religion, the second part of the test. As he pointed out, it would be difficult to argue that the benefit to religion of the crèche was greater than other examples of state support for religion which the Court had previously upheld, such as supplying textbooks to parochial schools or tax exemptions for church-owned properties.[215] Finally, he noted that the display involved no entanglement between the city and religious organisations, either in terms of finance or administration.

Behind the technical facade of the application of the *Lemon* test in *Lynch*, however, was the Court's recognition that much of American public life is imbued with religious symbolism. As the Chief Justice pointed out, both Christmas and Thanksgiving have been declared official holidays, despite their religious origins; Congress employs chaplains to lead members in daily prayers, a practice which the Court had upheld only the previous year;[216] and the statutorily prescribed national motto is 'In God We Trust'. He might also have alluded, as did the Reagan administration's *amicus* brief, to the fact that public sessions of the Supreme Court itself begin with the cry of 'God save the United States and this honourable Court'.[217] It is therefore as clear as anything can be that any interpretivist understanding of the Establishment Clause would permit insignificant, symbolic church-state involvement of the kind represented by the Pawtucket Christmas display. And as Burger pointed out, the Court had always claimed that its Establishment Clause jurisprudence '. . . has comported with what history reveals was the contemporaneous understanding of its guarantees.'[218]

Burger's opinion ended with what amounts to a plea to allow the Court the flexibility to distinguish between trivial church-state involvement and those which seriously threaten state neutrality in religious matters. He listed many of the cases in which the Court had struck down such practices and insisted that they demonstrated its continuing concern '. . . to protect the genuine objectives of the Establishment Clause.'[219] But as he had already noted, 'Any notion that these symbols pose a real danger of establishment of a state church is farfetched indeed.'[220]

Justice Brennan's lengthy dissent[221] seems out of proportion to an issue which he himself ackowledged involved, at worst, only a small step toward an establishment of religion. But as with Burger's opinion for the Court, there were indications that it was uncertainty over the future of the *Lemon* test which led him to strive so mightily in *Lynch*. He went out of his way to express his satisfaction that the Court had decided to apply the test here, even if it was only in a half-hearted fashion.[222] And although he proceeded to dispute each point of Burger's application of the test, he noted that while regrettable, it was at least understandable in the light of the particular facts of the case.[223] What disturbed him most, then, was the Court's broader intimation that symbolic church-state entanglement could not only be justified by a specific historical tradition supporting it, as with legislative prayers, but by reference to some general religious heritage. Unlike his handling of affirmative action cases, for example, Justice Brennan now celebrated the virtues of historical specificity as a weapon in the battle for judicial restraint: 'Without that guiding principle and the intellectual discipline it imposes, the Court is at sea, free to select random elements of America's varied history solely to suit the views of five Members of this Court.'[224]

What Justice Brennan more concretely feared was that a new majority on the Court was emerging in Establishment Clause jurisprudence, a majority which would tolerate state support for religious practices which could be deemed traditional. Such toleration could lead to discrimination against smaller religious denominations, whose practices had not entered the American mainstream.

The *Lynch* dissenters could take some comfort, however, from Justice O'Connor's concurring opinion. The Justice made clear her own view that much of the *Lemon* test was unsatisfactory and that its purpose and effect prongs could best be applied by asking whether a particular practice was intended to convey either an endorsement or disapproval of religion, or actually conveyed such a message. This, she pointed out, is a significantly different question from whether a particular practice advances or inhibits religion, as currently asked by the *Lemon* test. However, although she thereby struck a blow against the test, her new formulation was not intended to eviscerate it. Indeed, as she elaborated her endorsement standard, it appeared to echo Brennan's worry about future discrimination against smaller religious groups: 'Endorsement sends a message to non adherents that they are outsiders, not full members of the political community, and an accompanying message to adherents that they are insiders, favoured members of the political community.'[225] She also signalled her belief that all government acknowledgement or celebration of religion must be subjected to careful judicial scrutiny and judged on its unique circumstances.[226]

Five years later, in *Allegheny County v. Pittsburgh ACLU*,[227] Justice O'Connor demonstrated that her endorsement test had real teeth, though the net result was to throw the Court's Establishment Clause jurisprudence into even greater confusion. For Justice O'Connor now joined the four *Lynch* dissenters in holding that a crèche displayed alone in a county courthouse did violate the Establishment Clause; but then joined the other four members of the Court in holding that a Jewish menorah[228] displayed with a Christmas tree outside a county-city office building, did not. There were five opinions from the Justices, none of which commanded a majority: only two Justices, O'Connor and Blackmun, agreed that the menorah display, but not the crèche, was constitutional; three Justices, Brennan, Marshall and Stevens, thought neither was constitutional; and four members, Rehnquist,

White, Scalia and Kennedy, believed both were constitutional.

Justice Blackmun tried to bring some order to the Court's past decisions, noting that the *Lemon* test had been further refined in recent years by the notion of endorsement and disapproval of religion. More explicitly, he described the rationale for the majority decision in *Lynch* as 'none too clear' and contrasted it with Justice O'Connor's concurring opinion: 'The main difference is that the concurrence provides a sound analytical framework for evaluating governmental use of religious symbols:'[229] that is, whether people viewing a religious display would fairly understand if it communicates an endorsement of religion or not. And that depends on the particular features of each individual display.[230]

It was such factual differences that persuaded Blackmun and O'Connor to distinguish between the Pawtucket and Allegheny County displays: in the former, the crèche had been part of a larger display, including non-religious symbols, whereas in the latter, the crèche stood alone and included a banner proclaiming 'Gloria in Excelsis Deo'. Another important difference was that the Pawtucket crèche was displayed in a privately-owned park, whereas the Allegheny County crèche was placed on the main staircase of the county courthouse. Justice Blackmun concluded: 'In sum, *Lynch* teaches that government may celebrate Christmas in some manner and form, but not in a way that endorses Christian doctrine. Here, Allegheny County has transgressed that line. It has chosen to celebrate Christmas in a way that has the effect of endorsing a patently Christian message: Glory to God for the birth of Jesus Christ. Under *Lynch*, and the rest of our cases, nothing more is required to demonstrate a violation of the Establishment Clause.'[231]

The factual circumstances of the menorah display, on the other hand, persuaded Justices Blackmun and O'Connor that it conveyed no message of religious endorsement. Particularly important was the fact that it was displayed next to a Christmas tree, '. . . the preeminent secular symbol of the Christmas holiday season'; and, moreover, while the menorah was only eighteen foot high, the Christmas tree was forty-five feet high. Thus, 'Given this configuration, it is much more sensible to interpret the meaning of the menorah in light of the tree, rather than vice versa . . . In these circumstances, then, the combination of the tree and the menorah communicates, not a simultaneous endorsement of both Christian and Jewish faith, but instead, a secular celebration of Christmas coupled with an acknowledgement of Chanukah as a contemporaneous alternative tradition.'[232] As if to emphasise further the importance of physical aspects of the two displays, Justice Blackmun included a photograph of each at the end of his opinion.

Both the two other main blocs on the Court eschewed the Blackmun-O'Connor approach in favour of one based on more clear-cut principles. Justice Brennan, for example, reiterated his view that any government display of an object with a specifically religious meaning violated the First Amendment. And he poked fun at the emphasis on '. . . perspective, spacing and accent expressed in Justice Blackmun's opinion, (which made) analysis under the Establishment Clause look more like an exam in Art 101 than an enquiry into constitutional law.'[233]

Justice Kennedy's opinion quickly made it clear that here was yet another member of the Court who was dissatisfied with the *Lemon* test. In a highly disparaging tone, he wrote: 'In keeping with the usual fashion of recent years, the majority applies the *Lemon* test to judge the constitutionality of the holiday displays here in question. I am content for present purposes to remain within the *Lemon* framework, but do not wish to be seen as advocating, let alone adopting, that test as our primary guide in this difficult area . . . Substantial revision of our Establishment Clause doctrine may be in order.'[234] Indeed, five members of the Court had now clearly signalled their criticisms of the *Lemon* test.[235] However, Justice Kennedy was also convinced that both the creche and menorah displays were constitutional under the *Lemon* test. Permissible accommodation of religion only became impermissible advancement of religion when one of just two principles were infringed: '. . . government may not coerce anyone to support or participate in any religion or its exercise; and it may not . . . give direct benefits to religion in such a degree that it in fact establishes a state religion or religious faith, or tends to do so.'[236] Thus, as a general principle, where there is no direct or indirect coercion, the government may accommodate religion by a passive, symbolic acknowledgement of religion, such as the Allegheny County displays.[237]

The Brennan and Kennedy positions could hardly be further apart: the former would prohibit all governmental display of religious symbols, while the latter would permit any that did not involve coercion.[238] But there is little hope that the Court will rally around Justice O'Connor's intermediate position, especially as Justice Kennedy was quite as disparaging about it as he was about the *Lemon* test.[239] Ironically, like Justice Brennan, he too was critical of the Blackmun-O'Connor emphasis on the physical aspects of the displays under consideration, calling it 'a jurisprudence of minutiae'.[240] Such an approach was at odds with the very fundamentals of the judicial function: 'Deciding cases on the basis of such an unguided examination of marginalia is irreconcilable with the imperative of applying neutral principles in constitutional adjudication.'[241]

Given that Justice Kennedy's opinion commanded four votes in *Allegheny County* and the fact that since that case was decided, President Bush has appointed two more Justices to replace Brennan and Marshall,[242] it is probable that his vision of government use of religious symbolism will prevail. Consequently, the conservative cultural counter-revolution against the liberalism and secularism of the 1960s will have won a symbolic victory. Exactly how important this is in political terms is perhaps debatable: but if we turn now to look at a recent case belonging to the third category mentioned above, those involving attempts to read religion into substantive social policy, the significance of the conservative victory becomes apparent.

In 1981, Congress passed the Adolescent Family Life Act (AFLA). The Act's chief sponsors were two Senators closely identified with the New Christian Right, Jeremiah Denton of Alabama and Orrin Hatch of Utah.[243] The Act was clearly based upon strict traditional codes of sexual behaviour for adolescents. Its principal aims were to combat teenage premarital sex and abortion, by promoting chastity and adoption as an alternative to abortion.[244] It was also a symbol of the conservative counter-revolution in that it was designed to counteract the effects of Title X of the Public Health Service Act of 1970. Title X, passed at a time when 'enlightened' liberal attitudes to sex prevailed, provided contraceptives and abortion advice to adolescents, something which Hatch, Denton and other conservatives viewed as encouraging both immorality and the breakdown of traditional family life.[245] Just as Title X provided funding for groups such as Planned Parenthood, the AFLA would now furnish grants to public and private agencies to provide counselling to teenagers which was more in tune with traditional values. Thus, the AFLA specified that no funds should go to organisations which provided abortions or abortion counselling; nor to any group giving contraceptive advice, if such advice was available from other groups in the community. The AFLA further specified that applicants for grants must explain how they intended to involve religious and charitable groups, as well as other private groups, in their proposed programme.[246] It was this required involvement of religious groups in the expenditure of government funds which led the American Jewish Congress and others to file suit alleging a violation of the Establishment Clause.[247]

The suit reached the Supreme Court in 1988, in *Bowen v. Kendrick*.[248] The federal District Court had ruled that the Act did violate the Establishment Clause, both as written ('on its face') and as applied in practice: the Act failed the second prong of the *Lemon* test because it advanced religion by encouraging and permitting the involvement of religious organisations. In a 5–4 vote, however, the Justices reversed.[249]

Ironically, Chief Justice Rehnquist's opinion for the Court reviewed the AFLA under the *Lemon* test, despite the fact that not one of the five majority Justices thought it satisfactory.[250] He noted that there was no contention that the AFLA did not have a valid secular purpose – the reduction of social and economic problems caused by teenage sexual activity and its consequences – even if the Act was, in part, religiously inspired.[251]

The second element in the test was more difficult, as the District Court had detected several grounds for concluding that the AFLA had the effect of advancing religion. At the heart of the District Court's concern was the fear that religious groups involved in counselling teenagers under the programme would simply give advice according to their faith and dogma: and the federal government, in effect, would be financing and otherwise sponsoring such religious indoctrination. Indeed, as far as the 'as applied' review of the Act was concerned, there was considerable evidence on the record that this had, in fact, already occurred.

Rehnquist, however, argued that, at least on its face, the Act permitted only a *coincidence* of its secular purposes and any advice that might be given by religious groups. The services provided by the AFLA were secular and even though a particular view of adolescent, premarital sex was embedded in them, '. . . that approach is not inherently religious, although it may coincide with the approach taken by certain religions.'[252]

As for the requirement that applicants for AFLA grants must show how they intend to involve religious groups in their programme, the Chief Justice thought that this merely reflected the view of Congress that such groups had a useful part to play in the provision of these secular services. There was, moreover, no actual requirement that religious organisations be involved, and the Act clearly invited the participation of secular, as well as sectarian groups. Thus, '. . . nothing on the face of the Act suggests it is anything but neutral with respect to the grantee's status as a sectarian or purely secular institution.'[253]

He did acknowledge a heightened danger of religious advancement if funds went to groups which could be described as 'pervasively sectarian', such as parochial schools. With little evidence or argument, however, he asserted that few of the groups targeted by Congress could be described as 'pervasively sectarian', but were rather more likely to be merely 'religiously affiliated'. He therefore concluded that the risk of government funding of pervasively sectarian organisations was too remote to warrant a verdict of unconstitutionality.[254]

This conclusion also served to satisfy the majority that the third prong of the *Lemon* test – excessive entanglement of church and state – would not be infringed. For if the religious recipients of grants were not pervasively sectarian, then Congress need not engage in intense monitoring of their activities to ensure that they do not use federal funds to preach dogma.[255]

Up to this point, Rehnquist had dealt only with the challenge to the AFLA 'as written'. His opinion in this respect could fairly be described as one which leaned over backwards to find in favour of the Act: its philosophy was, after all, virtually identical with the teachings of certain religious groups, particularly fundamentalists and the Roman Catholic Church, and organisations affiliated to these churches were clearly invited and encouraged to propound that philosophy on behalf of the United States government. Nevertheless, given the traditional reluctance of the Court to strike down acts of Congress, a healthy dose of judicial self-restraint could also be seen as an important underlying factor in the Court's position.[256]

Such an interpretation is, however, seriously undermined by Rehnquist's handling of the 'as applied' challenge to the statute. For as he was obliged to concede, '. . . there is no dispute that the record contains evidence of specific incidents of impermissible behaviour by AFLA grantees . . .'[257] While he did not elaborate, Justice Blackmun, in dissent, provided several examples from the case record of what had been going on under the auspices of the AFLA. Thus, parents and teenagers were counselled: 'The Church has always taught that the marriage act, or intercourse, seals the union of husband and wife . . . Christ commits Himself to us when we come to ask for the sacrament of marriage. We ask Him to be active in our life. God is love. We ask Him to share his love in ours, and God procreates with us . . .'; and another described its family planning method as one designed to help couples '. . . to cultivate their matrimonial spirituality and to make themselves better instruments in God's plan (and) facilitating the evangelisation of homes.'[258] Not unreasonably in the light of such evidence, Blackmun argued:

> Whatever Congress had in mind . . .it enacted a statute that facilitated and,
> indeed, encouraged the use of public funds for such instruction, by giving
> religious groups a central pedagogical and counselling role without
> imposing any restraints on the sectarian quality of the participation. As the
> record developed thus far in this litigation makes all too clear, federal
> tax-dollars appropriated for AFLA purposes have been used, with
> Government approval, to support religious teaching.[259]

While Chief Justice Rehnquist could not ignore such evidence, he
nullified its constitutional significance by confining its relevance to the
legitimacy of individual grants, rather than of the Act as a whole. He
therefore remanded the 'as applied' challenge back to the District
Court for more specific investigation of these apparantly
impermissible grants. He also, however, did his best to ensure that the
District Court did not return with a finding that the number of such
grants condemned the Act as a whole: he squarely told the District
Court that the appropriate remedy for a finding that grants were being
made in violation of the Constitution would be to require the with-
drawal of those particular grants.[260] Thus did the majority Justices
seek to pre-empt the decision of the District Court based on factual
findings, in order to preserve the AFLA. Whether such a strategy will
work remains to be seen. On behalf of the dissenters, Justice Blackmun
encouraged the District Court to declare the Act unconstitutional, if
further factual investigation confirms what has already been found.[261]
And Justice O'Connor, not for the first time, ended her concurring
opinion on an enigmatic note, saying that if the District Court did
indeed find violations of the Establishment Clause, an appropriate
remedy would take into account '. . . the history of the programme's
administration as well as the extent of any continuing constitutional
violations.'[262]

Taken as a whole, the Court's decisions under the Establishment
Clause have significantly changed since the early 1980s. The *Lemon*
test has gone in all but name: as noted above, five Justices are on the
record as wanting either to revise it substantially or do away with it
altogether. It survives simply because there has until now been little
possibility of agreement on a new test with which to replace it.[263]
Whatever its flaws, the *Lemon* test was a significant barrier to governmental support for religion, especially as the failure of legislation to
satisfy just one of its prongs was enough to condemn it. In that sense, it
was 'hostile' to religion as conservative critics alleged, because it

required government policy to be essentially secular. As *Bowen* demonstrates, only a distorted and disingenuous application of the *Lemon* test would allow government to advance a religious platform.

It is also clear that the slow and agonising demise of the *Lemon* test was brought about by the placement on the Court in the 1980s of three new Justices nominated by President Reagan: nominees who, in turn, owed their appointment to the political influence of conservative religious groups within the Reagan coalition. Moreover, neither the fact that the 'wall of separation' between church and state has been dismantled slowly, nor that much of the conflict over it has been symbolic, should be allowed to detract from the significance of the conservative victory. Not only is symbolism important in its own right in politics, but *Bowen* may well turn out to be not the climax, but the spring-board of the conservative campaign to reassert religious values in public life through constitutional interpretation.

Notes

1 K. Karst, 'Religion, sex, and politics: cultural counter-revolution in constitutional perspective', *University of California, Davis, Law Review*, XXIV, 1991, pp. 677–734.
2 D. DeLeon, *Everything Is Changing: Contemporary US Movements in Historical Perspective*, New York, 1988, p. 181. See also R. Mohr, *Gays/Justice: A Study of Ethics, Society and Law*, New York, 1988, pp. 32–4.
3 See *Bowers v. Hardwick*, 478 US 186 (1986), Opinion of Justice Brennan, n. 6, p. 2855.
4 T. Smith, 'The Polls–A Report: the sexual revolution?', *Public Opinion Quarterly*, LIV, 1990, pp. 415–35, 424.
5 *Ibid.*, p. 424.
6 'Developments in the law: sexual orientation and the law', *Harvard Law Review*, CII, 1989, pp. 1508–671, 1512–14. See also DeLeon, *op. cit.*, p. 195.
7 Ibid., p. 186.
8 'Developments in the law', *op. cit.*, p. 1516.
9 Mohr, *op. cit.*, p. 61.
10 DeLeon, *op. cit.*, p. 196.
11 'Developments in the law', *op. cit.*, pp. 1516–17.
12 *Ibid.*, p. 1516, n. 44.
13 DeLeon, *op. cit.*, pp. 201–2.
14 425 US 901 (1976).
15 478 US 186 (1986). Justice Blackmun may simply have changed his mind about granting review in the intervening years; but with his *Roe* opinion under increasing pressure in the 1980s, he may have wished to strengthen the Court's privacy doctrine by expanding its reach. Justice Powell may also have changed his position, since he seems to have considerable difficulty knowing on which side to come down, *infra*.
16 M. Dubber, 'Homosexual privacy rights before the United States Supreme Court and the European Court of Human Rights: a comparison of methodologies', *Stanford Journal of International Law*, XXVII, 1990, pp. 189–214, 191; M. Urofsky, *The Continuity of Change: The Supreme Court And Individual Liberties 1953–1986*, Belmont, California, 1991, p. 262.
17 *Bowers*, Opinion of Justice Stevens, n. 11, p. 2859. On general non-enforcement of such laws, see 'Developments in the law – sexual orientation and the law', *op. cit.*, pp. 1520–1.

264 RAW JUDICIAL POWER?

18 *Bowers*, Opinion of the Court, n. 1, p. 2842.
19 *Bowers*, Opinion of Justice Blackmun, n. 1, p. 2849.
20 Dubber, *op. cit.*, p. 191. There were also a significant number of *amicus* briefs in this case. Two were filed on behalf of the state, including one by Concerned Women for America which stated that: 'We oppose any laws designed to grant special legal protection to those who engage in homosexuality. Such laws are an affront to public morality and our dedication to family life.': Brief of Concerned Women for America, *Transcripts of Records and Briefs*, CLVIII, 1985, pp. 1–2. Ten briefs were filed on behalf of Hardwick, including Gay/Lesbian groups, such as the Lamda Legal Defense and Education Fund, the National Gay Rights Advocates and the Lesbian Rights Project; women's groups, including NOW; professional health groups in the form of the American Psychological Association and the American Public Health Association; and religious/ethnic groups, including the Presbyterian Church and the American Jewish Congress.
21 *Bowers*, p. 2843
22 *Ibid.*
23 *Ibid.*, p. 2844
24 *Ibid.*, p. 2846
25 Justice White, of course, dissented in *Roe*, but others in the *Bowers* majority – Chief Justice Burger and Justice Powell – had not. Moreover, in legal theory at least, *Roe* has precedential weight, regardless of the dissenters' views.
26 *Ibid.*, p. 2846
27 For a more comprehensive critique of White's historical analysis and an interesting comparison with the approach taken by the European Court of Human Rights in similar cases, see Dubber, *op. cit.*
28 *Bowers*, p. 2849
29 *Ibid.*, p. 2851
30 *Ibid.*
31 *Ibid.*, p. 2852
32 'Developments in the law – sexual orientation and the law', *op. cit.*, p. 1523.
33 'This case does not require a judgement on whether laws against sodomy between consenting adults in general, or between homosexuals in particular, are wise or desirable.': *Bowers*, p. 2843
34 *Bowers*, p. 2847.
35 *Ibid.*, p. 2846.
36 'Developments in the law – sexual orientation and the law', *op. cit.*, p. 1524.
37 *Bowers*, p. 2853.
38 *Ibid.*, p. 2847.
39 388 US 1 (1967).
40 *US Supreme Court Oral Arguments*, XVII, 1985, p. 28.
41 *Ibid.*, p. 2856
42 Quoted in Dubber, *op. cit.*, n. 111, p. 213.
43 491 US – , 105 L Ed 2d 91, 109 S Ct – (1989).
44 It should be noted, however, that no matter how widespread adulterous sex may be in the United States, it is still overwhelmingly condemned at the rhetorical level. Between 1970 and 1989, the number of poll respondents believing that extramarital sex is 'always wrong' never fell below 65 per cent, and stood higher in 1989 (77 per cent) than in 1970 (72 per cent). Smith, *op. cit.*, p. 423.
45 The blood tests put the likelihood of Michael's fatherhood at 98.07 per cent, *Michael H.*, p. 100.
46 Victoria also made an equal protection claim, on the grounds that while the mother and natural father could rebut the presumption of paternity if done within two years of the birth, the child herself could not, *Michael H.*, p. 101.
47 Justice Scalia announced the judgement of the Court and wrote a plurality opinion in

which Chief Justice Rehnquist joined wholly and in which Justices O'Connor and
Kennedy joined with the exception of Scalia's critical footnote 6. Justice O'Connor
wrote concurring opinion, joined by Kennedy, to explain their reservations. Justice
Stevens concurred in the plurality's conclusion, but not their reasoning. Justice
Brennan wrote a dissent joined by Justices Marshall and Blackmun. And Justice White
wrote a dissent on the procedural due process issue, joined by Justice Brennan.

48 *Ibid.*, n. 6, pp. 108–9.
49 *Ibid.*, p. 109.
50 *Ibid.*, p. 108 (emphasis added).
51 *Ibid.*, p. 106. Scalia denied that he was using an excessively narrow definition of the term
    'family', saying that it included households of unmarried parents and their children, as
    well as the marital family, n. 3, p. 106.
52 Opinion of Justice O'Connor, *Ibid.*, pp. 111–12. Justice Brennan cited a long list of
    cases, including those involving the right of married and unmarried couples to use
    contraceptives, to show that the Court had not employed Justice Scalia's method in the
    past and, therefore, '. . . the novelty of the interpretive method that the plurality opinion
    employs today.', pp. 116–17.
53 *Ibid.*, p. 118.
54 'The Supreme Court 1988 Term', *Harvard Law Review*, CIII, 1989–90, pp. 43–393,
    185. Justice Brennan also thought he detected Justice Scalia's subjectivity in the latter's
    repeated description of Michael H. as the '*adulterous* natural father', *Michael H.*, p. 119
    (emphasis in original).
55 Smith, *op. cit.*, p. 419. Smith is not convinced that a major 'sexual revolution' actually
    took place, but it is worth stressing that his conclusion is based on attitudes expressed in
    opinion polls rather than Americans' actual behaviour, p. 416. One does not need to be a
    dyed-in-the-wool cynic to suspect that what people *do* in matters of sexuality may be
    rather different from what they *say*, especially when talking to pollsters.
56 Between the two dates, the number of those disapproving fell from 72.7 per cent to 55
    per cent; 80.5 per cent to 64.8 per cent; and 74.3 per cent to 58.7 per cent, respectively:
    Smith, *op. cit.*, pp. 424–5.
57 *Ibid.*, pp. 425–6.
58 G. Hawkins and F. Zimring, *Pornography in a Free Society*, Cambridge, 1988, p. 70.
59 D. Downs, *The New Politics of Pornography*, Chicago, 1989, p. 22.
60 Hawkins and Zimring, *op. cit.*, p. 78. All quotes from the two Commissions included
    here are from this source and can be found in Table 4.2, pp. 78–9 and Table 4.3, pp.
    80–1.
61 See n. 60, *supra.*
62 See *Ibid.*
63 See *Ibid.*
64 Downs, *op. cit.*, pp. 1–2.
65 Hawkins and Zimring, *op. cit.*, p. 76.
66 *Ibid.*, p. 99.
67 Downs, *op. cit.*, p. 2.
68 Hawkins and Zimring, *op. cit.*, p. x.
69 C. Mackinnon, *Feminism Unmodified: Discourses on Life and Law*, Cambridge, Mass.,
    1987, pp. 175–6.
70 This account of the ordinances is taken from Downs, *op. cit.*, except where otherwise
    indicated.
71 *Ibid.*, p. 44.
72 For a critique of magazines such as *Playboy* as pornography, see Mackinnon, *op. cit.*,
    pp.134–45.
73 Downs, *op. cit.*, p. 109.
74 *American Booksellers v. Hudnut*, 106 S Ct. 1172 (1986).
75 The Feminist Anti-Censorship Task Force was formed in 1984 with the specific aim of

opposing the Mackinnon-Dworkin ordinances: Hawkins and Zimring, *op. cit.*, p. 167. The Minneapolis CLU led the fight against the ordinance there and the national ACLU often submits briefs defending pornography rights in the Supreme Court. Citizens for Decency Through Law was founded in 1957 as Citizens For Decent Literature, Inc. Its leader is Charles H. Keating, who was also appointed to the Meese Commission.

76 354 US 476 (1957).
77 *Ibid.*, p. 489.
78 M. I. Urofsky, *The Continuity of Change: The Supreme Court And Individual Liberties 1953–1986*, Belmont, California, 1991, p. 80.
79 Woodward and Armstrong, *op. cit.*, p. 195.
80 *Kingsley v. Regents*, 360 US 684 (1959).
81 Woodward and Armstrong, *op. cit.*, p. 193.
82 *Ibid.*, p. 194.
83 388 US 184 (1964), p. 197.
84 Woodward and Armstrong, *op. cit.*, p. 198.
85 *Ibid.* p. 191.
86 *Memoirs v. Massachusetts*, 383 US 413 (1966), pp. 419–20.
87 Urofsky, *op. cit.*, pp. 83–4. The two cases apart from *Memoirs* were *Mishkin v. New York*, 383 US 502 (1966) and *Ginzberg v. US* 383 US 463 (1966).
88 Downs, *op. cit.*, p. 16.
89 394 US 557 (1969).
90 413 US 15 (1973), p. 24.
91 Downs, op. cit., pp. 17–18.
92 *Ibid.*, pp.18–22.
93 492 US – , 106 L Ed 2d 93, 109 S Ct – (1989).
94 *Ibid.*, n. 1 and 3, pp. 100–1.
95 Transcripts of Records and Briefs, CCLXXXI, Brief of Action For Children's Television *et al.*, p. 3.
96 Transcripts of Records and Briefs, CCLXXX, Brief for Citizens For Decency Through Law *et al.*, pp. 4–5.
97 *Sable*, pp. 103–4.
98 *Ibid.*, pp. 104–5.
99 *Ibid.*, p. 110. The other dissenters were Justices Marshall and Stevens.
100 *Ibid.*, p. 108.
101 He wrote: 'To the extent that the Government suggests that we should defer to Congress' conclusion about an issue of constitutional law, our answer is that while we do not ignore it, it is our task in the end to decide whether Congress has violated the Constitution. *This is particularly true where the legislature has concluded that its product does not violate the First Amendment.*' (emphasis added), *Ibid.*, p. 107.
102 501 US – , 115 L Ed 2d 504, 111 S Ct – (1991).
103 R. Marcus, 'Bump and grind: is it free speech?', *International Herald Tribune*, 7 January 1991, p. 3.
104 Section 1 of the Act made public displays of nudity a Class A misdemeanour and defined nudity as follows: '. . . the showing of the human male or female genitals, pubic area, or buttocks with less than a fully opaque covering of any part of the nipple, or the showing of the covered male genitals in a discernibly turgid state.': *Barnes*, n. 2, p. 523.
105 Marcus, *op. cit.*
106 Transcripts of Records and Briefs (unbound), Brief of People For The American Way *et al.*, pp. 3–4.
107 *Ibid.*, Brief for Concerned Women For America *et al.*, p. 1.
108 *Ibid..*, Brief for The American Family Association *et al.*, p. 12.
109 *Barnes*, p. 511 (emphases added).
110 'The Supreme Court 1990 Term – leading cases', *Harvard Law Review*, CV, 1991, pp. 287–97, 294.

111 391 US 367 (1968).
112 *Barnes*, p. 512.
113 *Ibid.*, p. 512–13.
114 *Ibid.*, p. 514. It is hard to take this aspect of the Chief Justice's argument seriously: the very fact that Indiana requires only these parts of the body to be hidden from view suggests that they are of more than 'slight' importance where eroticism is concerned.
115 *Ibid.*, p. 520. Justice Scalia argued that *Barnes* raised no First Amendment issue at all, because the Indiana law aimed at regulating nude conduct in general, not expression.
116 *Ibid.*, p. 527.
117 *Ibid.*, p. 517.
118 *Ibid.*, p. 530.
119 Marcus, *op. cit.*
120 Souter did not agree that the Indiana statute should be upheld pursuant to the state's interest in protecting morality, but rather because the state was entitled to protect society against criminal activities associated with such establishments as the Kitty Kat Lounge: *Barnes*, p. 521.
121 495 US – , 109 L Ed 2d 98, 110 S Ct – (1990).
122 *Osborne*, p. 107.
123 See n. 89, *supra*.
124 *Osborne*, p. 108.
125 *Ibid.*, p. 109.
126 *Ibid.*, p. 130. Brennan was joined in dissent by Justices Marshall and Stevens.
127 *Ibid.*, p. 110.
128 *Ibid.*
129 *Ibid.*, n. 8, p. 110.
130 *Ibid.*, pp. 130–1.
131 *Ibid.*, p. 132.
132 See, for example, R. Bork, *The Tempting of America*, New York, 1990, p. 333.
133 *Congressional Quarterly Almanac*, XLV, 1989, p. 308.
134 319 US 624 (1943).
135 Brief for Petitioner, Records of Transcripts and Briefs, CII, 1988, p. 7.
136 Brief for Respondent, *Ibid*, p. 3.
137 491 US – , 105 L Ed 2d 342, 109 S Ct – (1989).
138 Congressional Quarterly Almanac, *op. cit.*, pp. 307–8.
139 'The Supreme Court 1988 Term', *Harvard Law Review*, CIII, 1989–90, pp. 43–393, 249–50.
140 *Johnson*, p. 356, quotation marks omitted.
141 *Ibid.*, p. 359.
142 *Ibid.*, p. 362.
143 *Ibid.*, p. 363.
144 *Ibid.*, pp. 369–70.
145 *Ibid.*, p. 373.
146 *Ibid.*, p. 374.
147 Justice Stevens, dissent was largely free of the rhetorical flourishes of patriotic history and culture that characterised Rehnquist's opinion. Nevertheless, as well as describing the restriction imposed by the statute as a 'trivial burden', Stevens also subscribed to a view of the symbolism of the Stars and Stripes that is wholly unproblematic: 'It is more than a proud symbol of the courage, the determination, and the gifts of nature that transformed thirteen fledgling Colonies into a world power. It is a symbol of freedom, of equal opportunity, of religious tolerance, and of goodwill for other peoples who share our aspirations. The symbol carries its message to dissidents both at home and abroad who may have no interest at all in our national unity or survival.', *Ibid.*, p. 374.
148 *Congressional Quarterly Almanac*, (1989), op. cit., p. 293.
149 *Ibid.*, p. 307.

150 *Ibid.*, p. 314.
151 *Ibid.*, p. 311.
152 *Ibid.*, p. 308.
153 496 US –, 110 L Ed 2d 287, 110 S Ct – (1990).
154 Transcripts of Records and Briefs, CCCCXXXIX, 1989.
155 Brief for the United States, *Ibid.*, p. 41.
156 Brief for the American Bar Association, pp. 16–7.
157 *Eichman*, p. 296.
158 *Congressional Quarterly Almanac*, XLVI, 1990, p. 524.
159 *Cantwell v. Connecticut* , 310 US 296 (1940) and *Everson v. Board of Education*, 330 US 1 (1947), respectively.
160 See, for example, 'Developments in the law – religion and the state', *Harvard Law Review*, C, 1987, pp. 1606–1781; S. Bruce, *The Rise And Fall Of The New Christian Right*, Oxford, 1988; M. Feeley and S. Krislov, *Constitutional Law*, Boston, 1985, pp. 366–420; H. Abraham, *Freedom And The Court: Civil Rights And Liberties In The United States*, (4th ed.), Oxford, 1982, pp. 220, 306; L. Barker and T. Barker, *Civil Liberties And The Constitution: Cases and Commentaries* (3rd Ed.), Englewood Cliffs, 1978, pp. 11–61; L. Pfeffer, *Religious Freedom*, Skokie, Illinois, 1977.
161 333 US 203 (1948).
162 *Zorach v. Clausen* 343 US 306 (1952).
163 *Ibid.*, Opinion of Justice Jackson, 325.
164 370 US 471 (1962).
165 374 US 203 (1963).
166 393 US 97 (1968).
167 'Developments – religion and the state', *op. cit.*, p. 1661, n. 107.
168 D. O'Brien, *Storm Centre: The Supreme Court in American Life*, New York, 1986, p. 299.
169 Bruce, *op. cit.*, p. 157.
170 Abraham, *op. cit.*, p. 272.
171 'Developments – religion and the state', *op. cit.*, pp. 1612–3.
172 K. Elifson and K. Hadaway, 'Prayer in public schools: when church and state collide', *Public Opinion Quarterly*, IL, 1985, pp. 317–29, 321.
173 'Notes – rethinking the incorporation of the establishment clause: a federalist view', *Harvard Law Review*, CV, 1992, pp. 1700–19, p. 1716, n. 109.
174 L. Sigelman and S. Presser, 'Measuring public support for the New Christian Right: the perils of point estimation', *Public Opinion Quarterly*, LII, 1988, pp. 325–37. The authors reject an earlier analysis showing public support for the New Christian Right at 30 per cent and argue that it may be as low as 5 per cent. This study is based on four issues – abortion rights, sex education in schools, ERA and school prayer.
175 See, for example, Bruce, *op. cit.*; Peele, *op. cit.*
176 'Developments – religion and the law', *op. cit.*, pp. 1633–4.
177 'Notes – rethinking the incorporation of the establishment clause', *op. cit.*, p. 1702.
178 *Ibid.*, p. 49.
179 *Ibid.*, pp. 40–1.
180 Elifson and Hadaway, *op. cit.*, Table 2, p. 322.
181 *Ibid.*, Table 1, p. 321.
182 *Ibid.*, p. 326.
183 392 US 236 (1968).
184 403 US 602 (1971).
185 *Lemon*, p. 614.
186 *Ibid.*, pp. 612–13.
187 See Feeley and Krislov, *op. cit.*, pp. 287–93, for a list of leading cases and votes.
188 472 US 38 (1985).
189 'Developments – religion and the state', *op. cit.*, p. 1662.
190 L. Caplan, *The Tenth Justice: The Solicitor-General and the Rule of Law*, New York, 1987,

p. 102.
191 *Wallace*, pp. 42–5.
192 482 US 578 (1987).
193 *Epperson v. Arkansas*, 393 US 97 (1968).
194 K. O'Connor and G. Ivers, 'Creationism, evolution and the courts', *PS: Political Science and Politics*, Winter, 1988, pp. 10–17, 11.
195 *Ibid.*, pp. 12–13.
196 *Edwards*, p. 530.
197 O'Connor and Ivers, *op. cit.*, p. 13. There is a long tradition of interest groups participating in Religion Clause cases, both as *amici curiae* and as plaintiffs. See L. Pfeffer, '*Amici* in church-state litigation', *Law and Contemporary Problems*, XXXXIV, 1981, pp. 83–110.
198 *Edwards*, p. 587.
199 *Ibid.*, p. 589.
200 *Ibid.*, p. 591, n. 13.
201 *Ibid.*, pp. 599–604.
202 *Ibid.*, pp. 596–7.
203 *Ibid.*, p. 621 (italics in original).
204 'We have no basis on the record to conclude that creation science need be anything other than a collection of scientific data supporting the theory that life abruptly appeared on earth.', *Ibid.*, p. 629.
205 *Ibid.*, p. 634.
206 *Ibid.*
207 *Ibid.*, p. 639.
208 In typical tongue-in-cheek fashion, Scalia's list of possible motivations for supporting a bill ranged from a desire to foster religion, through being mad at one's wife who opposed the bill, to having accidentally voted 'yes' instead of 'no', *Ibid.*, p. 637.
209 *Ibid.*, p. 639.
210 Caplan, *op. cit.*, pp. 96–7.
211 465 US 668 (1984).
212 *Lynch*, p. 679.
213 Particularly Justices White and Rehnquist.
214 *Lynch*, pp. 680–1.
215 *Ibid.*, pp. 681–2.
216 *Marsh v. Chambers*, 463 US 783 (1983).
217 Caplan, *op. cit.*, p. 96.
218 *Lynch*, p. 673.
219 *Ibid.*, p. 687.
220 *Ibid.*, p. 686.
221 This was joined by Justices Marshall, Blackmun and Stevens.
222 *Ibid.*, p. 696.
223 *Ibid.*, p. 713.
224 *Ibid.*, p. 725.
225 *Ibid.*, p. 688.
226 *Ibid.*, p. 694.
227 492 US – , 106 L Ed 2d 472, 109 S Ct – (1989).
228 A candelabra used in the celebration of the Chanukah holiday, which occurs at about the same time as Christmas.
229 *Allegheny County*, p. 495.
230 *Ibid.*, p. 496.
231 *Ibid.*, p. 500.
232 *Ibid.*, p. 510.
233 *Ibid.*, p. 527.
234 *Ibid.*, p. 535. It is curious that a Justice who advocates self-restraint should treat the

basis of some twenty years of Establishment Clause jurisprudence as a mere 'fashion'.
235 White, Rehnquist, O'Connor, Scalia and Kennedy.
236 *Allegheny County*, p. 538.
237 *Ibid.*, p. 539–40.
238 Justice Kennedy did allow that a city could not erect a permanent, large Latin cross on
     the roof of city hall, since this would amount to government support of an effort to
     proselytise on behalf of a particular religion, *Ibid.*, p. 539.
239 He wrote: '. . . I submit that the endorsement test is flawed in its fundamentals and
     unworkable in practice. The uncritical adoption of this standard is every bit as troubling
     as the bizarre result it produces in the case before us.', *Ibid.*, p. 544.
240 *Ibid.*, p. 547.
241 *Ibid.*, p. 548.
242 Justices Souter and Thomas.
243 A. Petrich, 'Bowen v. Kendrick: retreat from prophylaxis in church-state relationships',
     Hastings Constitutional Law Quarterly, XVI, 1989, pp. 513–51, 513.
244 *Congressional Quarterly Almanac*, XXXVII, 1981, p. 488.
245 Petrich, *op. cit.*, pp. 513–14, especially n. 5.
246 *Ibid.*, p. 524.
247 *Ibid.*, pp. 524–5. The American Jewish Congress has a long history of involvement in
     litigation under the Religion Clauses: see Pfeffer, *op. cit.* A significant number of interest
     groups also participated in the case as *amici curiae*: support for the Act came notably
     from Catholic and anti-abortion organisations, including the US Catholic Conference
     and the National Right to Life Committee; on the other side were professional medical
     organisations such as the American Public Health Association and the American
     Psychological Association; pro-choice groups, including Planned Parenthood, the
     NOW-LDEF and NARAL; and groups who specialise in church-state matters,
     Americans United for Separation of Church and State. Altogether, seventeen briefs
     were filed in the case, representing dozens of organisations: *Records of Transcripts and
     Briefs*, 1988.
248 487 US 589 (1988).
249 The Justices in the majority were Rehnquist, White, O'Connor, Scalia and Kennedy; in
     the minority were Blackmun, Brennan, Marshall and Stevens.
250 For reasons discussed below, the Court must have felt the time was not right to fashion a
     replacement test for *Lemon*. For the moment, Rehnquist was content to say that the
     Lemon test 'guides the general nature of our enquiry in this area.', *Bowen*, p. 602.
251 *Bowen*, pp. 602–3.
252 *Ibid.*, p. 605.
253 *Ibid.*, p. 608.
254 *Ibid.*, p. 611.
255 *Ibid.*, p. 616.
256 See T. Marshall, *Public Opinion and the Supreme Court*, Boston, 1989, pp. 83–5, for a
     quantitative analysis showing that the Court is far more reluctant to strike down federal
     legislation than state legislation.
257 *Bowen*, p. 620.
258 *Ibid.*, pp. 625–6.
259 *Ibid.*, p. 626.
260 *Ibid.*, p. 622.
261 *Ibid.*, pp. 652–3.
262 *Ibid.*, p. 624.
263 Bearing in mind Justice Kennedy's dissent in *Allegheny County*, *supra*, and the sub-
     sequent replacement of Justices Brennan and Marshall by Justices Souter and Thomas,
     it may be that agreement will be found on a test which places far fewer limitations on
     governmental espousal of religious values and viewpoints. At the time of writing, the
     Court, including Souter and Thomas, are considering the case of *Lee v. Weisman*, in

which Solicitor-General Kenneth Starr has asked the Court to abandon the *Lemon* test: *The Washington Post*, 19 March 1991, p. A14.

Eight—Conclusion

> In my view, constitutional adjudication presents an insoluble dilemma. The extraordinary character of the questions put before the Court means that the Court cannot ignore the political aspects of its tasks – the public consequences of its decisions – yet the answer to the question 'what substantive result is best for the country?' is often inconsistent with the responses obtained by asking 'what is the decision according to law?'[1]

The United States Supreme Court has always been recognised as an institution whose work combines elements of both law and politics. The evidence of the foregoing analysis suggests that this is still true, though the stress should now be emphatically upon the political roots of constitutional interpretation. While the Justices nominated by Republican presidents since 1969 have been selected in part to 'rectify' this imbalance between politics and law, the cases examined here indicate only a partial achievement of that goal.

The Supreme Court is primarily a legal institution in its formal setting and language. Its formal procedures are those of the nation's highest appellate court and issues still come to it in the form of legal disputes arranged as concrete cases. Even here, however, the integrity of legal culture has been undermined by essentially political developments. Of great importance in this respect has been the rise of interest group litigants in almost every conceivable area of constitutional law, complemented by the prevalence of class action suits. Together, these two developments ensure that any interest group intent on stimulating, defending or reversing reforms on social issues is likely to end up trying its luck in constitutional litigation.

Of course, in theory, neither the courts in general, nor the Supreme Court in particular, are obliged to give them a hearing on the validity of their proposals. Interest groups are, however, highly skilled in framing their campaigns around the circumstances of real individuals who have 'rights' to assert; and, if there is a plausible basis for the claim in the Constitution, the Court cannot dismiss them without a hearing. Furthermore, there appears to be no shortage of such individuals willing to avail themselves of the skills and resources of groups specialising in litigation. The result is that individuals and groups are bound together by a partnership of need which may produce great mutual benefit. Interest groups must find an Allan Bakke, a Michael Hardwick or a Diane Johnson if they are to win an essentially political victory in the Courts; but today it is almost unthinkable that these individuals could take their case before the Supreme Court without substantial group support and guidance. Thus, individual constitutional claims are so inextricably bound up with political causes that the Supreme Court cannot adjudicate the former without advancing or retarding the latter.

A second factor undermining the Court's formal legal purity is the use made of it by the elected branches of government. We saw in the affirmative action cases, for example, that Congress was willing to leave the details of statutory schemes for the Court to work out, if only because this allowed legislators to avoid difficult issues. If Congress had been obliged to resolve them, legislative debates would have been more fractious and necessary compromises more elusive. Some legislation, including parts of the Civil Rights Act of 1964, might never have been enacted at all. In short, Congress sometimes sees the Court as a useful player in the legislative process, precisely because its formal legal and judicial setting enables it to resolve political disputes free of many of the constraints imposed upon elected politicians.

For all its assaults on the Court over such issues as flag burning and school prayer, Congress will continue to embroil the Justices in the legislative process whenever it is convenient. A sure sign of this is the current debate in Congress over a proposed constitutional amendment to require a balanced budget. The elected branches of the federal government have failed time and time again to deliver what they have promised to the American people on this matter. Finally, unable to make the political compromises necessary to achieve what virtually everyone claims to want, politicians at both the federal and state level are preparing to turn to the Court. While it is not clear exactly what will be required of the Justices should such an amendment be ratified, it is by no means impossible to imagine a situation in which the Court will directly or indirectly choose which budgeted programmes will be cut and which will go ahead. The mere fact that this debate is taking place at the end of a period when the Justices have been widely accused of systematically usurping the policy-making powers of the other branches of government suggests two things about the Court's role in the political system. First, that it is most likely to be called to play a legislative role when the elected branches of government have failed to fulfil their responsibilities; and second, that this in turn is most likely to occur when Congress and the White House are controlled by different political parties. Thus, in an era of bifurcated government and political failure, judicial power may provide the only available means of advance.

To a considerable extent, the activities of interest groups and the elected branches of government oblige the Court to make policy resolutions, whether the Justices will it or not. And they are called upon to play this role precisely because the formal legal setting provides uniquely attractive opportunities for these parties to get what they want without incurring the political and economic costs required by the normal legislative process. The simple fact is, then, that the Supreme Court is tacitly recognised as a branch of government with a legitimate legislative, and therefore political, role to play.

Hypocrisy aside, therefore, the serious accusation against the modern Court is not that it performs a legislative or policy-making role. It always has done to some extent and if today it performs that role with greater frequency and prominence, it is because the modern political system and culture objectively invites it to do so. Rather, then, criticism of the Justices focuses on two principal *subjective* aspects of their decisions. First, that they make policy resolutions when it is not necessary; that is, when other branches of government, either federal or state, are both empowered and willing to decide policy for themselves. Second, that when the Justices make their decisions, they do so on the basis of their political convictions rather than the imperatives of the Constitution and legal reasoning. The liberal jurisprudence of both the Warren Court and the Burger Court came under fire from conservatives on both counts and the counter-revolution they launched was supposed to end both tendencies. As already noted, however, success has only been partial, largely for reasons beyond the control of the Justices themselves.

The counter-revolution has been somewhat successful with regard to the aim of reducing the frequency with which the Court has provided the ultimate resolution of policy conflicts. The Warren Court rarely refused an opportunity to tackle an area of social policy involving individual or group rights and it laid the basis for the pioneering decisions of the Burger Court. Most obviously during those years, the Court wrested control of policy from the states and local government: in matters of procreation, sex and race discrimination, criminal law, censorship of pornography and religion, the Court undermined the authority of government and community and placed the 'rights' and autonomy of the individual largely beyond their reach. It was not simply that the Court pursued and enforced values that were often at odds with those of state and local government. More importantly, the Court supplanted elected government as the level at which authoritative policy decisions were made. Furthermore, the Court rarely had a clear constitutional mandate for arrogating these powers to itself.

Where the Court used its increased power to reach results which were generally favoured by the public, as with the striking of Connecticut's contraceptive ban in *Griswold*, no-one paid much attention either to the fact that the state had until then exercised authority over the issue, or to the fact that the Court had added yet another string to its bow – in this case, a right to privacy. Where, however, the Court's substantive decisions aroused the ire of significant sections of the public or legislative majorities, the Court's newly-claimed power also became the object of criticism. As well as individual decisions in cases like *Roe* and *Furman*, the cumulative effect of the Court's aggrandisement led not only to the conservatives' attempt to curtail judicial power, but also to disquiet among those generally favourable to its liberal tendencies.

The 1980s have witnessed the end and partial reversal of the growth of judicial power in this respect. As we have seen, the later Burger and Rehnquist Courts refused to usurp state authority in such matters as anti-sodomy laws, the status of natural fathers and the right to view pornography involving minors. In addition, it has greatly enhanced the power of the states to legislate in matters such as abortion, capital punishment and official support for religion. In short, the Court has returned considerable power over the Social Issue to the states and local communities.

While the policy consequences of this devolution of power may be deplorable to liberals and progressives, it is worth emphasising the point that the 'conservative' Court has thereby not only acted in accordance with democratic theory, but also has *not mandated* conservative policies. There is a crucial distinction between a Court which returns power to make, say, abortion policy to the states and one which declares the fetus a person from the moment of conception and bans all abortions. A decision of the latter kind is reminiscent of the conservative Court which threw out much of the New Deal; whereas a decision of the former kind recalls the liberal Justices who were critical of that judicial activism. The later Burger and Rehnquist Courts have made some substantively conservative decisions, particularly in the area of affirmative action. On the whole, however, it has practised judicial self-restraint: thus, states may allow, encourage and fund abortions, repeal anti-sodomy or capital punishment statutes, and permit public nudity wherever they wish. Regardless of whether the states use their powers to enact liberal or conservative policies, however, it is a fundamental misconception to characterise the Court by the ideological preferences of state legislatures.

If the conservative counter-revolution has led to greater judicial self-restraint on this score, however, it has not succeeded in its other aim of making judicial interpretation less subjective. First of all, no member of the Court practises originalism or strict intentionalism. None disputes the 'evolving standards' test in capital punishment cases; the incorporation of all important aspects of the Bill of Rights into the Fourteenth Amendment; at least some minimal validity of substantive due process or that the First Amendment protects pornography. These developments may well be beneficial, but they have little connection to what the framers of 1787 and 1868 thought they were protecting.

Without intentionalism, Justices of all persuasions inevitably engage in the process of redefining the meanings and applications of open constitutional phrases and unwritten constitutional concepts – cruel and unusual punishment, privacy, equal protection, and so on. Such interpretation is, by definition, subjective and political. Why, for example, is Justice Scalia's reference point of 'the most specific tradition' in *Michael H.* any more neutral than Justice Brennan's broader concept of substantive due process rights? What is the legal reasoning that persuades Chief Justice Rehnquist to afford varying levels of First Amendment protection to pornography, but none at all to political dissenters who burn the American flag? Or what peculiarly legal logic underpins Justice O'Connor's view in affirmative action cases that a history of societal discrimination is too vague to trigger remedial measures, but that a requirement of 'victim specificity' is unnecessarily restrictive? And, to take a somewhat different final illustration from the abortion cases, at what point does an allegedly wrong decision such as *Roe* acquire such precedential weight that it cannot be overruled? The answers to these questions lie in the realms of political and moral philosophy more than law. Constitutional interpretation is thus inevitably subjective and also political in the broadest sense of the term.

If politics is inherent to the interpretive process, the cases analysed here also suggest that the Court moves to the rhythm of the wider political world. For even though the Court does not exactly 'follow the election returns', it is responsive to political change in the wider

political world. Most obviously, the appointment process allows
politicians to place new Justices on the Court who will take it in new
directions. The presidential power to nominate new Justices is the
main factor in the appointment process, even though nominees are by
no means always confirmed by the Senate. As a result, a period of
domination of the presidency by one party can lead to a fundamental
reorientation in the Court's jurisprudence. As of 1992, only one
Justice, Byron White, had been appointed by a Democrat president,
John F. Kennedy, and that was thirty years ago. The result has been the
abandonment of liberal activism, although by no means in a straightforward manner. The impact of the four Nixon appointees was far less
than had been anticipated and it took the determined effort of the
Reagan-Bush presidencies, and five further appointments, to turn the
Court around.

The differential impact of the Nixon and Reagan-Bush nominees
suggests that something more than mere presidential will is needed to
achieve a constitutional counter-revolution. The conservative backlash
which began with President Nixon did not reach its peak until the
1980s. By that time, disillusion with both government activism and
liberal policies had set in and it is no surprise that the Court should
respond to that changed climate. More concrete and specific, however,
was the hostile response to particular decisions by the Court. Virtually
nothing remains of the great death penalty case, *Furman v. Georgia*,
mainly because the states simply refused to accept it. And while the
bare bones of the abortion right created by *Roe v. Wade* remain, the
Court now seems willing to allow almost any state 'regulation' of the
right which stops short of an outright ban. The 'raw judicial power'
exercised by the Court in those cases was insufficient to withstand an
onslaught that involved national, state and local government; well-
organised and wealthy pressure groups; and, in significant measure,
the opinions of academics, journalists and the public. When even the
Court's allies in Congress proved willing to allow measures like the
Hyde Amendment to pass, it must have been clear to the Justices that
the great days of judicial innovation were over.

It is tempting to conclude that the Court has created such constitutional muddle and controversy that it should retire to the background
of American politics, only exercising the power of judicial review in the
most egregious instances of constitutional violation. Above all,
perhaps, the issues of modern life and the perspectives Americans have
upon them are so far removed from the ideas of the framers that the
Constitution provides little meaningful guide for judicial decision

making. Without such guidance, it is difficult indeed to square the power of judicial review with democratic theory.

The main grounds for a defence of judicial review, therefore, rest on the functional considerations outlined in chapter two of this book: the Court is the institution best equipped to make policy on individual rights. Certainly one may concede that, on the whole, the Justices of the Supreme Court are more likely to base their policy making on reasoned principles of morality and political philosophy than elected politicians. For what is clear from the analysis of judicial opinions presented here is that the Court does, to a considerable extent, seek to justify its decisions by an appeal to the higher values and principles of political discourse. However, a *functional* justification of activist judicial review stands or falls on its results, not the means by which those results are achieved. On this score, the alternatives are not enticing. Judicial restraint will undoubtedly yield the most appalling substantive results in some cases: the notion that adult homosexuals have no sexual privacy in their own homes; or that women can be harassed and bullied into bearing children they do not want, even when as a consequence of misfortune or crime; or that the mentally retarded may be legally killed for having committed crimes whose gravity they do not appreciate – all these are the results of the current Court's self-restraint.

On the other hand, those who deplore these results must ask themselves whether the Court really is in a position to lead the fight for more enlightened social policies. It is quite possible that the Court's efforts to accelerate social policy on abortion rights and the abolition of the death penalty were actually counter-productive to those reform movements. The evidence of the 1960s was that both public opinion and state officials were moving in the direction of the reformers. While it is impossible to know if those trends would have continued without the dramatic intervention of the Court, it is clear that *Roe* and *Furman* catalysed reactionary trends. Moreover, in as much as these decisions fused the political conservative backlash with the attack on judicial activism, the Court almost certainly undermined its ability to promote reform on other issues and even brought discredit on those reform movements generally. Harsh as it may seem, the laudable intentions of the liberals and moderates on the Court may have done more harm than good.

Furthermore, whatever merits there may be to the functionalist defence of judicial activism, the acceptability of judicial policy making depends not merely upon the results achieved, but the legitimacy of the exercise of the Court's power. No progressive, never mind conservative, should welcome the prospect of unelected judges routinely acting as a super-legislature on social issues. Those who desire social reform should take their campaign to the people and their elected representatives, however difficult and frustrating that may prove. Success in the political arena is not only more legitimate than that achieved in the courts, it is also likely to prove more enduring.

Notes

1 A. Cox, *The Warren Court: Constitutional Decision as an Instrument of Reform*, Cambridge, Mass., 1968, pp. 4–5.

Epilogue—Law, politics and self-preservation: the Supreme Court in the 1990s

> If abortion is the Achilles' heel for Republicans, then affirmative action is the Achilles' heel for Democrats.[1]

As presidential hopefuls limbered up for the 1996 election, the Social Issue once again loomed large in their tactical thinking. Republicans, anxious to preserve their lead among white, male voters, attacked affirmative action with relish. Phil Gramm, for example, promised to abolish federal government affirmative action obligations for contractors on day one of his presidency. And Bob Dole, emphasising race rather than gender, promised a broad attack on affirmation action. He explained, 'why did 62% of white males vote Republican in 1994? I think it's because of things like this, where sometimes the best-qualified person does not get the job, because he or she may be one colour.'[2]

Abortion, on the other hand, was the last thing the Republican Party wanted to make a major campaign issue. Aware of the need to appeal to moderate voters, especially women, GOP strategists sought to distance the party from the extremist views of the pro-life movement. At the same time, however, fundamentalist Christian conservatives were striving to make a pro-life abortion policy a prerequisite for the party's nomination. Thus one of the most powerful of such groups, the Christian Coalition, threatened to desert the party if its presidential and vice-presidential nominees were not clearly opposed to abortion rights: 'Pro-family voters will not support a party . . . which has a national ticket that does not share Ronald Reagan's belief in the sanctity of human life.'[3]

Democrats can profit from Republican discomfiture over abortion, but the Social Issue threatens them too. Affirmative action is an electoral cross which they have little choice but to bear, given the need to retain the votes of African-Americans, feminists and liberals. In a bizarre twist to the politics of affirmative action, President Clinton spent the spring of 1995 considering whether he could turn the tables on his Republican rivals by championing affirmative action for women, while downplaying race-based preferences. According to one Clinton aide, 'it is useful to move the debate from 12 per cent to 51 per cent of the American people.'[4] Moreover, as the President discovered in the first days of his presidency over the 'gays in the military' issue, action on social issues demanded by party constituents may prove highly damaging with a broader audience. In short, the Social Issue continues to be an electoral minefield which politicians must navigate with extreme care.

Despite the absence of electoral pressures, the Supreme Court appears to have reached the same conclusion. Since the first edition of this book was written in 1992, it has become clear that the conservative counter-revolution on the Court has come to a halt for the foreseeable future. As was suggested, this has come about principally because of developments in the Court's political environment.[5] Most important, of course, was the election of Bill Clinton as president in November 1992. This meant that when Justices White and Blackmun retired from the Court, they were replaced by moderate liberals, rather than the moderate or radical conservatives who were appointed by Presidents Reagan and Bush. The initial impression, at least, is that the net effect of the appointments of Justices Ruth Bader Ginsburg (1993) and Stephen Breyer (1994) has been to strengthen the Court's centre at the expense of its conservative wing.[6]   As we shall see below, this has not entailed a complete end to politically conservative decisions. But it has ended any hope (or fear) that the Scalia-Thomas brand of radical conservative jurisprudence can dominate the Court. Instead, the cautious, moderate approach to constitutional adjudication exemplified by Justice O'Connor, sets the tone of the Court in the mid-1990s. As a result of its decisions during the 1993 Term, the Court was rightly described as 'risk-averse', as it sought to lower its own political profile by avoiding decisions that would provoke extreme responses from Congress, the President and the states.[7]

The same description could be applied to President Clinton in his choice of Supreme Court nominees. For all the sound judicial qualities of Justices Ginsburg and Breyer, it is clear that the President's selections were determined to a considerable degree by the desire to avoid a confirmation battle with Senate Republicans and conservatives. While the two Justices were duly confirmed with ease, the price paid is that neither is likely to provide the liberal intellectual leadership that disappeared from the Court with the retirement of William Brennan.[8]

The current Court majority, then, eschews judicial activism of either the liberal or conservative variety. This means that no bold extension of civil liberties is likely to occur, unless perhaps congressional or presidential approval of such a step has been clearly signalled. Even then, the deferential approach of the current Court makes it probable that such decisions would be couched in narrow, cautious terms. At the same time, however, the majority's judicial restraint ensures that no reversal of major liberal precedents is likely to occur. In short, the approach of the Court in *Casey*[9] provides the template for this Court's approach to the treatment of controversial past issues and cases: adherence to the essential elements of major precedents, combined with wide latitude for legislatures to intervene in the exercise of the rights involved.

This approach subordinates questions of constitutional interpretation to concerns with institutional legitimacy and self-preservation. In the wake of its exercise of 'raw judicial power' and the conservative counter-attack, the Court seems determined to re-establish its credentials as a legal body. Among other things, this means depoliticisation of its work by the avoidance of politically controversial decisions. Instead, the Court seeks to emphasise stability and predictability in an era of violent swings in political mood and partisan fortunes. This makes a great deal of sense from the perspective of institutional self-interest. Not only should it minimise attacks from the right or left on the Court, but may, over time, enhance its status as a body dedicated to law rather than politics.

There are dangers to this approach, however. If the Court is seen as avoiding its constitutional duty by excessive deference to the elected branches of government, it may lose credibility and cease to command respect. Nevertheless, for the moment at least, the Court's priority is the achievement of a low political profile.

If we turn now to examine the major decisions of the Court on social issues since 1992, we will see how exactly a majority of the Justices today are seeking to 'depoliticise' the Court by the avoidance of provocative, controversial decisions.

Capital punishment

We saw in chapter three that the Court went through two major stages in its capital punishment jurisprudence. The first began with its ill-fated decision in *Furman v. Georgia* (1972) declaring all existing death penalty statutes to be unconstitutional. The popular and legislative backlash to *Furman* was so great, however, that the Court beat a hasty retreat in *Gregg v. Georgia* (1976) and declared that capital punishment *per se* was not 'cruel and unusual' within the meaning of the Eighth Amendment. In the wake of *Gregg*, the Court's second stage consisted of two important but somewhat less momentous issues: for what kinds of crime and criminals is death the appropriate punishment? And what broad procedural practices will ensure that the penalty is not imposed in the arbitrary manner that characterised the pre-*Furman* era?

On the first question, the Court ruled that death was not an appropriate punishment for rape (*Coker v. Georgia*, 1977), but that it was constitutionally acceptable to execute the mentally retarded and juveniles (*Penry v. Lynaugh*, 1989; *Stanford v. Kentucky*, 1989). On the second question, the Court eventually decided that States must specify a limiting range of 'aggravating circumstances' which justify the death penalty for murder, while allowing defendants to introduce any arguments as 'mitigating circumstances' justifying an alternative punishment, (*Lockett v. Ohio*, 1978).

Many of these decisions were resolved by the Court's majority with reference to contemporary American views on capital punishment, particularly as these are manifested in state legislative action. Given both popular and legislative enthusiasm for the death penalty, of course, this has led the Court to adopt a permissive attitude to state capital punishment practices. Unfortunately for opponents of the death penalty, the last few years offer no grounds for optimism that 'the evolving standards of decency'[10] of American society are moving their way. Quite the reverse, in fact. In 1995, the state of New York reintroduced the death penalty, making it the thirty-eighth[11] to do so since *Furman*. The writing had been on the wall since the legislature had many times before voted for reintroduction, but Governor Mario Cuomo had always used his veto. However, Cuomo's defeat in the 1994 gubernatorial election by death penalty proponent George Pataki ended this last line of resistance.

Also in 1994, President Clinton signed into law a new crime bill that expanded the number of federal offences for which the death penalty could be imposed. Not content with that, the congressional Republicans' 'Contract with America' included 'The Taking Back Our Streets Act', promising more effective death penalty provisions.

Moreover, while actual executions are still infrequent in comparison with the number of death sentences imposed, there does seem to be a quickening of the pace in recent years. In the period from 1977–89, there were just 120 executions; but between 1990 and March 1995, there were a further 151.[12] Most of these took place in a handful of

Southern states, with Texas leading the way with 90 executions since 1977.[13] At the very least, these statistics suggest that there has been no general revulsion against actual executions and that Americans are becoming used to the idea of seeing murderers die by lethal injection or the electric chair.

In this political climate, it is hardly surprising that the Court has reduced still further its willingness to intervene in death penalty practices. It should also be noted that there is at the moment not one member of the United States Supreme Court who believes that capital punishment *per se* is unconstitutional. Ironically, Justice Harry A. Blackmun waited until his last year in office to conclude that inconsistencies which still characterise the imposition of the death penalty make it irredeemably unconstitutional.[14] None of his colleagues agreed, however, and his successor has already made clear that he will not challenge the constitutionality of capital punishment.

The Court is now in what may be regarded as the third stage of its death penalty jurisprudence. This involves the Justices in dealing with residual issues pertaining to particular cases rather than with broad issues of either principle or practice. And even here, the Court is generally reluctant to instruct states on how they should proceed.

The 1995 decision in *Harris v. Alabama*,[15] while perhaps not of wide constitutional significance, fairly reflects the current deference of the Court to the states. The case arose from the death sentence imposed on Louise Harris for the murder of her husband, a deputy sheriff. Harris asked her lover, Lorenzo McCarter, to help her kill her husband. McCarter duly recruited two accomplices. With all four acting in concert, Harris's husband was shot to death by one of the accomplices as he stopped his car at an intersection on his way to work.

Harris was convicted of capital murder. At her sentencing hearing, she put before the jury the mitigating circumstances that she hoped would render the death penalty inappropriate. This included good background and character, the fact that she was raising seven children and that she was an active member of her church. The jury voted 7–5 that she be sentenced to life imprisonment without parole.

At this point, a unique feature of Alabama's capital punishment statute came into play. Like just three other states with the death penalty, the jury's sentencing decision is only advisory in Alabama, with the trial judge having the ultimate sentencing authority. Unlike in those other three jurisdictions, however, an Alabama judge is not required to give 'great weight' to the jury's recommendation, but is merely obliged to 'consider' it. In Harris's case, the trial judge overrode the jury's advisory verdict and sentenced her to death. On appeal to the Supreme Court, Harris claimed that the latitude granted the trial judge in Alabama violated the Eighth Amendment's proscription of 'cruel and unusual punishments'. By an overwhelming vote of 8–1, the Court rejected her claim.[16]

Writing for the Court, Justice O'Connor rested her argument on two principal grounds. First, the Court had previously decided in *Spaziano v. Florida*[17] that states could vest ultimate sentencing authority in the judge rather than the jury, even though the great majority of states had chosen not to do so. In *Spaziano*, the Florida statute had been modified by a state Court ruling requiring the judge to give 'great weight' to the jury's recommendation, but Justice O'Connor did not accept that this obliged Alabama to do the same. Once a state had taken measures to avoid arbitrary imposition of the death penalty by guiding the sentencer on, for example, aggravating and mitigating circumstances, then it had met its constitutional obligations. For the Supreme Court to intervene further, said Justice O'Connor, would be to 'place within constitutional ambit micromanagement tasks that properly rest within the State's discretion to administer its criminal justice system.'[18]

This was not Justice O'Connor's only reference to the desirability of judicial restraint by the federal courts in these matters. For example, Justice Stevens argued in dissent that, since the purpose of capital punishment was to express the conscience of the community on matters of life and death, the jury should take ultimate responsibility for imposing the death penalty. Justice O'Connor countered as follows:

> What purpose is served by capital punishment and how a State should implement its capital punishment scheme – to the extent that those questions involve only policy issues – are matters over which we, as judges, have no jurisdiction. Our power of judicial review legitimately extends only to determine whether the policy choices of the community, expressed through its legislative enactments, comport with the Constitution.'[19]

Yet Justice O'Connor's appeal to judicial restraint seems less than persuasive in the light of Justice Stevens' reminder of the political realities of Alabama's death penalty practice. As he points out, 'Alabama trial judges face partisan election every six years.'[20] This means there is a danger that judges will bow to popular clamour for the death penalty, even where a jury has considered all the evidence and decided execution is inappropriate. Indeed, Justice O'Connor did not dispute statistics showing that on forty-seven occasions, Alabama trial judges had overridden a jury recommendation of life and imposed the death penalty. On the other hand, only five times had judges over-ridden a jury recommendation of death to impose life imprisonment.

Justice O'Connor thought these statistics might be misleading in that they didn't reveal how many more death sentences might have been imposed by judges had it not been for a jury recommendation of life. But in any case, she said, the statistics are not constitutionally relevant. As long as actual death penalties are not the product of whim, the 'unexpected' effect of statutory provisions are not a matter for the Supreme Court: 'If the Alabama statute indeed has not had the effect that we or its drafters had anticipated, such unintended results would be of little constitutional consequence. An ineffectual law is for the State legislature to amend, not for us to annul.'[21]

Only rarely does the current Court seem willing to challenge state capital sentencing procedures. Thus in *Arave v. Creech* (1993),[22] a 7–2 majority of the Justices took the view that, in the particular case, showing 'utter disregard for human life' during a murder was not unconstitutionally vague as an 'aggravating circumstance' permitting imposition of the death penalty. The majority's reasoning was some-what convoluted. The Court noted that the phrase 'utter disregard for human life' had been interpreted by the Idaho Supreme Court to connote 'the cold-blooded, pitiless slayer'. This phrase was in turn interpreted by the Justices to mean 'a killer who kills without feeling or sympathy.'[23]

Unsurprisingly, the dissenting opinion of Justice Blackmun took the Court to task for applying neither the statutory phrase nor the State Court's limiting construction of it, but rather one of its own concoction. Nevertheless, the heart of the issue was whether, in accordance with precedent, 'without feeling or sympathy' was capable of narrowing the class of murderers who were eligible for the death penalty. Justice O'Connor, writing for the Court, conceded that 'the question is close'.[24] Nevertheless, she argued that some killers do exhibit 'feeling', be it anger, jealousy, revenge or a variety of emotions. This 'aggravating circumstance' therefore succeeds in distinguishing between some murderers who are eligible for execution and some who are not.

Justice Blackmun flatly contradicted this argument by demon-strating first that the Idaho Court's phrase 'cold-blooded' was frequently applied to cases where the feelings listed by Justice O'Connor were emphatically present. Moreover, he attacked his majority colleagues' refusal to examine other capital cases in Idaho to see whether the state had applied the *Court's new reconstruction* of the statutory phrase, as opposed to the original Idaho court's construction, on a consistent basis. In dismissive fashion, he wrote:

> If, for example, a State declared that 'jabberwocky' was an aggravating
> circumstance, and then carefully invoked 'jabberwocky' in every one of its
> capital cases, this Court could not simply decide that 'jabberwocky' means
> 'killing a police officer' and then dispense with any inquiry into whether the
> term had ever been understood in that way by the State's courts, simply
> because the 'jabberwocky' construction had been reaffirmed.[25]

Blackmun also reminded the Court that even if the Idaho clause can
pass constitutional muster, it seems odd to apply it to the murder by
which the case arose. Thomas Creech had killed a fellow prison inmate
in circumstances which all conceded were unclear. But whatever the
background to the murder, it does seem that Creech's victim struck the
first blow.

At the very least, Justice Blackmun's dissent demonstrated that the
Court strained to save the Idaho clause. What may have been the
decisive factor then was not the murder at issue, but Thomas Creech's
past. For before being incarcerated, Creech had killed at least 26
people, with bodies recovered in seven states. Creech, therefore,
certainly fits the bill as a 'cold-blooded, pitiless killer' and there would
most likely have been an enormous popular backlash against the Court
had it overturned his death sentence. Added to the Court's established
norm of deference to state legislatures' sentencing procedures,
deference to public opinion may here help to explain the Court's
willingness to go out of its way to uphold Idaho's 'aggravating circumstance'.

The Court seems equally accommodating to state sentencing procedures when the issue revolves around 'mitigating circumstances'.
Although the *Lockett* decision established that a death-eligible
defendant must be permitted to introduce any evidence in mitigation, it
did not prescribe precise procedures governing this. In 1993, in
Johnson v. Texas,[26] the Court had to consider whether the Texas death
penalty statute allowed a convicted murderer sufficient scope to introduce his youth as a mitigating factor.

Dorsie Lee Johnson was 19 years old when in 1986 he robbed
Allsup's convenience store in Snyder, Texas. He took some $160 and a
carton of cigarettes. But having decided in advance that there should
be no witnesses to the crime, he ordered Jack Huddleston, the store
clerk, to lie on the floor and then shot him in the back of the neck.
Having convicted Johnson of murder, the trial jury was then required
to consider two 'special issues' in determining whether to impose the

death penalty. The first was whether the crime had been committed deliberately; and the second was whether there was a probability that Johnson would commit further criminal acts of violence which would constitute a continuing threat to society. The jury was instructed that, in considering both issues, it could take into account all the evidence submitted to it, whether aggravating or mitigating. Johnson was sentenced to death. He appealed on the grounds that the special issues did not allow the jury to give adequate mitigating effect to his youth. He argued that the jury should have been given a special instruction to consider his age as a mitigating factor.

The Supreme Court rejected his claim in a 5–4 vote.[27] Johnson's case was complicated by the fact that shortly after his trial, the Court had decided *Penry v. Lynaugh*. Although that case had ruled that the mentally retarded could constitutionally be executed, it also ordered that a sentencing jury needed to be given a special instruction on Penry's retardation.[28] In *Johnson*, however, the Court refused to extend the *Penry* rule to cover a defendant's age. The second Texas special rule, it reasoned, addressed the question of future dangerousness. Because mental retardation made it unlikely that Penry could learn from his past mistakes and change his behaviour, his condition could only be considered as an *aggravating* factor, unless the jury received a special instruction as to how his retardation might mitigate his culpability for the crime. There was no such barrier to the jury considering Johnson's youth as a mitigating factor, however.

States, Justice Kennedy said for the Court, cannot preclude jury consideration of any mitigating factors, but it can structure such consideration. Texas has chosen to do that by means of its 'special issues' and that satisfies Eighth Amendment standards. To rule in Johnson's favour would 'remove all power on the part of the States to structure the consideration of mitigating evidence – a result we have been consistent in rejecting.'[29]

For the dissenters, however, Texas' right to structure jury consideration of youth amounted to the right impermissably to limit such consideration. Justice O'Connor made the point that, at best, Texas permitted the jury to consider Johnson's youth as it affected his future dangerousness. Yet it permitted no consideration where it was most appropriate – on his culpability. Quoting from earlier cases, she argued that youth, with its associated immaturity and inexperience, could render a defendant less morally culpable than an adult convicted of the same crime. Consequently, 'In my view, the jury could not express a reasoned moral response to this aspect of Johnson's youth in answering any of the special issues.'[30]

Whatever the strength of the dissenters' argument, however, the Court's majority apparently has decided that in all but the most egregious cases of error, the States are constitutionally endowed with both power and moral responsibility for the execution of murderers.[31] Indeed, the Court has done much in recent years to avoid consideration of death penalty cases at all by limiting the number of federal habeas corpus appeals a death row prisoner may make.[32] In 1993, in *Herrera v. Collins*,[33] a 6–3 majority of the Court ruled that even a claim of actual innocence of the crime for which the death penalty was imposed, did not entitle Leonel Herrera to a second federal habeas hearing. Chief Justice Rehnquist remarked for the Court that '. . . federal habeas courts sit to ensure that individuals are not imprisoned in violation of the Constitution – not to correct errors of fact.'[34] Herrera's claim of innocence was admittedly unconvincing, but some of the majority Justices were clearly disturbed at the future prospect of executing an innocent person. This undoubtedly helped persuade them in *Schlup v. Delo* (1995) to distinguish *Herrera* on a technicality and grant Lloyd Schlup's much stronger claim to innocence a second federal habeas hearing.[35]

Despite the exceptional case like *Schlup*, the Court's strong tendency is to leave capital punishment to the states. While it would be too much to say that the Court has washed its hands of death penalty cases, it is nevertheless true that it grants the states so much leeway in determining capital procedures that *Furman v. Georgia* seems but a distant, almost irrelevant memory.

Abortion

In no area of constitutional law did Bill Clinton's election have greater significance than abortion. When originally announced in 1992, the 5–4 *Casey* decision reaffirming the central principle of *Roe v. Wade* seemed highly vulnerable to the next change in the Court's personnel. However, President Clinton's appointment of Ruth Bader Ginsburg to replace Byron White, a dissenter in *Roe*, has created a 6–3 majority supportive of the constitutional right to abortion. That majority has been furthered strengthened by the replacement of the aging author of *Roe*, Harry Blackmun, with another abortion rights supporter, Stephen Breyer. *Roe* is therefore safe for the foreseeable future. Of course, states are still free to regulate the exercise of abortion rights, as *Casey* made all too clear. But the possibility of successful legal opposition to fundamental abortion rights is now remote.

As a result, there is now even sharper focus on illegal efforts to stop the performance of abortions. The most notorious of such efforts have been the murders of abortion clinic personnel. In January 1995, John Salvi, an anti-abortion activist, was arrested for the murder of two receptionists and the attempted murder of five others, at Planned Parenthood clinics in Boston. The previous year, Paul Hill, another militant opponent of abortion, was sentenced to death for the murder in Pensacola, Florida, of an abortion clinic doctor and an assistant.

Below this extreme level of violence exists a long-running campaign to intimidate clinic personnel and pregnant women themselves into abandoning the exercise of abortion rights. We saw in chapter four that groups such as Operation Rescue aimed to block access to abortion clinics by practising civil disobedience on a scale that would overwhelm local law enforcement capabilities. So successful have these tactics been that pro-choice groups have sought both judicial and legislative remedies.

Their greatest success in the legislative realm once again owed a great deal to the election of Bill Clinton. Clinton had taken a clear pro-choice position in the 1992 presidential election campaign; and early in his administration, he reversed several of the executive branch restrictions on abortion services that had been imposed by Ronald Reagan and George Bush. Most notably he abolished the so-called 'gag rule' that prevented federally funded clinics from giving information and advice on abortion. He also permitted clinical testing of the French abortion pill, RU-486.

More important still, however, was the fact that the threat of a presidential veto was now lifted from pro-choice legislation in Congress. Ironically, this could not secure passage of the Freedom of Choice Act, which got lost amid wrangling over funding and other issues. Pro-choice interest groups actually split over the bill: NARAL and Planned Parenthood were willing to tolerate some state restrictions, while NOW and the ACLU were opposed to compromise.[36] Perhaps the loss of the Freedom of Choice Act was not critical given the recent reinforcement of *Roe* on the Supreme Court. But the Republican capture of Congress in 1994 makes it highly unlikely that a stronger version of the bill can be enacted any time soon.

Clinton was, however, able to sign into law the Freedom of Access to Clinic Entrances Act (FACE) in 1994, which made it a federal crime to use violence and intimidation to prevent access to abortion clinics. The passage of FACE gave notice to pro-life militants that, unlike the civil rights activists whose tactics they imitated, they could not expect the support of the federal government. Together with the *Casey* decision, it marked a significant turnaround in the abortion conflict. Whereas the momentum in the 1980s had clearly been with the pro-life movement, the first half of the 1990s saw the pro-choice movement regain the initiative. For the first time in many years, there appeared to be a consensus shared by all three branches of the federal government that basic constitutional abortion rights are here to stay.

FACE did not, however, resolve all the legal issues associated with clinic protest. Most importantly, the federal right of access to abortion clinics did not, of course, eliminate the First Amendment free speech rights of pro-life demonstrators. As a consequence, the principal abortion cases before the Supreme Court since *Casey* concern the clash between two conflicting assertions of fundamental constitutional rights.

Confronted with 'guerilla tactics' by pro-life groups, pro-choice litigants preferred to avoid a protracted clinic-by-clinic legal campaign based on local trespass laws and instead opted for a federal law strategy. This had the obvious advantage of a possible nationwide victory that would deal with 'rescue' activities wherever they occurred. The first such attempt reached the Court in *Bray v. Alexandria Women's Health Clinic* (1993).[37] This involved the clinic-blocking activities of Operation Rescue in and around the Washington, DC, area. Such had been the effort put in by Operation Rescue that, despite the arrest of some 240 demonstrators, police were unable to prevent the closure of a clinic in Falls Church for over six hours.[38] A group of pro-choice individuals, clinics and interest groups invoked the Civil Rights Act of 1871, otherwise known as the Ku Klux Klan Act, codified at 42 USC section 1985(3). The Act prohibits conspiracies depriving, either directly or indirectly, any person or class of persons of the equal protection of the laws – (the 'deprivation clause'); or preventing or hindering the constituted authorities of any state from securing to all persons the equal protection of the laws – (the 'hindrance clause'). Obviously aimed originally at protecting black Americans from conspiracies by the Ku Klux Klan, the question now was whether it protected pregnant women seeking abortions against conspiracies by Operation Rescue.

A 6–3 majority of the Court decided that the deprivation clause did not apply, while a 5–4 majority decided that the hindrance clause did not apply. Speaking for the Court, Justice Scalia interpreted relevant precedents narrowly. Like most members of the Court, current and past, he was anxious to avoid transforming the Ku Klux Klan Act into a general federal tort law.[39] Nevertheless, as the dissenting opinions showed, Scalia declined to accept the legitimate scope left by precedent to apply the law to the activities of Operation Rescue.

The key precedent was *Griffin v. Breckenridge* (1971).[40] There the Burger Court had expanded the reach of 1985(3) to cover purely private conspiracies. But in order to avoid a situation in which every tort became a federal violation, it required that such conspiracies must evince 'some racial, or perhaps otherwise class-based, invidiously discriminatory animus'.[41] Justice Scalia denied that Operation Rescue's campaign involved such an animus, since women as a general class were not the target, either directly or indirectly:

> A tax on wearing yamulkes is a tax on Jews. But opposition to voluntary abortion cannot possibly be considered such an irrational surrogate for opposition to (or paternalism towards) women. Whatever one thinks of abortion, it cannot be denied that there are common and respectable reasons for opposing it, other than hatred or condescension toward (or indeed any view at all concerning) women as a class – as is evident from the fact that men and women are on both sides of the issue, just as men and women are on both sides of petitioners' unlawful demonstrations.[42]

He also rejected the contention that, even without any intent by Operation Rescue to discriminate against women as a class, such discrimination was present simply by the fact that only women were affected by the conspiracy. Here he relied on the much-criticised decision in *Gedulig v. Aiello*. That had held that the Fourteenth Amendment was not violated by a disability insurance scheme that excluded pregnancy-related disability, simply because only women became pregnant.[43]

In their separate dissents, both Justice O'Connor and Justice Stevens criticised the Court for overemphasising the language of the gloss put on 1985(3) by *Griffin*, at the expense of the broader purpose behind the Act, and, indeed, the gloss. Justice O'Connor regarded the *Griffin* gloss of class-based animus as nothing more than 'a reasonable shorthand description of the type of actions the 42nd Congress was attempting to address'.[44] Instead of taking on a life of its own, it should be applied with the broad purpose of the original legislation in mind. And since the conspiracy is aimed at a group targeted because of their class characteristics, she was convinced that 1985(3) was intended to reach the activities of Operation Rescue:

> The statute was intended to provide a federal means of redress to the targets of private conspiracies seeking to accomplish their political and

social goals through unlawful means. Today the Court takes yet another step in restricting the scope of the statute, to the point where it now cannot be applied to a modern-day paradigm of the situation the statute was meant to address.'[45]

The decision in *Bray* is a reminder that, depending upon the interpretive method chosen, Justices may reach radically opposing substantive results. Yet it would be wrong to conclude that interpretive method acts merely or always as camouflage for policy predilection. For the next case involving anti-abortion clinic protests saw a unanimous Court decide that whereas the Ku Klux Klan Act could not be invoked against such demonstrations, the Racketeer Influenced and Corrupt Organisations (RICO) chapter of the Organised Crime Control Act of 1970 was applicable.

NOW v. Scheidler (1994) was a narrow but significant victory for pro-choice activists. The case was brought by the National Organisation for Women and two health care centres that provide abortions. The respondents were pro-life activists, including Joseph Scheidler, and a coalition of anti-abortion groups organised as the Pro-Life Action Network (PLAN). As well as engaging in typical 'rescue' protests at clinics, Scheidler had testified before Congress in 1987 that the protestors aimed to shut the clinics down.[46] The crux of NOW's case, therefore, was that Scheidler and PLAN were involved in a nationwide conspiracy involving a pattern of racketeering activity. This included the use of force, violence and fear to induce clinic employees to give up their professions and patients to give up their right to avail themselves of clinic services.

The District Court dismissed their claim, however, arguing that RICO violations were limited to those involving economic motives, and the Court of Appeals agreed. The Supreme Court, however, speaking through Chief Justice Rehnquist, held that the statutory language was unambiguous and required no such economic motive. Moreover, even allowing for the fact that RICO was aimed squarely at organised crime, they found nothing in its legislative history that clearly expressed an intent to limit its reach to economically motivated racketeering.[47] If the Court needed any further encouragement, then the Clinton administration provided it: the Justice Department intervened to argue that a narrow construction of RICO would hamper its efforts to prosecute terrorist and other non-economic conspiracies.[48]

Of course, the decision in *Scheidler* did not reach the issue of whether PLAN had indeed fallen foul of RICO, but merely that *NOW* could proceed with a RICO suit. Nevertheless, it is a significant victory

for pro-choice activists, if only because of the threat of massive
financial penalties that accompany RICO convictions. For not only can
this involve treble damages, but also liability for plaintiff's legal costs:
given that the *Scheidler* case began in 1986, these costs could be very
destructive.[49] Indeed, fear of incurring huge financial penalties for
engaging in illegal protest activities created some strange bedfellows in
Scheidler: the anti-abortion movement found itself supported by
amicus briefs from such groups as The PETA Gay and Lesbian Task
Force, Community for Creative Nonviolence, Feminists for Animal
Rights and Los Angeles Earth First![50] *Scheidler* could eventually turn
out to be anything but a substantively liberal decision if RICO is used to
chill First Amendment rights.

Six months after *Scheidler* was decided, the Court handed abortion
rights activists the best of another clinic protest case. *Madsen v.
Women's Health Centre, Inc.*[51] arose from a court injunction placed on
Operation Rescue demonstrations in Melbourne, Florida. By the standards of some pro-life clinic-blocking activities, those targeting the
Aware Woman Centre for Choice clinic were not extreme. The protestors chanted and displayed religious and anti-abortion slogans, such
as 'She Is a Child, Not a Choice' and 'Abortion: God Calls It Murder'.
Randall Terry, the national leader of Operation Rescue, gave a press
conference outside the clinic. More seriously, cars entering the clinic
were held up by demonstrators and 'sidewalk counsellors' trying to
persuade women occupants not to go through with abortions. The
number of demonstrators varied, sometimes reaching up to four
hundred. At times they used loudspeakers and bullhorns so that their
messages could be heard inside the clinic. Anti-abortion activists also
protested outside the homes of clinic staff and canvassed their neigh-
bours' houses identifying the staff as 'baby-killers'. There was, however, no direct violence and counter-demonstrations also took place
outside the clinic. Their chants included 'Right to life is a lie, you don't
care if women die' and 'Why don't you join the wacko in Waco?'[52]

The legal dispute began in 1992, when a Florida court issued a
permanent injunction, enjoining the pro-life demonstrators from
blocking or interfering with those entering or leaving the clinic. Six
months later, finding that the first injunction was not being observed,
the court issued a second, broader injunction. Among other things, the
second injunction banned the demonstrators from a thirty-six-foot
buffer zone around the clinic's property line; it banned protest noise
and visual images that were audible or observable from within the clinic
during hours of surgery and patient recovery; within three hundred

feet of the clinic, it banned demonstrators from approaching persons seeking the clinic's services, unless they indicated a desire to be approached; and a complete ban was made on protest activity within three hundred feet of the homes of clinic staff. The Florida Supreme Court upheld the injunction over the pro-life activists' claim that it violated their First Amendment rights to free speech. However, a separate challenge to the injunction had been successful in the federal Court of Appeals for the Eleventh Circuit just a few days before the State Supreme Court's decision was announced.

By a majority of 6–3, the Supreme Court upheld some key elements of the injunction, although it struck down others.[53] In so doing, the Court enhanced the judicial injunction as a weapon against clinic protestors, but, inevitably, only at some cost to First Amendment protection.

Chief Justice Rehnquist wrote the Court's opinion. The first critical step his argument took was that the injunction was not 'content based', but 'content neutral'. Rehnquist's rationale was simple enough: although the injunction applied to the anti-abortion protestors but not the pro-abortion demonstrators, this was because of the former's past conduct rather than their message. Thus, he wrote, '. . . the fact that the injunction covered people with a particular viewpoint does not itself render the injunction content or viewpoint based.'[54] The importance of this argument was that it absolved the Court from having to apply 'strict scrutiny' to the injunction. To survive strict scrutiny, a content-based restriction speech must be shown to serve a *compelling* state interest and be narrowly drawn to achieve that interest. A content neutral restriction, however, only requires an intermediate level of scrutiny – that it be narrowly tailored to serve a *significant* government interest. Whatever the semantic import of the two formulae, the practical difference is that speech restrictions almost never survive strict scrutiny, while they often satisfy intermediate scrutiny.

At this point, however, Rehnquist's opinion took a creative turn. Intermediate review, he argued, is appropriate where a statute or ordinance is at issue, but not where an injunction is concerned. This is so because there are greater risks of censorship of particular viewpoints with court-imposed injunctions than there are with generally applicable legislative measures. Therefore, he concluded, the standard of review in cases involving content neutral injunctions should be that 'the injunction burden no more speech than is necessary to serve a significant government interest'.[55]

There is some scepticism in legal circles about the value and purpose

296 RAW JUDICIAL POWER?

of such formulae. Robert Nagel, for example, argues that they obfuscate rather than explain and leave judicial subjectivity unfettered.[56] Unsurprisingly, then, Justice Scalia, writing in dissent, poked fun at the Chief Justice's new standard. He supposed that it could be called 'intermediate-intermediate scrutiny', though he confessed that its substantive distinction from 'plain old intermediate review' was too subtle for him to grasp.[57]

More seriously, Scalia argued that strict scrutiny should be applied to the Florida Court's injunction, regardless of whether it was technically content based or content neutral. For whatever the intent behind speech-restricting injunctions, the effect is to stifle the expression of a particular point of view: 'When a judge, on the motion of an employer, enjoins picketing at the site of a labour dispute, he enjoins (and knows he is enjoining) the expression of pro-union views.'[58]

Justice Scalia also bitterly condemned the Court's opinion for its failure to observe precedents. Although appearing Solomonic by upholding some but not all elements of the injunction, he said, it was in fact completely at odds with the Court's established jurisprudence. This, he lamented, was becoming typical in abortion cases. Pointedly quoting from Rehnquist's *Thornburgh* opinion, he wrote:

> 'This Court's abortion decisions have already worked a major distortion in the Court's constitutional jurisprudence. Today's decision goes further, and makes it painfully clear that no legal rule or doctrine is safe from ad hoc nullification by this Court when an occasion for its application arises in a case involving state regulation of abortion.' ... Today the ad hoc nullification machine claims its latest, greatest, and most surprising victim: the First Amendment.[59]

Rehnquist responded vigorously to Scalia's attack: not only did he stand by the distinction between an ordinance and an injunction, but also pointed out that Scalia had failed to cite a single precedent in which the Court had applied strict scrutiny to an injunction.[60] Just as the Chief Justice, therefore, could be accused of activism in his creation of a novel standard of review, Justice Scalia is vulnerable to the charge of activism in his disrespect for precedent. Once again, then, the question is raised whether appeals to the tenets of judicial restraint are anything more than tactical manoeuvres designed to buttress a conclusion reached for quite other reasons.

After the vitriol of the debate over standards of review, the actual substance of the Court's decision seems an anticlimax. Yet, in practical terms, for those seeking and providing abortion services it provides at least some relief from the harassment of pro-life militants. The Court found that the ban on protest activities within the thirty-six-foot buffer zone around the clinic's property line did indeed 'burden no more speech than necessary' to protect ingress to and egress from the clinic. It would require protestors to move to the other side of the street from the clinic and to keep off its driveway. However, the Court ruled that the buffer zone could not be applied to land abutting the clinic boundary but which was not used for access.

The Court also upheld the noise restriction during hours of surgery and recovery. Evidence on the record showed that such noise adversely affected the health and well-being of the patients and hence the ban was justified. The restriction on visual images observable from within the clinic, however, could not be sustained. For '. . . it is much easier for the clinic to pull its curtains than for a patient to stop up her ears . . .'[61]

Turning to the ban on approaches to clinic clients within three hundred feet of the clinic, unless invited, the Court held that this did burden more speech than was necessary to serve the ends of access to the clinic and preventing intimidation. The First Amendment required that Americans must tolerate insulting and even outrageous speech.

Finally, the Court continued its balanced approach in reviewing the ban on protest activities within three hundred feet of the residences of clinic staff. It upheld the ban of the use of sound amplification equipment within the zone. The size of the zone was too great for the picketing element, however. The state did have a legitimate interest in preserving the tranquillity and privacy of the home, but '. . . a limitation on the time, duration of picketing, and number of pickets outside a smaller zone could have accomplished the desired result.'[62]

Madsen bears the principal hallmark of much of the Court's abortion-related jurisprudence, namely, compromise. And for as long as a majority of the Court adheres to the basic right to abortion created in *Roe*, but that right continues to attract the deep hostility of some legislators and pro-life activists, it is difficult to see how else the Court can reasonably proceed. Although it decided in *Casey* that it should not 'surrender to political pressure' and abandon the basic right to abortion, the Court must nevertheless continue to accommodate that pressure if it wishes to avoid a repetition of the frontal assault it suffered in the 1980s.

Women will continue, therefore, to avail themselves of abortion services and pro-life militants will continue vociferously to protest that fact. *Madsen*, however, ensures that women will find it somewhat less of an ordeal to use the services of abortion clinics, while pro-life militants will find their tactics somewhat less effective. As Eleanor Smeal of the Feminist Majority Foundation put it, '(*Madsen*) establishes that a woman doesn't have to walk a gauntlet to exercise her right to abortion.'[63] Together with *Scheidler*, therefore, *Madsen* may represent a slight shift towards the pro-choice side in the political and legal struggle over abortion. But of the struggle itself, there is no end in sight.

Affirmative action and race

If abortion was the politically hottest social issue of the 1970s and 1980s, affirmative action may take its place for the 1990s. As already indicated, the Republican Party believes it is an issue that can carry it to the White House in 1996. It has good reason for doing so. One 1995 opinion poll showed 75 per cent of Americans opposed to race preferences in jobs and education. Whites polled 79–14 per cent against affirmative action and minorities themselves were only 50–46 per cent in favour.[64] Moreover, there is an attempt being made to put the somewhat misleadingly named 'California Civil Rights Initiative' on the state ballot for 1996. This referendum would end all preference programmes related to education, job hiring and government contracting, whether they involve race, gender or anything else.

While the passage of the Civil Rights Act of 1991 gave affirmative action a badly needed boost, the revival of Republican congressional fortunes in 1994 bodes ill for future legislation on affirmative action. In the spring of 1995, the House Economic and Educational Opportunities Committee scheduled hearings on the effects of affirmative action in the work-place. Its Chairperson, Bill Goodling (R-Pa.) set the tone for the hearings by arguing that, although affirmative action may have been necessary a generation ago, the time had now come to scale it back. Congressional Republicans have also promised to reform, or eliminate altogether, the Equal Employment Opportunity Commission, the Labour Department's Office of Federal Contract Compliance Programmes and even the 1964 Civil Rights Act itself.[65] Meanwhile at the White House, President Clinton ordered his own 'intense, urgent review' of affirmative action programmes.[66] It would, therefore, not be at all surprising to see the entire edifice of affirmative action in the nation dismantled in the 1990s.

As we saw in chapter five, the Supreme Court did much in the 1980s to accommodate the rising tide against affirmative action into constitutional law. Those decisions helped proliferate successful challenges to affirmative action programmes in the lower courts. Thus, '*Croson* ushered opponents of affirmative action into the courts, and they have taken the opportunity.'[67]

The Court has issued no landmark pronouncements on affirmative action in the race context since 1991, although in *AGC v. City of Jacksonville*, it made legal challenges to minority set-asides easier to pursue.[68] The Court has also agreed to hear another challenge by white contractors to a federal government scheme that provides incentives to contractors to hire minority subcontractors.[69] But in the current climate of popular and legislative hostility to affirmative action, the Court need do nothing further to ensure its demise.

The Court now appears to share the widespread enthusiasm among conservatives for the idea of a 'colour-blind' society, based, of course, on the foundations of a 'colour-blind' Constitution.[70] This was indicated in *Shaw v. Reno* (1993),[71] a case which received an enormous amount of publicity, although it actually decided little of substance. *Shaw* concerned legislative redistricting rather than the broad affirmative action programmes that concern us here. Nevertheless, it is worthy of note in this context, precisely because the Court's majority decided to import, for the first time on redistricting issues, the line of reasoning it used in cases such as *Wygant v. Jackson Board of Education* and *City of Richmond v. Croson*, discussed in chapter five.[72]

Shaw involved the constitutional legitimacy of 'majority-minority' legislative districts, that is, legislative districts in which the majority of the population is either African-American or Hispanic. The Court had long ago upheld the principle of such districts, in *United Jewish Organisations v. Carey* (1977).[73] And pursuant to the Voting Rights Act of 1965, states and the Attorney-General had encouraged their proliferation. Following the 1990 census, the redistricting of congressional seats produced a record 52 majority-minority districts. Generated by computer, these districts were often irregularly shaped in the extreme. Thus, Florida's 3rd District was described as 'a gnawed wishbone', Louisiana's 4th District as 'a Z with drips' and Texas' 30th District as 'a microscopic view of a new strain of a disease'.[74]

In *Shaw* a Court majority of 5–4 were very disturbed by such weird electoral architecture. The case involved North Carolina's 12th District, which stretched over 160 miles and was frequently described as 'snake-like'.[75] Justice O'Connor's opinion for the Court conceded that race-conscious districting was not unconstitutional *per se* and that, in this particular case, the white challengers to the plan had suffered no tangible harm, such as dilution of their own votes. (The first challenge to the District had been brought by the North Carolina Republican Party, and it participated in *Shaw* as an *amicus curiae*.)[76] Precisely for those reasons, the District Court had ruled that the plaintiffs had failed to demonstrate an Equal Protection claim and dismissed the case. Nevertheless, the Supreme Court broke new ground by reinstating the case because the North Carolina Assembly had adopted a reapportionment scheme 'so irrational on its face' that it could be challenged as an unjustified racial gerrymander.[77]

Justice O'Connor's opinion compared the North Carolina plan to 'the most egregious racial gerrymanders of the past' and 'political apartheid',[78] in spite of the fact that the plan had resulted in the election of the first black members of Congress from the state since Reconstruction. Citing cases such as *Wygant* and *Croson*, O'Connor argued that all racial classifications, intended as benign or not, are presumptively unconstitutional and can only be upheld by 'an extra-ordinary justification'.[79] And as for the point that even the plaintiffs had alleged no specific harm to their own voting rights, she retorted that,

> Racial classifications with respect to voting carry particular dangers. Racial gerrymandering, even for remedial purposes, may balkanise us into competing factions; it threatens to carry us further from the goal of a political system in which race no longer matters – a goal that the Fourteenth and Fifteenth Amendments embody, and to which the Nation continues to aspire.[80]

However, it seems that the decisive factor in *Shaw* was the shape of the 12th District, for this, according to the majority, ignored traditional districting principles, such as compactness and contiguity. Thus, wrote Justice O'Connor, '. . . we believe that reapportionment is one area where appearances do matter'.[81] She even pointed out that the Attorney-General had suggested the possibility of a more compact majority-minority District – perhaps a hint that less weirdly shaped 'racial gerrymanders' might pass constitutional muster.[82] The particular harm of the 12th District, then, was that its highly explicit race-consciousness sent the wrong message about the desirability of racial classifications in public life. And while a majority of the Justices were not ready to adopt the notion of a colour-blind Constitution in all cases, *Shaw* indicates that they may well wish to take further strides in that direction and away from the remedial practices of affirmative action.[83]

Gender equality

We saw in chapter six that the Court spent a good deal of its time analogising sex discrimination with race discrimination. The Court never found the two to be wholly comparable and therefore created different levels of judicial scrutiny in reviewing sex-based and race-based classifications. Whereas classifications by race are subject to strict scrutiny, those based on sex invoke heightened scrutiny: in order to be constitutional '. . . classifications by gender must serve important governmental objectives and must be substantially related to achievement of those objectives.'[84] Part of the Court's reason for not fully equating sexism with racism was the continuing debate, even among feminists, as to whether there were any 'real' differences between men and women, as opposed to 'artificial' differences based in custom or stereotyping.

In 1994, in *J.E.B. v. Alabama ex rel. T.B.*, the Court had occasion to revisit these issues and, in so doing, gave a strong reaffirmation of its commitment to constitutional gender equality.[85] The precise constitutional issue at stake in *J.E.B.* was whether the Fourteenth Amendment's Equal Protection Clause is violated when lawyers make peremptory challenges to potential jurors solely on the basis of gender. The context was a paternity suit brought by Alabama on behalf of T.B. against the alleged father of her child, J.E.B. Of thirty-six potential jurors called, twenty-four were women and twelve were men. Lawyers for the state used nine of ten peremptory challenges to eliminate nine men and one women. J.E.B.'s lawyer struck ten women and one man by peremptory challenge. The result was a jury of twelve women.

Both before and after the jury found J.E.B. to be the father and the Court ordered him to pay maintenance, he argued that the state's use of gender-based peremptory challenges violated his Equal Protection rights. Although he lost his case in the State courts, a 6–3 majority of the Supreme Court upheld his challenge.[86]

Writing for the Court, Justice Blackmun relied heavily on a line of cases stemming from *Batson v. Kentucky* (1986) which had outlawed race-based peremptory challenges.[87] He saw no problem in extending these precedents to cover gender. Thus, in response to the argument that women had never suffered discrimination on the same scale as African-Americans, he said: 'While the prejudicial attitudes towards women in this country have not been identical to those held towards racial minorities, the similarities between the experiences of racial minorities and women, in some contexts, overpower those

differences.'[88] He recited evidence in support of this argument,
though he also pointed out that, whatever the correct comparison
between discrimination against women and against blacks, the fact that
women had undoubtedly suffered a long history of discrimination was
enough to justify heightened scrutiny. Therefore, the only question the
Court needed to answer was whether gender-based peremptory challenges substantially furthered the State's important interest in securing
a fair trial.

He concluded that they did not. Such challenges were based on the
notion that male jurors would favour men in a paternity suit, while
women jurors would favour the mother. There is no evidence to
support such generalisations, said Blackmun, and 'We shall not accept
as a defence to gender-based peremptory challenges the very stereotype the law condemns.'[89] The prejudice which informs such stereotypes harms the litigants, the individual juror, who has a right to
participate in public affairs, and the community. Justice Blackmun
expressed the breadth and depth of the pernicious effects of stereotyping when he wrote:

> When state actors exercise peremptory challenges in reliance on gender
> stereotypes, they ratify and reinforce prejudicial views of the relative
> abilities of men and women. Because these stereotypes have wreaked
> injustice in so many other spheres of our country's life, active discrimina-
> tion by litigants on the basis of gender during jury selection invites cynicism
> respecting the jury's neutrality and its obligation to adhere to the law. The
> potential for cynicism is particularly acute in cases where gender-related
> issues are prominent, such as cases involving rape, sexual harassment or
> paternity.[90]

The Court acknowledged the importance of the peremptory challenge
in a defendant's right to a fair trial and intended no fundamental attack
upon it. Rather, it saw its decision in *J.E.B.* as simple confirmation of
the constitutional disfavour in which gender classifications stand:

> Today we reaffirm what, by now, should be axiomatic: Intentional dis-
> crimination on the basis of gender by state actors violates the Equal
> Protection Clause, particularly where, as here, the discrimination serves to
> ratify and perpetuate invidious, archaic, and overbroad stereotypes about
> the relative abilities of men and women.[91]

What the majority of the Justices viewed as a passionate commitment to
gender equality, Justice Scalia considered to be an expression of
'political correctness'. He began his dissent with the observation that:

> Today's opinion is an inspiring demonstration of how thoroughly up-to-
> date and right-thinking we Justices are in matters pertaining to the sexes (or

as the Court would have it, the genders), and how sternly we disapprove the male chauvinist attitudes of our predecessors.[92]

He also pointed out that the alleged victim of discrimination in this case was a man, not a woman, and that Blackmun's references to historical injustices against women were irrelevant. (In this, of course, Justice Scalia simply ignored the fact that the Court had long ago held that gender-based classifications were unconstitutional whether they disadvantaged women or men.)

More to the point, Scalia argued that, at worst, J.E.B. had suffered 'harmless error': he himself had employed gender-based peremptory challenges and, anyway, scientific evidence introduced at trial demonstrated with 99.92 per cent certainty that he was indeed the father of T.B.'s child. He saw no good reason, therefore, for limiting the vital right to make peremptory challenges.

Justice Scalia did not dwell long on the question of whether men and women really did bring different perspectives to jury service, though he did sarcastically observe that on this issue, '... unisex is unquestionably in fashion'.[93] It was left then to Chief Justice Rehnquist to counter the Court's view that gender-based peremptory challenges were based on prejudice and were akin to race-based challenges:

> The two sexes differ, both biologically and, to a diminishing extent, in experience. It is not merely 'stereotyping' to say that these differences may produce a difference in outlook which is brought to the jury room. Accordingly, use of peremptory challenges on the basis of sex is generally not the sort of derogatory and invidious act which peremptory challenges directed at black jurors may be.[94]

The solid majority against gender-based classifications in *J.E.B.*, and the ringing endorsement the Court's opinion gave to its precedents, indicates that the cause of formal gender equality is alive and well. Indeed, it mirrors the greater strength in the wider political world of the liberal movement for sex equality compared with that for race equality. As was noted at the outset of this chapter, it really is useful to be fighting a cause identified with 51 per cent, rather than 12 per cent, of the population.

Religion, sex and politics

In chapter seven a range of social issues was discussed under this rubric. Of these, the one which has undoubtedly attracted the greatest

304   RAW JUDICIAL POWER?

publicity and controversy since 1992 is that of gay rights. This is due,
however, not to any decision by the Supreme Court but to the actions of
politicians. Most prominently, President Clinton kicked off his presidency with a controversial attempt to end discrimination against gays in
the military.

Prior to 1993, servicemen and women could be dismissed through
expedited hearing for homosexual acts or even merely declaring themselves to be gay. In the decade up to 1993, some 14,000 had been so
dismissed, just over half of them Navy personnel.[95] Clinton had
received significant political and financial backing from the gay community in his presidential campaign and his action on the military ban
was seen as due reward for that support.[96] Congressional conservatives, including Chair of the Armed Services Committee Sam
Nunn, and military leaders themselves were appalled by Clinton's
proposal. Their principal argument was that allowing open and
practising gays in the armed services would inevitably lead to
breakdowns in discipline and a decline in America's defence capacity.
Clinton was forced to retreat and eventually, in July 1993, a compromise was reached, known as 'don't ask, don't tell'. In other words,
the armed services would cease asking their personnel if they were gay,
an affirmative answer to which meant automatic dismissal; and gay
personnel would keep their sexual orientation secret and thus avoid
triggering dismissal procedures.

Sooner or later, this issue will reach the Supreme Court, given the
very obvious Equal Protection concerns it raises and the fact that some
lower courts have already declared it unconstitutional on First Amendment free speech grounds.[97] It is impossible to predict how the Court
might decide it. On the one hand, it seems blatant and, to many,
irrational discrimination against a minority group. On the other hand,
the Court's decision in *Bowers v. Hardwick* (1986) suggests that gays do
not constitute a 'suspect class' and any restrictions on their rights,
therefore, will not be subjected to heightened scrutiny. Combined with
the fact that the Court has traditionally been highly deferential to
internal decisions taken by military hierarchies, this does not augur
well for a decision ordering the military to cease its discrimination.[98]

Perhaps the most ominous development for the gay community,
however, is the attempt by Speaker of the House, Newt Gingrich, to
use anti-homosexual sentiment against President Clinton. Undeterred
by the fact that his half-sister is a lesbian activist, Gingrich intends to
force Clinton to reinstate the complete ban on gays in the military.[99]

Neither can the Court count on the support of the public or state legislatures. There seems to be no let-up in the fear and dislike of homosexuals by heterosexuals that was noted in chapter seven. For example, in March 1995, only the Governor's veto stopped a Montana law coming into force that would have required gays to register with police. And even in relatively liberal Colorado, the battle continues over the anti-gay ordinance forbidding state laws that put homosexuals on a legal par with heterosexuals.[100]

As noted at the beginning of this chapter, the current Court seems strongly inclined to adopt a low profile. Gay and lesbian rights, however, seem likely to lead to a plethora of cases that the Court will find difficult to avoid. For example, in early 1995, the Court granted review in *Hurley v. Irish-American, Gay, Lesbian, and Bisexual Group of Boston*: this raises the issue of whether the organisers of the annual Boston St Patrick's Day Parade can ban gay organisations from participation in the event without violating their First Amendment free expression rights.[101] Thus, it maybe that, along with affirmative action, gay rights will become among the most politically prominent of the social issues in the years to come.

To those two issues should perhaps be added another: school prayer. As with affirmative action and gay rights, conservative politicians know that they have public opinion on their side in their push for illiberal policies. When necessary, therefore, there is no doubt that they will attempt to further their cause in the federal courts. On Establishment Clause issues, however, the Supreme Court remains in the state of confusion that was noted in chapter seven.

We saw that in the 1980s, the Court became less insistent upon a 'wall of separation' between church and state and more inclined to accommodate religious practices in public life. In particular, the so-called *Lemon* test, which imposed a rigorous scrutiny on state-supported religious practices, appeared to be destined for judicial oblivion.[102] Since 1992, the Court has continued to undermine the *Lemon* test to the point where it now seems virtually irrelevant to the Court's Establishment Clause jurisprudence, although Justice Scalia wrote amusingly of the Court's inability finally to dispense with it:

> Like some ghoul in a late-night horror movie that repeatedly sits up in its grave and shuffles abroad, after being repeatedly killed and buried, *Lemon* stalks our Establishment Clause jurisprudence . . . The secret of *Lemon's* survival, I think, is that it is so easy to kill. It is there to scare us (and our audience) when we wish to do so, but we can command it to return to the tomb at will.[103]

The real problem with the *Lemon* test, however, is that no alternative can be found which commands majority support. Indeed, as we shall see below, the Justices cannot even agree on whether any such test, or tests, are desirable at all. In the meantime, therefore, the Court examines and decides Establishment Clause conflicts on a case-by-case basis, giving little sense of any fundamental guiding constitutional principle.

In *Lee v. Weisman* (1992), the Bush Administration squarely asked the Court to abandon the *Lemon* test.[104] The Court declined to do so and declared unconstitutional the recitation of a religious benediction at a public school graduation ceremony. Neither, however, did the Court employ the *Lemon* test in reaching its decision.[105] Two subsequent cases confirm that most, if not all the Justices, are content simply to ignore the *Lemon* test. In *Zobrest v. Catalina Foothills District* (1993) and *Board of Education v. Grumet* (1994)[106] the Court failed to use the *Lemon* test, even though the lower courts had based their decisions upon it.

Zobrest concerned a deaf child in Arizona who transferred from public school to a private Catholic school. At public school, the state had provided him with a sign-language interpreter as required by the federal Individuals with Disabilities Education Act (IDEA) of 1988. His parents requested that the interpreter continue to be provided when he moved to Salpointe Catholic High School, claiming that this was required both by the IDEA and the Free Exercise Clause of the First Amendment. The state refused, however, on the grounds that such public assistance to a parochial school would violate the Establishment Clause. Its decision was upheld by both the District Court and the federal Court of Appeals, applying the *Lemon* test. However, a 5-4 majority of the Supreme Court reversed, arguing that Zobrest's request merely involved a religion-neutral benefit to pupils regardless of whether the school they attended was private or public, parochial or secular. It did not, therefore, constitute an establishment of religion, especially as the IDEA created no financial incentive for the Zobrests to send their son to a parochial school.[107] Among the precedents cited by Chief Justice Rehnquist to support this characterisation of the issue was *Bowen v. Kendrick*, the case which had upheld the religiously-inspired Adolescent Family Life Act.[108]

The dissenting Justices all detected an eagerness on the part of the majority to reach the constitutional issue raised in *Zobrest*. In separate opinions, both Justice Blackmun and Justice O'Connor argued that judicial restraint required the Court to settle the case on grounds of statutory interpretation. This chimed with the established principle that the Supreme Court should always avoid constitutional matters if another basis for decision is available.[109] Like most tenets of restraint, however, this one left the Court with an 'escape clause': here Rehnquist argued that since the lower courts had only heard arguments on the constitutional issues, the Supreme Court was bound to decide on that basis. In fact, of course, an alternative response could simply have been to remand the case for hearing on the statutory grounds that had not been litigated. Once again, then, *Zobrest* demonstrates that judicial activism is not the preserve of liberal judges, any more than judicial restraint is the preserve of conservatives.

If the conservative Justices won a victory for religious accommodation in *Zobrest*, however, they suffered a significant setback in *Board of Education v. Grumet*. The case involved a clear, if understandable, instance of state support for religion. An orthodox Jewish sect, the Satmar Hasidim, had been permitted under New York State law to form itself into the Village of Kiryas Joel. The Village boundaries were drawn precisely to include only the homes of Satmar adherents. Problems arose, however, over the education of the sect's handicapped children. The sect's private schools could not provide the special services needed for these children and initially the adjacent Monroe-Woodbury School District supplied teachers at an annex of a Satmar school. That service was withdrawn in 1985, however, following Supreme Court decisions indicating that such provision violated the Establishment Clause. The Satmar then sent their handicapped children to Monroe-Woodbury public schools, but the cultural shock and fear this induced led to all but one child being withdrawn. New York State resolved the problem in 1989 by enacting a law, Chapter 748, making the Village a public school district in its own right, with boundaries precisely conterminous with those of the Village. This meant that Kiryas Joel School District now received public funds to operate a public school for handicapped children. This was undoubtedly an ingenious and sympathetic attempt to solve a difficult problem – but it also raised problems under the Establishment Clause.

Indeed, in *Grumet*, a 6–3 majority of the Supreme Court struck it down.[110] Writing for the Court, Justice Souter said that Chapter 748 violated the neutrality of government toward religion that was required by the Establishment Clause. It had done this by effectively delegating civil government authority to a group designated by religious adherence, that is, the Kiryas Joel School District. He pointed out that the New York State legislature was perfectly aware that it was creating an exclusively Satmar school district; moreover, the creation of such a small district ran completely against the trend in the state to consolidate school districts within ever larger boundaries.[111] The result, he said, was 'a purposeful and forbidden fusion of governmental and religious functions'.[112]

Justice Scalia entered a vigorous dissent in which he disputed virtually every aspect of Justice Souter's argument. Thus he denied that New York had delegated any civic authority to a religious group, such as a church. Rather, he claimed, the Kiryas Joel School District designated citizens singled out for their cultural characteristics, not their religion. Noting that the residents of the Village School District are not only Satmar by religion, but also wear unusual dress, share unusual customs and refrain from mixing much with those culturally different from them, he asks, 'On what basis does Justice Souter conclude that it is the theological distinctiveness rather than the cultural distinctiveness that was the basis for New York State's decision?'[113] The implausibility of this argument failed to convince Justice Kennedy, an erstwhile ally in Establishment Clause cases: he asserted squarely that New York State had engaged in religious gerrymandering, just as North Carolina had engaged in racial gerrymandering in *Shaw v. Reno*.[114]

However, the essence of Justice Scalia's dissent was that even if the district had been designated for religious purposes, it was still 'a permissable accommodation' of religion by government. Justice Souter coolly dismissed this by reference to '. . . (Justice Scalia's) inability to accept the fact that this Court has long held that the First Amendment reaches more than classic, 18th century establishments.'[115] Scalia denied this, asserting instead that what the Establishment Clause prohibits are measures which favour one religion over another.[116] Since there is no evidence of such favouritism here, he says, the Court has no business assuming that New York State would not treat other religions on the same basis as the Satmars should they encounter similar educational problems.

Regardless of the merits of the arguments in *Grumet*, however, what stands out is the lack of any doctrinal coherence in the case. As noted above, the lower courts dealt with the issues within the framework of the *Lemon* test. Justice Souter's opinion, however, studiously ignored it. Justice Blackmun was so alarmed by this that he wrote a concurring opinion '. . . to note my disagreement with any suggestion that today's decision signals a departure from the principles described in *Lemon v. Kurtzman*.'[117] He then went on to argue that *Grumet* was effectively decided on *Lemon* criteria. But the fact that no other Justice joined his concurrence, and that Blackmun himself left the Court in 1994, suggests that the entire Court now agrees that the *Lemon* test was insufficiently accommodating to religious tradition and practice in the United States. It thus stands as a significant, if limited, success for the conservative backlash against the liberal jurisprudence of the Warren and Burger Courts.

The demise of *Lemon*, however, does nothing to alter the fact that the Court will continue to practise non-interpretivism in Establishment Clause cases. For whatever the weaknesses in Justice Scalia's dissent, he is surely right to say that the Court needs some fixed star by which to guide:

> To replace *Lemon* with nothing is simply to announce that we are now so bold that we no longer feel the need even to pretend that our haphazard course of Establishment Clause decisions is governed by any principle.[118]

Summary

The Court continues to negotiate its way out of the controversies it helped to create in earlier decades. It has done so partly by making concessions to the conservative backlash in the country, but also by trying to generate some kind of stability and predictability in accordance with legal and constitutional norms. The ultimate goal is to deflect political passions away from the Court and on to the legislative arenas at state and federal level. In this sense, there will be no exercise of 'raw judicial power' in the foreseeable future.

Yet this does not mean that the Court has rediscovered some lost art of interpretivism or some consensus on the original intent behind this or that constitutional clause. That, as was argued in chapter two, is well-nigh impossible. And as the Establishment Clause and abortion rights cases, for example, make only too clear, the Court is engaged more in improvisation than in meaningful interpretivism. It is simply, then, that the Court in the 1990s improvises with far greater caution, both judicial and political, than at any time since 1954.

Notes

1 Frank Luntz (Republican campaign strategist), *The Guardian*, 24 February 1995, p. 13.
2 *Ibid.*
3 Ralph Reed (Executive Director of Christian Coalition), *The Guardian*, 14 February 1995, p. 10.
4 *Newsweek*, 27 March 1995, p. 24.

5 See p. 117, *supra*.
6 At the time of writing, Justice Breyer has not yet completed a full Term on the Court. In her first Term, however, Justice Ginsburg provides an interesting comparison with Justice White, whom she replaced. In his last year on the Court, White was most likely to vote with Chief Justice Rehnquist and Justice Kennedy, and least likely to vote with Justices Stevens and Blackmun. Ginsburg, however, was most likely to vote with Justices Souter and Stevens, and least likely to vote with Justices Thomas and Scalia, 'The Supreme Court 1992 Term: The Statistics', *Harvard Law Review*, CVII, 1993, pp. 372–9, 373; 'The Supreme Court 1993 Term: The Statistics', *Harvard Law Review*, CVIII, 1994, pp. 372–9, 373.
7 W. Eskridge and P. Frickley, 'Law as equilibrium', *Harvard Law Review*, CVIII, 1994, pp. 26–108, 43.
8 Justice Ginsburg was confirmed by the Senate 96–3, and Justice Breyer by 87–9. The then-ranking Republican on the Senate Judiciary Committee, Orrin Hatch, welcomed the Ginsburg nomination as 'about as good as you're going to get' from a Democrat President, *CQ Weekly Report*, 17 July 1993, p. 1875. And Stephen Breyer was described as 'liberal enough on key issues to satisfy most Democrats and conservative enough on business and criminal law to placate Republicans', *CQ Weekly Report*, 21 May 1994, p. 1305.
9 See above, pp. 115–17, and below.
10 See above, p. 52.
11 The states which do *not* have the death penalty are: Alaska, Hawaii, Iowa, Maine, Massachusetts, Michigan, Minnesota, North Dakota, Rhode Island, Vermont, West Virginia and Wisconsin. *The Guardian*, 7 April 1995, p. 2.
12 *Statistical Abstract of the United States: 1994* (114th ed.), Washington, DC, 1994, p. 218; *The Guardian*, 7 April 1995, p. 2.
13 *The Economist*, 1 April 1995, p. 55.
14 *Callins v. Collins* (1994), Docket no. 93-7054. Blackmun dissented from a decision denying review of Callins' death sentence. He said that he had struggled for twenty years to help the Court to find the right balance between the conflicting demands of consistency across cases and individualised sentencing in particular cases. He and the Court had failed. Thus, 'Rather than continue to coddle the Court's delusion that the desired level of fairness has been achieved and the need for regulation eviscerated, I feel morally and intellectually obligated to concede that the death penalty experiment has failed. It is virtually self-evident to me now that no combination of procedural rules or substantive regulations ever can save the death penalty from its inherent constitutional deficiencies. The basic question – does the system accurately and consistently determine which defendants "deserve" to die? – cannot be answered in the affirmative.' *US Supreme Court Reports, Lawyers' Edition Advance*, 127 L Ed 2d No. 3, 25 March 1994, pp. 435–49, 438.
15 Docket no. 93-7659.
16 Justice O'Connor wrote the Court's opinion, joined by Chief Justice Rehnquist and Justices Scalia, Kennedy, Souter, Thomas, Ginsburg and Breyer. The dissenter was Justice Stevens.
17 468 US 447 (1984).
18 *Harris*, Opinion of the Court, p. 6 (NB pagination from Internet copy).
19 *Ibid.*, p. 5.
20 *Harris*, Opinion of Justice Stevens, p. 4 (Internet).
21 *Harris*, Opinion of Justice O'Connor, p. 8 (Internet).
22 507 US – , 123 L Ed 2d 188, 113 S Ct – (1993). Justice O'Connor wrote the Court's opinion, joined by Chief Justice Rehnquist and Justices White, Scalia, Kennedy, Souter and Thomas. Justice Blackmun wrote a dissent, joined by Justice Stevens.
23 *Arave*, p. 196.
24 *Ibid.*, p. 199.

25 *Ibid.*, p. 207.
26 509 US – , 125 L Ed 2d 290, 113 S Ct – (1993).
27 Justice Kennedy delivered the Court's opinion, joined by Chief Justice Rehnquist and Justices White, Scalia and Thomas. Justice O'Connor wrote a dissenting opinion, joined by Justices Blackmun, Stevens and Souter.
28 492 US 302 (1989). See also *supra*, pp. 72–3.
29 *Johnson*, p. 309.
30 *Ibid.*, p. 312.
31 See, for example, *Simmons v. South Carolina*, 512 US – , 129 L Ed 2d 133, 114 S Ct 2187 (1994). Here a 7–2 majority reversed a death sentence where the trial court refused to allow a jury considering the defendant's future dangerousness to be told that the alternative to the death sentence was life *without parole*.
32 See, for example, *McCleskey v. Zant*, 111 S Ct 1454 (1991).
33 506 US – , 122 L Ed 2d 203, 113 S Ct – (1993).
34 *Herrera*, pp. 216–17.
35 Docket no. 93–7901. The majority Justices were Stevens, O'Connor, Souter, Ginsburg and Breyer. Of these, only Justice O'Connor was also in the majority in *Herrera*, but Breyer had replaced Justice White in the intervening period.
36 *National Journal*, 5 March 1994, p. 522.
37 506 US – , 122 L Ed 2d 34, 113 S Ct – (1993).
38 *Bray*, p. 73.
39 *Ibid.*, see opinions of Justice Scalia, p. 45; Justice Kennedy, p. 57; and Justice O'Connor, p. 96.
40 403 US 88 (1971).
41 *Bray*, p. 35.
42 *Ibid.*, p. 47.
43 417 US 484 (1974) – see *supra*, pp. 200–2.
44 *Bray*, p. 97.
45 *Ibid.*, p. 102.
46 114 S Ct 798 (1994). Opinion of Chief Justice Rehnquist, p. 1 (NB pagination from Internet copy).
47 *Scheidler*, Rehnquist opinion, p. 7 (Internet).
48 *CQ Weekly Report*, 29 January 1994, p. 175.
49 *Harvard Law Review*, CVIII, 1994, p. 358.
50 *Ibid.*, p. 357, n. 42.
51 512 US – , 129 L Ed 2d 593, 114 S Ct 2516 (1994).
52 These facts are taken from the somewhat differing accounts of the protest activities contained in Chief Justice Rehnquist's opinion for the Court, pp. 603–4, and Justice Scalia's dissent, pp. 620–3.
53 Chief Justice Rehnquist wrote the Court's opinion, joined by Justices Blackmun, O'Connor, Souter, Ginsburg and, in part, Stevens. Justice Scalia dissented in part, joined by Justices Kennedy and Thomas.
54 *Madsen*, p. 606.
55 *Ibid.*, p. 608.
56 R. Nagel, *Constitutional Cultures: The Mentality and Consequences of Judicial Review*, Berkeley, 1993, p. 147.
57 *Madsen*, p. 624.
58 *Ibid.* pp. 624–5.
59 *Ibid.*, p. 620.
60 *Ibid.*, p. 609.
61 *Ibid.*, p. 613.
62 *Ibid.*, p. 614.
63 *CQ Weekly Report*, 2 July 1994, p. 1810.
64 The Newsweek Poll, 23–4 March 1995, as reported in *Newsweek*, 3 April 1995, p. 27.

65 *CQ Weekly Report*, 18 March 1995, p. 819.
66 *Ibid.*, p. 820.
67 *Harvard Law Review*, CVII, 1993, p. 303 and n. 3. *City of Richmond v. Croson* (1989) concerned set-asides for minority contractors, *supra*, pp. 158–64.
68 113 S Ct 2297 (1993). The Justices ruled 7–2 that a challenger to a set-aside progamme need not demonstrate that he would have won a contract had it not been for the minority preference: the denial of equal treatment in the bidding process is sufficient to give him standing.
69 The case is *Adarand Constructors v. Pena*, Docket no. 93–1841. *Congressional Weekly Report*, 18 March 1995, p. 820.
70 See, for example, Andrew Kull, *The Colour-Blind Constitution*, Cambridge, Mass., 1992.
71 509 US – , 125 L Ed 2d 511, 113 S. Ct. 2816 (1993).
72 *Supra*, pp. 151–6, and pp. 158–64.
73 430 US 144 (1977).
74 *1993 CQ Almanac*, XLIX, p. 326.
75 North Carolina had originally submitted a redistricting plan to the Attorney-General, as required by the Voting Rights Act, that contained only one majority-minority district. The Attorney-General rejected it on the grounds that the state could have created a second such district. North Carolina duly submitted a revised plan including the additional majority-minority 12th District.
76 *Shaw*, p. 521.
77 *Ibid.*, p. 536.
78 *Ibid.*, pp. 525 and 529.
79 *Ibid.*, p. 526.
80 *Ibid.*, p. 535.
81 *Ibid.*, p. 529.
82 *Ibid.*, pp. 535–6.
83 Early in 1995, the Court granted review in similar 'majority-minority district' cases from Louisiana and Georgia: *US v. Hays* (Docket no. 94-558) and *Miller v. Johnson* (Docket no. 94–631), respectively.
84 *Craig v. Boren* (1976), *supra*, pp. 192–3.
85 511 US – , 128 L Ed 2d 89, 114 S. Ct. 1419 (1994).
86 Justice Blackmun wrote for the majority, which also included Justices Stevens, O'Connor, Souter and Ginsburg, with Justice Kennedy concurring. The dissenters were Chief Justice Rehnquist and Justices Scalia and Thomas.
87 476 US 79 (1986). See also *Powers v. Ohio*, 499 US 400 (1991), *Edmonson v. Leesville Concrete Co.*, 500 US 614 (1991) and *Georgia v. McCollum*, 505 US – (1992).
88 *J.E.B.*, p. 101.
89 *Ibid.*, pp. 102–3.
90 *Ibid.*, p. 104.
91 *Ibid.*, p. 98.
92 *Ibid.*, p. 114.
93 *Ibid.*, p. 115.
94 *Ibid.*, p. 114.
95 *CQ Almanac*, XLIX, 1993, Washington, DC, 1993, p. 454.
96 One gay group, the Human Rights Campaign Fund, contributed an estimated $2.5 million to Clinton's campaign chest, *ibid.*, p. 455.
97 *Ibid.*, p. 461. See also, *The Guardian*, 4 April 1995, p. 12.
98 The case will pose interesting dilemmas for Justices Scalia and Kennedy, in particular, if it based on First Amendment rights. For as we can see from their votes in the flag-burning case of *Texas v. Johnson*, 491 US 397 (1989), *supra*, 240–3, both Justices are willing to swallow their personal distaste for certain types of behaviour if fundamental First Amendment rights are at stake.

99 *The Guardian*, 4 April 1995, p. 12.

100 For a detailed discussion on anti-gay laws, see 'The constitutionality of anti-gay ballot initiatives: a symposium', *Ohio State Law Journal*, LX, 1994, pp. 491–674; 'Stonewall at 25: a symposium', *Harvard Civil Rights and Civil Liberties Law Review*, XXIX, 1994, pp. 277–605.

101 Docket no. 94–749.

102 *Supra*, pp. 254–63.

103 *Lamb's Chapel v. Centre Moriches*, 511 US - , 128 L Ed 2d 229, 114 S Ct – (1993), p. 365. Here the Justices unanimously overruled a school board's decision not to allow a Christian evangelical church access to film screening facilities that were made available to other social and civic groups. What brought on Justice Scalia's scorn was an aside in the Court's opinion that allowing access would have satisfied all three prongs of the *Lemon* test, p. 363.

104 505 US – , 120 L Ed 2d 467, 112 S Ct – (1992). *Supra*, p. 270, n. 263.

105 Writing for the majority in *Lee*, Justice Kennedy said: 'This case does not require us to revisit the difficult questions dividing us in recent cases, questions of the definition and full scope of the principles governing the extent of permitted accommodation by the State for the religious beliefs and practices of many of its citizens . . . Thus we do not accept the invitation of petitioners and amicus the United States to reconsider our decision in *Lemon v. Kurtzman* . . .', *ibid.*, p. 480.

106 509 US – , 125 L Ed 2d 1, 113 S. Ct 2462 (1993) and 512 US – , 129 L Ed 2d 546, 114 S Ct 2481 (1994), respectively.

107 *Zobrest*, p. 11. Chief Justice Rehnquist was joined by Justices White, Scalia, Kennedy and Thomas. The dissenters were Justices Blackmun, Stevens, O'Connor and Souter, though they were not agreed on the grounds for dissent.

108 *Ibid.*, p. 10. For a discussion of *Bowen*, see *supra*, pp. 260–2.

109 *Ibid.*, opinion of Justice Blackmun, pp. 1–4; and opinion of Justice O'Connor, p. 20.

110 Justice Souter wrote the Court's opinion, joined wholly or in part by Justices Blackmun, Stevens, O'Connor and Ginsburg; Justice Kennedy concurred in the judgement only. Justice Scalia wrote a dissenting opinion, joined by Chief Justice Rehnquist and Justice Thomas.

111 *Grumet*, pp. 558–9.

112 *Ibid.*, p. 560.

113 *Ibid.*, p. 584.

114 *Ibid.*, p. 577.

115 *Ibid.*, p. 564.

116 *Ibid.*, p. 589.

117 *Ibid.*, p. 565.

118 *Ibid.*, p. 591.

Case index

The citation of Supreme Court cases can appear in four forms, depending on which reporting volume is used. A full case citation contains three references: the *US Supreme Court Reports*, the *Supreme Court Reporter (Interim Edition)* and the *US Supreme Court Reports Lawyers' Edition*, respectively. When finally published in all three, a full citation reads, for example, *INS v. Chadha*, 462 US 919, 103 S Ct 2764, 77 L Ed 2d 317 (1983). Normally a case is cited only by the reference to the *US Supreme Court Reports*, but where this is not yet available or only partly available, reference is also made either to the *Lawyers Edition* as well, or to the *Reporter*. A recent case not yet published in any of these is cited by the *Slip Opinion*, issued immediately after the case is announced by the Court: in these circumstances, the Docket Number is given in this Index.

General index

Coventry University